THE GREAT GODDESSES OF EGYPT

THE GREAT GODDESSES OF EGYPT

Barbara S. Lesko

UNIVERSITY OF OKLAHOMA PRESS : NORMAN

ALSO BY BARBARA S. LESKO

The Remarkable Women of Ancient Egypt (Berkeley, 1978; Providence, 1987, 1996)
(collab. ed.) *Dictionary of Late Egyptian* (5 vols.) (Berkeley, 1982; Providence, 1984, 1987, 1989, 1990)
(ed.) *Women's Earliest Records from Ancient Egypt and Western Asia* (Atlanta, 1989)

Published with the assistance of the National Endowment for the Humanities, a federal agency which supports the study of such fields as history, philosophy, literature, and language.

Library of Congress Cataloging-in-Publication Data

Lesko, Barbara S.
    The great goddesses of Egypt / by Barbara S. Lesko.
        p.   cm.
    Includes bibliographical references and index.
    Summary: The book presents in depth histories of the cults of
seven major goddesses and many excerpts from their literature—
hymns, prayers, and magical spells as well as descriptions of
ritual, temples and clergy.
    ISBN 0-8061-3202-7 (paperback : alk. paper)
    1. Goddesses, Egyptian.   2. Egypt—Religion.   I. Title.
BL2450.G58L47   1999
299'.31—dc21   99-11850
                                                        CIP

The paper in this book meets the guidelines for permanence and durability of the Committee on Production Guidelines for Book Longevity of the Council on Library Resources, Inc. ∞

Text design by Gail Carter.

1 2 3 4 5 6 7 8 9 10

For Leonard

CONTENTS

FIGURES

REFACE

In the pantheon of ancient Egypt, some deities held higher status and commanded more devotion than others. Among these were seven goddesses: Nut, Neith, Nekhbet, Wadjet, Hathor, Mut, and Isis. Their cults spanned most of Egypt's ancient history and were important to kings and commoners, women and men alike. Some of the greatest temples that tourists see along the Nile today—at Dendera, Philae, Abu Simbel, and Deir el-Bahri—were constructed to celebrate the cults of female divinities. The Egyptians credited the great goddesses with creation and with control over life and death. They won fierce loyalty from their faithful, and wherever Egyptians traveled the cult of Hathor or Isis was sure to accompany them and become established in foreign ports frequented by Egyptian traders, diplomats, workers, and soldiers. Their goddesses were not only motherly, they were protectors and workers of cures. They not only induced good harvests for farmers, brought couples together in matrimony, and helped women conceive, they helped miners and sailors in their quests. Most important, they held open the door to eternal life for all who were morally deserving of it and welcomed and guided the blessed dead through the uncertainties and dangers of the Netherworld so that reunion with the sun would reward the Egyptians with everlasting life. Faith in the divine, hope for everlasting life, and commitment to charity were first expressed in the land of Egypt. Surely the significance of these goddesses over thousands of years merits a book that introduces the student, teacher, and general reader to their stories and the beauty of their literature.

Song and story were very important to the ancient celebrations of the goddess cults, and fortunately some of the religious literature and much of the art and architecture that were produced in Egypt over three thousand years of its ancient history have survived, so we know the characteristics attributed to these divine beings and we can read the petitions, hymns of praise, and prayers of their devoted followers—both the humble and the mighty.

Ancient Egyptian religious literature is plentiful and derives from a long cultural life, spanning almost three thousand years. It should be recognized as of the utmost importance for any reconstruction of humanity's early religious beliefs, yet it remains largely unknown and unstudied by writers on spiritual feminism (a contemporary movement that seeks the Goddess as a living force) or by comparative religionists. However, studies of some of the first attempts to organize religious beliefs are surely relevant.

This study makes available accurate translations of original Egyptian theological writings—hymns, prayers, and personal statements of faith from ancient worshipers about what the goddess in question meant to people who knew her best. Too many of the seriously researched works on Egyptian goddesses remain beyond the reach of most readers, in scholarly series or European journals or monographs of small circulation, and are readily available to only the most determined researcher. Thus this book attempts a distillation of available resources and current scholarly writing. This last, however, sometimes disappoints. When even the most erudite of scholars of Egyptian religion fails to mention a single goddess among the leading deities of ancient Egypt, something is amiss. All too often Hathor, Isis, and other major female deities are discussed in limited terms, overlooking the well-researched studies on specific goddesses and the original ancient texts that have revealed their wide-ranging powers and roles that match those of the greatest male gods. It is not my intention to denigrate male deities but to bring into focus goddesses whose powers were equally great and whose attributes are sometimes astounding.

Women have worshipped goddesses for far more millennia than they have lived under the patriarchal monotheisms. One frequently hears the complaint that the religions of today have little relevance for women, but this was not always the case. Thousands of years ago, when people first began to form religious cults, female deities were very real and very much taken to heart by both women and men, who passionately followed what they perceived to be sympathetic and often-gentle immortals who helped the just and the repentant during life and offered eternal life to the good and deserving. At least this was true of the well-documented divinities of ancient Egypt, whose cults flourished for thousands of years and who were the object of joyous ritual and pious prayers. Women participated fully in the religious cults of ancient Egypt, and the followers of the goddesses especially held high ranks in the temple hierarchies. Indeed, they not only participated, they helped guide the development of the cults throughout their long histories.

Many women today are seeking spiritual life outside of mainstream religions, and women readers should appreciate female divinities who once supported women during the significant passages and trials of their lives, who were protectors, bestowers of happiness, and promotors of fertility. Contemporary technological society has severed a once-intimate relationship that humans had with the earth and all its creatures, but studying the sacred qualities that the Egyptians perceived in the natural world and the reverence they held for all life is itself inspiring and can be a guide toward better lives for all of us.

I plan to follow the documentation historically and to distinguish the goddesses so that their essential natures may become apparent. The Egyptians left us no written mythology, only titles, spells, hymns, and art. It is easy to become confused by the syncretism and baffling inconsistencies of the ancient texts so that distinctions blur. Trying to impose order and structure is a modern approach, but I am writing for contemporary readers, many of whom will have had no prior knowledge of ancient Egyptian religion. Clearly there should be something to bridge the gap between the paragraph entries of directories for Egyptian gods and the weighty academic tomes, some of which focus on a single goddess, or on votive offerings, or on hymns, or on temple personnel of individual cults.

For the past twenty years my research has led me down several paths as I have attempted to trace the female experience in one of the world's oldest and most impressive civilizations. I published the first book written in English on ancient Egyptian women as far back as 1977. The scope of my research expanded when, in the course of writing a chapter on women in the ancient Near East for the second edition of the women's history college textbook, *Becoming Visible*, I discovered that published resources were few and largely superficial. This led me to organize an international conference in 1987 on women in ancient Egypt and western Asia, with vital help from the National Endowment for the Humanities and the Mellon Foundation. The conference brought together thirty scholars who delivered and debated papers over a three-day period and resulted in the book, *Women's Earliest Records*. Since then many more Egyptologists have published articles and books concerning women's roles in ancient Egypt, but it is clear that we are not all of one mind regarding exactly how to evaluate the evidence, which remains sparsely scattered over a three-thousand-year history.

In this book I examine ancient women's religious needs and practices and the powers attributed to female deities. I have opted for a diachronic or chronological approach as much as possible, having become convinced from the evidence that the goddesses and their attributes were viewed differently over the millennia and suspecting that this can be indicative of social and political movements and changes in values and needs of the people. The synchronic approach generally followed by writers on Egyptian religion can lead to oversights and misunderstandings.

I have had the distinct advantage of being married for more than thirty years to a professor of Egyptology, Leonard H. Lesko, a scholar well acquainted with ancient Egyptian religious literature. I also have enjoyed the advantage of having at my disposal at Brown University one of the world's greatest libraries of Egyptology. My husband graciously provided new translations of many of the texts quoted in this book. However, all the conclusions reached in my study are mine alone and do not necessarily reflect his understanding of Egyptian religion.

I wish to thank my editor, Kimberly Wiar, for her early enthusiastic reception of the idea for this book and her continued interest and support. Many colleagues have come to my aid with photographs from their museum collections, and I thank them for their kind cooperation: Dr. Mohamed Saleh, Director General of the Egyptian Museum, Cairo; Dr. Vivian Davies, Keeper of the British Museum; Dr. Helen White-house, Ashmolean Museum at Oxford; Dr. Catharine Roehrig, Metropolitan Museum of Art in New York; Dr. Rita Freed, Museum of

Fine Arts, Boston; Professor David Silverman and Jennifer Houser, University of Pennsylvania Museum; and Sarah Wentworth, Walters Art Gallery, Baltimore. I am also grateful for the permission granted by the University Press of New England and the Trustees of Brandeis University to quote Louis V. Zabkar's translation of the Aretalogy of Kyme from his book, *Hymns to Isis in Her Temple at Philae.* My colleagues at Brown have my gratitude as well: Professor Lanny Bell, who allowed me to read an important article of his before it was published; my research assistant, Lee Payne, who produced the graphics and drawings for this book; and my husband, Leonard, Charles E. Wilbour Professor of Egyptology, who helped in so many ways. It is also my pleasure to acknowledge the assistance given to me over the past years of research by Brown University Reference Librarian Duane Davies, who was always ready to help track down particularly obscure volumes.

CHRONOLOGY OF ANCIENT EGYPT

PREDYNASTIC PERIOD
Badarian: 5500–3500 B.C.
Amratian (Naqada I): 3500
Early Gerzean (Naqada II): 3500–3300
Late Gerzean: 3300–3100

PROTODYNASTIC PERIOD
(beginning of the historic age, includes Dynasties 1–2):
3100–2660 B.C.

OLD KINGDOM: 2660–2180 B.C.
(Dynasties 3–6)

FIRST INTERMEDIATE PERIOD: 2180–2050 B.C.
(Dynasties 7–11)

MIDDLE KINGDOM: 2050–1786 B.C.
(Dynasty 12)

SECOND INTERMEDIATE PERIOD: 1785–1554 B.C.
(Dynasties 13–17)

NEW KINGDOM: 1554–1075 B.C.
(Dynasties 18–20)

THIRD INTERMEDIATE PERIOD: 1075–720 B.C.
(Dynasties 21–24)

NUBIAN PERIOD: 726–664 B.C.
(Dynasty 25)

SAITE PERIOD: 664–525 B.C.
(Dynasty 26)

FIRST PERSIAN PERIOD: 525–404 B.C.
(Dynasty 27)

LAST NATIVE RULERS: 404–341 B.C.
(Dynasties 28–30)

SECOND PERSIAN PERIOD: 341–332 B.C.
(Dynasty 31)

ALEXANDER THE GREAT'S DYNASTY: 332–323 B.C.

PTOLEMAIC DYNASTY: 323–330 B.C.

ROMAN CONQUEST

THE GREAT GODDESSES OF EGYPT

ABBREVIATIONS

Annales	*Annales du Service des Antiquités de l'Egypte, Cairo*
BD	Book of the Dead
CT	Coffin Texts
Diod.	Diodorus Siculus, *World History*, Book 1
Dyn.	Dynasty
Herod.	Herodotus, *Histories*, book 2
JEA	*Journal of Egyptian Archaeology*, London
LA	Lexicon
Metam.	Apuleius *Metamorphoses*
P	Papyrus
PT	Pyramid Texts
SAKB	*Studien zur altägyptischen Kultur Beihefte*, Hamburg
Sp.	Spell
Utt.	Utterance

ᴇARLY WOMEN AND THE FIRST EVIDENCE OF FAITH

Earth, they say, is the mother of all.
ARETALOGY OF MARONEA, 2D CENTURY B.C.

The traveler in Egypt is struck by the grandeur of its ancient temples and the multiplicity of its ancient deities. Perhaps it comes as a surprise that some of the largest and best-preserved temples are dedicated to goddesses. Who were these divine women? Were they merely consorts to powerful male deities, or did they too figure large in the cosmos and play major roles for the ancients in life and in death? Goddesses are often depicted as lioness-headed or as wholly human but wearing diadems of cow horns. What does this mean? And what are we to make of the depictions of divine animals—cows, cats, vultures, and snakes?

Today it is possible to follow the history of deities in Egypt using written records accumulated over three thousand years. The surviving data are not complete; indeed the gaps in the records are often enormous. This is in part a result of the accident of survival, but it is also indicative of a culture in which the spoken word, oral tradition, preserved mythological lore, folklore, and religious teachings and passed them to younger generations. Much did not need to be written down, for everyone heard stories while they were growing up about the deities who were present at one's birth and one's death and might lend help (or cause harm) during life's crises. The surviving records tell of goddesses who were creators, protectors, curers, and guarantors of eternal life. The waxing and waning of the goddesses' fortunes and their interconnections and developing personalities can be traced over the centuries and are fascinating to behold. The great temples and numerous statues of the greatest goddesses primarily date from the end of their stories, because time takes a toll on all things and Egyptians often recycled building stone. But millennia earlier, in prehistory, there were goddesses too.

The story of the goddesses may be seen as the story of women and the origins of civilized life. The earliest humans, as soon as they began to contemplate life, should have realized that women were special. Women created life, both female and male. This meant they possessed unique power. New human life could not be sustained without a woman's milk. This made women especially important. Women regularly sustained a blood loss that was not fatal. This surely made them mysterious. Women could also induce an involuntary sexual response in men. This made them dangerous. In earliest times, then, women may very well have seemed to possess powers men did not. Realization of this has led some to argue that "in the beginning" humans revered femaleness to such an extent that they conceived of a great mother goddess, and her worship was the first sign of religious life on earth.

Religious beliefs, of course, began long before civilization—characterized by organized statehood, writing, urban settlement, and large-scale buildings—as anthropological studies of primitive tribes document. The numerous small carvings of female torsos dating to prehistoric times in Europe and western Asia have persuaded many that our earliest ancestors in the Paleolithic period (before 15,000 B.C., during the stone tool age) revered a mother goddess. Not all archaeologists accept these figurines as necessarily indicative of a religious cult, however. It can be argued that men everywhere and always have enjoyed rendering the female body artistically. The earliest figurines are very small, personal talismans and need not have been religious in nature. Nonetheless, there are a number of ancient archaeological sites that have revealed incontrovertible evidence of some very early religious cults that focused on female divinity. Impressive structures and monumental sculpture dedicated to goddess cults survive from the two ends of the ancient Mediterranean world and antecedent to the beginning of Egyptian civilization. This evidence has been recovered and published by archaeologists working on Malta and on the Anatolian steppe.[1]

Artifacts, the material creations of human beings, do not date back as far as the Paleolithic in the area that became Egypt. Thus it is not possible to find evidence for a cult of a primeval mother goddess in the Nile valley contemporaneous with such an early period. A hundred thousand years ago and more, Stone Age people roamed the Saharan grasslands and oases over a wide area hundreds of miles west of today's Nile valley as foragers and hunters, but it was not until almost 12,000 B.C. that people in Africa began to develop a more organized and settled existence. There was more rainfall during the prehistoric millennia, and the great herds of wild cattle, gazelles, and ostriches it sustained guaranteed that early hunters would not go hungry. Closer to the great river, grassy plains and the then-forested steppe were the usual habitat for giraffes, elephants, and lions, and indeed, once it begins, prehistoric art testifies to their abundance during the formative stages of Egyptian civilization and still around the time of the political unification of Egypt (3100 B.C.) and the beginning of its historic age.

Even after the Nile receded into the river basin it has occupied throughout historic times, the presence of threatening animals such as lions (which continued to roam the boundaries of Egypt well into Roman times) and crocodiles and hippopotamuses (which inhabited the river and its swamps), along with the extensive floods that occurred annually, would have presented tribes of the Nile region with a world fraught with danger and difficulties. Did they face these dangers unarmed and unaided? Competing with large animals for food and depending on wild plants for balance in the diet is a precarious existence yet one that was followed for millennia before a more settled existence with domesticated plants and animals was attempted. Both men and women hunted game, but women—responsible for children— probably trapped smaller animals and foraged for edible plants closer to their settlements rather than join hunting parties that roamed farther afield for days or weeks at a time. It has been argued that the nurturing by mothers of their children would have stimulated human cerebral development, but also the greater amount of time for contact between females and children of the early tribes makes it likely that social organization developed and was passed along to the younger generation by the females of the group.[2]

Twenty thousand years ago people already had the same intelligence and physiques as today and thus were capable of learning which plants were edible, such as wild grapes, or useful, such as rushes and branches that could be worked into baskets to help in collecting and storing the gathered produce of the earth. Daily contact with wild plants would have led to the recognition that new shoots sprang from some of the seeds that had been left on the ground. This in turn would have led early women to deliberately sow more seeds to increase the yearly harvest.[3]

In time the vast increase of the harvest through using larger tracts of land that had not previously yielded food crops must have won for these first farmers the awe and appreciation of their communities. Domestication of animals and farming reduced dependence on hunting and possibly lowered the comparative status of the big game hunters in these early communities. The earliest graves from the prehistoric age in Egypt seldom contain weapons, except for a few arrowheads, which may indicate that defense was not a major concern of these first communities, and thus neither food production nor defense made males absolutely essential as leaders.[4] Indeed, archae-ologists report that in the earliest Egyptian prehistoric period, known as the Badarian (ca. 4500–4000 B.C.), women's graves were "in general larger than those of men."[5] Population growth was now an asset, not a liability, for in farming the more hands there were to help, the better off everyone was. The status of the mothering female thus may have risen, and the need for divinities concerned with fecundity of field, flock, and family would have been felt.

With the help of radiocarbon dating, the beginning of agriculture in the Near East has been placed at about 8000 B.C. The women, around whom families gathered and who produced the food, taught the best way to do myriad practical tasks, and passed on tribal lore, would not necessarily have found awesome powers and divinity in males. In animals, perhaps. In the stars and the moon certainly, but if asked by their children the sex of the Milky Way, or the moon, or the sky itself, early mothers may well have replied "Female."

If women won the admiration of their neighbors and families for feeding them, perhaps women also won political supremacy in the communities of prehistoric times. From our vantage point, we cannot know if this was true, or, if true some places, whether female leadership was possible in other places or long-lasting anywhere. It seems reason-able, however, to assume that female shamans or priestesses were behind the goddess cult attested by the shrines of Çatal Hüyük in ancient Anatolia, and the stories that women told and retold from generation to generation explaining the celestial phenomena to their children probably were the basis for the later formalized beliefs in sky goddesses, which are found contemporaneously in both ancient Sumer (in southern Iraq) and ancient Egypt.[6]

Because writing does not appear anywhere before 3100 B.C., the earliest religious beliefs of the Sumerians and Egyptians cannot be known except by projecting their earliest written mythology back in time. This is a dangerous if tempting methodology, and I am more interested in describing the cults of the female divinities in Egypt in the historic period, during which they are well documented. However, some Egyptian goddesses did have cults already in prehistoric times.

First Evidence of Faith

One can say nothing definitive about Egyptian religious beliefs before 4000 B.C., due to sparse artifactual remains and the absence of identifiable cemeteries. Before that time people along the Nile were predominantly hunters, fishers, and foragers and apparently did not bury their dead but laid them out to be disposed of by carrion or threw them into the river.[7] This suggests that the concept of an afterlife, for instance, had not yet developed.

By 4000 B.C., when agriculture was established, the people of the Badarian culture lived in settlements and laid their dead in well-formed graves. The graves were outfitted with pots that contained food and implements used in daily life, such as small copper tools and pins as well as slate palettes used in the preparation of cosmetics. Devoting time, energy, and expertise to digging graves and donating some of the wealth of the community to the dead indicate an already strongly established faith (or hope) in life after death. Also from this time, the presence of numerous figurines of animals, such as cows, bulls, and sheep, like the portrayals of the hunted beasts in the Paleolithic caves of France, suggests rituals to ensure a food supply and may indicate an appeal for an increase in herds. Threatening animals such as snakes and hippopotamuses, also found among the pottery models, may have been regarded as divine powers worthy of esteem or as powers requiring ritual exorcism. Few early amulets have been found, but at least two are known from this early Badarian period.[8] One was the head of an oryx or gazelle carved from stone and tied to the ankle of a male skeleton. Another, a pendant, was in the shape of a hippopotamus. In the first instance, we can surmise that the wearer hoped to be made swift as a gazelle; in the second, perhaps protection against the dangerous hippopotamus was sought. There were also clay vessels in the shape of birds, frogs, fish, and hippos, whether for ritual purposes or whimsy we cannot now know, but magic was undoubtedly a part of these peoples' daily lives, as it is in the lives of most of the world's indigenous peoples studied by ethnographers and anthropologists for decades.[9]

The Egyptologist Erik Hornung believes that ancient people did not see themselves as superior to the animal kingdom but as partners.[10] Certainly our remote ancestors were not masters of their universe. To be a "partner" was the very most one could hope for in a land populated by dangerous beasts. The superiority of beasts over humans could often be felt, and for this reason respect for the animal kingdom could flourish and may have spawned the idea that divinity was inherent in certain animals. Even at the height of their civilization, in the second millennium B.C., the deceased Egyptian on the day of judgment was expected to "avow not to have maltreated any cattle," and, as Hermann te Velde has pointed out, "in Egyptian ethics charity towards humans could be mentioned in the same breath with the feeding of animals."[11]

The Badarians entered Egypt from the south.[12] Like the Nilotic tribes of the Sudan today, they were both subsistence farmers and herders. Because herds "were an important investment or insurance against crop failure and hard times," they were "most valued for their dairy products."[13] Thus most cows would have lived out their lives providing milk. Our "earliest friend," the dog, was also an integral part of the Badarian community, signaling the approach of strangers and chasing predatory animals from the campsite and its storage places. Carefully wrapped and buried bodies of cows, sheep, and dogs have been found in Badarian cemeteries.

Because the cow later is equated with important goddesses, some prehistorians have stated that already in the Badarian period the cow represented a divine mother or fertility goddess. The prehistorian Elise Baumgartel has cited as evidence the female form of a few pottery vessels and the "cow-mother goddess" amulets (understood by some other scholars to be bulls' heads).[14] The greater usefulness of the cow in providing her milk for various products, her nurturing characteristics, and the life-giving maternity she symbolized would indeed seem to weigh in favor of these vessels and stone carvings commemorating cows rather than bulls. Henri Frankfurt was among the first to draw attention to how Egyptian culture reflected its closeness to bovines in many respects.[15] Baumgartel was also convinced that some women served as magicians or diviners in this early society. At several sites impressive graves whose dead were bedecked with jewelry (denoting high status) contained a variety of unusual implements that Baumgartel identified as professional ritual equipment connected with fertility magic.[16]

At one such grave at El-Mahasna a woman was laid to rest in a large square grave containing the richest furniture of all those excavated in the cemetery. On her skeleton was found a large number of ivory bracelets and around her neck several strings of carnelian and green-glazed steatite beads. Nearby lay two pairs of tusks, one hollow and one solid tusk in each pair, emblematic, Baumgartel suggested quaintly, of "the male and female element." Other objects in this grave point to fertility rites as well: a red pottery bowl on whose rim is modeled a line of four hippos (the hippo goddess of historic times was a protector and promoter of pregnancy) and a rare ivory statuette of an ithyphallic male. Such equipment and such a large, wealthy grave suggested to Baumgartel that here was a princess or a priestess or both, a woman of great consequence who carried out the necessary rites to keep her community healthy and growing.[17] Women's graves equipped richly and similarly were found at other early predynastic sites as well, so the female role in ritual seems to be well established in the prehistoric period in Egypt.[18]

Even the more modest tombs contained artistic objects that probably have religious significance. These are pottery figurines, usually but not exclusively female. The figurines often lack facial details (the head being just a knob or pinch of clay), and the majority have raised or outstretched arms. Most of them are not overtly sexual. Although the females have pendulous breasts, very few of the figurines show sex organs or even the pubic triangle. Nor are their legs usually delineated, but from the waist down the figure is simply conical in shape, perhaps to allow it to be grasped easily by the human hand. Although some of the female figurines exhibit wide hips, even most of these do not resemble steatopygous fertility figurines known from other cultures, where the buttocks as well as the abdomen are proportionally grossly oversized. The so-called Venus figures of Europe, many of which exhibit such exaggerated physical features, date from the much earlier upper Paleolithic and are not associated with graves.[19]

The agricultural revolution improved the lives of everyone, but it also made society conscious of the need for more people. An increase in workers could facilitate an increase in food production. To ensure human fertility, ancient women of the later historic period took votives to the shrines of appropriate goddesses, as we shall see later. Baumgartel thought the same happened in prehistoric times, but the earliest deities may have been chthonic, that is, dwelling in the earth.[20] Indeed, the appearance of new plants emerging from the soil may well have given early people the idea that a force below ground was pushing them upward, and serpents emerging from holes in the ground may have also encouraged the idea of an earth deity. Thus it may well have been, as Baumgartel suggested, that people felt the grave was a conduit for communicating with deities of fecundity. That most of the later Egyptian female figurines were found in graves was used by Baumgartel as support for their having religious significance. She suggested that they represented a donor (or surviving person), usually a woman, who wanted to petition the mother goddess for children.[21] We do not know for certain, but it is also possible that they represented a deity (they are not all female) whose image would protect or help the dead as did later, historic deities, especially goddesses. In the historic period elite Egyptians were often buried with servant statues who would be available to do any tasks required of their owners. However, the prehistoric figurines lack hands or fully formed arms and legs and thus probably do not represent servant statues.[22] Scholars have referred to some of the female figurines of later times as "concubines" who were placed in the grave to render sexual service in the Beyond. However, a large number of the predynastic figurines were found in the graves of women and children. P. J. Ucko has suggested a range of possibilities for the anthropomorphic figurines: children's playthings, vehicles of sympathetic magic, representations of deceased twins, or sorcerers' agents.[23] But none of these scenarios explains why the overwhelming preponderance of figurines is female in form, unless females (divine or not) were originally regarded by that society as more important, more powerful, and more essential for the survival of Egyptians, both living and dead.

Once graves and grave goods appeared, it is logical that grave rituals also developed. Judging from their historic roles and the equipment found in some prehistoric graves, women were very much a part of the rituals and beliefs concerning death and resurrection. Recently the Egyptian archaeologist Fekri Hassan added his voice to those who believe that the main cult of the predynastic period was dedicated to a goddess associated with death and resurrection "as well as with the plants, domestic animals, and the cycles of nature."[24]

GOD THE MOTHER?

Although she makes no such claim for it, the prehistorian and archaeologist Barbara Adams has published a remarkable little figurine from the predynastic cemetery at Qau, which, more than any of those surviving from predynastic Egypt, might be taken as a representation of a goddess of fertility.[25] She is a well-modeled and graceful image of good proportions. Her arms were never extended beyond the shoulders, and her legs are now broken off. Her breasts are ample but not exaggerated, and a pubic triangle is delineated. Thus, without the arms, the woman's sexuality seems to be emphasized by the artist (who, Adams believes, was a female potter). Uniquely and significantly, on the back of the woman is incised a fanlike pattern that seems to represent vegetation, as Egyptians of the historical period often portrayed clumps of plants in a fan-shaped grouping. Perhaps in the mind of this artist the divinity of fecundity of the earth was female. A larger pottery figurine, this one with its raised arms partially preserved, was found by W. M. F. Petrie at Naqada and recently republished by Hassan. She has animal, grain(?), and water designs all over her body.[26] Similarly, animals of the savanna (ruminants and ostriches) are associated with female figures (of larger size) on the decorated pots of the last prehistoric cultural phase, the Gerzean period (3300–3100 B.C.). It would seem likely that here indeed are early representations of a goddess of fecundity.

Scholars studying other cultures have been convinced that goddess worship was strongly connected, and that it expanded, with the growth of sophisticated agriculture, advances in animal domestication, and even the emergence of settled urban life. Linking a female deity with the fertility of the earth is an idea that spans the globe and still persists among us to this day, yet this concept came to be denied, as we shall see.

The sacred status of womankind may have begun tens of thousands of years ago, reflecting the mysterious and remarkable powers that human women possessed and human males did not. But the goddess of fertility would more likely have taken shape at the dawn of the agricultural revolution and the domestication of animals—both of which could easily be the legacies of our prehistoric ancestresses. As mothers are on the whole typically more approachable and nurturing than fathers, it is not surprising that the idea of a divine mother is encountered all over the world, possibly going back more than twenty thousand years, and is still present today, as in India, where goddess cults are very much alive. In respecting the fertility of women, the ancient Egyptians could have seen divine femininity as the power that made the plants grow and the herds multiply. Later the historical goddesses indeed possessed such attributes. They fed humankind, cured, protected, and brought forth new life, and were the guardians who received the dead and led them into a new and better world. As they ruled in this world and the next, it is not surprising to find goddesses linked intimately with the human who sat on the throne in earthly life. This relationship is well documented for historic Egypt, as will be shown, but is not as clear for the prehistoric period from which only artifactual evidence survives. However, the goddesses of dynastic Egypt must have antecedents in the prehistoric period, which is not so culturally distinct at its later stages from Egypt at the time of the pharaohs.

OUT OF AFRICA

There is much evidence from ancient Egypt contradicting the opinion commonly held by historians that all women of all earlier cultures were relegated to the private sphere. In pharaonic times Egyptian women were regularly called up to do national service, as were men. In religious life women were active participants in the cult, serving in many ranks of the clerical hierarchy, and certainly did not require a male to mediate between them and a deity. Similarly, Egyptian women were independent legal persons and did not need a male cosignatory or legal guardian. They were free to earn wages and make purchases in the marketplace. Ancient Egyptian women owned and had complete control over both movable and immovable property such as real estate. This right could not be claimed by women in some parts of the United States as late as the 1960s.[27]

The independence and leadership roles of ancient Egyptian women may be part of an African cultural pattern that began millennia ago and continued into recent times. In the 1860s the famous Dr. David Livingstone wrote of meeting female chiefs in the Congo, and in most of the monarchical systems of traditional Africa there were either one or two women of the highest rank who occupied a position on a par with that of the king or complementary to it.[28]

Anthropologists who have studied tribes and records of early travelers and missionaries tell us that "everywhere in Africa that one scrapes the surface one finds ethno-historical data on the authority once shared by women."[29] Recent work with traditional African societies has revealed that both men and women were recognized as having important roles in the public sphere. Thus it is not too surprising to find that in Egypt in several excavated cemeteries from the early cultural periods the richest tombs were those of women. In another grave at Badari (grave no. 3740) a woman was buried with a weapon that was commonly used in sacrifice, a "knobbed mace-head of pink limestone," as well as a slate cosmetic palette.[30] These were valuable objects and indicated high status as well as wealth.

If prominent roles for females were the norm for many African societies and for this reason show up already in ancient Egypt, perhaps there are other indications of an African cultural heritage pertinent to our study. Early Egyptologists, such as E. A. Wallis Budge and Flinders Petrie, seemed to be reluctant to credit much cultural development to the indigenous inhabitants of the Nile valley and were quick to attribute the arrival of agriculture and important deities to the incursions of western Asiatics into the region. However, the most recent research indicates that Egyptian agriculture was started in the western oases centuries before the agriculturalists migrated east toward the Nile Valley.[31] Such a bias against the creativity of an African culture is reflected even by more recent writers and scholars such as E. O. James, who did not consider Africa pertinent for his study of the pancultural cult of the mother goddess. He claimed that even the sun god of the Egyptians, Re, was an import from the cloud-covered eastern Mediterranean, a claim unsubstantiated by any evidence (James provides none) and illogical for the sun-drenched land of Egypt.[32] It might be argued that the sun's heat was a destructive force and the sun would be more appreciated in a cooler and damper climate, but the harmful aspect of the sun was seldom acknowledged later in Egypt and its benign aspect more often emphasized. The sun's disk is frequently encountered in Egyptian religious iconography, and the sun god Re was the supreme deity in the pantheon during much of pharaonic history.

Recently the archaeologist Barry J. Kemp has considered some of these early claims for the importance of cultural importations and argues for an Upper Egyptian origin for Horus, the falcon god of the sky, which had been proposed by others as an Asiatic import.[33] Kemp also realistically points to the "unlimited agricultural potential" of the Egyptian landscape in which the sustenance of a settled life by the growing of crops found nothing but encouragement and could have developed naturally.[34]

It is most helpful to search among surviving Nilotic tribes, such as the Dinka of the White Nile, to gain insight into the material and spiritual life of the early predynastic Egyptians. The Dinka, who were studied intensively by anthropologists during the first half of the twentieth century, were a herding society that did some farming and a little hunting. Their value system and social life revolved, to a large extent, around their cattle, which provided them with food, drink, and clothing as well as inspiration in song and dance. While there were rich pasture-lands along the riverbanks, during floods the herds had to be moved to the unsettled savanna at a higher elevation. Human settlements were on outcroppings that kept the villagers dry.

Although the Dinka tribespeople interviewed by the anthropologist Godfrey Lienhardt professed belief in a supreme divinity, they also had clan divinities, which often took the emblem of a particular animal. As the Dinka explained it, if a clan took a giraffe or an elephant as its clan divinity, it did not mean that divinity was present in all such animals, but it did require that such animals be treated with respect. The divinity represented by the animal is one and apart: if all giraffes were to be somehow exterminated, the spirit of ancestral Giraffe would endure and would help to protect the clan. Thus it was not the individual animal member but the concept Giraffe that belonged to a wider class of powers. "It seems that the Dinka themselves often think of them as acquired by chance— a chance association, though an important one, between the founding ancestor of a clan and the species, which then becomes the clan divinity of all his descendants."[35]

Because the surviving emblems from predynastic Egypt show falcons and cows, hippopotamuses and gazelles, and among the names of the first kings of the historic period are Catfish and Scorpion, and later deities appear as crocodiles, lionesses, vultures, and ibises, it is tempting to see here the vestiges of early clan divinities. The prehistoric schematic clay figurines of human shape (and of both sexes) with arms gracefully raised and bent inward, usually above the head but sometimes positioned more forward, bear a striking resemblance to the Dinka photographed by Leinhardt. In these photographs the Dinka dance with just such curved, raised arms. According to Lienhardt, the Dinka are portraying the sweeping horns of a "display ox."[36] So important and central to their society are the cattle they keep that Dinka youths are reported, when sitting by themselves alone with their herd, as holding their arms extended and curved in just this position. This could explain why the few predynastic figurines that appear to be seated still exhibit this formation of the arms.

The Primeval Cow Goddess

Although Baumgartel believed the Badarian conical-bottomed figurines with raised arms were images of humans, not deities, she saw the image of a bovine fertility goddess in some of the pottery of the succeeding Upper Egyptian cultural phase (ca. 4000 B.C.), the Amratian/Naqada I culture. There is a vase dating from the end of Naqada I "on the exterior of which are represented in relief a human head flanked by two cow's horns and a pair of arms holding the breasts which descend from the rim of the vase behind the head."[37] Other vases from the period are known which also show arms holding breasts. Such artifacts have been used to argue for a maternal or fertility goddess in the prehistoric period. In my opinion, this concept would also fit in with the flora- and fauna-engraved female figurines described above.

Figure 1. Predynastic female figureine from Naqada, possibly a goddess of fecundity. After Petrie and Quibell 1896. Drawing by Lee Payne.

There are still those (not only some Egyptologists) who charge that the idea of a prehistoric and widely venerated mother goddess (suggested by the hundreds of so-called Venus figurines found across Europe) is merely a fantasy.[38] It is obvious, however, that the female role not only of giver of birth (life) but also of sustainer of early life would naturally have had a profound impact on the earliest humans. Of course, their world was populated by all sorts of forces, many life threatening, which needed to be recognized and propitiated, and this calls into doubt the concept of a lone goddess or even a supreme mother goddess dominating all other divinities. The more explicit evidence from Asia Minor and southern Europe and other Neolithic cultures suggests that a similar very early African or Egyptian earth mother or mother goddess is surely possible even if it is not substantiated by physical evidence in Egypt and even if she was not venerated alone.

Archaeological and anthropological data from the ancient Near East and Africa suggest that when and where the female principle was venerated, it often assumed aspects of the cow.[39] The cow is a domesticated animal; it can stand, anywhere at any time in history, as the very image of the homestead, of settled agricultural life—an image evoking warmth and security. The cow is surely the embodiment of nurturing motherhood. Gentle with her young and sharing her milk with humans as well, the cow is venerated even today in herding societies throughout the world. In Sri Lanka, for instance, a milk-overflowing ceremony invokes the goddess who stands for "matrilineal kinship, mother's blood, bodily health, and integration of community."[40]

The earliest clear representation of a cow goddess is found on a slate palette of the Gerzean Period that bears a relief of a cow's head (facing forward) and five stars just above the tips of the horns. Hornung suggests she is to be equated with Bat, the cow icon of Upper Egypt.[41] Baumgartel thought this was the first representation of the sky as a deity,[42] and surely the stars do suggest a celestial goddess. Mehet-Weret, known from the historic period's literature but often appearing as a precursor to the sky goddess Nut, is another possible identity for this starry head.

The curved cow horns are reminiscent of the lunar crescent, but there was no moon goddess in pharaonic Egypt. However, the crescent moon, as I have seen it in Luxor, hanging low over the western hills with points turned upward, certainly evokes a celestial bovine's horns. Thus we may have in this early rendition of a sacred cow one of the few hints of a moon goddess who might have flourished as far back as the Neolithic or early Chalcolithic but who disappeared, or was suppressed, during the early historic period. From the archaeological evidence it is clear that not one but several religious cults were established long before the Two Lands were unified and a documented Egyptian history began.

In about 3100 B.C., when the Upper Egyptians celebrated what may have been their final victory over the delta and united Egypt into a strong kingdom of the Two Lands, they placed the cow (or possibly buffalo) goddess of Upper Egypt, Bat, prominently at the top of both sides of a large commemorative shield-shaped slate. This palette with its relief scenes commemorating the victory of King Narmer and the Upper Egyptians—known today as the Narmer Palette—is an important historic and artistic monument. Given her dominant position on both sides, it seems that the goddess, who promoted the birth of humans, now presided over the birth of a nation.

Figure 2. The two heads of Bat from the Narmer Palette. Drawing by Lee Payne.

With the absence of texts from Egypt's prehistoric period we cannot understand all the nuances of the early goddess's meaning for her people, but in the literature of Egypt's historic period, as we shall see presently, the image of the cow goddess is prominent and she has many important roles to play. James suggested that not until animal husbandry was practiced and the role of the male found to be essential in breeding was a male divine role imagined. This, if true, would give primacy to the cow clan divinity but would not explain the presence of other animal divinities unless they were predated by only one (female animal) divinity from a time too early to have provided any artifactual evidence.

Clearly goddesses did not have exclusive command of humanity's loyalty or fear, however. The same rich female's grave (page 9) that contained the slim male figure also contained an ivory carving of an animal, later identified with the god Seth, and in the next cultural phase, the Gerzean period, pot paintings indicate that a multitude of cults were flourishing before 3200 B.C. The buff pottery of the Gerzean age with its red line paintings gives us the best insights into the culture of the late predynastic period. Various deities known from later times are suggested by the totems portrayed. Among the divine symbols are the harpoonlike spear or phallic symbol of the fertility god Min, the falcon of Horus, who was later known as a sky god, and the crossed arrows of the goddess Neith. While large female figures are found on a number of Gerzean pots, a large male ithyphallic figure is depicted, adjacent to the totem for Min, on a least one pot known to me (found in a grave at Ballas).[43] Thus the male role in fertility was probably recognized in Egypt contemporaneously with the female.

The Egyptologist Jaroslav Černý believed that anthropomorphism in the portrayal of deities developed when intellectual rather than purely physical qualities became most valued by people. This he connected with the flowering of civilization; "Gods, to whom a high degree of power and intelligence was attributed, were, therefore, bound to assume human form."[44] Humans, both men and women, are portrayed on Gerzean pot paintings. Among the portrayals of birds, landmasses, and huts or shrines, many Gerzean pots have a female figure, usually with arms raised as in the pottery figurines, who is portrayed on a larger scale than other closely associated female and male figures. Baumgartel interpreted the major female figure as the great mother goddesses, and others have been equally convinced.[45] However, because there is often more than one female figure and a number of smaller figures portrayed, the concept of a goddess and her lover/son that is found in other cultures (and suggested by Baumgartel and, more recently, by Hassan) does not quite fit.[46] Again, the presence of a lone ithyphallic male figure on other pots argues persuasively for both male and female deities concerned with fertility and not a single dominant female deity.

It is just as legitimate—if one wanted to build on this very tenuous evidence—to suggest that the larger female in the vase paintings is a human, perhaps a politically important person. Indeed, in historic period art, the more important figure, whether in a family or a national scene, whether human or divine, is portrayed on a larger scale. The frequent prominence of a female figure in the Gerzean paintings could indicate a goddess, a priestess, or a chieftainess; nothing more can be said with certainty. There is no absolute evidence for a prehistoric monotheism, whether based on a female or a male principle. Indeed, Hassan believes strongly in the "complementarity of the male and female principals" in the mythic thought of predynastic Egyptians.[47] The recognizable totems of that age give ample evidence of both male and female deities. As in historic times, the earliest inhabitants of the Nile valley seemed to have preferred a multiplicity of choices.

Also it should be recalled, but seldom is, that deities themselves (as opposed to their standards or totems) were very rarely portrayed by Egyptian artists until much later, not at first in tombs, not very extensively in sculpture, only in royal contexts, and not until the Middle Kingdom in representational art associated with commoners. Egyptologists who have not even considered the possibility of political importance, or temporal power (such as clan leaders or priestesses for such female figures), perhaps have been biased by the patriarchal societies in which they themselves live. They also reveal a lack of familiarity with African political history, as known from later periods. Numerous regions in sub-Saharan Africa have experienced generations of rule by females, and Egypt's southern neighbor, the kingdom of Meroe, exhibited this at its height in the last millennium B.C.

Female leadership in society or in cults certainly does not rule out female deities; just the opposite would be expected. It will be seen that the queens of the First Dynasty had close ties to the goddess Neith, whose presence is documented by representations of her totem in the late prehistoric period. They incorporated her name in theirs and oversaw her cult. No doubt at her original cult center, the town later known as Sais, this goddess was supreme, and some might have claimed "alone." It was when the many petty city-states became consolidated into one nation that the multitude of cults had to be sorted out.

What happened when civilization and the Egyptian state developed in about 3100 B.C.? Hassan suggests the following interpretation of events. The predynastic myths and rituals, concerned with birth, death, and resurrection, had been associated with goddesses. Now these goddesses' sacred powers were absorbed by the male leaders of the consolidated state of the First Dynasty. The early state "was most likely not the result of a single battle, but the culmination of wars and alliances, as well as fragmentation and re-unification over a period of at least 250 years." The few major kingdoms that emerged between 3400 and 3200 B.C. included, among others, Naqada and Hierakonpolis in Upper Egypt and Sais in the delta. Each locale had its own principal deity (Seth at Naqada, Horus at Hierakonpolis, and Neith at Sais in these cases). But as a unified state was created from local or "tribal" (to use Hassan's term) societies, so too a shift in emphasis from local deities to cosmic gods was necessitated. Early women had found their power in kinship-based relations, but their roles were now undermined by the emergence of a nonkinship organization, composed of male-dominated political groups related to defense and economic activities "beyond the traditional (territorial) domain of females."[48]

Now too occurred a "transition from a focus on female-linked vegetation and regeneration cults to male-linked myths and rituals of legitimation." The king took on, as a reflection of his cosmic role, the "guaranteeing of prosperity, the orderly transition of the seasons, and plentiful harvests." There was no more need for a goddess of the herds or a mother goddess of the earth who assured bountiful crops. The king himself would uphold Maat, the divine order of the universe, and assure that all was well in Egypt. Divine kingship became the cornerstone of the Egyptian state, and the king was given a divine genealogy by the priests of Heliopolis, the chief cult center of the sun god, Re. The king found himself equated with Horus, the great god of the sky, revered for centuries by the town whose leaders took credit for the unification of the Two Lands. Myths now provided "a cosmic rationale for the rule of a male king and hereditary succession."[49]

The old goddesses could not be ignored, however. That would have been dangerous. So it was necessary for them to legitimize the king. He is affiliated with the Two Ladies, the vulture goddess Nekhbet of El-Kab in Upper Egypt and the cobra goddess Wadjet of Buto in the delta or Lower Egypt. They would protect him as divine mothers or serve him as nurses, just as would the bovine goddess Bat, who appeared on the top of the Narmer Palette. Later Isis, the throne, and Hathor, the divine genealogy of the king personified, would nurture and protect and even revive the king when dead. Hassan suggests that the god Osiris gained the "funerary role of the goddess" when he became god-king of the dead.[50] Nut the sky goddess developed out of the earlier Mehet-Weret, as will be seen shortly. Over the centuries the goddesses found themselves with new roles but with staying power as well, because the theologians of the sun god and the priests of the king were not the only worshipers in the land.

$\mathcal{T}$HE SKY GODDESS NUT

In the beginning were air and moisture, and from their union came the earth and the sky, and the sky was named Nut, and she was a goddess who would give birth to all of the gods. This was one of many creation stories the historic Egyptians devised to explain the age-old, universal human quest for understanding of how the universe of beings and forces came into existence. How should we interpret this particular cosmogony? Does it prove that from the very beginning of their intellectual stirrings the Egyptians believed in a supreme mother goddess? If so, did they represent her in sculpture and worship her in shrines? Did she accompany them even in death? Was she supreme over all other beings? At the time that the cosmogonies, or genealogies of gods, were written down, the patriarchal state and professional priesthoods had already developed. The priesthoods made sure that air and moisture were preceded by a male creator. For the priests of the sun at the city of On, this male creator was Atum; for the priests at Memphis, it was Ptah, the god of craftsmen; and at Hermopolis, it was Thoth, god of wisdom and chief deity of that community. Nonetheless, the sky goddess Nut (pronounced Noot) was acknowledged universally as mother of all the gods who came after her.

As we have seen, those whose lives center around animal husbandry and agriculture are likely to project the image of their favorite animals onto the larger, divine scale. The cow is known to have been the manifestation of the great goddess at one of Egypt's earliest and holiest shrines: the city temple of Nekhen, later Hierakonpolis, home of Egypt's first kings. This was the largest predynastic settlement in Upper Egypt, home to the falcon god Horus and also to the bovine goddess whose image dominates the large and beautifully carved palette commemorating the defeat of the North by the Upper Egyptians (ca. 3100 B.C.).[1]

Scholars consider Bat to have been a sky goddess. Her four legs were the four pillars that supported the heavenly canopy, her star-studded belly. Interestingly, the name seems to mean "female soul" or even "female power,"[2] and it is tempting to interpret this as the deification of the very essence of femininity, cast large against the sky. The two faces of Bat on the Narmer Palette correspond to the two faces on the handles of sacred rattles (sistra) and mirrors used later in temple ritual and seem to be a sign of power, the ability to see before and behind. This is expressed in the earliest funerary literature, known as the Pyramid Texts, which were inscribed on the inner walls of royal pyramids of the Fifth and Sixth dynasties (ca. 2500–2180 B.C.).[3] Later the goddess Nut, who most frequently was portrayed as a completely human woman, is sometimes herself represented as a cow: May Nut the Great put her hands on him / She the long of horn, the pendulous of breast (PT Utt. 548). Nut represents a move from predynastic clan divinities that express reliance on the superior physical powers of certain animals to cosmogonic deities. She was a member of the original family, the daughter of the first couple, Shu and Tefnut, air and moisture. These divinities received less attention from the Egyptians, perhaps because they were so amorphous. However, a text on the coffin of a woman who lived in about 2000 B.C. states that Nut was "already glorious and powerful in the womb of her mother Tefnut even before she was born."[4] Nut was much more tangible, if distant.

It is typical of ancient Egyptian religious beliefs that several competing mythologies, only small snippets of which survive, coexisted in the Pyramid Texts. Allusions to these also appear in the later written religious books that guaranteed the attainment of a successful afterlife to any deserving deceased person. From these later texts we learn of another cow goddess who was a personification of the primeval waters out of which the first life arose. This is Mehet-Weret, the Great Flood, who is credited as the first entity of existence. In a land such as Egypt where a great flood covered much of the inhabited Nile valley and delta each year following a long, dry season and left, as it receded, a refreshed earth sprouting with life, it seems natural that a primeval watery abyss would be conceived of as having predated all life. Confusingly, however, later theologians conceived of this Great Flood as a *celestial* cow goddess. Thus in Spell 124 of the Book of the Dead, which was probably not composed until the second millennium B.C., Mehet-Weret is associated with other sky deities.[5] This may have come about because by the historic period, when theologians were attempting to systematize a confusing array of early myths and divinities, deities were merged or at least caused to share many attributes and concerns. Furthermore, the surviving religious books all pertain to the cults of the funeral and afterlife of the worthy deceased. The Netherworld was understood by the Egyptians as being in the sky. Thus, simply put, the earth represented life, and the sky was the domain of the dead. The watery abyss on earth engendered life, and the sky goddess received the dead. Thus all deities who would find a role in funerary prayers and rituals had to be, somehow, associated with the sky, but placing Mehet-Weret in heaven vacated space below, so that the theologians could hand it over to a male deity. Before we leave the subject of Mehet-Weret, it is interesting to note that although primeval, she was never completely forgotten, for Egyptians seldom discarded anything that had proven worth in the past. Thus in the New Kingdom (1567–1085 B.C.) she reappears in the Book of the Celestial Cow, a recorded myth preserved in texts in royal tombs.

The Book of the Celestial Cow is found in the tombs of kings who ruled after the iconoclastic Amarna period, under the pharaoh Akhenaton and Nefertiti, who so drastically affected the pantheistic religious establishments of their time. The traditional theologians, who regained control subsequently, resurrected older mythological concepts out of nostalgia for earlier, more orthodox times. The outermost golden shrine over the sarcophagus of Pharaoh Tutankhamun and the walls of the tombs of Seti I, Ramses II, and Ramses III all preserve the myth that tells of the aged and tired sun god desiring to retire from the responsibilities of earthly rule and ascending into heaven on the back of the celestial cow. The concept of the sky itself as a gigantic celestial cow is also preserved and is graphically portrayed on Tutankhamun's golden shrine, one of four that, one within the other, surrounded his sarcophagus.[6]

The cow was not the only way the Egyptians conceived of the sky, however. There are indications in the Pyramid Texts that at least in some parts of the country the sky was thought of as a great vulture.[7]

We cannot know how early the Egyptians began to formulate the origins of the gods of the cosmos, but there is no reason to believe that they waited until their writing system was developed. Surely there was a rich oral tradition long before the start of the historic dynasties. The innumerable and often-incomprehensible (to us) allusions in the Pyramid Texts of the Old Kingdom (surviving examples date only to about 2350 B.C.) bear this out. There is no doubt that early people were very much aware of the sky and studied the stars at night. Even today in the less urbanized areas of Egypt, the night sky is very black and the stars vivid; before industrial pollution, the celestial orbs would have been even more visible to the naked eye. Indeed, nineteenth-century authors have written of their vividness:

> The blue of the sky is dotted with stars—they are almost like fires—the sky is aflame—a real oriental night.[8]

> The stars gave as much light as the moon in Europe.[9]

Several scholars have suggested that Egyptian myths were created to explain what early people saw in the sky, for example, that Nut was created to personify the Milky Way.[10] This may be true, as tomb paintings of the Ramesside period (thirteenth century B.C.) display stars not only on Nut's body but also alongside it, suggesting that she was sometimes regarded as representing only part of the sky, not the entire canopy.[11] Furthermore, Spell 176 in the Book of the Dead refers to the Milky Way, and Spell 177 begins by invoking Nut. If Nut was the Milky Way, the yellow-white elongated mass of stars would easily lend itself to being interpreted as the naked yellow skin of a woman (women were almost always painted yellow by Egyptian artists, and men reddish brown).

A professional astronomer has recently published maps of the pre-dawn Egyptian sky as it would have appeared in the predynastic period on the morning of the winter solstice. The Milky Way exhibits an amazing likeness to the outstretched figure of the goddess Nut, with her feet on one horizon and her hands touching the other (see fig. 3). The sun would have appeared at the winter solstice in the correct area

Figure 3. The goddess Nut bending over her husband, Geb, the earth, from the Inner Coffin of Nany. Rogers Fund, 1930. Courtesy of the Metropolitan Museum of Art, New York.

of the figure's anatomy to suggest to observers that it was being born by Nut. Nine months earlier, at the spring equinox, the sun began to rise an hour and a quarter after sunset in such a position that it appeared to fall into Nut's mouth, which would have easily suggested the idea that the great female in the sky was swallowing the sun, only to bear him nine months later during the last days of what is now December.[12]

The Pyramid Texts honor Nut with epithets such as "Great Protector," "Grand Horizon," and "Mother of the Gods." Nut was the most prominent sky goddess of the historic period, but she was probably not the first or only goddess in the sky. Indeed, some infer that she was a creation of the Heliopolitan priests of the sun god in the Old Kingdom, although the "sky religion" itself was doubtless much older.[13] However, the early and well-known images of the bovine goddess Bat and of Mehet-Weret were intentionally downplayed in the historic period in favor of a goddess in human form who, like a heavenly mother, would

Figure 4. The Pyramid Texts inscribed on the interior walls of the Pyramids of Unis, Fifth Dynasty. Photo by L. H. Lesko.

receive into her realm the blessed dead (who became stars) and who would also be the mother of the sun Re. The place-names of the sun's voyage inside Nut suggest aspects of the goddess's anatomy, as Leonard H. Lesko has pointed out: "winding waterway," "nurse canal," "field of reeds," "doors thrown open."[14] Such double entendres are commonly found much later, in New Kingdom love songs,[15] and various plays on words, including puns and alliteration, abound in the Pyramid Texts, which were originally chanted aloud.

The purpose of the Nut sequence of spells in the Pyramid Texts (some Middle Kingdom coffins found at the same site, Saqqara, contain these texts as well) was to empower the deceased to rise into the sky and to become an imperishable star throughout eternity. Texts that describe the sky goddess Nut as stretched out over the deceased come from either the sarcophagus chamber of the royal pyramid or from the lids of the coffins found in the great cemetery at Saqqara. The deceased comes to "mother Nut in her name of sarcophagus" (PT Utt.

364). Throughout the historic period Nut was firmly associated with receiving, reviving, and protecting the dead.[16] As she herself says in the mortuary texts engraved on the interior walls of royal pyramids from about 2350 B.C. on and probably deriving from preceding centuries of theological thought:

> I enclose your beauty within this soul of mine
> for all life, stability, dominion and health for the king.
> May he live for ever! (PT Utt. 11)

There are texts that describe the entire coffin as the goddess, so that it serves as the body, actually the womb, of Nut from which the deceased will emerge, that is, be born again (PT Utt. 325). The concept of the sarcophagus as Nut's womb fits well with the identification of the deceased with the god Osiris, Lord of the Dead, who mythology tells us is Nut's son, and also with Re, the sun god, as Nut bore the sun every day. Pyramid Text Utterances 466 and 697 tell us that Nut bore the constellation Orion (which thus came to be understood as Osiris) and daily gave birth to stars. She is given a strong image, said to be more powerful than Shu, her father, and to take the gods to her.[17]

Nut was usually portrayed as an attractive, svelte, naked woman, which is very unusual for an Egyptian deity. Indeed, the nude was never popular in historic period Egyptian art. Nut may have been portrayed this way in religious iconography because she was to be thought of as a woman about to give birth. From the Coffin Texts—a compilation of mortuary texts written inside wooden coffins of the Middle Kingdom— comes a reference to Nut having braided hair (e.g., Sp. 77), which may indicate as well the image of a woman in labor who keeps her hair from being a nuisance at a difficult time. Also, her light skin is suggested by the white streak in the sky. One of Nut's characteristics was her outstretched arms. Bending over the earth with her fingertips on one horizon and her feet on the other, Nut embodied the heavens. As part of the first generation of gods, with her brother Geb, Nut was the ancestress of the holy pantheon and by inference mother to all living creatures. From this earliest preserved religious literature come repeated assertions that the dead king or queen will ascend to heaven, join mother Nut, and become one of the imperishable stars of her realm:

May you go forth with your mother Nut; that she may take your hand and give you the road to the horizon, to the place where Re is. (PT Utt. 422)

The King will not die . . . for the King is an Imperishable Star, [son] of the great sky in the midst of the Mansion of Selket. (PT Utt. 571)

By 2000 B.C., commoners had acquired, seized, or were offered the once exclusively royal mortuary religious texts and concepts for themselves and forever after represented the sky goddess Nut—the protective mother who embraces the deceased and imparts eternal life—on the inside of their coffins. A woman of the Twelfth Dynasty had this inscribed on her coffin: "She imbues the Mistress of the House, Senebtisi justified, with life, stability, and power so that she not die ever."[18] Professor Černý believed that the stars that spangled the sky goddess's body had to represent not only the royal dead but also all worthy spirits: "Nut was the 'one with a thousand souls' (kha-bawes); certainly all the numberless stars did not belong to dead kings, but included other humans as well."[19] From this distance in time, we cannot know the details of what ordinary people during the earliest dynasties believed, hoped for, or were permitted to anticipate concerning an afterlife.

There are still other puzzling characteristics of Egyptian religion. For instance, it is very unusual for a people to have a goddess of the sky and not of the earth.[20] Some references in the Pyramid Texts to Isis and Nephthys being the two banks of the River Nile have been interpreted as vestiges of the goddess-as-earth concept in predynastic Egypt.[21] This idea was replaced in the Old Kingdom by the Heliopolitan cosmogony, which names the earth god Geb and the sky goddess Nut as parents of the two pairs of deities who contended for rule of the world. Why did the historic Egyptians promote the earth as male and the sky as female? Worldwide sky deities are much more commonly male. It seems that the Egyptians were denying the more obvious fertility of the childbearing female, but, as Susan Hollis also points out correctly, Nut does bear the gods and thus is not a lifeless heavenly roof.[22] In Egypt life-sustaining water does not come from the sky but from the river, which the ancients saw as part of the earth, but this does not explain why in pharaonic Egypt the divinity of the earth was deemed a male.

Those who have studied the Great Mother-goddess cults found throughout the world are convinced that such a goddess representing the fertility of the land and its people existed in predynastic times in Egypt (perhaps reflected in the female figurine from Qau described above or in the concept of the Great Flood as a cow) but was intentionally removed from serious consideration by the professional (male) theologians of the historic period.[23] The fertility bestowed by the Nile inundation was personified now by the androgynous Hapi, or Nile spirits, and would often be associated with the dead god Osiris who rose again. The earth god Geb received little attention, enjoyed few if any cult places, and had little acknowledged connection with nature's fertility; he was honored more as father of gods, by virtue of being the mate of Nut. Nut's mothering vis-à-vis humans was associated with receiving the dead and causing them to be reborn after death. Thus the role of a fertility goddess or mother goddess outside the realm of the dead was greatly diminished by Old Kingdom theologians. However, as will be seen later, the Egyptians acknowledged more than one goddess as the divine mother.

Although the first royal funerary literature known as the Pyramid Texts describe Nut in flattering terms—as powerful while yet in the womb of her own mother (PT Utt. 430), as having power over her own father, Shu (PT Utt. 434), as filling every place with her beauty (PT Utt. 432), and even as king of Lower Egypt (PT Utt. 431)—it is interesting that these Nut spells are not found among the Pyramid Texts on the earlier royal tombs; they appear only in the Sixth Dynasty pyramids of the kings Pepi I, Merenre, and Pepi II. It may well be that Nut was an example of a phenomenon we will encounter again: the deliberate construction, during the formative years of the Old Kingdom, by theologians of a pantheon that banished the more primitive chthonic deities (like Mehet-Weret) to lesser status and put in their place new, or newly improved forms of, deities that fitted in better with the concept of divine kingship and "civilized life" in general. Such a manipulation was not unique to the Egyptians. It has been suggested for ancient (contemporary to the Old Kingdom) Sumer, where an apparent "fall" of the supreme mother goddess in the "divine pecking order" occurred in the Sumerian theological system very early.[24] The deliberate destruction of the original female creator is even more clearly described in later Babylonian religious texts.[25] Thus the idea that the same thing occurred in Egypt, with the establishment of the organized state and the development of the cult of divine kingship, should not be surprising.

Kemp has suggested that Egyptian religion, as we know it from the formal, state-approved written texts, is an intellectually manipulated construction of the historic period, most likely of the middle or late Old Kingdom.[26] While he places more emphasis on developments in religious iconography, it is probable that intellectual intervention was devoted as much to religious teachings and that the religion known from the historic period's monuments and written documents does not necessarily reflect much of the original religious beliefs of the pre- and protodynastic Egyptians (or the vast majority of unlettered Egyptians of the historic period for that matter) but new concepts designed mainly to promote the divinity of the king of Egypt. Indeed, in 1959 Rudolf Anthes proposed that "the historical concept of Horus as the ruler of the sky or lord of heaven was speculative rather than natural and came into existence in consequence of the unification."[27] Thus up until approximately 3000 B.C. the sky may well have been generally considered female, but, for political purposes, afterward Nut had to coexist with a heavenly counterpart, Horus, who became a more prominent deity in the historic period. Who was Horus?

THE MYTH OF DIVINE KINGSHIP

Egypt is itself hardly a geographic unity but an expanse of delta in the north and a long river valley along which communication was slow. Regionalism was a factor in the formation of Egyptian religions. It can be argued that historic period funerary concepts reveal religions dedicated to Thoth (god of wisdom, associated with the moon, the sacred ibis, and the sacred baboon), Re (the sun), and Osiris (god of the flood and king of the dead). As Nut was originally considered the mother of Osiris, she was very much a part of the religion that worshiped him. Each presented different goals desired by its faithful in the afterlife. Thus uniformity of religious concepts was never total or desired. From the beginning, there were various ways of thinking about death and the hereafter as well as creation, and the dominant deities were quite individual or localized. It became the concern of the tightly centralized state to formulate religious concepts, promoting certain ideas from various regions of the country and discarding or diminishing others. Placing the king at the center, as son of the supreme gods, was the goal of this manipulation.[28] Archaeologists have called attention to the profound cultural differences between Upper (southern) and Lower (northern) Egypt from earliest times.[29] By the late predynastic period the two separate areas, delta and valley, had consolidated enough politically to become two large kingdoms. When the delta was overrun and secured by the forces of the king of Upper Egypt, it became possible to forge a potentially rich and powerful united kingdom out of the two states. While the conquest took place successfully, the challenge for the Upper Egyptian royal house was to continue to hold the delta, to win for itself and posterity the continued loyalty and support of the northerners and indeed all people of the large state. The best way to do this effectively was, not to try to dominate the northerners with a ruthlessly repressive regime that would forever quell opposition (an impossible task), but to win their respect and adherence by casting the new king of the united Two Lands not as a king of Upper Egypt but as a ruler from the realm of the gods. As a result almost all of the Egyptian myths that have come down to us from inscriptions on royal monuments were intended primarily to bolster "the greatest myth of all," divine kingship.[30]

By late Prehistoric times, the divine falcon was appearing frequently in the iconography. The falcon god Horus from the southern town of Edfu apparently had emerged as the favorite deity of the Upper Egyptian ruler and his followers at Nekhen, which, as we have seen, also venerated a bovine mother goddess. The fierce bird of prey, who can soar so high he seems to commune with the sun, was regarded as a sky god, and later cosmogonies place him as a grandson of Nut, the son of her children, Isis and Osiris. When the need arose to propagandize the existence of a divine kingship for Egypt, the king, or Lord of the Two Lands, became equated with Horus, although among the Pyramid Texts one can find passages reflecting an earlier time when Horus was a distinct and all-powerful god who received and protected the king on his death:

> O King, do not languish, do not cry out, for Geb has brought
> Horus to you. . . . He has brought all the gods to you

together without an escapee from him among them. Horus has protected you, and his protecting you will not stop. (PT Utt. 357)

I am a great one, the son of a great one. It is from between the thighs of the Two Enneads that I have come forth. When I worshipped Re, I worshipped Horus, the Easterner. (PT Utt. 504)

However, by the time they were compiled from diverse sources and engraved on the inner walls of royal pyramids of the late Fifth and Sixth dynasties, these funerary ritual spells also equate the king of Egypt with the god Horus:

O Great Sky, give your hand to the King; O Great Nut, give your hand to the King. This divine falcon of yours is the King. The King has come that he may go forth to the sky and open up the cool place. The King will greet his father Re. He from whom the King has come has made him powerful as Horus, so that he may give the King a new appearance in glory and set in place for the King his two divine eyes. (PT Utt. 681)

Note that now Re, the sun, has become the father of the king of Egypt, giving the earthly ruler a second, distinguished pedigree. Not only is the king, as Horus, the grandson of Nut by way of being the son of Osiris, he is now also the son of Re—the sun born of Nut—and thus in two ways the king is descended from Nut, Mother of All the Gods.

By the Fifth Dynasty the sun god seems to have become the preeminent deity in Egypt. Now the sun temples actually equaled, if not exceeded in some cases, the size of the royal pyramids. Likewise the king, while still known as Horus, seemed to have slipped in esteem somewhat by being called Son of Re. Political as well as theological changes are detectable in the Fifth Dynasty too. Whereas in the Fourth Dynasty all the highest administrative positions of government were held by members of the royal family, this is definitely not the case in the Fifth, when the ever-growing bureaucracy is staffed by common people. Now too, for the first time in any great number, the statuary of ordinary people abound, and throughout the land their tombs are as large and as impressively decorated as they could afford to make them. Thus significant theological and political developments were affecting the royal family, but what exactly precipitated these alterations in the status quo, who was behind them, and how they came about we will probably never know for certain.

The more widely disseminated funerary texts of the subsequent dynasties, the Coffin Texts, refer to three classes of people: patricians, plebes, and sunfolk. It is possible that the sunfolk were followers of the Re theological system, which had successfully exerted pressure on the royal house of the Old Kingdom to bring about both theological and political changes. Thus the sunfolk would have felt themselves a people set apart and particularly blessed with power and influence in this world and the beyond. I point this out to show that in the long history of Egypt changes occurred constantly even in the conservative realm of religion, and it is only prudent to proceed chronologically in attempts at reconstructing the ancients' beliefs.

It must have been almost from the start of Egypt's history as a united kingdom that its king was equated with Horus, the sky god inherited from his ancestral Upper Egyptian forebears.[31] Presumably the two large celestial orbs represented Horus's eyes. The sun was brilliant and sharp, the moon less so. Thus the myth "The Contendings of Horus and Seth" evolved to explain the "damaged" eye which became part of the widely dispersed myth of Osiris and the divine kingship. Given the existence of Nut, also a widely acknowledged sky deity, some sorting out of roles had to be done by theologians.

Thus Geb and Nut (earth and sky) had two girls, Isis and Nepthys, and two boys, Osiris and Seth. As within many families, sibling rivalry between the sons arose. Later mythology, possibly influenced by memories of actual events such as the killing of an early king by a hippopotamus,[32] tells how Seth, who in Ptolemaic temple art is portrayed as a hippo, became jealous of his popular brother who was a much-beloved king. By a ruse he succeeded in killing Osiris, but Isis, whose magical powers were great, succeeded in reviving her brother-husband Osiris long enough to conceive their son, Horus (see chapter 7).

Horus grew up to challenge successfully his wicked uncle for the throne of Egypt. Thus Egyptian kings were equated with Horus, and their deceased fathers were called Osiris (as in the Pyramid Texts).

Scholars point out that succession to the throne is not universally from father to son. In some cultures it is from brother to brother (as today in some Arab countries). Thus the story of Horus and Seth settled for all time that a king's son should succeed to the throne of Egypt. It also, of course, makes clear that kingship is a right held only by the males of the line. However, the vital role played by the sister-wife in the story and the careful upbringing of Horus by his mother reflect the importance of the mother of the king of Egypt throughout history. Also, because this story is comparatively late (i.e., from the historic period) it need not reflect predynastic political conditions, which could have varied around the country when it was still split into many self-ruling clans. Nor does it reflect theological structures that predated the dynastic period, as the divine kingship was a construct to support the continued effectiveness of the rule of a single king over a united kingdom, which was founded in about 3100 B.C.

I have pointed out that probably very early, in the predynastic period, a segment of the population was engaged in closely watching the heavens.[33] Orion was seen to disappear (or die) for a time and then reappear (or be resurrected). Whether this gave rise to the myth of Osiris being killed by Seth or whether the myth predated and was affixed to the recognition of the celestial activities we cannot know. Egypt ended up with two Osirises: the god of vegetation (resurrected after the dry season by the receding waters of the Nile) and the sky god, identified with Orion and part of a more elaborate "sky religion." As Osiris was believed to be the father of the reigning king, identified with Horus, this placed the goal of the deceased in the heavens as well.

I believe the idea of the sky goddess—at least as a celestial cow or vulture—predated the king's need to be descended from the gods. Once the myth of divine kingship was established, it was, perhaps, deemed more appropriate that the sky goddess have the form of a human mother, for she would become understood as the ancestress of the king. However, in the Pyramid Texts, some of which are believed to date to predynastic times, there are a few Utterances that describe the sky goddess as "the Great Wild Cow who dwells in Nekheb" (412, 675). With the establishment at Memphis of the temple of Ptah, who was patron of craftsmen and in a late text was credited with creation, Nut had a rival and lost, if she ever had it, universal acknowledgment of seniority.

The later Re religion, like the Ptah religion, gave primacy to a male creator. Kings created temples and priesthoods, and it was through constructed myth that the king came to be related in one way or another to many gods, temples, and religions in ancient Egypt."[34] The Pyramid Texts not only record early beliefs, they reflect cosmology drawn up during the historic period by the priests of Heliopolis, Re's cult place across the river from Memphis, which placed Atum, the aged sun god, as first god, supreme creator of the Ennead:

> Atum Khoprer, you have come to be high on the primeval hill, you have arisen on the Benben stone in the mansion of the Benben in Heliopolis, you spat out Shu, you expectorated Tefnut, and you put your two arms around them as the arms of a *ka* symbol so that your *ka* might be in them. O Atum place your arms around the king, around this edifice, around this pyramid. . . .
>
> Oh Great Ennead which is in Heliopolis—Atum, Shu, Tefnut, Geb, Nut, Osiris, Isis, Seth, Nephthys—children of Atum, extend his goodwill to his child in your name of nine bows. Let his back be turned from you toward Atum, so that he may protect this king, so that he may protect this pyramid of the king, so that he may protect this edifice of his from all the gods and from all the dead, and so that he may guard against anything happening evily against him forever and ever. (PT, Utt. 600; Lesko translation)

THE FALL OF FEMALE POWER

In the historic period we now have a creator god who is male, Atum, who, we are told, began creating the gods by spitting out Shu and Tefnut, air and moisture. Atum creates by himself; he is not female, and he needs no female mate or consort according to the priests of Heliopolis. What has happened to the logical idea of a female partner in propagation or even a creator goddess as seen in Nut? Nut, Mother of the Gods, has become the granddaughter of Atum. Through the deliberate manipulation of logic she has been superseded by a male priesthood working to give a stronger basis to the sovereignty of the Horus king and wishing to give priority to their own cult place of Heliopolis,[35] where the very icon of the sun god was the wide obelisk known as the Benben—what might be termed a phallic symbol. Now the king of Egypt was regarded as descended from a form of the aged sun, Atum.

Similarly at Memphis just twenty miles away, the god Ptah held sway, and his influential priesthood put him at the head of the divine Ennead, explaining in a more sophisticated conception that Ptah created by first thinking and planning and then merely enunciating the names of the first gods. This creation ex nihilo reminds one of the later Hebrew Bible wording "and God *said,* let there be light" (Gen. 1:3). It is also reminiscent of the New Testament's Logos doctrine in the Gospel of John 1:1. And so through deliberate intellectual interference, the story of creation was altered to exclude the divine female creative element that had existed from prehistoric times. In fairness, I should point out that it may be inferred that Ptah was androgynous, as he was said to incorporate both Nun and its female counterpart, Naunet—the primeval morass of chaos that preceded creation. However, Ptah is always depicted in art as masculine and is husband to more than one goddess in the mythology. As mentioned above, the promotion of another younger, male deity over an all-powerful female creator has been reconstructed as well for ancient Sumer, the only other civilization we have written records from that existed at this same time in southern Mesopotamia.

Samuel Noah Kramer has written how the Sumerian goddess Nammu, originally credited with creating the gods and the universe, lost status when theologians began to systematize their pantheons and devise lists of deities in order of importance. The theologians gave Nammu's powers as goddess of the sea to her son Enki, and Nammu's equally high-ranking daughter Ki, the mother earth of the ancient Sumerians, eventually was reduced to fourth place among the highest deities.[36] The Babylonians preached that the original mother goddess Tiamat, "she who bore them all" was a monster who was killed by Marduk, the king of the gods.[37] Much later we find a similar adjustment of the pantheon by the Greeks, as can be gleaned from the Eumenides of Aeschylus, who has the chorus of ancient and holy mothers mourn their loss of status before the rise of a sexless Athena:

O shame and grief, that such a fate
should fall to me, whose wisdom grew
within me when the world was new!
Must I accept, beneath the ground,
a nameless and abhorred estate?
O ancient Earth, see my disgrace
O Night, my mother, hear me groan,
Outwitted, scorned and overthrown
By new gods from my ancient place![38]

Certainly the male role in procreation had been discovered many centuries earlier, so this should not, by itself, have effected the fall of the goddess as some theoreticians have posited. Indeed, the understanding of the role of both sexes in reproduction was achieved long before the advent of the dynasties. Thousands of years earlier in Anatolia both male and female principles were celebrated at Çatal Hüyük and other early shrines to the primal earth goddess. The partnership of both sexes in the divine sphere and in the annual renewal of the earth and promotion of all life should not have ended, but it did in Egypt, at least among those who controlled the greatest theological centers and their wealth. Thus I believe the promotion of male divinities to a more senior position and to responsibility for creation was politically motivated.

NUT, MOTHER OF THE DEAD

Nut remained important for the dead, as seen in the Coffin Texts that were products of the late Old Kingdom, the First Intermediate Period and the Middle Kingdom. The texts once engraved only on the walls of royal tombs now were penned on the wooden boards of a common person's coffin. Any Egyptian who could afford a well-prepared coffin was thus assured of the attainment of a desirable afterlife. Just as was true previously for their king and queen, common-born persons at death became equated with Nut's son, the god Osiris himself, and even with the great sun god Re, a remarkable illustration of a "democratization of the hereafter" as was recognized long ago by America's first professor of Egyptology James Henry Breasted.[39] Although it is unverifiable, it is tempting to see in this a profound expression of mankind's discovery of self-worth and a move toward questioning the concept of the divine right of kings. The unrelenting autocracy that had extracted from the people of Egypt the enormously costly efforts (in lives and resources) of ensuring an effective afterlife for the royal family (embodied in the stone mountains we call pyramid tombs) now had yielded to sharing the same hopes and expectations for eternal life with their subjects. Surely this was the second greatest revolution in human history.

In the Coffin Texts Nut is called "she of the braided hair who bore the gods"(CT Sp. 77), and she is described as fashioning daily the deceased who is now also identified as the sun god Re (CT Sp. 306), just as the king previously was. Identification between the coffin owner and Osiris, son of Geb and Nut, is also made clear (CT Sp. 644). As holy mother (and coffin) of the deceased, Nut says, "I am Nut, and I have come so that I may enfold and protect you from all things evil" (CT Sp. 792). Nut institutes offerings for the deceased (Sps. 33–35) and resurrects the dead before pulling him up into heaven: "Nut has come so that she may join your bones together, knit up your sinews, make your members firm, take away your corruption and take hold of your hand, so that you may live in your name of 'Living One'" (CT Sp. 850).

Once in the heavens, the deceased is "encircled by Orion, by Sothis and by the Morning Star" who set him within the arms of mother Nut and save him from damnation, from the "rage of the dead who go head-downward" (CT Sp. 44). "Nut the great will raise you in your beauty, she will enclose you in her arms"(CT Sp. 765). The deceased's role in heaven is dramatically described as, for instance, a dawn god who sees Nut every day: "The plumes tremble when Nut ascends, / those who are in the Storm tremble" (CT Sp. 720).

In the Coffin Texts Nut was also called Mother of the Gods (Sp. 864) and Uniter of the Two Lands of Geb and the Land of Your West, but her exalted rank and ubiquity in the religious literature of the early periods is diminished in the next major historic period, the New Kingdom. This period, at mid-second millennium B.C., saw the expansionist ambitions of warrior pharaohs propel Egypt to preeminence in wealth and political and cultural influence in the eastern Mediterranean. Now funerary spells were being sold on papyrus scrolls, and people were being buried in anthropoid coffins. Nut was still their protector and resurrector, but her name is not invoked quite so often in their Books of the Dead. From the surviving artifacts alone, however, it is obvious that she is still the great mother in the heavens and protector of all the virtuous dead. Her image was frequently painted on the inside bottom or cover of the coffin. In that way every dead Egyptian could be laid to rest in the embrace of this goddess. From her coffin, found in the late New Kingdom tomb of Hattiay at Thebes, the Singer of Amon Henut-wadjebu begs, "O my mother Nut, stretch yourself over me, that I may be placed among the imperishable stars, which are in you, and that I may not die."[40]

In a fine private tomb dating to the reign of Amunhotep III of the Eighteenth Dynasty and belonging to his royal herald, Kheruef, who was also the chief steward of his queen, Tiy, the goddess Nut assures Kheruef that he "shall [proceed] to the sky in front of the stars which are in my belly. He shall never die but shall be glorious in the sky . . . breathing nourishment through the four winds that come forth from the belly of Nut."[41]

In the wall paintings of Tutankhamun's tomb, the deceased king approaches Nut after his successor performs the Opening of the Mouth ceremony (a rite meant to revivify the dead king) on Tutankhamun's mummy. Because the king goes on from Nut to appear before Osiris, king of the dead, the image of Nut here may symbolically suggest the coffin that the royal body was interred in just after the mummy received the last rites.

The royal dead also still sought the great goddess's help in attaining eternal life among the imperishable stars. From the Eighteenth Dynasty's brilliant tomb assemblage created for King Tutankhamun come the words of Nut herself, engraved on the exterior of one of the golden shrines that enclosed the royal sarcophagus, expressing her commands that made possible this resurrection: "Raise yourself on your right side, my son Osiris, King Tutankhamun, ruler of Southern Heliopolis, justified. May you stand up and go forth! May you make all the transformations you wish, may you live forever!"[42] This reads like the reassuring response to the king's own prayer on the ceiling of shrine IV: "Mother Nut, may you spread your wing to my face. May your two arms embrace me in health and in life, that I may exist inside you, and that you may provide my protection!"[43]

On the front panel of the innermost of the four great shrines Nut is depicted spreading her wings over the deceased king. In this

Figure 5. Nut inside coffin of the God's Wife Ankhnesneferibre. © British Museum. Courtesy of The British Museum.

Eighteenth Dynasty text the great goddess is called "The Effective One," which seems to equate her with the eye of the sun god,[44] a new extension of her attributes with connotations of power but also of subordination to the supreme god of this age.

Nut speaks to Tutankhamun (and now to us) frequently from these golden shrines about her proud lineage and seems not to concede to any attempts to diminish her prestige:

> I spread myself out over this my son, in my name of the Mysterious One, the one whom Geb establishes. . . . I am Nut the Great, the Mighty, the Uraeus-serpent, the soul of the Glorious One, for I was powerful in the body of my mother Tefnut, in my name of Nut, in order to be powerful over my mother. It is with my beauty that I have guided everyone. Moreover, the earth is under me to its limit, I having seized it, having taken hold of the South and the North. What my arms embraced is inside my two arms, that I may make Osiris live. May you live forever and ever, King of Upper and Lower Egypt.[45]

After the tumultuous period of the Eighteenth Dynasty, the Nineteenth Dynasty seems to have relapsed into more conservative religious modes. It has been called the age of personal piety. Now the royal tombs had ceilings decorated elaborately to portray the heavens, either with constellations, as in the magnificent tomb of Seti I at the beginning of the Nineteenth Dynasty, or with a giant image of Nut swallowing the sun, as on the ceiling of the tomb of Ramses IV of the Twentieth Dynasty. Such an image, was also used by Seti I's artists when they decorated the ceiling of his cenotaph at Abydos. Here the winged sun disk is shown at Nut's mouth, but the text accompanying the vignette seems to indicate that the sun was not actually swallowed by the sky goddess until the third hour of the night.[46]

The reassuring idea of the heavenly mother to whom the deserving would return in death, the holy mother who could resurrect the dead, the sacred womb from which the dead would be reborn—these concepts first expressed at the beginning of their historic age in the third millennium B.C. were maintained by the Egyptians to the very last (perhaps despite the theologians). The funerary rites and preparations of the common people were part of the folk religion and were long enduring. The image of Nut still adorns the great stone sarcophagi of the Persian Period (fifth century B.C.) and was adopted by the Greeks and Romans who settled in Egypt as well. The last coffins of the pre-Christian period still are adorned on their interiors by Nut's outstretched naked body and the sun disk she bore. The Papyrus Carlsberg I, which dates probably to the second century A.D., depicts Nut supported by Shu and contains texts dealing in mythological terms with the movements of the sun and stars. Nut is continually called "Mother of the Gods" who daily gives birth to Re. Stars disappearing at night are described as piglets eaten by the great Sow, that is, Nut. In this papyrus Geb becomes angry at Nut because she ate their piglets and Shu must intervene by supporting Nut high above Geb.[47]

Although as a heavenly and protective mother Nut is the most pervasive image of the goddess, it was not her only manifestation for the Egyptian. Perhaps the wood of their coffins influenced the idea of Nut as a tree goddess, but no matter the origin, by the New Kingdom, especially in the Nineteenth Dynasty, one meets the lady emerging from the branches of the sycamore tree in the wall paintings in private tombs. Usually Nut's legs are hidden in the trunk of the tree as she holds a tray of bread and a water jar from which the deceased husband-and-wife (and/or mother) tomb inhabitants will partake gratefully. Sometimes the full figure of the goddess is rendered with a tree projecting from the top of her head. In other contexts, such as stelae and stone offering tables, an entire tree with only the arms of Nut extended from it is depicted. It is this form that survives the longest; it is found even on offering tables of the Ptolemaic Dynasty which followed Alexander the Great's conquest and ruled Egypt in the last three centuries B.C. (until the death of Cleopatra VII). Chapters from the Book of the Dead pertaining to drinking water were often engraved on these as accompanying texts for the figure of the tree goddess, but an association of Nut with the presentation of food and drink to the dead has been traced back to the Middle Kingdom.[48] Throughout their history the Egyptians provided their dead with the basics of sustenance, and it is interesting to find the celestial goddess coming down to earth to play a role in the most basic, humble needs of her people. The association may stem from the fact that the coffin, equated with Nut, was generally of wood, and thus Nut was the stuff of trees.

While Nut figured in the coffins, tomb scenes, funerary papyri, and offering tables of the common people, some of the most dynamic graphic portrayals of the great goddess of the heavens survive in the tombs of the pharaohs of the Twentieth Dynasty. On the vaulted ceilings of the large burial chambers are painted back-to-back images of the naked heavenly goddess. The red disk of the sun is shown gliding along her svelte yellow body on its daytime course and being swallowed at evening so that it may reemerge (be born again) from her loins at dawn. The goddess of the night sky has a long row of stars painted on her belly. The goddess exists not only in the sky that people can see above them, but her interior is equated with Duat, the Netherworld, that which is below the earth, into which the sun descends. Here Nut, or at least her belly, is equated with a "secret cavern" from which the sun will be born again.[49] The sun god is shown as a winged disk at Nut's mouth. She swallows it, and the sun slowly traverses her interior to be born at the twelfth hour of the night, at which time he enters the solar bark.[50] The "daily miracle of the sun's transformation and rejuvenation" is the central theme of the texts and images on the walls of the tombs in the Valley of the Kings. "Each dawn signified a general renewal of all creation, and the Egyptian perceived an analogy in the daily transformation and rejuvenation of the dead."[51]

The well-preserved and imposing temples built by the Ptolemaic Dynasty that ruled Egypt after Alexander the Great's conquest of the country often contained chapels to Nut, as seen at Esna and Edfu. The largest, most famous, and most dramatic image of the sky goddess is carved on the ceiling of the grand Ptolemaic Period temple of Dendera, but by that late date (early Roman empire) Nut's aspects had been assimilated by the goddess Hathor, of whom I shall have much to say later.

I have proceeded chronologically through the history of Nut, that is, what can be reconstructed from the minimal texts and images that survive. She has left us no temples of her own, and perhaps she did not have a cult as such, except in the hearts of her people and the literature of her theologians. Now we cast ourselves back to the predynastic age to consider a goddess whose standard is portrayed at least as early as the late predynastic or Gerzean period, Neith.

CHAPTER 3

𝒩EITH, LADY OF SAIS AND CREATOR OF ALL

There is evidence from before recorded history of a powerful if mysterious goddess who was associated with weaponry. This is Neith, the most revered goddess at the beginning of Egyptian history. Although an ancient Egyptian writer of the second millennium B.C. referred to Neith as being important in "primeval time," she is not documented before the last phase of the predynastic period, the Gerzean, where her emblem appears on some decorated pottery.[1]

The earliest portrayal of what is believed to be a sacred shrine is associated with the cult of Neith.[2] Although Neith has always been associated with the northern city of Sais in the eastern delta, this early drawing was found in Upper Egypt. It occurs on an ivory label from the burial site of King Aha, perhaps the first ruler of a united Egypt, who would have reigned about 3100 B.C. Depicted is a walled compound at one end of which is a vaulted roofed hut, and in front of this stands a large totem pole bearing the symbol of the goddess, two end-to-end ovals and crossed arrows. Two flag poles at the opposite end of the compound indicate the holiness of the place, as this was the hieroglyph for "deity." Although Hornung has pointed out that there is "no certain evidence for the worship of anthropomorphic deities in pre-dynastic Egypt," he accepts that deities such as Neith and the male gods Min and Onuris, who generally take human form and are familiar from the early historic age, enjoyed cults in the predynastic age.[3]

Neith was apparently originally related to the click beetle, which is commonly found in the Nile valley as well as in oases. Her symbol consisted of two click beetles, head to head, over two crossed arrows. Why the goddess Neith was associated with this large beetle is unknown. However, the Egyptians were keen observers of nature, and they must have been impressed by the dexterity and energy of the click beetle, which was able to save itself from the rising flood waters of the Nile by its jumping ability. As it propelled itself along, it emitted a noise that has given the beetle its modern name. That the click beetle escaped the hazards of the annual inundation may have encouraged the ancients to find divinity in such a remarkable power. Neith then became a flood goddess, keeping the lives and property of Egyptians safe during a hazardous if beneficial period of the year.[4]

That the ancients themselves forgot that the bilobate symbol represented two beetles is certain, for later in her history this central image was interpreted as a shield. The image of the insect is clear on the early objects, however.[5] One of these is a shallow oval plate with decoration on its exterior that shows an upright click beetle with human arms holding a sacred *was* scepter (a staff topped with an animal's head) in each hand. These sacred scepters are later frequently shown with Neith and other deities and express dominion. The insect suggests that this goddess began her existence as a clan divinity. It is difficult to understand how the *was* scepters and arrows could have been associated with an insect alone. Whether the image of a woman, a huntress or warrior, was recognized and honored from the very start of this cult is not known, but surely the weapons were not associated with an insect.

Also in the First Dynasty another cult sign, a tied pair of bows, was associated with Neith, and later she was known as Mistress of the Bow and Ruler of Arrows. Thus weaponry was clearly part of Neith's equipment, which is not surprising as the end of the predynastic period was a time of political turmoil that saw a succession of battles as the leaders of Upper Egypt strove to conquer the entire Nile valley and delta and establish a single large country under their control. Thus a war deity would meet their needs. Moreover, in later periods numerous fierce lioness goddesses were recognized, so a warlike goddess is not surprising this early. The most important goddess, perhaps the most important deity, of the northern kingdom, Neith lent her Red Crown (the crown of Lower Egypt) to the ruler who thereby signified his dominion over Lower Egypt. Because the pharaoh was Lord of the Two Lands he wore a double crown comprised of the red and white crowns—the symbols of Lower and Upper Egypt.

Because hieroglyphs lack symbols representing vowels, it is impossible to know exactly how any ancient name or word was pronounced. We are dependent on late Greek sources and their references to Egyptian deities and kings to reconstruct the original pronunciations. However, the great German philologist Kurt Sethe argued that the original name of the goddess Neith may have been Nr.t (*i* sometimes being a modification of the letter *r*), and her name would thus mean "the terrifying one."[6] There is, interestingly, a major goddess of neighboring Canaan whose name contains the same simple *NT* root as historical Neith. This is Anath, known for her bloodthirstiness and passionate love of war. Although paired with a male deity, the important Ba'al Hadad, Anath's role is more as his partner in warfare than as his wife or lover. Indeed, Anath is often referred to as a virgin.[7] It would not have been impossible for the Egyptian goddess from the delta, a region that had continual contact with the people outside of Egypt's boundaries, to influence the development of foreign pantheons long before the phenomenal spread of the cult of Isis.

Although Neith's cult shrine is first documented at Abydos, judging from other evidence, it was probably not her chief or even original cult place. Later periods connected her particularly with the northern town of Sais (Sa el-Hagar) in the western delta, but the pottery depicting her standards was much more widely dispersed. Thus her cult could not originally have been so limited. In the historic period there was a temple at Memphis dedicated to Neith of Sais, and there is reference to Neith in the later Coffin Texts as Mistress of Mendes, another prominent central delta town (Sp. 408). Hermann Kees describes the northwestern part of the delta as being, at the beginning of history, inhabited primarily by Libyans and points out that during the Old Kingdom Neith was characterized by Egyptians as Neith from Libya, "as if she was the chieftainess of the neighboring people with whom the inhabitants of the Nile valley were at all times at war."[8] Other Egyptologists dispute this connection, however, and the first appearance of Neith is purely Egyptian.

Neith's earliest documented appearance as an image in human form seems to fall sometime between the reigns of King Djet and Nynetjer, between the middle of the First and the middle of the Second dynasties).[9] As she was later frequently depicted wearing the Red Crown of Lower Egypt, it is generally thought that Neith personified the kingship of Lower Egypt (the entire delta of the Nile) before the unification of the Two Lands and was regarded as the protectress of the Red Crown and the king: "May the terror of you come into being in the hearts of the gods like the *Nt*-crown which is on the King of Lower Egypt" (PT Utt. 412).

Among his numerous titles the king of historic Egypt was He of the Sedj Plant and the Bee, and Neith's temple at Sais was sometimes known as the House of the Bee. Thus the royal title must emphasize the connection with the preeminent goddess, who was guardian of one of the two large political entities or regions that made up historic Egypt.

The religion of the historic Egyptians has been recognized by scholars as having been strongly influenced by political circumstances,[10] and thus it is likely that Neith was the chief divinity of the delta leadership who were finally conquered by the Upper Egyptians, leading to the foundation of a kingdom of the Two Lands. By arrogating to themselves their crown, their royal title, and their patron divinity, the conquering dynasty assumed all the powers of the conquered royal house of the North. The goddess of the delta was still a power to be feared and propitiated.

An important and politic undertaking of the founding rulers of the First Dynasty was the creation of a new capital at the natural frontier between Upper and Lower Egypt, at a point near where the delta and the long Nile valley of Upper Egypt come together. The founding of the temple of Neith, north of Memphis's white walls, and of the god Ptah to the south of the walls may well go back to the beginning of the First Dynasty.[11] Reference is still made in the Coffin Texts of the Middle Kingdom to a mansion of Neith and Ptah, meaning a temple probably continued to exist where the powerful Lower Egyptian goddess was paired with the great god of the capital city of Memphis (CT Sp. 635).

It is intriguing that at the beginning of their recorded history Neith seems to have enjoyed a dominant role at the Egyptian royal court. From the First Dynasty come numerous stelae of priestesses of Neith, and there are a number of queens whose names demonstrate that they identified with her: Mer(it)-Neith, Her-Neith, Neith-hotep, and Nakht-Neith. Neith-hotep, which may be translated as "Neith be appeased," was the queen of the first king of the First Dynasty, Aha, who was credited with building a temple of Neith at Sais. It seems that Aha, once he gained control of the northern kingdom of Lower Egypt, had joined in a diplomatic marriage with a woman of the vanquished royal house. She was probably from the chief city of Pe, which was also the cult city of Neith, and she may well have been a priestess of the mighty goddess. The popularity of the cult of Neith continued, because Aha's successor's daughter was Mer(it)-Neith, whose name means "Beloved of Neith." This princess became the wife of her father's successor, Djet, and mother of the next king, Den, for whom she was regent in his youth.[12] Some of the early queens had tombs as large or larger than the male rulers, and Neith's symbol surmounts the palace facade design (*serekh*) that encloses the names of two prominent queens of the First Dynasty, Neith-Hotep and Merit-Neith, just as Horus, the falcon god of the sky, is found perched on the kings' serekh. This has suggested to some that these early dynastic royal women held some powers comparable to the king's.

With the divine image of a strong, arms-bearing female close at hand, it is easy to believe that the queens took the goddess as their special deity. The importance of this goddess to the queen of Egypt is evidenced by Neith's symbols in the design of the gold-covered chair of Queen Hetepheres, mother of Khufu, builder of the Great Pyramid in the Fourth Dynasty.[13]

Neith rarely shows up in the Pyramid Texts, which supports the idea that she was not originally associated with death and resurrection like Nut and Isis but was more of the world of the living, involved with power and politics. Certainly Neith was by far the favorite deity acknowledged in the personal names of the earliest dynasties, for she appears in almost 40 percent of all theophoric names.[14] She apparently was felt to have a beneficent side, indicated by some personal names such as "One whom Neith protects," "Neith is my mistress," and "She loves Neith."[15]

Thousands of years after the founding of her cult, the Roman Plutarch wrote that this goddess claimed, "No mortal has ever lifted my veil," which has been interpreted more recently as meaning no one has ever appreciated the true nature of her divinity.[16] Certainly she is difficult to fathom, and there is little textual material dating from the early dynasties, yet Neith was undoubtedly the most important goddess during the earliest historic period.

When the object bearing her arrows was deemed a shield, it was usual for scholars to pronounce Neith a patroness of warfare. After some time the original association with the click beetle was forgotten, and the "shield" referred to by the ancients eventually linked Neith with Athena. Both were women whose activities and powers challenge gender distinctions, but the similarity is quite limited when the earlier Egyptian references to Neith's attributes are recalled, including motherhood.

From the beginning Neith's arrows were very much a part of her imagery, and thus we assume Neith was a deity with special significance for warrior kings and their wives. Whether known as a successful huntress or for her prowess in battle, Neith's support in winning victories for the tribe and later the nation would have made her a most important and powerful goddess. At the very least Neith should be understood as a strong and independent female image, one not subordinated to any male deity.[17] Neith did not depend on a male partner for her creative powers, which encompassed the entire universe of gods, animals, and humans. Indeed, a later text tells that she created the world by herself.

Neith is conspicuous from her near-absence in the Old Kingdom's royal funerary literature. Throughout the Pyramid Texts there are scattered mythological allusions whose significance we can no longer grasp. When the deceased says, "It is as Sobek [crocodile god of the inundation] looks at Neith that I looked at you" (PT Utt. 308), we cannot know if more than the mother-son relationship is being stressed, a kinship mentioned in Pyramid Text Utterance 317. None of the Egyptian goddesses seem to have escaped motherhood. The fearsome goddess Neith apparently bore the man-eating crocodile, and in some texts she, like Nut, bore the sun. Her involvement with crocodiles and water is reiterated in several spells in the later Coffin Texts, for example, "The crocodile goes forth from under the Heights of Neith and from under the riverbanks" (CT Sp. 407). Neith was most likely associated with the waters of the inundation: "Water was measured out for you by the Nile-god, so that Neith would come to you with her nurses" (CT Sp. 358). In some statues from a much later period, Neith is shown as a woman with a crocodile's head, so her connection with the dangerous reptile was not forgotten.

The waters referred to in funerary literature can be associated with Nun, the waters of chaos, which were also the origin of all life. Thus the priests of Heliopolis boosted their god Atum-Re as the creator, with all living things emerging from Nun. Because water gives life, the dead were offered water at the tomb to revivify them. This may be the meaning of the above-quoted text. Neith, like most other deities mentioned in the funerary literature, had a role beneficial to the deceased.

This goddess continued to be paired with Sobek in the religious literature. For example, Spell 71 of the Book of the Dead says, "Sobek is situated on his hill, Neith is standing on her shore," which locates the two deities on the river. While it is not emphasized in the mortuary ritual literature, the crocodile was an extremely dangerous animal that plagued everyone who approached the river and its streams and canals. Crocodiles are well camouflaged by their color and texture, can move swiftly, and can capture and consume large animals, including humans, in a few seconds. Indeed, early chroniclers such as Africanus and Eusebius maintained that a Ninth Dynasty Egyptian king was killed by one. Thus a goddess having an intimate relationship of any sort with crocodiles could not escape the suspicion of terror and bloodthirstiness. However, all surviving images of Neith are very staid; in most she is a short-haired woman wearing the Red Crown of Lower Egypt. Her role vis-à-vis the king and the sun itself was one of protector, thus her fierce powers are put to a respectable purpose. There may have been myths or folklore that stressed the more frightening aspects of her potential, but these have not survived.

In the Pyramid Texts the goddesses Isis, Nepthys, Neith, and Selket appear as protectors of the throne (Utt. 362) and as guardians of the king and his mortal remains:

> My mother is Isis
> My nurse is Nephthys. . .
> Neith is behind me and
> Selket is before me. (PT Utt. 555)

Centuries later, this group of guardian goddesses appeared on the corners of royal sarcophagi of the Eighteenth Dynasty or as freestanding images, arms outstretched, shielding the canopic shrine of the king from harm (as so beautifully rendered in the tomb of Tutankhamun;

Figure 6. Bronze figurine of Neith standing, Egyptian Late Period. Courtesy of the University of Pennsylvania Museum of Archaeology and Anthropology, Philadelphia.

see fig. 7). The idea of protection by Neith must have been very old, because a small Old Kingdom golden box or casket is in the shape of a click beetle, as if to ensure safety or divine protection for its contents. Similarly, the symbols of this goddess on the back of the golden chair of Queen Hetepheres would have extended divine protection to the queen.

Neith and Selket are paired elsewhere in the Pyramid Texts in a context that calls for strength, for Selket was the scorpion goddess whose poisoned sting was very potent. In Utterance 580 Seth, the enemy of Osiris, is sacrificed and his spine given to Neith and Selket.

The cult of Neith, Who Opens the Ways North of the Walls (of Memphis, Egypt's capital city), is associated with the royal court of the Old Kingdom through textual documentation as well and in the tombs of the Fourth and Fifth Dynasty kings. The rulers of the Fifth and Sixth dynasties also erected sun temples not far from their pyramids, and it is at King Userkaf's temple that a sculpted stone head attributed by the excavators to the goddess Neith was recovered. The beardless face under the Red Crown bears a remote resemblance to the ruler, but such was true of portrayals of divinities in the previous dynasty. Userkaf is believed to have reemphasized the cult of Neith within the royal context after the late Fourth Dynasty rulers had replaced her with another goddess, Hathor.[18]

While Neith may not have had an important role in the texts recorded in royal pyramids at the end of the Old Kingdom, she does appear once again in the funerary literature on the coffins of commoners during subsequent centuries, which indicates that many sources for these texts existed. Funerary priests probably chose from a large volume of available spells, many of which could only have been written on scrolls that were appropriated by scribes of later centuries for their client's coffins. Among the earliest Coffin Texts are those from one of the cemeteries of the central Egyptian city of Hermopolis, cult center of the god Thoth. It is particularly on the Hermopolitan coffins that Neith is prominent.

There are spells, for example, Coffin Text Spell 669, that equate the deceased with the goddess Neith in the realm of the dead, thus conveying to the deceased all the power of the awesome goddess. In the Coffin Texts the goddess's name is associated with the delta towns

Figure 7. Neith, Isis, and Selket, the canopic equipment from Tutankhamun's tomb. Photo by Harry Burton. Courtesy of the Metropolitan Museum of Art, New York.

of Sais and Mendes, and she is also linked with both Ptah and Thoth, creator gods of their own cities, Memphis and Hermopolis, respectively. Perhaps most important, Neith is presented as one who judges the dead:

The Elder Gods rejoice and the two great Enneads are
  happy
when they see the appearances in glory of this Neith, the
  Great,
Lady of Sais.
For she has taken for herself the document of
the Great Ones in her following. (CT Sp. 281)

Judgment has been made in the presence of Neith.
  (CT Sp. 630).

In some versions of Spell 15 Neith is presented as a protector of
Osiris (the dead person in the coffin as well as the god himself) and is
described as if a bovine sky goddess—"The Great Lady [whose (?)]
horns [are] adorned with two stars" (CT Sp. 846)—which recalls the
image of the cow's head on the much earlier predynastic palette, which
may thus depict this early and powerful goddess rather than Mehet-
Weret.

All this hints at an extensive body of myth or religious stories in
which an invincible goddess played many roles. But, unfortunately,
aside from the rather cryptic Coffin Texts, few other early writings
survive to provide us with a full picture of Neith. It seems that other
"junior" goddesses stole some of this senior deity's attributes. The
goddess Sekhmet, who usually took a lioness's form and was a companion of Ptah, already in the Middle Kingdom was described as a
shooter of arrows and maintained her association with ferocity even
more than did Neith. Neith was not to remain a war goddess but one
known for her protective powers and thus more benevolent in spirit
than Sekhmet.

Although her temples of the period do not survive, Neith is depicted
in the great terraced temple of Queen Hatshepsut, the female pharaoh,
where she and the scorpion goddess Selket support the bodies of the
king of the gods, Amun-Re, and the queen mother in the famous scene
of the divine conception of Hatshepsut. The scorpion is regarded in
the ancient Near East as a symbol of motherhood (apparently the
female scorpion carries her young on her back), and in Mesopotamian
art the scorpion is shown under the marriage bed at a sacred marriage.[19] This is why she is portrayed under the bed of Hatshepsut's

mother when she received her husband in his guise of Amun-Re. Thus the positive, protective, and creative powers of these goddesses were not only associated with the throne or the sarcophagus but were also constantly called on by the royal family.

Neith was also regarded as the divine patron of weavers, and one Eighteenth Dynasty tomb's text mentions the linen wrappings of the mummy having been produced by the weavers of Neith.[20] Hundreds of meters of cloth generally were needed to wrap the mummy, and these came under the protection of Neith, regarded as the spiritual source of the woven fabric. Through the women weavers she extended her protection to the deceased.

Neith may appear in Tutankhamun's tomb in still another guise, that of a golden serpent. Such a figure, a rising cobra, bears the same design on its hood as Neith's headdress on her anthropomorphic guardian statue from this famous tomb.[21] The serpent imagery and the relationship to linen mummy wrappings are both found in Book of the Dead Spell 185K:

> Neith will come to you as the coiled one, provided with her
> raiment.
> She will adorn your face with strips of white, green, bright
> red and [(dark)red] linen.

And in the Hymn to the Diadems, Neith's Red Crown is described in relation perhaps to Wadjit, the serpent guardian of Lower Egypt from which both goddesses hail: "O Net-crown, O In-crown, O Great Crown, O Sorceress, O Serpent!"[22]

As a mortuary goddess, together with Isis, Nephthys, and Selket, Neith took care of Osiris himself, but also every deceased worthy Egyptian who was identified as an Osiris after death. However, in Coffin Text Spell 669 the deceased could become Neith in the realm of the dead as well. This too reveals the importance this goddess retained during periods from which her temples do not survive. Texts, however, can be even more significant than hewn or constructed monuments because they better reveal the inner workings of the mind, the value systems of a people, and the accumulated wisdom of the ages.

MOTHER OF THE GODS

Although not as well represented in historical art or literature as some of her divine colleagues, Neith was still highly regarded throughout history as illustrated in an intriguing piece of literature, from the Ramesside period of the New Kingdom (1304–1075). This long, rambling text purports to be a myth of the Contendings of Horus and Seth for the right to rule Egypt.[23] It is iconoclastic, as it makes the important gods look childish, ribald, and ridiculous, and may have been a piece of literature to be read for amusement rather than a religious document. Nevertheless, the only deity who is treated with respect by the author is the goddess Neith, who is called "the eldest, the Mother of the gods, who shone on the first face," implying that she predated everyone else. Although this last statement may be intended as flattery (she is also called "hale and young"), it is perhaps significant because there were few deities whose cults survived into the New Kingdom from such an early age as the predynastic. That the Egyptians of the second millennium recalled this is surely significant in demonstrating the long-lasting importance of this great goddess. Because Neith is their mother, the gods write a letter to her asking for advice and guidance in settling a quarrel that has confounded a jury of deities. When Neith replies, it is to support Horus's claim to the throne of his father Osiris. Indeed, she threatens to topple the sky to the ground if the company of gods does not follow her directive. In this context, regarded as a sky goddess and mother of all the gods, Neith seems to have been interchanged with Nut, but again— as the Middle Kingdom Coffin Texts suggest—we may have lost much of the mythology of this very early goddess.

By the Nineteenth Dynasty of the New Kingdom theologians were crediting Neith with astounding powers. She is present on the walls of the great hypostyle hall at Karnak where King Ramses II is depicted at his coronation. As he kneels before Amun-Re, King of the Gods, to receive his crown it is Neith who stands beside the enthroned god.[24]

On the great stone sarcophagus of King Merneptah of the Nineteenth Dynasty a text refers to Neith as a creator deity: again she is the mother of the major gods Re and Osiris, the One who was present at the beginning.[25] This is the earliest-known reference to Neith as a creator, which is spelled out clearly again much later in her history. That a female deity could be accepted by the Egyptians as a creator is surely significant, but scholars have tended either to overlook this fact or to downplay it by forcing Neith into an androgynous persona. However, Neith is no virgin goddess like Athena even if a husband is not associated with her. Her motherhood is clearly stated, and her priesthood was originally mainly, if not exclusively, female.

The elaborately decorated tombs of the kings of the Nineteenth and Twentieth dynasties with their numerous vignettes from the books of funerary literature designed to aid their occupants in gaining eternal life with the sun god necessitated the inclusion of Neith in the underworld. As mother of the sun god she is part of the crew of his boat. "The Book of That Which Is in the Beyond" describes the course of the sun god through the underworld during the twelve hours of the night.[26] Neith appears at the fourth, tenth, and eleventh hours wearing her Red Crown for identification. In the eleventh hour she appears in four forms—as a child, as queen of Upper Egypt, as queen of Lower Egypt, and as a pregnant goddess. If it was necessary for the dead king to be reborn to have eternal life, it is obvious that Neith was the goddess chosen to carry him to gestation, as his mother, the Lady of the Two Lands did in life, so that this goal could be met. Again, this is surely a very womanly role for the "androgynous" Neith. Whereas archaeological work has shown her to be a protector of the dead, it is obvious from the textual material that the Egyptian public still knew Neith to be a goddess of great seniority and awesome power.

RULER OF THE GODS

It was at Sais that Neith's cult flourished for millennia and that she was regarded as the leader of all the gods. She was often called Neith of Libya, for her province in the far west was a gateway to the Libyan desert. When finally the princes of Sais became rulers of the entire kingdom of Upper and Lower Egypt in the sixth century B.C., Neith replaced the longtime supreme state deity, Amun-Re, at the head of the pantheon as the ruler of the gods. The Twenty-sixth Dynasty rulers at Sais ruled as quislings for the Assyrians who had invaded and ravaged

Egypt. People of that sorry time cast their eyes back to Egypt's days of glory and decorated their tombs with art of the early style of the Old Kingdom and excerpts from the Pyramid Texts. King Psamtik, founder of the Twenty-sixth Dynasty, began the enlargement and enhancement of the temple of his dynasty's patron goddess. The work was carried on by his successors and included major engineering feats such as hewing a gigantic naos from a single block of granite at the Aswan quarry and transporting it the length of the country to its final resting place within the temple. This transport alone took three years. Amasis, one of the last kings of this dynasty, erected beautiful propylaea in honor of the goddess.

Not long afterward, when he visited and wrote about his experiences in Egypt, Herodotus described the great festival held at Sais for Neith as an occasion when many lamps were lighted in the town to mark a night of sacrifice. He claims also to have seen the sacred image of the goddess, a kneeling cow with a sun disk between its horns, when it was carried in public procession covered by a purple robe.[27] From the Twenty-seventh Dynasty, which experienced Persian domination, comes a text exalting the greatness of the city of Sais: "I caused that His Majesty know the greatness of Sais. It is the place of Neith-the-Great, the mother who bore Re and began birth when birth had not yet happened, and (caused him to know) the nature of the greatness of Sais . . . that it is the mystery of all the deities."[28]

Clearly, the claim to primacy of position in creation, first encountered on the royal sarcophagus of the Nineteenth Dynasty, was being maintained by Neith's priests as they usurped for her the maternal role of Nut, the one who bears Re. Of course, the same primacy of position was claimed for Atum, for Ptah of Memphis, and for Thoth of Hermopolis when their followers placed them at the head of the Ogdoad (the four pairs of primeval gods who existed before any others). It was perhaps with more justification that this was done for Neith, for she, at least, was female and can be documented much earlier than any of the aforementioned gods.

On a papyrus scroll dating to the Ptolemaic Dynasty (that spanned the last centuries B.C., and ended with the death of the famous Cleopatra VII) are preserved lyrics of the lamentation of the dead god Osiris that refer to Neith as the mother of Osiris and to her city Sais as his city:

Come to Sais in order that you may see your mother Neith.
Good child, you shall not separate from her!
Come to her breasts that have abundance in [them].
Good brother, you shall not separate from her! . . .
Come to Sais, your city!
Your place is the Mansion shrine,
You shall rest beside your mother forever!
She will protect for your body, she will drive away your
    enemies,
She will be a protection for your body forever!
O good Sovereign, come to your house,
Lord of Sais, come to Sais![29]

This late text recalls Neith's role as the guardian and protector of the dead king, as when she joins Isis, Nephthys, and Selket to surround the sarcophagus and canopic chest. It also reflects the importance of the delta city of Sais in the Twenty-sixth Dynasty and suggests that its writer may have come from there.

CREATRIX

Although she began her history as a goddess from Lower Egypt, Neith was soon honored widely in Egypt. The Ptolemies erected many grandiose temples to Egyptian deities throughout the land, hoping in this way to make the native population more amenable to foreign rule. In the southern town of Esna, on the east bank of the Nile, they erected a temple to the ram-headed god Khnum, lord of the Nile's cataract region, which begins about fifty miles farther south. Either because of her association with crocodiles and the annual flood or because the priests of Sais were highly influential and demanded it, a Neith cult was also celebrated in this great southern temple. On its interior north wall, west of the doorway, the Esna creation myth presents Neith emerging, in the form of a cow, from the primordial waters (Nun) and bringing into existence the first land. She accomplishes this ex nihilo, that is, by uttering a command. As the following text indicates, Neith is recognized as a goddess—but one who incorporates both male and female properties and power. She is unique and mysterious and is credited with creation.

> You are the Lady of Sais . . . whose two-thirds are masculine
>   and one-third is feminine
> Unique Goddess, mysterious and great
> who came to be in the beginning
> and caused everything to come to be . . .
> the divine mother of Re, who shines in the horizon
> the mysterious one who radiates her brightness.[30]

Neith was credited with calling forth the flood that brought the land back to life, for which Khnum, also a creator god, was celebrated too. Khnum and Neith do not seem to have been paired in a sexual sense. Indeed, throughout her history Neith has no obvious husband, and that is why she was thought to be able to produce her children without male assistance.

Although it probably had its origins in Sais and much earlier, our only text for the story of Neith as the creator of all is on the walls of the temple at Esna:

> Father of the fathers and Mother of the mothers, the
>   divinity who came into being was in the midst of the
>   primeval waters having appeared out of herself while
>   the land was in twilight and no land had yet come forth
>   and no plant had yet grown.
> She illumined the rays of her two eyes and dawn came into
>   being.
> Then she said: let this place become land for me
> in the midst of the primeval water
> in order that I might rest on it.
> And this place became land in the midst of the primeval
>   water, just as she said,
> and thus came into being "the land of the waters" [= Esna]
>   and Sais. . . .
> Then she was pleased with this mound,
> and thus Egypt came into being in jubilation.[31]

Everything Neith conceived with her heart came into being, including thirty gods, and then she went on to create the "august god" Re, who himself created mankind from the tears of his eye. It is difficult to accept this goddess as androgynous when again and again the text refers to her as "the cow goddess" and she is called Mother. Probably the reference to being both Father and Mother was merely to stress that Neith created the first land and the first gods all by herself. In all, seven creative utterances were used by this amazing goddess. Texts that date to the Roman Period, indeed the first three centuries A.D., engraved on the walls of the temple at Esna tell us that Neith's major festival occurred at Esna on the thirteenth day of the third month of the summer season, lasted all day, and commemorated the arrival of Neith, in her boat shrine, after saving her son Re, the sun god. The goddess of course used her bow and arrows to defeat the sun's enemies. In the third hour of the day the high priest announced the arrival of the goddess in solemn procession. The statue of the goddess was then placed in the sunlight, to reunite her with her son. The goddess's retinue, the temple personnel, arranged themselves on both sides of the large hall and were purified with water. Hymns were sung, sacrifices were offered, and the daily ritual of the temple was performed.

For the masses of faithful in the city the highlight of the festival was the public appearance, or epiphany, of the goddess. As Neith's festival lasted into the night, there was a second series of rites performed with a public appearance at the quay of a statue representing Neith as the celestial cow after it had been adorned at the temple. The cow form of her divine statue is not surprising as Neith was closely associated with the waters of chaos, or Great Flood (Mehet-Weret), characterized by a cow who rose from these primeval waters, as seen in the Pyramid Texts and as she is portrayed in the Esna creation text.

Along with the recitation of appropriate texts, four arrows were shot toward the cardinal points to signify that the power of Neith was universal and that her and Egypt's enemies everywhere could expect to be annihilated.[32] One can imagine that these awesome and colorful events were followed by a night of feasting and rejoicing. Although the town of Esna is very ancient and doubtless contained earlier temple structures, today only the hypostyle hall of the Ptolemaic-Roman temple is preserved, and the temple itself is several meters below the level of the modern town, which is built on the accumulation of centuries and the annual laying down of silt from the time when the Nile annually flooded its banks.

The festival being completed, Neith left Esna to settle in Sais, undertaking the journey as a cow with Re between her horns.[33] Whether this same power of creation was credited to Neith at her temple in Sais (which doubtless would also have claimed to be her original hometown) we cannot be sure, but it seems likely from the text quoted above. Thus, even late in Egypt's ancient history, we have an example of the primacy of rank and power in the pantheon credited to a female deity who needed no male help with her creative acts. Although competing cults credited other, male, gods with the first creation, it is interesting that as late as the Roman Empire Egyptians were open to crediting a goddess with this vital role. Presumably, because Neith was one of the few deities documented for the prehistoric age, she may also have been the first acknowledged creator god in Egyptian history. By the end of her story, she was interpreted as an androgynous creator, as one text at Esna specifically states.[34] No male partner is portrayed for Neith and thus some, like C. J. Bleeker, regard her as a virgin mother goddess.[35]

The Esna myth, doubtless borrowed from Sais, may actually preserve the original, millennia-old creation myth, but we cannot be sure. The other famous ex nihilo creation story (see chapter 2) seems to have been the product of the historic period and could have influenced the theologians of Neith's cult. Indeed, a number of Egyptologists seem to subscribe to the idea that the Late Period was the heyday of Egyptian mythology. Without any early evidence we cannot know whether the creation story of Neith as it survives at Esna was composed by priests of the last dynasties or earlier by some during the New Kingdom or reflects the original concept of the prehistoric worshipers of this goddess. Neith's high regard among the ruling class of the first two dynasties encourages the belief that this was part of her story from the beginning.

CHAPTER 4

HE TWO LADIES

Vestiges of the Remote Past

The Two Ladies—the vulture and the cobra—appear as protectors of the king of Egypt, important enough to be part of his series of formal titles. The title He of Two Ladies, placed second among his five titles, was known since the commencement of the dynasties,[1] but the cobra and the vulture goddesses to which it refers probably enjoyed their individual cults long before the historic period. Indeed, they would seem to be clan divinities: the vulture from the very ancient town of Nekheb in southern Egypt and the cobra from the twin towns of Pe and Dep in the delta, later known collectively as the township of Buto. Thus the Two Ladies are vestiges of a remote past. Once they were worshiped as supreme deities in their respective locales and probably viewed as the Great Mother in each place. When the united state was founded, these early holy mothers were absorbed into the cult of divine kingship and would forevermore be given the responsibility of nurturing and protecting the king, whether in text or iconography, but they also remained the focus of worship for people of their hometowns.

NEKHBET

"She of Nekheb" was the goddess of the Upper Egyptian town of Nekheb, modern El-Kab, on the east bank of the Nile, just up-stream from Esna and roughly halfway between Luxor and Aswan. Here habitation dates to at least 6400 B.C.[2] Usually presented as a vulture, Nekhbet most likely had a predynastic cult reaching far back in time, and could well have been regarded as a creator or supreme mother goddess in the entire southern half of Upper Egypt at least. She probably had close ties to the predynastic ruling house of Upper Egypt, whose capital city of Nekhen was situated just across the river from her own town. When the rulers of that town established their hegemony over all of Upper Egypt and went on to subdue the North and create a united kingdom of the Two Lands, Nekhbet became the tutelary goddess of the king, in partnership with the serpent goddess Wadjet from the delta. Nekhbet's earliest appearance is as a flying figure hovering protectively above the king on objects, such as the mace head now in Oxford, belonging to the "first king," Narmer.[3] Interestingly, this early king is depicted wearing only the Red Crown of Lower Egypt when sitting on his throne atop a high dais, and the vulture goddess is the only deity present. The vulture goddess would more clearly come to represent the White Crown of Upper Egypt later.

Nekhbet the vulture may have been a primeval goddess of the sky, rival to Horus the falcon god, but in a resurrection text in the Pyramid Texts Nekhbet is also visualized as a great wild cow:

> Your mother is the great wild cow
> who dwells in Nekheb,
> white of head-cloth,
> long of plumes,
> and pendulous of breasts;
> she suckles you and will not
> wean you. (PT Utt. 412)

Although she came from the town immediately across the river from the early capital of Upper Egypt, Nekhbet would not have had quite the same appeal as that town's falcon god Horus, with whom the successful Upper Egyptian leader, in conquering the Northern Kingdom, identified strongly.[4] It is not surprising that a male political leader would identify with a male deity rather than a female one. Nonetheless, throughout Egyptian history one of the titles of the king, indeed a basic element of his titulary, is He of the Two Ladies, or Two Mistresses. Each ancient goddess (vulture and serpent) is vesting her sovereignty over her respective kingdom in the pharaoh.

It may seem odd that a vulture would be regarded as a mother goddess or a protectress. The hieroglyph of the vulture, read as *mt* (transliterated now as *mwt*), was used for writing the ancient Egyptian word for "mother," and the similarity of sounds may have at first suggested the connection. Some have suggested that the Egyptians, astute observers of the natural world, saw that the vulture was very attentive to her young, but surely this is true of most birds and most species. However, other cultures (such as the very early Anatolians) also worshiped a vulture as supreme mother goddess, the all-powerful goddess who both bestows and takes away life.[5] Thus it is possible that the same was true in Egypt: a primeval fearsome goddess of the southern region of Upper Egypt existed who in time was not discarded but deliberately transformed from an all-powerful deity to a supportive deity of the ruling class. In dynastic Egypt Nekhbet was seen as the protector of the king and indeed as his mother. Early slate palettes that purport to show historic or quasi-historic scenes show vultures attacking the fallen enemy on the battlefield. This may have been a realistic portrayal, but it could also be symbolic of the might of the Upper Egyptian ruler, who was thus identified with the emblematic goddess of his kingdom.

In addition, Nekhbet was depicted as a unifier of the Two Lands on monuments of the Second Dynasty, so it appears that the ruler was as assimilated to her as he was to Horus the falcon. An interesting combination of the male and female principles would thus be officially sanctioned for the king of united Egypt. Perhaps this was an attempt to win the loyalty of the (mostly female?) adherents of the powerful Nekhbet cult. The vulture goddess did not appear exclusively in bird form in the official iconography. In a royal funerary temple of the Fifth Dynasty she is depicted in human form, nursing King Sahure at her breast, thus emphasizing her role as divine mother.[6]

In the late Fourth Dynasty (ca. 2500 B.C.) the chief queen of Egypt had begun to wear a headdress in the form of a nesting vulture whose wings spread down on the sides of her head and whose head was at her brow. It has been suggested that the bearing of the goddess's symbol on their heads meant that the royal women were united with the goddess. These crowns survived throughout Egyptian history, into the Ptolemaic period, so their significance must have been great. As long as Nekhbet could be considered the mother of the king, the chief wife of a king, who might be expected to bear the next king, could easily have been identified with her.[7] Nekhbet is referred to as a mother of the king and a personification of the White Crown of Upper Egypt in the Pyramid Texts: "I have not forgotten my mother the White Crown, splendid and stout, dwelling in Nekheb, . . . Lady of the Secret Land, Lady of the Field of Fishers, Lady of the Valley of the Blessed" (PT Utt. 470).

At Nekheb the shrine of the goddess was known as the Per-wer, or House of Greatness, and consisted originally of a light frame construction with an animal skin for a roof.[8] Stylized representations of this are found as early as 3100 B.C. but remain in the religious iconography much longer. Structures of this type were rendered in stone at the jubilee court of the funerary complex of King Zoser of the Third Dynasty. Later in the Old Kingdom, with the advent of the solar religion (ca. 2350 B.C.), the Per-wer housed the protective serpent Weret-Hekau. This Per-wer was the holy shrine into which the king stepped at his coronation to have the uraeus officially affixed to his brow.[9] A copy of it, clad in gold, was placed among the tomb treasures of Tutankhamun.[10] On the roof of Tutankhamun's Per-wer are engraved images of fourteen flying vultures, showing that its original inhabitant was not forgotten.[11] The birds hold the hieroglyphic sign *shen*, which stands for infinity, in their talons.

Great goddesses could assume many forms. As is shown below, the serpent is associated worldwide with the divine female. Thus it is not surprising that Nekhbet could take the form of a serpent. For example, in the Pyramid Texts of the Old Kingdom the king is addressed thus:

> You have no human father and you have no human
>   mother,
> for this mother of yours is the great *hwrt*-serpent, white of
>   head-cloth,
> who dwells in Nekheb, whose wings are open, whose
>   breasts are pendulous. (Utt. 703)

The motherly protection extended by the vulture goddess to the pharaoh is exemplified by two spectacular necklaces among the treasures of Tutankhamun's tomb. One, found on the chest of the king's mummy, takes the form of a flexible collar: the great wing expanse of the vulture goddess is worked in many interlocking pieces of gold inlaid with colored glass.[12] Its antecedents can be seen many centuries earlier in the amuletic collars of similar design that were painted on the walls of the wooden coffins of the Middle Kingdom.[13] Nekhbet also appears as a pendant, with a very realistically modeled head in pure gold, set with obsidian eyes and a lapis lazuli beak. The vulture holds the signs for infinity in her talons. Again, the gold is inlaid with blue and red glass.[14]

Nekhbet's township El-Kab was a major center of Upper Egyptian life for millennia and served as the capital of the third Upper Egyptian nome, or province, during the New Kingdom. El-Kab's ancient brick walls, encompassing an area of about 550 square meters, still stand. Within this enclosure was the main temple of the goddess with subsidiary structures including a birth house and a sacred lake. King Amunhotep II of the Eighteenth Dynasty rebuilt a temple for this venerable goddess there. Interestingly, its foundation deposits yielded numerous faience ears, eyes, and fertility figurines of the New King-dom,[15] showing that the motherly aspect of Nekhbet had not been forgotten over the millennia and that common people still were drawn to her cult, even though she and Wadjet the cobra of the delta kingdom were preeminent royal goddesses. Amunhotep III built a small temple for the goddess in her home territory which may be visited today east of El-Kab at the mouth of a desert wadi. She is depicted assimilated to Hathor, patroness of love and sex, again suggesting her importance for guaranteeing fertility. The Ramesside kings also added to Nekhbet's town temple, and the Ptolemies built her a temple in the vicinity later. A number of tombs cut into a cliff face survive from the New Kingdom and may be visited today. One of the best-preserved belongs to the mayor Paheri of the Eighteenth Dynasty. Outside its entrance door on a flat space is carved a hymn to the goddess Nekhbet who is here known as Lady of the Valley:

> Homage, O Lady of the Mouth of the Valley, Mistress of
>   Heaven.
> Mistress of the gods,
> beautiful tiller for him who has no rudder
> judge in heaven and on earth
> beautiful star invisible except in good times.[16]

From the Twentieth Dynasty at Nekheb survives a tomb of a high priest of Nekhbet named Setau. On its walls is portrayed a water procession during which the sacred bark shrine of the vulture goddess is towed by a boat under full sail northward to attend the Sed festival, which was celebrated in the twenty-ninth year of Ramses III. This was such a great occasion that all the gods and goddesses of Egypt attended the ceremonies at Per-Ramesses, founded by Ramses II, where the king now had his residence. The prow of the goddess's boat was decorated with two heads of an antelope or oryx and carried the red shrine of the goddess. Perched on top was the figure of the vulture painted blue and green with white legs and a red band around the wings. Possibly a living bird is portrayed here with wings confined so that it could not fly off. The long trip to escort their goddess to the far northern part of Egypt and the royal residence must have been the highlight of the careers of the high priest and his wife, who was chief of the sacred entertainers in the goddess's temple. That the king sent his chief minister, the vizier To, to escort the goddess speaks to the importance of this venerable goddess's participation in one of the most important ceremonies in Ramses' long reign.[17]

WADJET

The cobra goddess Wadjet was the titulary goddess of the North, where cobras and other snakes abounded. Wadjet (or Edjo, as her name may also have been pronounced) had a long history in Egypt, but her story may have its origins deep in Africa. Among the Bari tribe of the southern Sudan survives the belief that the female ancestor of all mankind appeared in the form of a snake.[18] The earliest portrayals of serpents in Egyptian art associate them with elephants in a mutual relationship, not a hostile one.[19] Serpents seem to lead or protect the elephant, which may have been meant to stand as the image of the chief, if not of a clan divinity, which afterward disappeared from Egyptian belief systems.

Serpents are associated throughout the world with goddess cults and fertility.[20] They must have astounded early people with their ability to shed their skins and thus be reborn—a unique capacity among animals and thus worthy of awe. This may have encouraged the Egyptians'

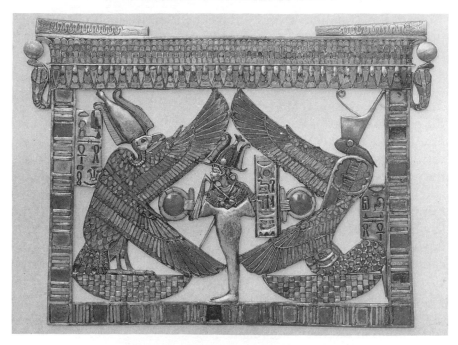

Figure 8. Nekhbet and Wadjet on a pectoral of Tutankhamun. Photo by Harry Burton. Courtesy of the Metropolitan Museum of Art, New York.

belief in the possibility of all living things being reborn after death, a goal they sought for millennia. For this reason serpents were honored more than feared by the Egyptians, and the striking cobra motif is found associated with royal burials, as in the architectural frieze at the Step Pyramid complex of King Zoser of the Third Dynasty.

Serpents are also earthbound creatures. For this reason the serpent deity is often the deity of the earth, and yet in historic Egypt the earth divinity is a male god named Geb, shown in human form. Ancient Egypt is unusual in not having an earth goddess; it is possible that originally Wadjet (and her serpent sisters in other parts of Egypt) was that earth divinity. Even her name, meaning "the Green One," evokes the idea of plant life and the fertility of the earth. Because Egyptian theologians of the historic age rewrote many beliefs and redrew the cosmogonies, the religious literature of the historic age no longer reflects the earliest beliefs of the people in the Nile valley. As we have

Figure 9. Sacred serpents protecting the Southern Tomb at the Zoser Stepped Pyramid Complex, Saqqara. Photo by B. S. Lesko.

seen, some scholars believe that the powers once residing with early goddesses were taken over by the divine king once the state was founded. Cosmogonies reflecting a more patriarchal family structure (a male creator god and a limited number of children of both sexes) dispensed with some early clan divinities and reduced the number of the most important deities. Thus Geb became Father Earth to Nut's Mother Sky. Throughout Egyptian history, however, the cobra is associated with goddesses rather than gods. This is seen in iconography devoted to Hathor and the two sisters Isis and Nepthys, the daughters of Geb and Nut, and other popular goddesses we shall examine shortly. This suggests that the cobra was considered female from the beginning of religious beliefs.

Wadjet's chief cult place was in the Nile's northwest delta. She was associated especially with the very ancient adjoining towns of Pe and Dep, which came to be called Buto collectively (modern Tell el-Fara'in). The two goddesses, cobra and vulture, sitting atop their baskets are engraved on a tablet from the First Dynasty.[21] They would come to be known as *nebty*, the Two Ladies or Two Mistresses. Nebty remained part of the titulary of the Egyptian ruler forever after. The Two Ladies also appear together on the base of a statue of the Third Dynasty king Zoser. The cobra's body is arranged in a double loop with a fully expanded hood and a curved tail hanging over its basket's edge.[22] The royal title He of the Two Mistresses indicates that the royal house remembered its roots and the goddesses' importance as protectors of the royal family of the Two Lands of Egypt.

From the First Dynasty the cobra is combined with the king's *nemes* headdress, actually a head cloth with lappets, such as is seen on the Great Sphinx at Giza.[23] The king of Egypt also wore a double crown of red (Lower Egypt) surrounding a loftier white (Upper Egypt); the cobra adorned the Red Crown of Lower Egypt, and the head of the Vulture was attached to the White Crown of Upper Egypt. Even when the king did not wear his double crown, a golden vulture and serpent were on his brow, as divine protectors, although the two goddesses were often both represented as two cobras. Rows of serpents protected the royal burial place, seen in the frieze of upright cobras along the roof line of the southern tomb at the magnificent Step Pyramid complex of King Zoser at Saqqara. Here too the ancient national shrines of both goddesses, representing the two "halves" of the country, are preserved in stone.

Wadjet, like Nekhbet, does not play a major role in the Pyramid Texts, but two Utterances preserve parts of a ritual for the handling of the Red Crown. When the officiating priest opens the door of the tabernacle that holds the crown, he addresses it as a goddess:

> O *Nt-*crown he has come to you, O Fiery Serpent
> He has come to you, O Great One
> He has come to you, O Great of Magic." (PT Utt. 220)

The risen serpent (Egyptian *i'rt*, interpreted by the Greeks as *ouraios* and Latinized as Uraeus) is to be understood as a divine cobra protector of royalty, guardian of the crown. From 1600 B.C. come ten hymns to the royal crowns that convey the power of the serpent on the royal brow. I quote from one:

> Hail to you, Eye of Horus, who cuts off the heads
> of those in the following of Seth.

May she tread them down, may she besprinkle the gods
with that which came forth from her—
in her name of Mistress of the Atef-crown.
Awe of her is greater than that of her foes—
in her name of Mistress of Awe.
The fear of her is produced in them that conspire against
 her—
in her name of Mistress of Fear.[24]

It was through the strength of the goddess on his brow that the king could rule over his people. She inspired fear of him and gave him the magical power to keep Egypt and the universe in order. Without the uraeus the king was powerless, and that is why even when he is portrayed as a youthful and future king, the prince wears the uraeus serpent on his brow. In time princesses and queens too were similarly protected.

By the Sixth Dynasty and the establishment of the cult of Re, the sun's disk is commonly shown flanked by two uraei. The sun's consort, Hathor, also is shown with a uraeus hanging from the horned sun disk on her head. The cobra also quite regularly accompanied the canine known as Wepwawet, Opener of the Ways, again as a guardian but also as a sharer in the concept of divine aggression and protection of the kingship. Such standards usually accompanied the king in Sed festival processions or in ceremonial smiting scenes.[25] Wadjet the cobra was more often found alone on the brow of the king as his divine protectress. The largest example of this was the cobra that originally protected the brow of the Great Sphinx at Giza. Its fragments, including the head, are now kept at the British Museum after being discovered lying between the sphinx's paws by a Captain Caviglia, who presented the cobra head to the Museum in 1817.

Occasionally Wadjet appears in human form with a winged cobra on her head accompanying the king as a protective mother. At the pyramid temple of King Neuser-Re of the Fifth Dynasty, she stands with her arm around the king and the epithet Wadjet of Pe is written above her head.[26] She was meant to inspire fear before the king but also to einsure his continued power and vitality:

O, Great Crown!
O, Crown great of magic!

O Fiery Serpent
Grant that the dread of me be like the dread of you
Grant that the fear of me be like the fear of you. (PT Utt.
   221)

The title Weret-Hekau meaning "Great of Magic" or "Great Enchantress," was given to some goddesses. It is written in hieroglyphs with the
determinative of a coiled serpent, the animal becoming synonymous
with the concept goddess. In the Pyramid Texts there is no mistaking
the identification of the uraeus and the crown of Lower Egypt with
Weret-Hekau, the Great Enchantress. The dual cult place of Wadjet
carried over to a dual cult for the cobra goddess, who was often
presented as dual guardian of the sun disk. It is interesting that the
vulture and the cobra goddess, the Two Ladies, were the most popular
theophoric element in the construction of personal names, after
Hathor and Maat, in the Old Kingdom.[27] They were both regarded as
the mothers of the king of Egypt. Senusert I of the Twelfth Dynasty was
called "son of the Two Ladies,"[28] thus enjoying the same relationship to
them as to Hathor and Isis. The Two Ladies lived on throughout
Egyptian history, both in the titulary of the king and in more tangible
form adorning his crowns, necklaces, and architecture. For instance,
there is an elaborate golden pectoral once worn by the Twelfth Dynasty
Pharaoh Aunemhet III (ca. 1850 B.C.) that features the solar cow
Hathor (shown as two symmetrically facing each other) topped by a
rearing serpent.[29] Their conjunction here has been interpreted as a
"manifestation of the same solar life energy" that itself is inseparable
from royal power. This is conveyed well in a granite statue originally
from the Temple of Karnak but now in Cairo which shows the
Eighteenth Dynasty pharaoh Amunhotep II wearing the White Crown
standing before a gigantic rearing serpent whose identity, if there was
any doubt, is proven by the papyrus stalks carved on either side of her.[30]
   The marvelous tomb assemblage of the young king Tutankhamun
included a small golden shrine, mentioned earlier as a copy of
Nekhbet's Per-wer, in which was found the image of Weret-Hekau, the
Great Enchantress: a female head on a snake's body nursing the king
of Egypt.[31] The goddess thus has a maternal role in relation to the king.
This image may already be found in the Pyramid Texts where the dead
king says:

I have laid down for myself this sunshine of yours as a
    stairway under my feet
on which I will ascend to that mother of mine, the living
    uraeus which should be upon me, O Re.
She will have compassion on me and will give me her
    breast that I may suck it. (Utt. 508)

Interestingly, this Utterance begins with an acknowledgment of both
Wadjet and Nekhbet who will rejoice on the day that the king ascends
to heaven.

Weret-Hekau is mentioned ten times in the inscriptions on the walls
of the shrine, which seems to commemorate the king's coronation and
is meant to provide the process for a renewal of the coronation in the
afterlife. Certainly the king's coronation was not complete until the
uraeus was placed on his brow. Both King Horemheb of the Eighteenth
Dynasty and Ramses III of the Twentieth mention this rite in their
inscriptions.[32] From Horemheb's it is clear that the affixing of the
sacred serpent to the brow of the king took place within a shrine known
as the Per-wer, of which the small golden shrine in Tutankhamun's
tomb is a model. The walls of the great hypostyle hall at Karnak display
many scenes illustrating the coronation of Ramses II of the Nineteenth
Dynasty. Ramses is crowned by Amun-Re, the king of all the gods at this
period, but is flanked by fully human images of both Nekhbet and
Wadjet after he is seated on his throne wearing the double crown of
Upper and Lower Egypt, which these goddesses personify.[33]

The Two Ladies were retained in royal iconography throughout
Egyptian history, judging from the funerary jewelry of Tutankhamun.
On one pectoral appear both Wadjet, wearing a red crown, and Nekhbet,
wearing the lofty Atef crown with its dual feathers, flanking a sacred
udjat eye.[34] Vultures wearing the Atef crown are depicted on the ceiling
of the hypostyle hall of Ramses II's rock-cut temple at Abu Simbel. In
all cases these great goddesses are the protectors of the royal body and
guardians of the sovereignty of the state. The theme of nursing the
pharaoh, as seen in the image of Weret-Hekau, is found again much
later in the Ptolemaic period at the temple of Hathor in Dendera,
where Wadjet, the Lady of Pe and Dep, is presented in the role normally
associated with Isis, as the mother of Horus, making a shelter for her
son Horus and raising him in the papyrus marshes. Clearly Wadjet, like

Nekhbet, Isis, and Hathor, was always one of the mothers of the Horus king of Egypt, endowing him with her divine strength and protection.[35]

RENENUTET

Besides Wadjet, the most prominent cobra goddess was Renenutet, goddess of the harvest and mistress of victuals. Apparently it was common for granaries to have a small shrine to this goddess nearby, most likely to protect the vital grain supplies from natural predators such as mice and birds, against both of which a snake would be a useful ally. Propitiating the power of the divine cobra to ensure that she would work her venom for rather than against the cultivators was surely an inspiration for the popularity of the cult of Renenutet. Even on the national level the goddess was propitiated in a shrine at the granaries of the great temple of Amun-Re, King of the Gods, during the New Kingdom, or Egyptian Empire period. Scenes that survive in private tombs show that the queen of Egypt herself mediated at the blessing of the harvest. The queen's role as a priestess, transmitting offerings to the goddess in return for the generous Egyptian harvest, may have been ages old. One thinks of all the serpent associations with the earliest goddess cults and their priestesses, such as the famous images of Crete, who were adept at handling serpents. It is very possible that due to early women's role as food producer and the queen's sex kinship with the cobra goddess, an Egyptian queen, going back as far as the predynastic age, would have been regarded as the natural mediator between her people's need for a bounteous harvest and the divinity who controlled it. The king too is shown officiating at the cult of Renenutet in a Twelfth Dynasty temple, but, significantly, he is accompanied by his young daughter.[36]

MERETSEGER

In the New Kingdom most members of the royal family were buried in the necropolis of Thebes on the west bank at what now is Luxor in Upper Egypt. Here their tombs were not pyramids but rock-cut tunnel-like sepulchers often penetrating deep into the sides or floor of desert valleys and easily hidden. The quarrymen and artisans who produced these large, well-decorated tombs lived as civil servants in a separate community, founded in the Eighteenth Dynasty, on a low desert escarpment in the shadow of a pyramidlike peak above the Valley of the Kings. This Peak of the West, as it was known, was believed to have been home to the goddess Meretseger, a serpent who was widely venerated in the workers' village. Hymns to Meretseger, Lady of the Western Mountain, have survived, and so have her cult images. Like Renenutet, she was apparently looked to for both safety and sustenance. However, some prayers written by the villagers show that she was a powerful force in both private and public life. If villagers fell ill or suffered eye problems, they felt they were being punished by Meretseger for some transgression.

The draftsman Neferabu dedicated a stela to Meretseger depicting her on the right side of the slab as a serpent with one human head and two serpent heads, and he engraved a hymn in seventeen columns that salutes her but also explains her power to punish as well as forgive the truly penitent:

> An ignorant man (I was), without my heart, who did not
> know good from evil.
> I was doing misdeeds against the Peak and she taught me a
> lesson.
> I was in her hand night and day, sitting on bricks like the
> pregnant woman. . . .
> Behold I will say to the great and small
> Who are in the (artisan) crew,
> Beware of the Peak!
> Because a lion is within it!
> The Peak strikes with the stroke of a savage lion
> She is after him who offends her.[37]

THE LAST MILLENNIUM

The Two Ladies were still venerated during the final centuries of Egypt's ancient story and throughout Egypt's empire. Successive dynasties, often with no legitimacy except military force, would pay homage to the greatest divinities in the hope of gaining their support. Today the

Figure 10. Head of a large snake statue and fragmentary colossal stone vulture (the Two Ladies) from the Sudan. Courtesy of the Ashmolean Museum, Oxford.

Ashmolean Museum of Oxford owns two finely sculpted heads of the Two Ladies originally commissioned by the prolific builder King Taharqa of the Kushite or Sudanese Dynasty whose Napatan kings controlled Egypt as the Twenty-fifth Dynasty. Taharqa built a temple closer to his home in the Sudan, at Sanam abu Dom, where these sculptures were recovered by archaeologists. Here, portrayed in a highly polished granite, both Nekhbet and Wadjet, the titulary goddesses of Egypt, were honored in art and in cults as ancestresses of a legitimate ruler of Egypt so far in time and space from their original Egyptian seats.

At Philae, in Isis's temple dating to the late Ptolemaic dynasty and Roman period, Nekhbet was not forgotten. She was still called "White One, Lady of Nekhen, Lady of Heaven and Mistress of All the gods."[38] Nekhbet's history continued into the Greco-Roman Period: she was equated with the Greek Eileithyia, and the Roman emperors added to her temple in Nekhen/El-Kab.

As for the late chapters of Wadjet's story, Psamtik, the second ruler of the Twenty-sixth Dynasty (ca. 664–525 B.C.), dedicated at Buto, the chief cult city of Wadjet, a large limestone statue of the goddess, on display today at the Museum of Archaeology and Anthropology at the University of Pennsylvania.[39] The upright cobra body has a human female's head with the long, tripartite archaic hairstyle seen on goddesses and also in portrayals of queens when the intention was to stress the royal woman's role as manifestation of a goddess. The cobra here wears as well a double-plumed diadem fronted by a sun disk flanked by horns, for which a band of uraei form a platform. The similar headgear often seen on Hathor and Isis at this time suggests this was

Figure 11. Cobra goddess (Wadjet?), limestone statuette, Twenty-sixth Dynasty, Thebes. Courtesy of the University of Pennsylvania Museum of Archaeology and Anthropology, Philadelphia.

viewed as a proper adornment of important goddesses. Indeed, Hathor and Isis are sometimes depicted as serpents, but the identity of this statue is narrowed due to its being carved in two dimensions on the upper part of the back of the monument with the figure of a vulture holding the *shen* sign for infinity in each of its claws. On either side of the serpent figure Nekhbet and Wadjet appear in low relief, and the inscription refers to Wadjet as Mistress of Pe and Dep. There is every likelihood that the statue was a votive offering of Psamtik in the temple of this great and very ancient goddess in Pe/Buto.

The Ptolemies still honored the titulary goddesses of yore, and at Philae Wadjet joined Nekhbet in holding out the sign of life toward the royal falcon and the name of Ptolemy.[40]

$\mathcal{H}$ATHOR, GODDESS OF LOVE

The early female divine power is personified in extant monuments from the earliest historical period as the two-faced goddess Bat, whose name meant "Feminine Power" or "Feminine Spirit."[1] Her two faces suggest the impressive power to see forward and behind and thus be protected from all threats. Bat's front-facing head with bovine ears and inward-curving horns is duplicated at the top of the monumental Narmer Palette and may be seen as well decorating the belt of the king represented there. The only other deity on the palette is the falcon, Horus, who was meant to represent the king himself. Other contemporary early monuments show the vulture Nekhbet and the symbol of the goddess Neith. Some scholars have suggested that the deity on the Narmer Palette is actually Mehet-Weret; others believe it is Hathor, who came to be the best-known cow goddess. There is no actual reference to Hathor until many centuries later, and her earliest representations do not stress bovine attributes. Hathor apparently had a temple in Gebelein as early as the Third Dynasty,[2] but it is not until the Fourth Dynasty (2613–2498 B.C.) that she appears in text and image.

During the Fourth Dynasty Hathor became a major deity on a par with the sun god, who represented in Egyptian religious thought the Great Power. Utterance 405 of the Pyramid Texts described Hathor as the Eye of the Sun, that is, the radiant heat and light emanating from the center of the solar disk. Hathor became the chief of all the goddesses, divine mother of the king of Egypt, and the special deity of women, but men too paid homage to her. Although rarely mentioned in the Pyramid Texts (which leads to the suspicion that she arrived late on the religious scene), Hathor was described therein with bovine features. Thus she may have already absorbed Bat, although Bat's image continued to adorn cultic instruments such as the mirror and the sistrum. In a rare instance of recalling this most ancient deity, Bat appears in the royal funerary literature, when the deceased king identifies himself with her: "I am Bat with her two faces" (PT Sp. 506).

HATHOR AND THE CULT OF THE SUN

The kings of the first three dynasties were buried in tomb complexes of many acres enclosed in walled compounds that imitated their palaces and parade grounds. By the Fourth Dynasty the royal tombs were constructed in the form of the first true, smooth-sided pyramids. The first was built by King Snefru in about 2700 B.C. As Kemp has argued, these pyramid tombs may convey a "radically different view of the nature of the monarchy." Whereas the earlier tomb complexes celebrated the king as a supreme *territorial* claimant and perpetuated the pageantry associated with his reign on earth, now the magical mound was preserved in stone and proclaimed the king's absorption "into the mystic symbol of the sun."[3] A new cult, the Re religion, had come to the fore.

In creation myths the sun god Re was associated with the aged sun god Atum. But, more important, the king of Egypt, originally identified as the earthly Horus, was now known as the Son of Re. Perhaps because existing cults of great goddesses refused to take a subordinate position, that of wife, to this new god, Re's priesthood found it necessary to introduce a specially created goddess as his consort. Re's partner was to be a goddess who would personify the entire Ennead, (the gods who made up the genealogy of the king), Hathor, whose name may be translated as "House (or Mansion) of Horus," "House" meaning genealogy.[4] It is possible that "House" is to be understood as a simile for the womb, as Hathor was also the mother of Horus.[5] In the Pyramid Texts we find what must be a reference to the goddess as a personification of Horus's home: "He shall ascend to the Mansion of Horus which is in the sky" (Utt. 485). However, the Ennead was also in the sky, depicted with Re on his solar bark. The goddess Hathor was likely invented to be a divine "right hand" or helpmate, a spouse who nurtured the divine child, the king of Egypt, who was the earthly manifestation of Horus. Perhaps her supporters would have already claimed for her the role of "universal feminine principle."[6] Hathor certainly played a major role in the cult at the royal sun temples of the late Old Kingdom. Even before the royal funerary literature was engraved on the interior of royal pyramids starting at the end of the Fifth Dynasty, the earliest kings of that dynasty were honoring the cult of Hathor with statue dedications and with endowments of land for her temples.[7]

The Fourth Dynasty witnessed the pinnacle of ancient Egyptian culture. The greatest attainments in science, math, engineering, and medicine had been reached. Thus the state's construction of Hathor—assuming it took place in the Third Dynasty—occurred rather late as a cultural and intellectual development. Certainly Hathor was not (contrary to what some authors have carelessly claimed) one of the earliest deities but rather one whose origins cannot be traced to before the Old Kingdom proper, and this reinforces the suspicion that she was deliberately created by the Re priesthood.

The earliest artistic representations of Hathor show her in wholly human form, wearing a headdress of the sun disk plus the outward-turned horns of a cow, suggesting that her attributes were borrowed from earlier goddesses.

In sculpture, the sun disk on Hathor's head clearly associates her with the other two important solar gods, Re and Horus. These three deities, in fact, were the preeminent deities of Egypt's golden age, the Old Kingdom. Hans Goedicke has suggested that Hathor, House of Horus, was meant to be understood as the "personification of the ordered cosmos, that is, the domain where Horus rules. . . . Hathor is the receptacle of life in a lawful, organized fashion."[8] This helps to explain why she is a prominent in both state art and religious literature from the beginning of her existence.

There have always been many aspects to Hathor, however. She is often identified in inscriptions of the Old Kingdom as Lady of the Sycamore. An early Fourth Dynasty monument of a woman priestess of Hathor, Mistress of the Sycamore, is the first evidence of the existence

of this goddess.[9] Typical of Egyptian religion, "new," or newly prominent, deities assumed aspects of older, better-known ones. Thus those
promoting their favorite female deity would naturally attach to her the
symbols and attributes of other early popular goddesses. Hathor
probably absorbed attributes of an earlier tree goddess. The Egyptian
tree goddess (whether identified as Hathor or another goddess) is
often shown dispensing water to the birdlike *bas* (souls) of deceased
persons in later papyrus and tomb paintings. Interestingly, near the
Giza plateau there still survived in the 1950s a deep and very ancient
well in the midst of a grove of sycamores.[10]

What is the significance of the sycamore tree? Such trees are long-
lived, grow large, and have strong wood. Sycamore wood used as architectural elements still survive from the Old Kingdom, more than four
thousand years ago. The sycamore was the only native tree of useful
size and sturdiness and thus the most important, but very early (before
Hathor) the Egyptians were trading with the area of present-day
Lebanon for the coniferous timber produced in that mountainous
country. Sycamores in Egypt grew along the desert edge, near the
burial grounds that were the special concern of Hathor. In the Pyramid
Texts Utterance 568 the sycamore seems to stand for the landscape of
the Beyond, the goal of the blessed dead: "The King has grasped for
himself the two sycamores which are in yonder side of the sky." But the
cult of the Mistress of the Southern Sycamore was surely not confined
to the funerary realm alone. Other possible explanations for the deification of the sycamore are discussed later.

It is obvious from inscriptions on private tombs of the Old Kingdom
that a woman could hold clerical positions, even major ones, in the cult
of more than one goddess. In an investigation of records of elite women
in the Old Kingdom, Marianne Galvin discovered women who held
positions in the cults of both Hathor and Neith. A number of these were
priestesses of Hathor, Mistress of the Sycamore.[11] For example, a priestess with a tomb at Dahshur and another buried at Saqqara officiated in
the cults of both Hathor, Mistress of the Sycamore in All Her Places, and
Neith, North of the Wall and Opener of the Ways.[12] These two goddesses' cults were centered at the capital city of Memphis and its
environs, which included, of course, the great royal cemeteries.

Hathor's importance for the royal family of the Fourth Dynasty is
apparent from the fact that the king's chief wife was her priestess; also

it is likely that the queen was already viewed as her earthly manifestation. For this reason the sculptured images of the queen and the goddess in Menkaure's pyramid complex are similar and the golden armchair of Queen Hetepheres, mother of Khufu, builder of the Great Pyramid, exhibits clusters of papyrus as arm decoration placing the queen between the papyrus clumps, as the cow of Hathor was traditionally portrayed. Queen Mersyankh, the granddaughter of a king and wife of Khafre, who built the second Great Pyramid at Giza, records in her tomb her role in the cult of both Hathor and the moon god Thoth.[13] She held the title God's Wife of Hathor, which indicates she was the chief officiant in the cult of this very important goddess. In her tomb at Giza she is seen with her mother, Queen Hetepheres II, in a boat "shaking the papyrus for Hathor," a ritual that is seen later in commoners' tomb scenes as well. The sound of the rustling papyrus plants must have evoked the presence of the goddess moving among the plants, and it has been suggested that in the mortuary beliefs of the Egyptians, the swampland, which was the favorite habitat of Egypt's cattle, was the final stage of the journey the deceased would take before entering the Blessed Beyond.[14] In the tomb context at least, Hathor is to be understood as the deity who welcomes the worthy dead and leads them into Eternity.

The goddess is impressively portrayed in the sculptural art made for the mortuary temple of King Menkaure's funerary complex at Giza's third pyramid. In one statue now in Boston the goddess is seated and is portrayed much larger in scale than the king, who stands like a dutiful son beside her. It is clear that her cult was designed as a support for and an instrument of the royal house, which promoted the king as the earthly form of Horus. Hathor was the mother of the king; the women of the royal family, her priestesses.

Other goddess cults had to be absorbed into Hathor, who thus acquired more than one identity. For instance, as Mistress of All the Gods, Hathor is not only being credited with the highest rank but must also be arrogating to herself attributes of the goddess Nut, who in the old Memphite theology was referred to as Mother of All Gods. The Book of the Dead, a development of the funerary literature first published in the fifteenth century B.C., may recall this in Spell 82, where Hathor and Ptah of Memphis are invoked and the deceased says: "I have recalled with my mouth the speech of Atum to my father when he

*Figure 12. Seated
Hathor. Triad of King
Mycerinus and two
goddesses, Giza, Fourth
Dynasty. Museum
Expedition. Courtesy of
the Museum of Fine
Arts, Boston.*

destroyed the majesty of the wife of Geb [Nut], whose head was broken at his word."

In Memphis many Old Kingdom inscriptions refer to Hathor, Lady of the Sycamore, who must have existed previously as a tree goddess, and Hathor is still recalled by this description in the New Kingdom's Book of the Dead: "You shall sit under the branches of the tree of Hathor, who is preeminent in the wide solar disk" (Sp. 82). We also know of a Hathor, Mistress of the Date Palm, in a town to the north of Memphis. In Egypt's hot climate the cool shade of a palm grove or of a wide-spreading tree like the sycamore would have been especially appreciated. The Middle Kingdom sage Ipuwer observed, "It is good when men build tombs, dig ponds, and groves of trees are planted for the gods."[15]

The tree of life is a theme commonly encountered in Near Eastern art of all ages. In the second half of the twentieth century there was still, near Cairo, an ancient sycamore tree associated with the Virgin Mary. Thus its sacredness endured until modern times. Most Egyptian towns probably had their local sacred tree, temples had gardens, and trees and gardens were often planted in the parched earth of the cemeteries too. The reference to Hathor as Lady of the Sycamore has been understood to refer to a particular old tree that grew to the south of the temple of Ptah in Memphis during the Old Kingdom.[16] Certainly a tree that outlasted the centuries was a marvel worthy of reverence. Such a sacred phenomenon was readily appropriated by those who were bent on building up the importance and pervasiveness of their new goddess. The presence of Hathor's name on an entrance to King Khafre's Valley temple, near his Great Sphinx at Giza, underlines the great goddess's role in the afterlife of the royal family. References to Hathor's roles with respect to royalty come almost exclusively from a funeral context in the Old Kingdom, so one must approach the question of religious beliefs in this early period with great caution.

In the Fourth Dynasty the king of Egypt became the son of the sun god Re. The Re element appears in the names and titles of the rulers of the mid-Fourth Dynasty, and the smooth-sided pyramid tombs may well be linked with his cult. The Pyramid Texts, from the late Fifth and the Sixth Dynasty, probably reflect an earlier understanding of the destiny of dead royalty as well as ideas newly added by the priests who directed their engraving on the walls of the royal burial chambers. The growing importance of Re's cult during the Fifth Dynasty is manifested in sun temples built almost adjacent to the king's funerary monuments and of proportions equal to the royal tomb. In these royal temples—which should reflect the state cult of the Fifth Dynasty—Hathor and Re were so closely associated that numerous priests had titles combining the two.[17] The Sixth Dynasty ruler Pepi I called himself the Son of Re and the Son of Hathor, sometimes using only the latter in his documents. This places Hathor on equal footing with Re. In the Pyramid Texts the solar eye of Re is described as located "on the horns of Hathor" (just as in art the goddess wears the disk between her horns) and is credited with allowing the deceased to be born again:

> That Eye of yours which is on the horns of Hathor,
> which turns back the years from me;
> I spend the night and am conceived and born every day.
> (PT Utt. 705)

At this time Hathor is referred to as "The Golden One"—undoubtedly a reference to the color of the sun disk—and the king is "Horus who came forth from the Golden One".[18] The one body of religious texts we have from this early period are the above-mentioned Pyramid Texts, or funerary spells, engraved in large blue hieroglyphs on the stone walls of royal burial crypts in the Fifth and Sixth dynasties, but these are mainly spells intended to propel the dead king or queen into the arms of the gods in the heavens.

In the Fifth and Sixth dynasties royal pyramids became more modest in size and in construction techniques. (Today some are mere piles of rubble.) This has been interpreted by Egyptologists as evidence that royal power was waning or that a rethinking of both economic and religious priorities had occurred. At this same time numerous private tombs on a grand scale were built throughout the country and statuary of nonroyal families proliferated. Unlike the Fourth Dynasty, power was no longer concentrated in the royal family; capable men of humble origin sometimes ended their careers in extremely powerful positions. It is a pity that no records survive to explain what might be called the first social revolution.

In terms of religion, it is clear that the important cult of Hathor was no longer confined to the patronage of the royal family. High officials as well as nonroyal women served as her clergy at the sun temples of the king at Abu Gurob and elsewhere. From the Nile delta to Aswan in the far south, Hathor had numerous cult places. The adherents to her cult were men and women alike, but in the Old Kingdom many more women than men were associated with the Hathor shrines. The expression "venerated before Hathor" appears on hundreds of Old Kingdom tomb inscriptions, because she was associated with the Re religion's mortuary cult accommodations. Later, in the second millennium, at Thebes, there is additional evidence that Hathor became an important mortuary goddess.

Galvin believes the goddess's widespread popularity in the Old Kingdom can be attributed to her identification as the proprietress and promoter of love, sexual life, music, and, it might be suggested, human happiness in general.[19] Leonard H. Lesko is of the opinion that the goddess's cult became widespread and attractive in the Old Kingdom for political reasons—primarily because of her close association with the king: everyone in Egypt would find it in their best interests to support the kingship by supporting the cult of his divine mother.[20] Whatever the reason for her popularity in the Fifth and Sixth dynasties, there is no doubt that women originally dominated the priestly ranks of Hathor's cult. Over them all stood a priestess of Hathor in All Her Places, under whom were numerous cult places in Giza-Saqqara, Dendera, and Kusae. Some cults were dedicated more specifically to Hathor, Mistress of the Sycamores. Galvin has documented about four hundred women who were involved in the cult of Hathor during the Old Kingdom and subsequent First Intermediate period.[21] She believes that, judging from the monuments they left, these women represent a socioeconomic cross-section. There is no doubt that women were the actual celebrants in this important cult: "The very fact that this priesthood was supported by 99% female enrollment indicates that certainly it was the women, the priestesses, who performed the rituals for Hathor."[22]

In the paintings inside temples and tombs of the later New Kingdom period Hathor is often depicted wearing a patterned red dress and a long, narrow, red scarf, which apparently identified the priestesses of Hathor during the Old Kingdom. The scarf was tied tightly around the neck and hung down the back. Millennia later an inscription at the temple of Edfu gives Hathor the title Mistress of the Red Cloth.[23] The

Coffin Texts of the Middle Kingdom have the deceased state that she has woven a dress for Hathor (Sp. 486), whereas in the preceding spell it is four gods—Horus, Thoth, Osiris, and Atum—who have woven the dress. On the second shrine that enclosed the sarcophagus of Pharaoh Tutankhamun, a goddess, who must be Hathor, is described as "She of the red cloth."[24] It is probable that presentation of clothing was a part of the daily ritual for Hathor as this has been documented for other deities. A hymn in the Coffin Texts that may have been used in the cult of the Middle Kingdom supports this:

> I have come that I might kiss the earth, that
> I might worship my mistress, for I have seen her beauty
> I will give praise to Hathor, for I have seen her beauty.
> I will give her the fabric, for her form is more
>   distinguished than the gods,
> I will see her beauty, for she makes my beautiful going.
>   (Sp. 484)

Surviving from the later New Kingdom are items of linen clothing, usually shirts, often painted with Hathoric designs, that were left as votives at the goddess's shrines. One cloth shows ten women worshipers of the sacred cow all wearing red dresses, and Hathor herself often appears in a red dress in painted scenes.[25] While women dominated the cults during the Old Kingdom (and the following period, which saw the breakdown of the centralized government and the rise of competing dynasties), male priests begin to show up in the documents more frequently and finally seem to take charge of the priestess clergy, becoming Overseers of Priests, a new title from the Sixth Dynasty through the First Intermediate period. Women continue to serve as priestesses, but in fewer numbers and no longer in positions of highest authority.[26]

That the governor, or local prince, of a province headed the cult of the local Hathor temple, however, would indicate that Hathor remained the most powerful of goddesses and to serve her meant enormous prestige. That men vied for this priestly position with women—and often won—demonstrates the importance of the goddess cult to both sexes. The wife of Intef-O, Great Prince of the Southland, was a high priestess. Another governor of the Thebaid, who controlled Upper

Egypt just before the successful Theban conquest of the north, was married to a priestess of Hathor. Thus the goddess's nonroyal clergy during the late First Intermediate Period and the Middle Kingdom tended to come from the highest echelons of Egyptian society. That men moved into the administration of the cult suggests they appreciated its importance and the social prestige attached to the higher clergy. The literacy of the elite males would have made them invaluable from an administrative point of view. However, the wealth that accrued to the temples was surely also a factor in attracting men to the cults.

By the time the Theban ruler Nebhepetre-Mentuhotep was in control of both Upper and Lower Egypt (ca. 2134 B.C.), his principal wife served as a priestess of Hathor, and it is clear from their royal tomb complex that Mentuhotep's other wives were also importantly involved in the celebration of the goddess's cult. Invariably the queen of Egypt was portrayed in sculpture as wearing the old-fashioned, long, tripartite wig characteristic of goddesses, as if to underline the role of the queen as a manifestation of Hathor on earth (this is seen in royal statues for twenty-five hundred years, from the Old Kingdom through the Ptolemaic Period). Evidence from the Thirteenth Dynasty also suggests that the wife of the king continued to act as a chief priestess in the Hathor cult. Royal patronage of her cult would continue in the New Kingdom.

Although Hathor was initially promoted by theologians who were developing and refining the myth of divine kingship, she become a very popular goddess, which is reflected in the frequency of references to her in the Coffin Texts. Now she rises and shines and thus is equated with the sun itself (CT Sps. 61, 482) or with sunbeams (Sps. 300, 710). She rides in a celestial bark, like Re, and is paired with Re as an equal in a number of spells, for example, 224, 334, 496, and 720. And although she may have been designed by theologians as a wife or helpmate of the supreme god Re, over time Hathor became "too impressive, dynamic and independent a figure to be fettered in any mythological system or to be bound to a husband."[27] The Coffin Texts refer to her as the Great Goddess, and the inference is that in Hathor we have a female creator. "The Great Goddess has fashioned you," the worthy dead are assured in Spell 44.

In Spell 331 Hathor is called "the Lady of All." Similarly, in the novella "The Story of Sinuhe," which dates from the beginning of the Twelfth Dynasty (ca. 1900), the *Nbet r-djer*, or Mistress of All, is identified with Hathor.[28] Sinuhe's story indicates that Re, Horus, and Hathor were still the three most important Egyptian divinities at the beginning of the Twelfth Dynasty. The name of the king, Senusert, means "Man of the Great Goddess," and Sinuhe means "Son of the Sycamore."

Because Hathor was manifested in a sacred cow, milk was important in her cult's rituals. The Old Kingdom temple at Dendera maintained a herd of cattle. The priestesses of Hathor who were buried at the Eleventh Dynasty funerary monument of their husband, King Mentuhotep II, at Deir el-Bahri, farther south on the west bank of Thebes (modern Luxor), are portrayed drinking from bowls of milk.[29] In the painted statues of the goddess from the New Kingdom she is depicted as a reddish brown cow with roughly star-shaped white spots. A white cow is known to have been the sacred animal associated with Hathor's Memphite cult much later, and a white calf seems to portray Hathor in Theban Eighteenth Dynasty tombs.

Already in the Old Kingdom Hathor's temple cult had attracted lay people, and she also figured in the ceremonies at the tomb door even at the funerals of commoners. Complicated dances by both men and women are recorded in several Sixth Dynasty tombs.[30] In the tomb of Iy-mery texts explain the dancing was for the Festival of Eternity and references to the "gold movement" hint at an invocation of Hathor, elsewhere known as the Golden One of Women. Later Hathor's connection with the deceased's hope to be "reborn" would be more explicit, but it is likely that in the Old Kingdom she was already "present" at funerals. As we have seen, her statues figured prominently in the funerary temple of Menkaure's Fourth Dynasty pyramid complex. In the Middle Kingdom's Coffin Texts, the religious spells that ensured the commoner of a blessed hereafter, Hathor is credited with having her own solar bark and later was depicted in the solar bark on walls in royal tombs, (see fig. 15 below). A goal of the blessed deceased, who hopes to serve the goddess forever, would be to serve as a rower: "I will go aboard your bark. I will acquire the thrones, I will ply my oar in those happy monthly festivals of yours of the summer" (CT Sp. 623). Private tombs of the Twelfth Dynasty, both at Thebes and farther north at Meir, ancient Kusae, clearly show that Hathor was the most important goddess invoked at funerals. Female flute players and drummers accompany dancers in the tomb built by Antefoker, a vizier of Senusert I, and used by his wife. The lyrics they sing invoke Hathor: "The doors of

Heaven open and the deity comes forth / The Golden Goddess has come."[31]

HATHORIC TEMPLES

By the Sixth Dynasty there were many temples up and down the Nile dedicated to the cult of Hathor, several erected by Pepi I (ca. 2400 B.C.) in Middle Egypt. He must have particularly favored the cult of Hathor of Dendera, for it is this form of the goddess who figured in his and his successors' titularies as Son of Hathor, Mistress of Dendera. Hathor was also associated with Atum, Lord of Heliopolis, during the reign of Pepi's I,[32] perhaps because of the similarity of the names of the cult places of the two deities (*Iwnu* for Heliopolis and *Iunut* for Dendera). The Egyptians loved puns even in writing serious religious texts, and a very late text in the Ptolemaic temple seen at Dendera today states that "Dendera was made for her as a substitute for Heliopolis." This tallies with the theory that Hathor was "invented" by the priests of Re at Heliopolis as a mate for the sun god.

Hathor's cult at Dendera would flourish for millennia. While Hathor came to be associated most strongly with the town of Dendera in Upper Egypt, a day's sail north of Thebes, she does not appear to have been the first deity there. The nome emblem for Dendera from the earliest records was a crocodile. Already in the Fifth Dynasty private monuments recorded a cult of Hathor of Dendera,[33] and there is also a Horus of Dendera known from a Sixth Dynasty inscription. It has been argued that this Horus is an ancient falcon sky god who became known later as Horus the Elder. He is mentioned in a Sixth Dynasty inscription as Horus of Dendera, but Hathor had two sons, one of them Horus Sematawy (Harsomtus) or Horus, Uniter of the Two Lands—an ephithet for the king. This corresponds well with Hathor's epithet, House of Horus, indicative of her role as mother or ancestress to the king of Egypt, who was the living Horus. Hathor was also mother to Ihy, the divine musician known as the "sistrum player" usually depicted as a very young boy still sucking his finger. The sistrum was an important cultic instrument especially, although not exclusively, associated with Hathor's cult. The Eleventh Dynasty king Nebhepetre-Mentuhotep erected a chapel at Dendera in which he is called Beloved of Hathor, Lady of Dendera, and Son of Re. Centuries later the Old Kingdom temple was rebuilt under Thutmose III of the Eighteenth Dynasty and refurbished by his successors in the Nineteenth and Twentieth dynasties. Hathor's cult was still very much alive at the end of Egypt's ancient history, when the immense temple for the Mistress of Dendera, begun by the Ptolemies, was finished by Roman emperors.

The magnificent temple of Hathor at Dendera, much of which is well preserved today because of its remote location, was built on the west bank of the Nile north of the larger modern town of Qena.[34] Today the pylons are missing but the "temple proper," as the roofed building beyond the large court is termed, is intact and contains a huge hypostyle hall of twenty-four soaring columns with a second hall of six columns followed by two smaller halls that lead to the dark central sanctuary of the goddess. All the central rooms beyond the first hypostyle are surrounded by numerous smaller rooms and chapels whose inscriptions suggest they were used for housing the cult statues of other deities resident in the temple as well as for storing the offerings, such as linen and perfumes, and ritual implements and temple furniture. It

Figure 13. Hathor's Temple of Dendera. Photo by L. H. Lesko.

Figure 14. Rear view of Temple of Dendera showing Hathor icon. Photo by B. S. Lesko.

is said that when Napoleon's men first came upon this ancient temple at Dendera on their military excursion into Upper Egypt, they scrambled over the sand dunes engulfing its lower half to rejoice in its enormous roofed halls. Vivant Denon was the first to describe it to the European public: "What uninterrupted power, what wealth, what abundance, what superfluity of resources must have belonged to a government that could raise an edifice like this, and that could find in its nation men capable of conceiving, executing, decorating and enriching it with all that speaks to the eyes and to the mind."[35]

There is no mistaking that this jewel of a shrine belonged to a goddess. The blue-haired female heads with little cow ears form a row on the top of the front colonnade above the stone wall of the facade. The interior walls and ceiling are covered with relief scenes and hieroglyphic texts, mostly intact except for the faces of the deities that have been damaged by squatters. On the ceiling are gigantic images of the goddess Nut swallowing the sun. In the center of the outer rear wall is the huge face of Hathor, which probably was once sheathed in gold (its surface has been destroyed by those trying to retrieve the precious metal). Immediately behind, inside the temple and approachable only by a ladder, is the small cell, or holy of holies, where the sacred image of the Golden One was kept. The temple's roof is accessible by interior stairways, and supported chapels for Hathor and Osiris. Outside, the spacious grounds once contained two Mammisi, or birth houses, for Hathor commemorating the birth of her child Ihy, and to the rear of the great temple was a small temple to Isis built by Augustus Caesar, to the west of which is a sacred lake. Now nearly dry, it looks like a walled garden full of vegetation. Mud brick buildings, now in ruins, immediately to the west of the Hathor temple served as a sanitarium, a feature of these later temples. Here the sick would come to drink the temple's water and spend the night, hoping to receive, in their dreams, divine prescriptions for their recovery.[36]

The great terraced temple built at Thebes by Nebhepetre-Mentuhotep II, who held the longest reign of the Eleventh Dynasty, was closely associated with his tomb and cenotaph, and is thus usually considered a funerary temple. However, Hathor is the most frequently portrayed deity there; the king's wives, who were her priestesses, were buried on the premises. Thus Hathor was honored by the Eleventh Dynasty's royal family as the preeminent goddess. Their temple at Deir el-Bahri can be considered her chief cult place at that time, because we can trace her worship at Karnak across the river only to the reign of Senusert I of the Twelfth Dynasty.

Much farther north in Middle Egypt, and thus closer to the royal capital at Memphis, was the town of Kusae, where Hathor was the chief deity as Lady of Kusae, at least from the early Middle Kingdom. The great tombs belonging to local princes at Meir testify to their devotion to this goddess, who was also referred to there by a priestess's text as The Gold.[37] The governors themselves served in Hathor's cult at Kusae. In the early New Kingdom the female pharaoh Hatshepsut had a rock-hewn shrine in the area, Speos Artemidos, dedicated to the lioness Pakhet who expressed the fearful side of Hathor, who is also evoked in the design of the sistrum columns there.[38] The Greek name refers to the fact that in the last centuries of the last millennium B.C. the goddess Artemis was equated with the ancient Hathor. The Middle Kingdom Coffin Texts contain a reference to the "old women of Kusae who are in the train of Hathor" (Sp. 61), which suggests a myth, or at least a religious tradition, now lost to us.

HATHOR IN ALL HER PLACES

Hathor was so widely loved that she was present everywhere Egyptians were found. The first indication of relations with Egypt exists in a fragment of stone bearing the cartouche of a Second Dynasty king, Khasekhemui, found at Byblos.[39]

The ancient seaport of Byblos worshiped a local goddess, Baalat-Gebal, and it was her temple that was its first large building in 2800 B.C. A few centuries later (corresponding at the latest to the Fifth Dynasty in Egypt but possibly earlier) this goddess appears in the art of Byblos depicted exactly like Hathor, dressed in a slim sheath of a dress and wearing on her head the solar disk and cow's horns. The constant visits by Egyptian officials and seamen and the probable establishment of an Egyptian mercantile and diplomatic community at Byblos would have introduced the Egyptian's most popular goddess to the host community, which itself was ruled by a powerful goddess. Obviously the two communities came to think of their goddesses as one and the same, and the Egyptians referred to theirs as Hathor, Lady of Byblos. This title became well known in Egypt, and there are numerous monuments to Hathor in Egypt which cite her as Lady of Byblos and also Lady of Punt, another exotic trading partner located in Africa on the southernmost Red Sea coast. Locally produced art at Byblos showed its rulers in the same relationship to the great goddess as the Egyptian kings were portrayed: being suckled by the golden cow who wears the solar disk between her horns. Gold cow hoofs were found in the vicinity of the ruins of the great temple, suggesting that a magnificent wooden bovine statue was the focus of the local cult during the middle Bronze Age.[40] The Egyptians came to exert such political influence at Byblos that local rulers began to write their names in hieroglyphs, used Egyptian titles, and allowed the Egyptian government to maintain a vast forest preserve from which any number of trees might be harvested to serve construction needs in Egypt.[41] Some massive wooden beams can still be seen in the wonderfully preserved boat of King Khufu of the Fourth Dynasty, reconstructed near where it was found beside his Great Pyramid at Giza. The close trade and political relationship between the two countries was not limited to the Old Kingdom but continued for the next fifteen hundred years, with only brief breaks. Hathor's epithet Mistress of Both Banks leads one to wonder whether this refers to the Nile or to the two shores on which she was worshiped—Egypt and the Levant. Hathor as Lady of Foreign Lands is also known from the Old Kingdom.[42] Hathor in All Her Places, which is an appellation for the goddess found then as well may correspond to the fourteen Hathors found years later in scenes on the walls of the great hypostyle hall at Karnak and to the multiple depictions on the walls of the still later Ptolemaic temple at Edfu. The state cult of Hathor thus did not long remain exclusively centered on the interests of the royal family.

Perhaps one of the most frequently encountered Hathors is that of Lady of Turquoise, for Hathor's temple at Serabit el-Khadim high in the Sinai has attracted many visitors in recent years. The Egyptians had long exploited the turquoise and copper mines of the region, and because large numbers of workers and administrators were stationed there a cult to a favorite Egyptian deity was established. Of all the possible goddesses it was the very popular Hathor who was selected for honor and worship at Serabit el-Khadim, at least from the Middle Kingdom's Twelfth Dynasty. A temple and many votive stelae from the caves that lined the approach to the temple have been found there. Evidence of animal sacrifices exists as well, and it is thought that a peculiarly Semitic type of worship took place here.[43] One text from the area refers to Hathor as Lady of Heaven as well as by name and credits her with a good yield from a season's work in the turquoise mine.[44] Even the Coffin Texts take note of Hathor's connection with the beautiful turquoise: "The mountain was broken, the stone was split, the caves of Hathor were opened up, the eastern horizon was opened for Hathor, so that she might go forth in turquoise and be clothed in her *Nemes* headdress" (Sp. 486). The shrine was established early in the Middle Kingdom and maintained into the late New Kingdom. Here as elsewhere the chapel for Hathor was cut into the rock, and there were caves in the vicinity in which, it has been suggested, the faithful slept so that their dreams, inspired by the goddess, could tell them where best to search for the precious turquoise.[45]

Hathor also helped her faithful in much more intimate ways. It is obvious, from the votives left by the ordinary men and women who came to the Hathoric shrines in the Sinai and other areas, that Hathor was the divinity who presided over fertility. Wooden phalli, pottery, and metal plaques showing breasts as well as nude female figurines were

Figure 15. Temple of Hathor, Serabit el-Khadim, the Sinai. Photo courtesy of Joseph J. Davis.

among the humble talismans left by those hoping for fertility and future offspring. Of course, in an agrarian country the fertility of flock and field was always of prime concern as well, but the votives found at numerous Hathor shrines and temples do point to Hathor as presiding over human sexuality.[46]

While references were made in votive stelae and graffiti to other deities elsewhere in the Sinai, Hathor had the only temple in the entire Sinai Peninsula, which surely testifies to her importance and popularity. Indeed, when Egyptians traveled abroad and encountered the local population's cult of a goddess, they assumed it was just another manifestation of their beloved and all-powerful Hathor.

MISTRESS OF THE WEST

Much archaeological testimony to the popularity of Hathor of Dendera comes to us from the Theban area, which was the royal capital for the

Eleventh Dynasty and a great religious center for the New Kingdom and later. A Hathoric cult must have existed at Thebes as early as the Sixth Dynasty, as inscriptions in Old Kingdom tombs in the area indicate that the wives of local officials were priestesses of Hathor.[47] An Old Kingdom shrine, now lost, was probably built into the cliffs here. Starting in the Eleventh Dynasty Hathor of Dendera was clearly involved with the necropolis on the west bank at Thebes. One of its kings, Wah'ankh-Inyotef, apparently took the initiative in the local cult of Hathor, for he tells us in a tomb inscription,

> I am indeed the one who causes the morning awakening of the sistrum player of Hathor every day, at whatever hour she wishes. May your heart be content with the sistrum player. May you travel well in peace. May you rejoice in life and in joy with Horus who loves you, who chews on your offerings with you, who eats from your provisions with you. May you allot me to it every day. Horus, Wah'ankh, revered by Osiris, the son of Re Intef, born of Nefru.[48]

The ruler wanted to be sure that Hathor would be his protector in his journey into the Beyond, and he felt he would win her support through the provision of not only offerings at her cult place but also the music she loved. The sistrum (most surviving examples are in bronze, but surely other metals were used as well) was a looped instrument with thin crossbars set loosely to allow a tinkling sound when shaken. The sistrum was more than a musical instrument; it became the symbol of the goddess, and her power was believed to emanate from it. Mirrors were also used in her cult starting in the late Old Kingdom. They caught the sun's light and thus came to be thought of as one of the implements in which the great goddess was manifest. Her priestesses danced with mirrors, and mirrors were portrayed on Middle Kingdom coffins (and sometimes deposited in the coffin) along with Hathor's necklace of many rows of beads, which also would have emitted a rustling sound. Perhaps these implements were thought to leave with the body of the deceased some of Hathor's power that would be needed if the quest for eternal life was to be successful.[49]

Although Hathor is still associated with the sun god Re, it is now in his form as the aged Atum. The inscription from the tomb of Wah'ankh-

Inyotef shares a stela with a hymn to Re at his setting, which is appropriate as the Netherworld was located in the west, and the best hope for the royal dead (and later all worthy Egyptians) was to be in the sun god's entourage in his nocturnal journey. Thus Hathor's epithet Mistress of the West.

The largest monument to survive in Thebes from the Eleventh Dynasty is the temple-tomb complex of King Nebhepetre-Mentuhotep called Akh-isut, located in the great bay of cliffs at Deir el-Bahri. Mentuhotep called himself Son of Hathor, Lady of Dendera, but replaced or incorporated the Hathoric shrine that already existed at Deir el-Bahri with an elaborate funerary complex that included a unique temple, tomb, and cenotaph for himself.[50] An early building of his (which he later expanded) encompassed the tombs of his wives. From wall inscriptions of her funerary chapel, of which only fragments survive, we learn that his Great Royal Wife, Queen Ashyt, was a priestess of Hathor, Mistress of Dendera. The tombs of Mentuhotep's lesser wives on the premises also give their titles as Priestess of Hathor, so it may be assumed that a major cult place existed for the goddess here in western Thebes during this time and that the royal mortuary temple itself was the focus of Hathor's cult.[51] It would remain so for generations.

It has recently been asserted that the entire region of Deir el-Bahri had special mystical significance to the ancients.[52] Archaeologists have discovered evidence that people frequented the high hills above the Theban plain, especially the western mountain known today as the Qurn, since Paleolithic times. The so-called Peak of the West formed a natural pyramid over the plain and foothills where many cemeteries were created during the historic period, and it overlooked the secret desert ravines and valleys in which for centuries royal families laid their dead in deep rock-hewn tombs.

We have seen that the citizens of Western Thebes honored the serpent goddess Meretseger, who they believed inhabited the Peak. Both tomb paintings and drawings on the funerary papyrus's Chapters of Coming Forth by Day show the cow of Hathor emerging from these western cliffs. Chapter 186 in the Papyrus of Ani has the hippo goddess Taweret standing in front of the cow, although she is not identified separately (only Hathor is named in the text) and both may be meant to be taken as varying forms of Hathor. Also, from the cemetery at Saqqara hundreds of miles to the north comes a papyrus scroll fragment with a drawing depicting a man worshiping before two well-known goddess figures who stand on what is surely a mountain. Its publishers at the Royal Museum in Leiden, which owns the document, have identified the terrain as Deir el-Bahri, and the inscription identifies the figure of the cow at the highest elevation as Mehet-Weret and the figure of Taweret, the upright hippo goddess wearing Hathoric horns and sun disk, as Hathor.[53] One of Hathor's many roles was as a motherly being who promoted fertility, which could be manifested through the identity with Taweret, whose chief concern was for pregnant women. Mehet-Weret, although very likely preceding Hathor historically, was now absorbed by her too but could still be understood as the personification of the primeval water—source of all life. The drawing on the papyrus, then, is a simplified rendition of the idea that the western mountain is the abode of the goddess. Indeed, it is very possible that the remarkable natural pyramid, the Qurn, was held to have been imbued with the holy presence of a great goddess from time immemorial. Was this their earth goddess later absorbed by and identified as Hathor?

If the recent reconstruction suggested for the Eleventh Dynasty temple of Mentuhotep by Rainer Stadelmann is correct, the small grove of trees on top of the earth mound at the temple's center and highest point could identify it as a chief cult place of the goddess.[54] Dieter Arnold reports that "the Mentuhotep Temple is one of the few Egyptian sanctuaries whose Temple garden was completely preserved."[55] The remains of trees found by the excavators reveal them to have been the tamarisk and the sycamore fig. This too points to Hathor, Lady of the Sycamore. It should be remembered that Thebes during the Eleventh Dynasty was a provincial town quite possibly in the shadow of Hathor's Dendera and Kusae and that it had yet to become famous as the cult city of Amun-Re, King of the Gods, who was promoted during the Egyptian empire. Hathor and her funerary functions are also documented for the Middle Kingdom period in tombs at other sites, as will be shown shortly, and even at Hathor's temple at Serabit el-Khadim in the Sinai, which was flourishing as a source for turquoise in the Middle Kingdom, one finds royal as well as some private stelae with the typical supplication for food and drink to sustain the deceased. Hathor's role in funeral rites is thus recalled, perhaps on behalf of those who perished on mining expeditions. The same type of offering formulaes are found on stelae dedicated at her temple of the Middle Kingdom at Deir el-Bahri, where Hathor's cult was probably of more importance than is generally credited.

Egyptian religion may have centered on ritual. Although most temples of the Middle Kingdom and early New Kingdom were torn down to make way for the grander edifices of the Empire period, some evidence of celebrations from earlier periods survive from the Memphite area, where Ptah was associated closely with the falcon god of the necropolis region Sokar, who became identified with Osiris. During the Middle Kingdom, a festival of Sokar was enacted in the fourth month of Akhet at both the political capital, Memphis, and the royal residence, Ith-tawi, on the edge of the Fayum near the Royal Pyramid. A "navigation of Hathor" and dancers and singers were part of Sokar's festival, indicating that Hathor played a role at that time in the glorification of Sokar-Osiris and the quest for eternal life.[56]

It is from a private tomb at Thebes dating from the Middle Kingdom that we have better visual images and more information about Hathoric cult celebrations. Wall paintings in the tomb of a Hathor priestess named Senet (the wife of an important Twelfth Dynasty official buried near the pyramid of his king far in the north of the country) show that a ritual involving song and dance was performed as a means of welcoming the funeral cortege as it entered the cemetery of the west bank, the realm of the Mistress of the West.[57] The chorus sang hymns to Hathor:

> Hail to thee, Lady of fragrance,
> Great Sekhmet, Sovercign Lady
> Worshipped one,
> Serpent who is upon her father . . .
> Your rays illumine the Two Lands,
> The two Regions are beneath your sway.

The musical accompaniment was provided by two harpists (a woman and a man), a female flute player, a group of men wearing menats and sounding clappers, and six elder women beating time as they stood in two lines of three each forming an avenue for the exuberant dancing of four younger, lightly clad (loincloths only) women. The rebirth the Egyptians hoped for after earthly death could not logically be disassociated from the sexuality necessary to begin human life. From a governor's tomb at Meir we learn that the necropolis ceremony of Hathor was meant to resurrect the deceased and give to her or him prolonged life in the hereafter. To this end the sacred *snw*-bread of Hathor was offered up, the sistrum rattled, and the menat necklace shaken to ensure the goddess's power would be present for the prolongation of life and the defeat of enemies. Here Hathor is called the Mistress of All, Mistress of the Two Lands. The dancing girls wear her sacred menat necklace and hold it out with one hand while in the other they rattle the naos-type sistrum as they sing:

> The Menat of Hathor, Mistress of Kusae
> that She may show you favor
> that She may prolong your life
> that She may overthrow your enemy.[58]

Hathor was invoked even as the mother of deceased commoners, indicative of the democratization of the hereafter that had taken place by the early Middle Kingdom. The following Twelfth Dynasty rulers saw the advantage of having a capital close to where the Two Lands of Upper and Lower Egypt joined and abandoned Thebes, but not before promoting the cult of a "new" god, Amun, and his consort on the east bank at Karnak. Amunemhet I, founder of this dynasty, did not fail to consecrate a shrine to Hathor at Dendera, however.

Most of the drama of the Middle Kingdom was played out in the north. The next great period in Egyptian history, the New Kingdom, was ushered in by a noble family from the southern Theban area. The women of this family were strong personalities, and the first kings hastened to honor their grandmothers and mothers, whom they credited with playing significant roles in the victory of the south over the north at the end of what historians call the Second Intermediate Period and in founding the new and dynamic royal family line of pharaohs who would conquer much of the known world of their time. Certainly one would expect that this dynasty's royal women would express an affinity for Hathor, and the most illustrious of these women, she who made herself king, Hatshepsut (reigned 1489–69), included a large shrine for Hathor, Chieftainess of Thebes, in her own mortuary temple on the west bank, built immediately north of Mentuhotep's

temple, in the great bay of Deir el-Bahri. Hathor, Chieftainess of
Thebes, had already been worshiped on the east bank in the town of
Waset, later Thebes, since the early Twelfth Dynasty. A later chapel
dedicated to Hathor within the Ptah temple rebuilt by Hatshepsut's
successor, Thutmose III, exists today.[59] Queen Hatshepsut's large, lovely
chapel dedicated to Hathor makes up the southern wing of the terraced temple of Deir el-Bahri, where pillars topped by the goddess's
head (which combines a human face with cow ears) still stand. On
nearby walls is an exquisite rendering, in low relief once painted, of
the sacred cow suckling the female pharaoh as a child and also licking
the hand of the enthroned woman.[60] Here again was a rock-cut chapel
for the cult statue of the goddess in the form of a cow.

The imposing royal temples built in the Eleventh and Eighteenth
dynasties against the cliffs at Deir el-Bahri were not the only testaments
to the holiness of the place. At some time, possibly in the reign of
Hatshepsut, a colossal natural pillar of rock that juts out vertically in
front of the cliff face just above her temple would seem to have been
carved or embellished to appear like a gigantic serpent before which
stands a royal figure.[61] Such a rearing cobra protecting a smaller image
of a king is seen in sculpture at the Cairo Museum.[62] Far to the south in
the Sudan at Napata, the flat-topped mountain Gebel Barkal exhibited
a similar rocky pinnacle that is also believed to have been decorated to
appear as a giant serpent. Here too, at the base of the sacred mountain,
was a rock-hewn sanctuary to Hathor-Mut, the consort of Amun to
whom was dedicated a nearby large temple.[63] Among other known
shrines to Hathor was a rock-hewn sanctuary, suggesting that a grotto,
home to either a snake or a wild cow, was an essential feature of Hathor's
cult.[64]

Clearly, Hathor's most popular cult place at Thebes was on the west
bank at Deir el-Bahri, and archaeologists have found numerous small
monuments left as votives by the common people for many centuries
after Hatshepsut's reign. Statues and stelae, libation basins and offering
tables, were all dedicated by men and women who beseeched the
beloved goddess and deities associated with her for recognition of their
good deeds and for help in their quest for eternal life. Sometimes her
worshipers tried flattery to attract the goddess's support. One royal
artist who served in her priesthood paid homage to the cow of gold,
the beautiful one, with numerous colors, the only one in the sky."[65]

Figure 16. Hatshepsut's Deir el-Bahri Temple and the Peak of the West. Photo by L. H. Lesko.

Hatshepsut's funerary temple was not only a place of homage to the great goddess and the focus of the rites and offerings on the female pharaoh's behalf; it was also a place where Hatshepsut chose to state emphatically in stone that she was divinely sired by Amun-Re, King of the Gods, and nursed by Hathor and thus the most legitimate heir to the throne of her ancestors.[66] Her artists recorded the union of her mother, Queen Ahmose, and Amun-Re in the guise of King Thutmose I. The two sit together on a marriage bed supported by the goddesses of procreation and protection. The god Khnum then created baby Hatshepsut and her identically formed ka on his divine potter's wheel. Goddesses, including Isis and Nephthys, attend Queen Ahmose at her delivery. The Seven Hathors take turns suckling the baby, and then Hathor presents the newborn to Amun, her father. On the walls of the large Hathor chapel, at the southern end of the Middle Terrace of this magnificent temple, are recorded several short speeches of Hathor, addressing Hatshepsut. Hathor is labeled "the divine cow, the divine mother, the lady of the sky, the queen of the gods." She says to Hatshepsut: "I kiss your hand, I lick your flesh. I fill Your Majesty with

Figure 17. Hathor as a cow nursing the pharaoh, north wall, Hathor Chapel, Temple of Deir el-Bahri. Photo by L. H. Lesko.

life and happiness as I have done to my Horus in the nest of Khebt. I have suckled Your Majesty with my breasts."[67]

Hathor's role as mother of the king, first documented in the Fourth Dynasty, is thus recalled in the Eighteenth Dynasty, one thousand years later. Hatshepsut had an intimate relationship with Hathor, and she built other chapels to her, as at Gebel el-Silsileh in Upper Egypt and at Qasr Ibrim far to the south in Nubia. At Speos Artemidos, near Beni Hasan in Middle Egypt, Hatshepsut left a lengthy inscription in which she describes how she found the local temple of the Mistress of Kusae in ruins following years of neglect of the goddess's cult—a neglect she principally blames on the Hyksos (Canaanite) dynasty and its political domination of the northern part of Egypt during the Second Intermediate Period (1785–1544 B.C.): "The temple of the Mistress of Kusae was fallen into ruin, and the earth had swallowed its august sanctuary while children danced on its roof. The serpent-goddess no longer gave terror . . . and its festivals no longer appeared. I sanctified it after it had been built anew. . . . I fashioned *her* image from gold, with a barque for a land procession."[68] The mention of Hathor as a serpent goddess

Figure 18. Hathor in the sun bark with the divine Ennead, Tomb of Seti I. Photo by L. H. Lesko.

underlines the myriad powerful forms that Hathor could assume, including that of the fiery uraeus who protected royalty.[69]

Hatshepsut's successor, Thutmose III, the great warrior king, also hastened to revere Hathor at Deir el-Bahri. He erected a chapel just next door, to the south, where Hathor was depicted in her human and bovine form. Thutmose III's temple included a grottolike shrine with the sacred cow's large sculpted image within, so that the cow goddess appeared to be emerging from a crevice in the stone cliffs, from inside the mountain itself.[70] V. A. Donahue proposes that because the western mountain was the site of unusually intensive occupation during the middle and late stages of the Paleolithic, throughout the Neolithic, and into the historic period, it may have been regarded as "an embodiment of divine fertility which offered hope of rebirth for those who came to rest in its matrix."[71] As the cult statue of Hathor consistently appears as if emerging from a hillside into which her shrines were constructed, Hathor indeed seems to embody the powerful spirit of the mountain.[72] Some Gerzean pots show a religious totem in the shape of hills, so the mystical quality of the western hills (where the sun drops below the horizon into the Beyond) may have been appreciated very early. Perhaps Hathor's epithet Lady of the West was first suggested by her intimate relationship with the western mountain in which so many of Egypt's revered dead were laid. In Thutmose III's grotto a statue of the king stood before a large and remarkably well preserved cow, under her head, emphasizing the king's role as "son" under the protection of his divine "mother." A huge menat necklace, probably of precious metals, surrounded the king's figure.[73] The cow goddess is flanked by tall bunches of marsh plants, which identify her as the divine nurse of Horus, son of Osiris, who was born in the marshes of the delta. The king of Egypt was identified with the god Horus, as texts in Hatshepsut's temple recall when Hathor says,: "I have wandered through the northern marshes, when I stopped at Khebt, protecting my Horus. . . . I am thy mother who formed thy limbs and created thy perfection."[74] The vignette illustrating Spell 186 in the New Kingdom's Book of the Dead also shows the Hathoric cow emerging from a mountainside and parting clumps of papyrus plants.

In a private tomb from the reign of Thutmose III, the owner praises Hathor as the very sun itself: "When you rise you come in peace. One is drunken because of your beautiful face, O Gold, O Hathor!"[75] In another Theban tomb from the next dynasty, a white calf stands beneath a large red sun disk and between two trees receiving the homage of the deceased tomb owners.[76] The equation of Hathor with the sun found in the Coffin Texts was thus still understood by Egyptians of the New Kingdom. Yet in the late Eighteenth Dynasty a religious movement, instigated, it seems, by the reigning king himself, underscored the masculine "father" identity of the disk. This is the Aton cult of Pharaoh Akhenaton about which much has been written. This patriarchal theology follows on the development of the Egyptian armed forces and an imperialistic foreign policy and perhaps was as antithetical to the ascendance of great goddesses like Hathor as it was to the cult of Amun-Re.

Thutmose's temple of the Eighteenth Dynasty was destroyed by rock slides, but Hathor eventually received a newer shrine built by Pharaoh Seti I of the Nineteenth Dynasty adjacent to the community of artisans who hewed and decorated the royal tombs in the desert valleys to the west of Deir el-Bahri. This artisan colony flourished for almost five hundred years. Many were the holidays and copious was

Figure 19. Hathor worshiped as the sun, Tomb of Iry-nefer, Thebes. Photo by L. H. Lesko.

the beer that helped its inhabitants commune with the greatest of their goddesses.

The walls of the royal tombs of the Eighteenth and Nineteenth dynasties show that a great trinity of gods with mortuary concerns existed: Hathor, Anubis, the jackal-headed guardian of the cemetery and patron of embalming, and Osiris, King of the Dead. Hathor is sometimes distinguished from other goddesses by a red ribbon around her hair and a large menat necklace. She is also seen wearing the hieroglyphic symbol for "West" on her head.[77] As she was a guarantor of continued life in the Beyond, Hathor is often depicted on private tomb walls and, as mentioned in the Book of the Dead vignettes, emerging from the Theban mountain or a papyrus thicket on the west bank of the river to take the dead under her motherly protection.

The Coffin Texts had called Hathor Mistress of the Northern Sky, as she shared Nut's role in receiving the dead into her entourage. By the Twenty-first Dynasty, Hathor has moved into the coffin iconography, and may be found on the floor of the coffin; appropriately, Nut is over the deceased on the inside of the lid.[78] In the New Kingdom Hathor more commonly bears the title Mistress of the West, which refers to the domain of the setting sun, the Beyond in the sky where all the blessed dead are destined to go. Sometimes her title is "the one who is over the western desert," which generally marked the cemetery area traditionally on the western side of the Nile as seen in the case of the extensive necropolis for Memphis and Thebes.

We have more information on funerals and special memorial days at Thebes. Most important was the annual Festival of the Valley, celebrated in the second month of summer when Amun of Karnak (King of the Gods in the Egyptian Empire period) sailed across the Nile to visit western Thebes and stopped at most of the royal mortuary temples, including those at Deir el-Bahri, where he spent the night with the delightful goddess. The crowds who came out to hail the god and his brilliant entourage left offerings and picnicked at their family tombs, during which time female musicians of Hathor's cult visited each group to extend to them the holy cult implements that some scholars believe evoked Hathor's power to revive the dead. The women who served in Hathor's cult are often described as musicians or chantresses, but this may not adequately convey their importance. Music and dance were necessary features of Hathor's cult, and the women who held the sacred cult implements were to be understood as impersonators of the goddess. That a very highly placed woman in the cult of Amun-Re, a chief of the concubines of Amun in the mortuary temple of Ramses II, and wife of the presiding *sem*-priest there was also a chantress of Hathor illustrates this.[79]

The goddess Nut, the original welcomer of the dead, was not forgotten in the New Kingdom cither. She and Hathor can be seen together, for example, in the tomb of Amunhotep III. Hathor is depicted on the left leading the divinities that greet the dead king, and Nut is on the right leading other gods. The goddesses embrace the dead king like mothers. The presence of both Hathor and Nut in one tomb testifies to the king's acceptance in both spheres of the Beyond: the heavens and the West.[80]

HATHOR, GODDESS OF LOVE

Because she was a goddess of love, sexuality, and happy family life, Hathor's festivals were certainly not limited to the necropolis. For instance, the first day of the fourth month of Inundation Season celebrated Hathor with drunken revelry (Hathor was also known as Mistress of Drunkenness, and vessels containing wine and beer were often decorated with her image). The ruins of the rambling palaces built by the pharaohs of the late Eighteenth Dynasty have yielded many broken beer jars decorated with three-dimensional blue-haired heads of Hathor (perhaps a reference to turquoise).

At Hathoric festivals sexual dalliance was probably the order of the day. New Kingdom Egypt was a permissive society, and the immensely popular Hathor was looked to for help in sexual relationships and the conceiving of offspring. As children were highly desired, it followed that heterosexuality was healthy and good, not something to be ashamed of or deemed a highly private activity. In her fertility aspect Hathor was extremely important to the populace, and this is why we find more votive offerings to her than to any other deity in the New Kingdom. But even beyond helping with fertility, she heard prayers and thus was a focus for personal piety.[81] The inscriptions found as late as the Twentieth Dynasty at her temple in the Sinai now use the old formula to introduce requests for life, prosperity, health, skill, favor, and love in the presence of the sovereign. Thus their priorities are different from those revealed on the stelae found at Hathor's shrine of the Middle Kingdom and are more related to the donors' earthly lives.[82]

Hathor's relationship to the sycamore tree is recalled in the following observation by an important member of the Napoleonic expedition, Vivant Denon:

> In the east, where indolent repose forms one of the chief luxuries, the tents or kiosks are pitched under the thick branches of a cluster of sycamores, and open at pleasure upon a fragrant underwood of orange and jessamine. To this is added the voluptuous pleasure of enjoyments still but imperfectly known to us, but which we may easily conceive; such, for instance, as to be attended by young slaves, who unite to elegance of form gentle and caressing manners; to be indolently stretched on vast and downy carpets, strewed with cushions, in company with some favourite beauty, breathing perfumes, and intoxicated with desires.[83]

Under the sycamores Vivant Denon and Napoleon Bonaparte lost their hearts to Egypt and the "voluptuous pleasure" of the East. Perhaps it was always thus, for the tree in the pleasure garden is invoked in the love poetry of the second millennium B.C., as a friend to lovers:

> The little sycamore . . . opens her [mouth] to speak . . .
> Come, spend time where the young people are:
> the meadow celebrates its day.
> Under me are a festival booth and a hut . . .
> Come spend the day in pleasure,
> [one] morning, then another—two days,
> sitting in [my] shade. (Turin Love Song, 28–30)[84]

The spreading branches of the sycamore and its dense shade provide a perfect trysting spot for young lovers. Is this why Hathor, promoter of love, was associated with the sycamore tree?

It trivializes Hathor to describe her, as so many have, as a joyful goddess of music and dance. Music and dance were an important part of Hathor's cult but mainly because dance is a sexual activity, whose power was manifest in her. Because Hathor's cult had many female clergy and many adherents among the common born, she must have been accepted as the supreme female goddess. She responded to women's needs for support in the different stages of life. She certainly was the most popular major divinity at the civil service community unearthed by archaeologists at Deir el-Medina which was inhabited primarily by women during the workweek when the artisans who produced the spectacularly decorated royal tombs were encamped at their worksites in the Valley of the Queens and the Valley of the Kings.

Through Hathor's support girls became women, found mates, and were fertile. Hathor was present at the birth of their children and protected family life. She was not primarily a mother goddess, however, a role that more clearly belonged to other goddesses, such as Mut and Isis. Through the dance and songs of the joyous Hathor cult, women celebrated their feminine mystique and thanked Hathor. The strong images of women in Egyptian art project this self-satisfaction and positive feeling.

While they embodied Hathor's magical powers, the sistra and menats were also musical instruments, and many women throughout the land served as musicians in her popular cult. They thus represented the goddess, holding out her sacred instruments to the crowds of faithful and conferring on all the goddess's favors. Some scholars feel that the sistrum and menat necklace were life-bestowing instruments; others see them as objects that appeased angry deities or conferred on the king powers of attraction. The Egyptians left us no dictionaries to explain such phenomena, but it is obvious from their use by both priestesses and goddesses that these instruments were not merely musical but endowed with magical powers. The people at such festivals responded by clapping their hands, snapping their fingers, and leaping for joy, judging from the scenes in the Eighteenth Dynasty tomb of Amunemhet at Thebes. The Egyptologist who edited the publication of this tomb wrote, "On this public holiday there may have been a temple celebration and a procession; and after these things the priestesses of Karnak doubtless paraded the town, stopping at one house after another in order to bestow upon their owners the blessings of Hathor, as symbolized in song and dance. From the eastern bank of the Nile they may have passed over to the Necropolis in the western hills, there to accomplish for the dead that which had been accomplished already on behalf of the living."[85] An artist-priest explained in his votive inscription, "I am the priest of Hathor, who hears the requests of all maidens who weep,"[86] and tells us that Hathor listens to the miserable. Another statue addresses the inhabitants of Thebes: "Go! . . . tell your requests to the Cow of Gold, to the Lady of Happiness, to the Mistress of [all the gods], . . . may she give us excellent children, happiness, and a good husband. . . . If cakes are placed before her, she will not be angry."[87]

Thus the lovely cow goddess was viewed as sympathetic to single women, particularly those who were unhappy, and she would help those seeking the universal goals of a happy marriage and healthy children. Her cult had become enormously popular by the late Old Kingdom. She was adored for herself and the power she held over human sexual life. For this reason I disagree with Bleeker, who regards Hathor as a virgin mother on the same plane as Neith.[88] Above all, Hathor was viewed as the mother of the king, and every Egyptian knew the king was the son of the supreme god, whether it was Re in the Old Kingdom, Amun-Re in the Eighteenth Dynasty, or Pre-Harakhty in the Nineteenth Dynasty. Moreover, Hathor was too involved in sexual allure, erotic dance, romance, and human fertility to be either androgynous or virginal by nature.

When Hathor came to be known as the patroness of love and bestower of fertility is not known, but I believe these important attributes went along with her increasing popularity. While later love poems credit Hathor with bringing couples together romantically, she also was known as Mistress of the Vulva, and wooden phalluses were left as votive offerings at her sanctuary at Deir el-Bahri by men who hoped to avoid impotence or to sire children.[89] The following text is written on a votive cloth left at the major shrine of the goddess at Deir el-Bahri during the New Kingdom: "Hail to you, who shines as Gold, the Horus Eye upon the head of Re, may you give life, prosperity, health, skill, favor and love for the ka of the Mistress of the Household, Mutemwia."[90]

A number of informal drawings, on leather, ostraca, and papyrus, from the New Kingdom settlement of the tomb artisans near the Valley of the Kings portray erotic situations. In one a woman plays a harp while a naked man dances.[91] The erotic papyrus from here seems to depict a brothel, but some of the women hold cultic sistra in their hands.[92] Whether the illustrations are meant to be accurate or sardonic (as some other drawings from this artist's colony clearly are) we cannot be sure. From temple texts of much later times we learn that at one of Hathor's feasts a phallus was carried in a procession and another feast was called "the opening of the bosoms of the women."[93] We can well imagine that the feast days of the goddess who was the promoter of human sexuality were noisy, exuberant celebrations awash in beer and wine and often resulted in orgies.

The cults of dead pharaohs might fall into neglect but not the cults of favorite goddesses. Hathor received the prayers and votive offerings of men and women seeking attractive spouses as well as sexual potency and pregnancies. A childless man might dedicate a votive with a prayer written on it beseeching Hathor for an heir. One text on a stone phallic votive offered by a childless male scribe appealed to Hathor as "thou desired one, cause me to receive a compensation of thy house as a rewarded one."[94]

Hathor was said to have seven kas (Re had fourteen and sometimes Hathor did too), while the king had two and ordinary folk had one. Hathor was credited by her faithful with their long lives, and the Seven Hathors attended the birth of babies and determined their fate.[95]

The love poetry of the Egyptian Empire (ca. 1300–1100 B.C.) reminds us that the goddess of love was credited with bringing lovers together, finding people their future mates, and thus giving them the possibility of lifelong happiness. One ardent woman's song laments:

> He does not know my desire to embrace him
> [or] he could write to my mother,
> Lover, I am destined for you
> by the Golden One of women,
> Come to me that I may see your perfection!
> (Chester Beatty I, Group A, No. 32)[96]

A man sings of his hope for a reunion with his mistress, telling us:

> I praise the Golden Goddess
> I exalt Her Majesty
> I raise high the Lady of Heaven
> I make praise for Hathor
> and chants for my Mistress. . . .
> I'll make a vow to my Goddess,
> so she'll give me my lady love as a gift in return! (Chester
> Beatty I, Group A, No. 35)[97]

HATHOR AND THE PHARAOH

Hathor led the deceased king into her realm in the West where eternal life beckoned, but she was also important to the king at his birth. Hathor's connection with the divine kingship is prominent in art and literature, and it has dominated most scholarship on her.

It has been argued that Hathor's embodiment of sexual attraction was put to a respectable use: she imbued the king, her son, with the "power of attraction," the power he needed to rule a large country with a dispersed population.[98] The power of Hathor, which evoked a joyful response among her followers, when extended to the king would give him the ability to win the hearts and loyalty of his people. The king was to be regarded as a god on earth and thus was meant to be adored.

The "attractive aspect" of the ruler, Alison Roberts has argued, was what was symbolized by the cultic necklace, or menat, of the goddess. The frequent image of Hathor holding out her menat to the ruler has been understood as "symbolic of the ability of the king to compel all lands to serve him through either the emanation of his attraction or his terrorizing qualities."[99] For Hathor, like Bat long before her, had two faces, or two sides to her disposition—positive and negative. She could attract with her brilliant warmth and sexual allure, but she could turn on her transgressors with the full ferocity of a lioness (even a cow can be belligerent). A story from the Middle Kingdom tells of a herdsman who encounters a terrifying half-female, half-animal goddess and then later encounters her as an alluring all-human woman.[100] Possibly the dual nature of Hathor—dangerous and seductive—was the inspiration for this tale. In the later New Kingdom Hathor is sometimes paired with Sekhmet, the lioness goddess who personified brute power. The power of Hathor to exhibit both attractive and offensive qualities is believed to have been encompassed by her cult implements. Priestesses and royal family members who used these sacred implements could work the power of Hathor through them. Perhaps we should think of the sistrum and menat as magic wands, even though other curved ivory implements associated with Hathoric religion and magic have already received this label from scholars. The sistra and menats were musical instruments, but their power clearly went beyond sound. In the Middle Kingdom tale of Sinuhe, the contrite courtier returned to Egypt after years in exile to face his king at the palace. The king, Senusert I, was already well disposed toward him, but, just to make sure, the royal children extended their menats and sistra to their father beseeching him to forgive and forget. The beneficent power of Hathor's magic, which flowed from her sacred cultic instruments, was expected to work in Sinuhe's favor: "May the Golden One give life to your nostrils / and may the Lady of Stars be joined to you."[101]

When the royal burial place became reestablished in Upper Egypt, Amun was joined with the greater god Re in a new syncretistic deity Amun-Re, and Hathor became the daughter/wife of Amun-Re, as she had been the consort and wife of Re previously. At least this was the case in the early Eighteenth Dynasty, when we find Hathor prominently worshiped at the temple Hatshepsut erected for the funerary cults of herself and her father, Thutmose I.

Several depictions of the ruler with Hathor also show him encircled by her sacred menat necklace. The necklace has been interpreted by scholars as the means used by Hathor to ensure the ruler's rebirth after death. Thus the composite drawing of the sacred cow both suckling and surrounding the ruler with her menat was meant to indicate that the great goddess assured life both on earth and in the Hereafter.

Without the support of the gods and goddesses, the ruler would fail and his realm would sink into chaos. To avoid the chance that their claim to the throne would be deemed weak or inappropriate, the kings of Egypt emphasized their divinity from the moment of their conception. Toward the back of the Temple of Luxor is a suite of rooms devoted to the divine birth of Amunhotep III of the later Eighteenth Dynasty, and here the complementarity of his earthly mother Queen Mutemwia, and the great goddesses is stressed.[102] Neith and Selket are present at the marriage bed, and Hathor and Mut attend the future king's birth and join to present the newborn to his divine father, Amun-Re. Much later in his life Amunhotep celebrated a jubilee marking the thirtieth year of his reign. It also seems to have been the occasion for his official, public declaration of his transformation into a deity, the sun disk itself.[103] He is shown in the sun bark with Hathor, and his artists rendered him far more youthfully during his last eight years, as if to stress that the king had been reborn.

This event had its origins in prehistory, and originally marked the ritualistic or symbolic death and resurrection of the ruler. There are only fragments of inscriptional material that illustrate this event before Amunhotep's reign, but even those from the Old Kingdom share significant features of Hathoric ceremonies. After the fall of the Old Kingdom these were taken over and imitated in the tomb scenes of private persons, who hoped thereby to be reborn after death, just like the kings. Apparently Hathor's presence and her magical power were necessary to ensure this rejuvenation. Lioness-masked priestesses using the curved ivory wands that were ritual objects of Hathor are depicted in Middle Kingdom private tombs and in the representations of this significant and memorable royal event in the tomb of Kheruef, a courtier of Amunhotep's queen, Tiy. He had been present at the royal jubilee and recorded in his tomb the presence of the goddess Hathor, about whom it was sung: "Make jubilation for The Gold and good pleasure for the Lady of the Two Lands that she may cause Nebmaare

(Amunhotep), who is given life, to be enduring. . . . Adoration of The Gold when she shines forth in the sky. . . . [T]here is no god who does what you dislike when you appear in glory. . . . [I]f [you] desire that he (Amunhotep) live, cause him to live during millions of years unceasingly."[104]

Amunhotep III also seems to have claimed divinity for his wife, Queen Tiy. Artists altered existing statues of the queen to give her the blue hair and diadem of Hathor; others portrayed her from the start as this goddess, suggesting she was the earthly manifestation of Hathor. The king was worshiped at several temples in Egypt and Nubia, and we know the queen had a cult at least in Nubia and at Serabit el-Khadim. Both the king and the queen were identified with other major deities as well. Amunhotep was worshiped as Thoth at his cult city of Hermopolis, as Osiris at Abydos, as Amun-Re at Karnak, and as Sobek Re at Armant. Besides Hathor, Queen Tiy was identified with Isis, Mut, Ma'at, and Sekhmet, among other goddesses.[105]

Soon after his royal jubilee, Amunhotep passed on permanently into the realm of the sun, and Egypt convulsed. His son and successor, Amunhotep IV, would change his name to show reverence to a rather obscure deity, Aton. This was the sun disk, but it had no relation to Hathor, and, indeed, the old pantheon seems to have been banished by the new religion. Aton was actually androgynous and was not given human form. Only the sun disk with rays terminating in hands extending the *ankh* sign of life to the royal family was portrayed during the new king's reign. Other gods were ignored and their temples closed. The sudden religious revolution orchestrated by the palace did not find ready reception in the larger community of pious and traditional people and did not long outlast its chief prophets. However, the Amarna interlude (as the period from 1366 to 1348 is called, after the site of the new capital and Aton's chief cult city in Middle Egypt) does seem to have occasioned some lasting theological changes. At least there are differences in the iconography in the royal tombs at Thebes, after the Valley of the Kings again received the burials of New Kingdom pharaohs.

There seems to be more emphasis now on Hathor as merely a daughter goddess. In the royal tombs she is seen leading the king into the presence of her father, Amun-Re, although she does hold out her sacred menat necklace to Seti I in the gesture assuring him of her power to cause his rejuvenation in the Beyond.[106] Also now, in the great state cult temple at Karnak across the river, the goddess Mut is more prominent as Amun-Re's wife (her name means "mother"), and here too Hathor is the daughter of Re, emanating from his brow just as the Greek Goddess Athena would later emerge from the brow of Zeus. However, Hathor, like Mut and unlike Athena, was unmistakably feminine, and both goddesses were credited with the ability to take on all the female roles: mother, wife, and daughter.[107] Hathor's role as a daughter goddess may be a Theban phenomenon, as we have only scant ruins of temples in the northern capital of Memphis and thus no comparable material to judge by. The Hathoric columns of what must be a temple to that goddess still protrude from the earth, awaiting excavation, at the site of Memphis.

By the Nineteenth Dynasty Hathor was described more frequently as the Eye of Re or his fiery uraeus. The flying sun disks above each temple doorway, to give one example, are accompanied by raised cobra heads. This uraeus is then the god's protection and is equated, not only with the Two Ladies but also with Hathor.[108] Some scholars have suggested that this demonstrates the aggressive aspect of the female and is the power that protected the great god Re, her father, Amun-Re, and the king of Egypt as well. As a daughter, Hathor propitiates her father for the benefit of mankind. In one earthy tale, probably written to scorn the gods and not to be taken seriously, the sun god falls into a sulky mood and retires to his pavilion. None of the deities know what to do. His saucy daughter Hathor, lifts her skirt in front of him, which restores the god to good humor, and all is well with the world once more.[109]

Hathor does not have a shrine in the great temple built by Seti I at Abydos; Mut and Isis are the only goddesses represented among the state gods. Hathor had started her career as wife of the sun god Re, but when Re was linked with Amun in the Eighteenth Dynasty and that "new god" acquired a wife, the goddess Mut, Hathor was left more on her own. Osiris's wife, Isis, also moved into increased prominence in the funerary context by the Nineteenth Dynasty, so Hathor may have become much more often associated with sexuality and fertility and the concerns of the people, as the records of the common folk from this time indicate. However, she still was identified with Egypt's queens.

HATHOR AND THE QUEEN OF EGYPT

In the reign of Ramses II, often referred to by historians as Ramses the Great, the claim of royal divinity, which probably was never dropped completely, was again entertained seriously. With it is evidenced more reverence of the goddess Hathor, whose power seems to have been necessary to work this wonder.

The most frequently visited Hathoric temple today is Abu Simbel, at Egypt's southern boundary. It was Ramses II who caused to be hewn from the living rock of the western cliffs above the Nile two magnificent temples, one celebrating Ramses the Great and the other his queen, Nefertari. There is no doubt that the royal couple are represented as deities at Abu Simbel, as they are of equal size and on an equal plane with other major deities. In the inner sanctum of Ramses' temple, he is sculpted sitting with the great gods of his empire: Ptah, Re-Harakhty, and Amun-Re. In her temple, Nefertari is crowned by two goddesses, Isis and Hathor, with the same solar crowns (with lofty double plumes and sun disk) as theirs.[110] This is in the vestibule preceding the holy of holies, or inner sanctum, in which a relief scene shows the enthroned divine king and queen receiving offerings from Ramses himself.

Hathor appears most frequently in the iconography of the queen's temple, whose facade is carved with gigantic figures of the queen or goddess alternating with those of Ramses. Queens of Egypt, from the Fourth Dynasty on, were often portrayed in sculpture wearing the archaic, tripartite wig of Hathor to express the idea that they were the earthly manifestation of this great goddess.[111] This idea is surely carried out here at Abu Simbel, where the goddesses received Queen Nefertari as one of their own. This is both Hathor's temple and Nefertari's memorial. Each of the pillars of the hypostyle hall within is topped with Hathor's head. There are numerous offering scenes of the king and queen before this goddess, who is identified either as the local goddess Hathor, Lady of Ibshek, or as the goddess of Heliopolis, the chief cult city of the sun, and Lady of Heaven and Mistress of All the Gods. Sometimes the goddess is offered flowers by the royal couple; at other times, a libation. Hathor promises continued life and dominion to both the king and the queen. Carved from the rear wall of the inner sanctum of the temple was a large statue of the cow goddess, emerging from

Figure 20. Abu Simbel, the queen's Hathoric temple. Photo courtesy of David Larkin.

the western mountain, as she was shown at Deir el-Bahri centuries before, with the image of the standing kind under her head.[112] Hathor was here acknowledged and worshiped as mother of the divine king and mistress of all the gods, and it was by his close association with her that the king truly became divine.

HATHOR'S ROLE IN LATER PERIODS

Their fondness for Hathor can be seen repeatedly in the monuments of private people of the Ramesside age and subsequent Third Intermediate Period. A large cow hovers over the small images of a husband and wife in a rather humble statue group from the Nineteenth Dynasty, now in Leiden, showing that ordinary people believed in the power of the goddess to protect them in their daily lives and, no doubt, hoped she would aid them in the transition from life to death to eternal life. Throughout the New Kingdom and later, high officials commonly were portrayed kneeling, holding a large Hathoric idol in front of them, and

Figure 21. Woman chantress holding sacred menat necklace and sistrum, Theban Tomb of Sennefer. Photo by L. H. Lesko.

their wives had themselves portrayed in statuary and tomb paintings holding the menat instrument of devotees of Hathor's cult. The involvement of women of all ranks with the cult of the popular goddess Hathor continued.

The popularity of the goddess persisted among the leadership class for centuries and caused many male officials of the Late Period to have themselves portrayed with obvious attributes of Hathor's cult, demonstrating their faith in her. A block statue of a Twenty-second Dynasty priest wears a large amulet of a Hathor head, as if it dangles from a cord which crosses his drawn-up knees. In the Twenty-fifth Dynasty, a royal princess was a priestess in her cult. We learn this from a poem dedicated to one Mutirdis.

> Sweet, sweet of love,
> the priestess of Hathor, Mutirdis.
> Sweet, sweet of love,
> says King Menkheperre,
> Sweet, say men,
> Mistress of love, say women.
> A princess is she, sweet of love
> Most beautiful of women:
> a lass whose like has never been seen.[113]

From the tomb of Psamtik at Saqqara, late Twenty-sixth Dynasty, comes a magnificent three-dimensional rendition on the theme encountered at Deir el-Bahri and Abu Simbel many centuries earlier—the sacred cow looming behind the standing king. Elegantly modeled, an idealized cow, sensually smooth of body, yet with a serious, thoughtful face, it is probably the loveliest cow ever created and authentically presents the divine in animal form. E. R. Russman calls the eyes "humanized," and perhaps this is what allows us today to accept the spirituality of this animal rendition of the great goddess.[114]

Animal worship seems to have increased during the Late Period, when Egypt was almost always under the political control of a foreign power (Assyrian or Persia) or its native quislings. It was now that Herodotus of Halicarnassus, on the west coast of Turkey, visited Egypt. His "eyewitness" accounts of Egyptian religious festivals tell of the playful violence between rival towns when a sacred cat or other animal of one town was harmed by the neighboring settlement.

A steatite bowl in the British Museum, dating to around 525 B.C., provides a visual record of a Hathoric feast. Oryx and bull seem ready to be sacrificed; a line of male and female musicians, wearing lotus flowers on their brows, form a procession to the temple. Tambourine, lyre, and double pipes are played by the men. One woman wields a pair of clappers, long associated with Hathor's cult, and another woman hitches up her skirt to bare her bottom, which she seems to be slapping rhythmically. This last lends the scene a bacchanalian theme in keeping with what other earlier documentation has led us to expect.[115] From the Late Period comes this song of praise for the popular goddess:

> We laud you with delightful songs
> for you are the Mistress of joy,
> the Mistress of music,
> the Queen of harp-playing,
> the Lady of the Dance.[116]

By that later time, the Hathor of the temple erected by the Ptolemies and completed by the Roman emperors at Dendera seems to have been a composite goddess, embodying the eminence of another greatly beloved female deity, the sky goddess Nut. Nut is portrayed on its ceiling bearing the sun. Dendera had long been Hathor's home, but her cult seems to have dominated Middle Egypt for millennia as it was found at several locations during the Middle Kingdom. While Hathor was known as Lady of the Sycamore at her cult place south of Memphis, in the region of Dendera she was known as Lady of the Acacia. She had a documented cult place at Ballas, south of Dendera, during the last centuries before Christ.[117] The chief repository for knowledge of the rituals and festivals of Hathor in the Late period is, however, her huge and well-preserved temple at Dendera, completely published by the French scholar Émile Chassinat. Its extensive wall surfaces are engraved with scenes and texts, as are the columns, stairwells and crypts.[118] The depictions of lines of priests with elaborate ritual objects and the pervasive darkness lend a somber air to the temple today, but the texts reveal that song and dance still celebrated the goddess of sexuality and fertility.

> Oh beautiful one, Oh glorious cow, Oh great one,
> Great of Magic, Oh glorious lady, Oh mistress of the gods!
> May the King respect you! As for Pharaoh, may you cause
> that he live!
> O Lady of the gods, may he respect you, may you cause
> that he live!
> Look upon him, Hathor, his mistress, from the cool
> region,
> See him, Hathor, his mistress, from the horizon,
> Hear him, flaming serpent, from the primeval waters!
> Look upon him, Lady of the gods, from the sky, from the
> earth,
> from Asia, from Libya, from the Western Mountain, from
> the Eastern Region,
> from every land, from every place, where your majesty
> shines![119]

From the gateway of the temple of Medamud comes a hymn that was sung at the celebration of the return of Hathor, Eye of the Sun, to Egypt from the far-off southeast where the winter sun rose:

> Come, oh Golden One, who feeds on praise,
> because the food of her desire is dancing,
> who shines on the festival at the time of lighting [the
> lamps],
> who is content with the dancing at night.
> Come! The procession is in the place of inebriation,
> that hall of traveling through the marshes.
> Its performance is set,
> its order is in effect,
> without anything lacking therein.[120]

From this it is clear that religious festivals usually took place at night when lights could direct the goddess to the place where she would be honored. The "hall of traveling through the marshes" seems to be a reference to the hypostyle hall of the temple, where the great columns resembled water plants. Hathor, the solar goddess, was present on the roof of the Temple of Dendera at the festival of the New Year when a

Uniting with the Disk ceremony would take place. There too she was regarded as the sun's eye returning to her father, the sun, an identity assumed by Horus, the old sky god of Edfu, who was now known as Re-Horus, assimilated with the sun. It was the sun god's great love for his daughter that was said to inspire him to cross the sky each day. Without her there would have been no sunrise. Inscribed in the propylons of the Hathor temple on the sacred island of Philae, where Hathor was worshiped in the late Ptolemaic Period, there is a hymn that expresses this relationship between Hathor and Re:

> Re exalts without ceasing,
> His heart rejoices when he joins his daughter,
> He swims in his firmament, in peace.
> He turns and takes his course.[121]

Two weeks before the new moon appeared in the third month of the summer season, Hathor of Dendera began her journey south by a dazzling river procession to Horus of Edfu, stopping and visiting the deities of temples along the way. On arriving at Edfu, on the day of the New Moon, her entourage was met by Horus and his following. The couple removed to an adjacent temple where they were presented with Ma'at, the sacred image of universal perfection, and offered the first fruits of the field. The gods then reboarded their boats and, accompanied by officials and townsfolk, sailed on to the temple of Horus at Edfu, where a sacred marriage took place between Hathor and Horus. Great crowds met the brilliant entourage of the goddess and conducted her to the temple. The "wedding" was celebrated with two weeks of drinking and feasting.[122] There was a serious side to the festivity, as H. W. Fairman determined in his study of the Edfu records. The rites bore so many similarities to a harvest festival that, even though not performed at the proper time, they could be considered as such. However, harvest festivals had for centuries been Osirianized and had taken on the semblance of funerary festivals. Hathor and Horus visited a nearby necropolis and the Divine Souls of Edfu, ancestral gods, on their annual journey. Fairman concluded that "Horus and Hathor brought these dead gods life and light." [123] Thus throughout her history Hathor was called on to ensure eternal life to the deserving dead.

As was often the case with major Egyptian temples, the vast temple of Horus at Edfu housed the cults of other deities as well, as shown in a document that records that the statue of Ptah from Edfu sailed north to visit Hathor at Dendera. This would have been occasioned by the Memphite cult of Ptah, which revered Hathor as Ptah's daughter. In the north, Ptah of Memphis journeyed by water to visit his daughter, Hathor, Mistress of the Sycamore, at her cult center south of Memphis as well.[124] Hathor also went by flotilla north to present-day Beni Hasan, where the Seven Hathors, the fairy godmothers who decided every newborn's future, were celebrated.

Through much of Egypt's history, Thebes had been the principal city of Upper Egypt and the realm of Amun-Re, King of the Gods. Since the Saite period, which had seen the resurgence of Neith, Mistress of Sais, his supremacy was a thing of the past. And although the later Ptolemaic dynasty did not ignore his cult city of Thebes entirely, they honored other divinities and on the west bank they built an attractive temple to Hathor on the ruins of a temple that dated to the Nineteenth and Twentieth dynasties. Hathor's old role as guardian of the dead was probably still being acknowledged in this temple in the midst of the cemetery region.

All the Ptolemaic Hathor temples share a feature indicative of union with the sun's disk. At certain designated times of the year, such as New Year's or the change of seasons, the sacred statue of Hathor of Dendera was carried to the roof, away from the mysterious darkness of the sanctuary. There her divine image was exposed to the rays of the sun so as to receive its cosmic energy.[125] This in turn allowed the divine image, once returned to the darkened holy of holies, to spread her powerful magic for the betterment of the world. When this cosmic union occurred at the beginning of the inundation season, in late summer, it restored life to the parched land. It is significant that Hathor, known for her benevolence and promotion of fertility, would play a significant role in the drama of renewal of the land of Egypt. The other cosmic union also took place on the holy day that fell on the twentieth of the month of Thoth, the moon god and patron of wisdom and letters. At Hathor's Dendera, at least, this feast was called the Festival of Drunkenness. We can imagine that ecstatic and erotic dances took place at this festival.

It is likely that the Festival of Drunkenness commemorated the following mythical episode. Long ago Re sent his daughter to chastise mankind and then repented. To distract the goddess from her attack, which had already cost many lives, huge quantities of beer dyed red were poured out on the ground before her. Thinking it was blood, Hathor began to lap it up, only to become drunk and sleepy. Thus she was pacified. And thus her followers drank red beer on her festival of inebriety. Perhaps the plagues that devastated ancient populations and mysteriously ended as suddenly as they had begun were explained by the sudden wrath of divinities like Hathor. It was the quelling of this wrath, the propitiation of the immensely powerful deities, that was the work of the clergy and their cult objects. Rattling the sistrum and dancing before the goddess, Hathor's priests propitiated her, dispelled her temper, and won her love and support for the king.

There was also a myth about Tefnut, a savage goddess from the south who was invited north by the Egyptian pantheon. On the island of Philae, where Egypt ends and Nubia begins, a small Hathor temple was built to commemorate the spot where the savage southern goddess was transformed by the wise and gentle scholar Thoth into a benevolent sister deity of Hathor. The southern goddess has been equated by some scholars with the scorching eye of the sun that can cause drought, famine, and death. She is a powerful agent of Re, for she can destroy his enemies, but she might also be vulnerable, as at the time of the rare solar eclipse. How did the ancients explain these? The goddess-eye quarreled with her father, the sun god Re, and left for another land, her homeland in the south, far away. Thoth, the moon god, was the persuasive agent who "brought back" the sun's eye and restored the world to normalcy.[126] Thus great, terrifying, and mysterious events—plagues and eclipses—were explained, rationalized, and accepted by the people of the ancient world.

It was here at the Temple of Philae, which we shall study more closely in chapter 7, that Hathor's history comes to an end. Although the Ptolemies had erected the great temple for Hathor at Dendera, the goddesses of that period were merging into one preeminent deity, Isis. Thus at Philae Hathor and Sekhmet along with Mut, Nekhbet, and Neith are assimilated with Isis to bestow on her all their power and historical stature.

CHAPTER 6

ℳUT AND THE SACRED CATS

Although most Egyptian goddesses can be traced to at least the beginning of history, Mut seems to have been "born" well into the historic period. Along with Amun and Khonsu, she formed the great Theban triad that is depicted so prominently on the major temples that survive today in the Luxor area.

Mut was the Egyptian word for "mother," written with the hieroglyphic sign of the vulture. For the goddess Mut, this vulture often holds a royal scepter. Unlike Nekhbet, Mut is never portrayed as a vulture goddess, and she does not appear in religious iconography or texts until sometime between the Middle Kingdom and the New Kingdom, or the Second Intermediate Period (ca. 1780–1550 B.C.), which is a fascinating time of political changes, only imperfectly understood by scholars.

By about 1780 B.C., Egypt was politically fragmented and probably in economic decline, which offered the opportunity for new families to vie for control of the provinces. In the Nile valley a plurality of political centers emerged. The northern delta regions had accepted foreign infiltration for a long time, but many Egyptologists accept the word of a later ancient historian, Manetho, that foreign invaders took advantage of political chaos in Egypt to invade and control at least the eastern delta after the close of the Thirteenth Dynasty. Archaeological work in the last decades of the twentieth century has seemed to verify this scenario, for it has revealed Canaanite installations at a delta site called Tell el-Dab'a.[1]

The prominent families of Upper Egypt were probably quite autonomous, although there were attempts to tax them under the strongest of the Hyksos, or foreign dynasties', rulers. From at least the Twelfth Dynasty (1900 B.C.) Thebes was the cult place of Amun, a god of obvious fertility characteristics. His theologians claimed he was one of the eight original beings of primeval chaos, which the Egyptians (with their orderly minds) conceived of as four couples. Amun's consort was Amunet, and the pair represented "hiddenness."[2] This primeval wife was later overshadowed, if not replaced, by the more identifiable goddess Mut, who may have been promoted first in the north of the country at Heliopolis, the venerable city of the sun (ancient Iunu, or On in the Bible). There Mut was described as a celestial cow who took a newly born Amun on her back and carried him south to Thebes. Heliopolis was home to professional theologians and the holiest city in the vicinity of the great capital of Memphis. The southern city of Thebes was, by contrast, something of a cultural backwater at the beginning of the New Kingdom.

In the late Second Intermediate Period Mut appears as one of several uraeus goddesses that included Wadjet of the Two Ladies. The earliest representation of her, however, is believed to be as a lioness-headed figure on a so-called magic wand of ivory dating to about 1730 B.C.[3] In the Middle Kingdom she is called Mistress of Megeb, a location in the tenthh Upper Egyptian nome in the midsection of the country. This form of Mut was still commemorated five hundred years later in the chapel for Mut at the temple Ramses III of the Twentieth Dynasty built for himself on the west bank at Thebes.[4]

It was the great Eighteenth Dynasty, the Upper Egyptian family that reunited Egypt under strong central rule based at Memphis, that accepted Mut as a proper consort for their favorite god, Amun. These rulers honored their origins even though political reasons necessitated their abandoning Thebes as their capital city for the more strategically located Memphis at the apex of the Nile's delta. They embellished the Temple of Karnak at Thebes so that it grew to be the largest and wealthiest of all temples. They promoted Amun to the head of Egypt's pantheon, calling him King of the Gods and fusing him with the old sun god Re as Amun-Re to emphasize his supreme power. Thus Thebes retained its splendor as the leading city of Upper Egypt, and its role as a great religious center grew. The Eighteenth Dynasty royal family built extensively there (both palaces and temples on the east bank) and laid their dead across the river in the embrace of the Theban hills. Perhaps the great triads of deities at the old religious centers to the north inspired the Thebans to decide that their favorite god required a family.

MISTRESS OF CROWNS

Amun had no elaborate mythology, and thus his priests were free to develop a family for him. However, the centers of political and religious power lay far to the north at Memphis and Heliopolis, respectively. Indeed, Thebes was often called Southern Heliopolis. The influential priesthoods at these cities could easily have imposed priestly appointments and theological dictums on the provincial Thebans. At any rate, Amun gained a spouse Mut, and a son, Khonsu, the moon god, who reflected links with an old moon cult that had been favored by this ruling family's Nubian ancestors.[5] One story indicates that Mut did not bear Khonsu but adopted the younger god to produce the holy triad for Karnak.

This corresponds to Mut's image in the Eighteenth Dynasty as mature goddess, both in art and in description, as when the epithet *wrt*, "great," is frequently added to her name. As Herman te Velde has stated, "This characterizes her as a person of consequence as a matron, as she is as the stately lady with the crowns."[6] The Eighteenth Dynasty restored and indeed exceeded the glory of the past and spread Egyptian political and cultural influence over a wider geographic area than ever before. It can be said, then, that Mut was the mother of her country, but by the next dynasty she is also called Ruler of the Gods in an inscription from Karnak dating to the reign of Ramses II. Here, in the company of Amun-Re and Khonsu, Mut addresses the king and says, " I place the diadem of Re on your head and give you years of festivals, while all the barbarians lie beneath your feet."[7]

Mut's role at Karnak has been described as the goddess who bound together the great luminaries of the sky, Amun-Re, the sun, and Khonsu, the moon.[8] Interestingly, however, Mut maintained some independence

Figure 22. Colossal head of the goddess Mut. Courtesy of the Egyptian Museum, Cairo.

from this familial unit. As was typical of other important Egyptian goddesses, Mut had the advantage of more than one husband, for she is associated with the great state god Ptah of Memphis as well. We know she had temples in the north at Giza and at the seat of the sun god in Heliopolis. Indeed, it is in the company of both Ptah and Amun that she made her first appearance in Thebes, during the reign of the Seventeenth Dynasty king Antef-Nubkheperre, in the Temple of Ptah at Karnak.[9] Thus the possibility exists that Mut had a lengthier history in the north, but the documentation for this has not been found. As Ptah was not a local Theban god, he was being "hosted" by Amun and Mut at Karnak, but Mut was not clearly designated in this Temple of Ptah as exclusively Amun's consort. Indeed, Mut could appear alone just as easily, and thus her independence seems to be stressed. The same text that calls Mut Ruler of the Gods speaks of her as Lady of Heaven. At least originally, however, Mut was preeminently a political goddess. She is identifiable as the Mistress of Crowns in that she often was portrayed wearing the double crown (*peschent*) of the pharaoh of Egypt, the only goddess to do so. It is difficult to believe that such an obviously manufactured goddess, conceived possibly as a political ploy allowing the priestly hierarchy of the north to exert control in Upper Egypt, would have won a devoted following and joined the ranks of the greatest goddesses, but Mut's subsequent history was long and distinguished.

Unlike most other major goddesses, Mut played only a minor role in the mortuary literature. She seems to be more concerned with this life and the integrity of the state: she had a temple oracle to which the living would come to seek solutions to critical problems,[10] and a ritual known as the Overthrowing of Apop was carried out in her temple at Heliopolis (as well as at the temple of Osiris at Abydos and probably other major temples). Apop was the demon who threatened the sun, but this identity was extended to anything that threatened Egypt, natural or political. For this ritual at the Mut temple, wax models were made of the enemies of the state who were identified by name and then destroyed.[11] Apop was visualized as a serpent, and his enemy was the cat, sometimes portrayed by artists as a tom and sometimes in texts as a she-cat.[12] Goddesses associated with cats (or lionesses) are commonly given the epithet Daughter of Re.[13] The conqueror of the demon that threatened the sun would need to be a solar deity. Thus Mut, daughter of the sun god Re, probably fought Apop (an eclipse?) with her powerful father. This cooperation is expressed in a song dating to the Third Intermediate Period (ca. 1075–664) from Mut's ritual: "Let us dance and shout for our mistress in her form in which she was when she was found at the splitting of the ished tree together with Re in Heliopolis."[14]

There seems to be no doubt that Mut's sacred animal was the cat. Te Velde has pointed out jars decorated with cats and Hathoric emblems that are shown as being used in the ritual for Mut at the Temple of Luxor, where they are depicted on the north wall of her part of the triple shrine of the Theban triad in the great court. He suggests that these decorated vases would have been filled with an intoxicating beverage, because "festivals of Egyptian goddesses could be celebrated exuberantly and feasts of Mut formed no exception to the rule."[15] Mut was also the recipient of cat statues dedicated by royalty as votives. There is a painting from the New Kingdom that shows a cat with an "arm" affectionately around the neck of a goose, the bird associated with Amun, suggesting the happy domestic arrangement between Amun and Mut.

Unlike the sensual Hathor, Mut was a respectable wife and house-hold manager. The Greeks later identified her with Hera, the wife of Zeus, perhaps not only because they associated Zeus with Amun. As consort of the king of the Egyptian pantheon, Mut also was the Mistress of the Temple of Karnak in an administrative sense. As S.-A. Naguib has pointed out, the relationship between Amun and Mut may have been familial, but the sexual aspect is definitely downplayed.[16] When Amun, whose powers were generative—fertility and fecundity—was portrayed as an ithyphallic god, if a goddess is present, she is Isis, not Mut. Isis and Hathor were goddesses with sexual powers, but Mut was an older woman, a crone who wielded power and influence as Mistress of Heaven, Mistress of Karnak, and Mistress of Diadems. This is seen not only in her crowns but also in the scepters she held, the *was* symbol of dominion and the *wadj* with its papyrus umbel as the finial. Mut was usually portrayed as a human female wearing a vulture-shaped cap, complete with wings and head. This headgear was commonly seen on queens since the Old Kingdom and thus has no original connection with the goddess Mut but rather with divine motherhood.

Mut's temple also supported a school, which reminds us of the role of the Egyptian mother in socializing the young. The mother is the

Figure 23. View of the Temple of Karnak from the east. Photo by L. H. Lesko.

parent specifically credited by the wise man Ani in his Maxims with sending sons off to school.[17]

From the beginning of the Eighteenth Dynasty, Mut is firmly established in Thebes, her sacred precinct built to the south of the main Karnak precinct of Amun.

Although Mut's precinct was referred to in the reign of Amunhotep I, Mut came to the fore in the reign of Queen Hatshepsut, who also wore the double crown of Egypt. As we have seen, Hathor was divine nurse to Hatshepsut, but Mut is referred to at Deir el-Bahri as bearing and rearing the ruler of Egypt, because her partner Amun-Re was the divine father of the pharaoh. Hatshepsut's mother and Hatshepsut herself share in the divinity of Mut, the mother as the earthly spouse of the god Amun-Re and Hatshepsut as a divine child of a mystical union. She is the first pharaoh said to be "born of Mut and Amun."[18] Of course, Hatshepsut, like Mut, was also the mistress of the crowns of Egypt. We can assume that all other Great Royal Wives and mothers of kings could claim to be earthly manifestations of Mut because the divine husband of the queen of Egypt was Amun-Re, Mut's consort.

Hatshepsut may have been the first pharaoh to claim to have been born of Mut, but surviving records suggest that she was not the last to make the claim. This close association between pharaoh and goddess seems to have influenced those officials of Hatshepsut's government who were ambitious to show special veneration for their pharaoh's divine mother. The reality for her devotees of this comparatively new member of the pantheon is clear from the story of one Kiki, who changed his name to Sa-Mut (Son of Mut) and bequeathed all of his property to the goddess. In his tomb he tells us that he found Mut to be at the head of all the gods and is pleased to consider her his personal protector:

> As for the one whom Mut will make a protégé,
> no god will be able to assail him
> the favorite of the king of his time,
> being one who passes on to the revered state.
> As for the one whom Mut will make a protégé,
> no evil will attack him,
> and he will be protected every day,
> until he reaches the necropolis.
> As for him whom Mut will make a protégé,
> who issues from the womb, favor and fate are his,
> and perfection upon the brick. He is destined for the
>   revered state.
> As for him whom Mut will make a protégé,
> how happy is he whom she loves,
> No god will cast him down,
> being one who does not know death.[19]

Because Mut was a member of the Theban triad and Karnak was their religious center, Hatshepsut demonstrated her veneration of this goddess, who characterized female possession of supreme authority, by building her a temple of her own to the south of the Temple of Amun at Karnak alongside a crescent-shaped sacred lake, called an Isheru. This precinct covered some twenty-two acres. Such Isherus are associated with cult places of lioness goddesses throughout Egypt—a form in which Mut had appeared during the Middle Kingdom. This may have suggested Mut's close and enduring association with the goddess Sekhmet, the most famous lioness of all.

The most prominent men of Hatshepsut's reign left their votive statues within the walls of Mut's precinct. Hatshepsut's chief of works, Sen-Mut (Brother of Mut), took credit for building there, and it is possible that he, like Sa-Mut in the same reign, expressed his loyalty to his queen's favorite goddess by changing his name to honor her.[20] Sen-Mut left an impressive carved relief inscription of himself there, measuring some five feet in height, which mentions his work on the Temple of Mut.

In Eighteenth Dynasty texts Mut is called The Great, Mistress of Heaven, Mistress of All the Gods, and Mistress of the Two lands. This last title is one borne consistently by the great royal wife, the queen of Egypt. Mut is often found in the religious iconography as completely human and wearing the double crown of Egypt. Although this crown belonged to the king of Egypt and was not worn by his consort, Hatshepsut, the first woman during the history of Mut to be crowned as pharaoh, wore it. Still, it is an unusual and marked characteristic of this goddess, a feature that long outlasted the image or even the memory of Hatshepsut, for the female pharaoh was regarded by later generations as an aberration, and her monuments were desecrated and her name was struck from most official king lists.[21]

Because Mut's history seems to be bound to the royal family of the Eighteenth Dynasty, a family whose women were undeniably formidable,[22] she should probably be understood as female royal power deified, indeed even the deification of the concept of royal power. That would partly explain her borrowing of the queenly title Mistress of the Two Lands. Mut's emergence into great prominence at Thebes on the east bank, or City of the Living side, of the river, coincided at Thebes with the relegation of Hathor to the west, the necropolis region where Hathor had had a major cult place since the Eleventh Dynasty and where she played the prime role in the royal mortuary religion of welcoming the deceased into the hereafter. Mut's connection with royalty is suggested by the fact that principal officials were quick to show their veneration to her, whereas Hathor remained popular not only with this official class but also with ordinary women and men. As we have seen, Hathor promoted human fertility, and her shrines were located in many small towns throughout the country. Mut was venerated at fewer places, more in keeping with the state religion's cult and her concern for royalty and the security of the kingdom.

Hapuseneb, the high priest of Amun during Hatshepsut's reign (who was also her chief political officer, or vizier) dedicated a statue of himself in Mut's precinct in southern Karnak.[23] In its inscription he also invokes Sekhmet, the lioness, and Bastet, the cat, who throughout history formed a partnership with, indeed were often seen as different manifestations of, Mut. Sekhmet was strong and fierce and represented Mut's aggressive side; Bastet personified the nurturing characteristics of femininity and motherhood. All were aspects of Mut.

The Temple of Mut became an important part of the great religious center of Karnak and was embellished by subsequent rulers in the Eighteenth Dynasty, notably Amunhotep III, who built a great series of granite statues of a seated lion-headed goddess on the shores of the crescent lake. Today remains of this collection of more than seven hundred lioness statues (the standing Sekhmet statues were also added by a later king) are scattered among museums and private collections all over the world. Why Amunhotep surrounded the lake and filled the Mut precinct (and possibly other temples) with hundreds of images of the sacred lioness is a mystery, although it has been suggested that he built one for each day of the year as a type of votive by which he hoped to be cured of his ailments or to rid Egypt of plague. Sekhmet could bring on illness or cure it, and texts exist of incantations to be spoken over a figure of Sekhmet in a time of plague.[24] Her part-time lay priests known as *wab* were medical specialists, skilled in magic. Indeed the chief of the king's physicians was also the overseer of the priests of Sekhmet.[25] Papyrus Ebers, one of the few surviving medical books from ancient Egypt, is essentially a book of spells to be recited by any physician or priest of Sekhmet. A small collection of medicomagical spells on papyri was discovered at the bottom of a tomb shaft dating to the Middle Kingdom, placed there along with magicians' paraphernalia, perhaps after the scrolls and objects became worn out, as they were discovered damaged. "Most of the prescriptions and spells deal with procreation, pregnancy, birth and newly born children; one is a birth prognostication."[26] Among the collection of papyrus scrolls, statuettes, apotropaic knives, amulets, and the like, was an unusual statuette of a nude woman wearing a lioness mask and holding serpent wands in each hand. She has been variously interpreted, but Robert Ritner deems this an image of the female Bes, or Beset, a household deity who protected women and children especially. Considering its date, an identity with Mut of Megeb, an early lion-headed form of Mut known from an atropaic wand of the Middle Kingdom, is also a possibility. The statue then would have been the magician's conduit for divine power.[27]

Lionesses were still present on the periphery of Egypt's populated areas in pharaonic times. The female of the species is a hunter who tracks and kills her prey and brings the meal back to her mate. Sekhmet was associated with the dangerous scorching sun's eye, which could bring drought and disaster to Egypt. Thus Sekhmet was seen as being able to annihilate her enemies, and to appease this goddess and the forces she could unleash became the object of the nation, especially during the last five days of the year, a particularly dangerous time. Litanies were recited to Sekhmet at year's end to prevent the goddess from threatening the security and well-being of all. The goodwill of this fierce goddess was certainly desired, and inscriptions on the statues set up along the lakeshore at the Mut precinct suggest that they were donated from various parts of the country, as if an all-out national effort was being made to respond to a crisis. However, there is another possible explanation for this unusual and excessive adulation of Mut-Sekhmet by Amunhotep III.

Amunhotep III was not in line for the throne, having been born of a lesser wife of Thutmose IV, who had two Great Royal Wives and other sons. Egyptian historical records, unfortunately, are most often pure propaganda, recording only what the reigning king wished to have remembered and thus containing little information on political strife and intrigue. That Amunhotep became king is odd enough, but it is also known that he came to the throne while still a boy. Thus, most likely, he did not seize rule for himself; it must have come to him through the efforts of others. Coincidental with his reign is the rise to prominence of a family of courtiers originally from Akhmim, one hundred miles north of Luxor. They are regarded by many Egyptologists as having been the parents of Amunhotep's mother, Mut-em-wia. In any case, this Akhmim family seems to have had a hand in the promotion of Mut-em-wia's son over the claims of others. Whether murder and conspiracy played a part in Amunhotep's succession we will probably never know. His mother was named after the goddess of Karnak, Mut-em-wia, and this could have occasioned Amunhotep's special honoring of the goddess Mut, who would have been understood as being the divine supporter of his mother and his own rise to power.

Commemorating this goddess as a lioness, her fiercest form (the equal of Sekhmet who was more commonly found as the spouse of Ptah), may be a recollection and justification for the use of force to gain the kingship.

All that can be said with certainty is that Mut is first found closely associated with Sekhmet at this time. The womanly image, wearing the king's double crown over the queen's vulture-shaped cap, continues to appear prominently in monumental art. There is a famous colossal head from a statue of the reign of King Horemheb at the end of the Eighteenth Dynasty which may reflect the features of his queen, Mutnodjmet (Mut Is Sweet), where the goddess is wearing the double crown (see fig. 22, above). The Temple of Ptah at Karnak dates at least to this royal couple's reign at the end of the Eighteenth Dynasty. This is not surprising as much of their lives was spent at Memphis where Ptah reigned as supreme god. Although Mut could be thought of as "sweet," also in the reign of Horemheb we find her described as the Lady of Terror. This was a way in which her awesome power could be extolled.

The name Mut-em-wia, which was held by many ordinary women as well as the mother of Amunhotep III, refers to the golden boat shrine in which each member of the Theban triad made his or her public appearances. A fine statue of Amunhotep's mother, now on exhibit in the British Museum, shows the queen (or Mut) seated in a bark on the prow and stern of which is a head similar to Hathor's. The figure of the woman is broken off and lost above the waist, so we do not know what type of headdress she wore originally, but she is embraced from behind by a great bird, probably the vulture, just as in statuary pharaohs were sometimes embraced at the back of the head by the divine falcon Horus. The statue is obviously a rebus for the name of the queen: Mut in Her Divine Bark. Most likely the goddess's figure would have resembled the Chief Royal Wife, Amunhotep III's highly influential mother.

Water festivals, great and glittering flotillas of large sacred boats covered with gold, were a magnificent feature of the cult of Mut and other deities as well. In her golden boat Mut accompanied Amun-Re, her divine husband, during their visits to the Temple of Luxor for the annual Feast of Opet. The first Temple of Luxor had been constructed in the reign of Sobekhotep I of the Thirteenth Dynasty, but this gave way to more ambitious buildings of the New Kingdom. Today what exists of this temple is mainly the work of Amunhotep III and Ramses the Great, but scholars believe that Hatshepsut had begun building here earlier in the Eighteenth Dynasty and that this is where she first chose to announce and depict the miracle of her divine conception and birth (as she also did at her mortuary temple across the river at Deir el-Bahri).[28] It was Hatshepsut who was a prime promoter of the goddess Mut. The female pharaoh developed the processional way that connected the Karnak and Luxor temples, supplying it with six stations for the divine barks and providing them with figures of her deified self. Thus the sacred way must have had a temple terminus in her day.

Hatshepsut's royal ka statues explain that the Temple of Luxor was a place where the divinity of the ruler was acknowledged by the great gods of the Theban triad. The oldest references to this Festival of Opet are recorded on Hatshepsut's monuments, her Red Chapel in Karnak, and her mortuary temple at Deir el-Bahri. During the Festival of Opet Amun, Mut, and Khonsu traveled from Karnak to Luxor. During the reign of Hatshepsut their sacred boat shrines, each containing the cult image of the deity, were carried on the shoulders of priests. The visit to Luxor occupied some eleven days. A huge dyad, or double statue, of Amun-Re and Mut dating from the reign of Amunhotep III may be seen today just inside the entrance to the great colonnaded hall where the festival would have taken place at the Temple of Luxor. Amunhotep III is responsible for the building of the main body of the temple, which included in its southeast corner a chamber commemorating his divine conception and birth. The cult of the reigning king's ka during the Festival of Opet was an important part of the celebration. This transformed the mortal king into a god and in every subsequent year reaffirmed his divinity and miraculously rejuvenated him, strengthening his powers to rule and reconfirming his right to rule as a god over men.[29] Back in Karnak, just outside of the Mut precinct, south of the Tenth Pylon, was located the shrine of Kamutef, the self-generating fertility god, a form of Amun-Re, who created the king and his ka. Additions to Amunhotep III's temple were made by Tutankhamun, who completed the decoration of the side walls of the colonnade with the scenes that illustrate the Opet festival. Horemheb and the Nineteenth Dynasty kings Seti I and Ramses II continued the embellishment and expansion of the temple, or Southern Sanctuary as it was called.

Mut continued to be a preeminent goddess throughout the New Kingdom. By the reign of Amunhotep III she had acquired the sacred menat of Hathor for her own use, evidence of her magical powers and possibly evidence too of a slight diminution of Hathor's stature, at least in the Theban area. The Nineteenth and Twentieth Dynasty rulers continued to embellish the seat of the King of the Gods at Karnak on the east bank at Thebes with treasure from their foreign campaigns and expeditions and built many halls, pyloned gateways, and whole temples, within the confines of Karnak commemorating their piety. At this time Mut was the preeminent goddess of the state religion. She personified the kingship, and in some Ramesside texts she is hailed as King of Upper and Lower Egypt and thus unique in the holy pantheon.[30] This proves that Mut's earthly concern is with the kingship and by wearing the double crown incorporates this authority.

Leadership and wisdom were characteristics found not only among kings and goddesses but also among the wise women of the villages. The wise or knowing woman was something like a local shaman, and she is mentioned in ancient private letters and other informal documentation but never named.[31] She was no doubt a fixture in the society of many villages and towns in ancient Egypt: the person in the village, perhaps sometimes the midwife, who knew the herbal recipes for cures, who gave advice, solved problems, predicted fortunes, found lost articles, and was, probably as she is today in the Near East, venerated and feared for her knowledge and special powers. Again it is this wise, older woman who best conveys the role and personality of Mut. She is not the nubile fertile girl, at the height of her sexual powers, embodied in Hathor, or the devoted young wife and mother personified by Isis. Mut may be regarded as the mature, wise, and public-spirited woman of middle age. A Late Period text, Papyrus Insinger, draws a comparison between Hathor and Mut, stating that Mut is the goddess of the good women and Hathor of "the bad women," by which the writer probably meant promiscuous women.[32] Mut was "the stately lady of the crowns standing behind Amun and placing a protective hand on his shoulder."[33]

Egyptian goddesses took many forms and played varying roles, however. Titles and attributes were shared by more than one goddess. This is a feature of polytheism but also probably reflects regionalism at a time when Egypt was far less united in a practical sense because of slow communication. This can be seen in the various forms Mut took during the Eighteenth Dynasty. It is clear that Mut and Sekhmet were "united," as one of the inscriptions on a Sekhmet statue of Amunhotep III mentions. Mut had been a consort of Ptah of Memphis early in her career, but Sekhmet was also his consort. Mut was the consort of Amun-Re, but he and Ptah were the chief gods of the two great cities of Egypt. Thus "together the two goddesses could symbolize the unity of Egypt conceived as a duality."[34]

EYE OF RE

Ramses II dominated the political history of the Nineteenth Dynasty and made such an impression during his long reign (1279–1212) that many subsequent kings of the Twentieth Dynasty assumed his name when they came to the throne. In the Twentieth Dynasty, under Ramses IV, we first encounter the epithet Eye of Re bestowed on Mut. This title appears in the inscriptions on the massive columns of the great hypostyle hall of Amun's temple at Karnak. The hall was erected during the reign of Ramses II, but it is so immense (it could easily accommodate all of the floor space of St. Peter's in Rome) that engraving of inscriptions was still going on years after construction had ceased. The Eye of Re epithet is repeatedly associated with Mut here, and would continue to be hers for centuries, through the Third Intermediate Period, the Kushite, Saite, and Ptolemaic dynasties, down to Roman times. This may be attributed to her greater prominence than Sekhmet, but it may also indicate the decreasing importance or popularity of Hathor in the Theban area by the Ramesside period, even though Hathor had a long history as a solar goddess. The Daughter of Re, a lioness-headed goddess, otherwise unnamed, is depicted accompanying Amun and Mut on a stela dating to the early Nineteenth Dynasty, thus indicating Mut's alter ego.

As mentioned above, the Eye of Re refers to the first female being and solar goddess, often identified with Tefnut, Hathor, or Mut-Sekhmet, who left Egypt in a rage and traveled south where she remained until she was reconciled and brought back to Egypt amid rejoicing. The role of propitiator, the god who brought her back to Egypt, was generally bestowed on a related male divinity who varied according to the form of the goddess. For instance, Shu would propitiate Tefnut, his twin sister, but Onuris or Thoth would propitiate Hathor, and Ptah would visit Mut to bring about reconciliation. Possibly the solar goddess's "enragement" and leaving Egypt in the form of an angry lioness alludes to the occasional cold spells that Egypt experienced. Winter in Egypt can be quite uncomfortable, occasionally even as far south as Aswan and certainly at Thebes and points north, and the rare drenching rainstorm can destroy mud brick buildings and cause flash floods. It is in the winter of the Northern Hemisphere that the sun reaches its southernmost position on the winter solstice. Thus references to the sun's eye returning from the southeast suggests the coming of spring. The arrival of spring would be an occasion for great festivity. Today an annual spring festival is widely and enthusiastically celebrated throughout Egypt, and it would not be surprising if this reflects an ancient celebration of the return of the sun's heat.[35] A Ramesside hymn to Amun describes the arrival of the Eye of Re thus: "Her Majesty returned as the beneficial Udjat Eye. . . . She has come to rest and has stopped in Isheru in her form of Sekhmet."[36]

Sekhmet clearly was thought to have a dual nature. Here it is her protective nature, the image of a lioness protecting her young, which implies her ability to extend powerful protection to the nation as well. All Egypt could be relieved to know that Sekhmet was "home" in her Isheru, quiet and content. Always there loomed, however, the potential for her dangerous, indeed deadly, rage. To help propitiate such a goddess, a new cultic instrument was designed in the late New Kingdom: the aegis, a collar surmounted by the head of a deity, rendered in metal. The head often was that of a lioness, surmounted by a solar disk. Attached to the menat counterpoise (from the necklace of Hathor, which had a long magical history), this aegis would serve its owner with a protective function but could be a votive offering for the goddess. It is associated in particular with the feline deities Sekhmet, Bastet, and Tefnut.[37]

Among the common people of Thebes in the Ramesside period, however, Mut was often viewed as simply the wife of Amun and affectionately depicted as a household cat, "the good cat," just as the favorite male local deity, Amun, was viewed as "the good goose." This divine pair appears on the votive stelae of humble pious people who hoped to stay in the good graces of the gods and be aided by them in life and death.[38] On one is written,

Praise to Mut, Lady of Heaven, Mistress of Amun's House
Beautiful of hands, carrying the sistra, Sweet of voice
O singers, be content with all that she says, pleasant to the
    heart.[39]

From the reign of Ramses VI in the later Twentieth Dynasty comes a stone stela found at Karnak in 1817 and now in the British Museum which contains a lengthy hymn to Mut presented as an acrostic.[40] Whoever composed this detailed text was a fanatic follower who saw all other major goddess manifest in Mut, who is here presented as all-powerful. At the top of the stela are figures of at least nineteen other deities in attitudes of adoration of Mut. The most repeated descriptions of Mut identify her with the sun itself: "Who illumines [the entire land with] her rays . . . [and] causes the land to prosper."[41] Mut is called Re's daughter, but it is he who rejoices in her and who is protected by her, as is all mankind and the gods "their lives are of her giving." "She gives sun-light. . . . She who is great in heaven, like the horizon." "Sun-rays belong to his daughter, since power has been given to her. . . . When Mut shines, sun-beams fall from her, the sole one in the midst of the lands." As the daughter of Re "she has no equal, since eternity belongs to her . . . she who causes the lands to live by means of her sun-rays. This *Udjat* Eye of Re."[42] Mut is also called "mistress of heaven, ruler of the two Lands, great of dread, foremost in the Ennead. . . . [S]he illumines our faces, when she shines as Re."[43]

It is clear here that Mut, like Hathor and a few other special goddesses, is equated with the life-giving and life-taking powerful sunlight. The other goddesses the writer mentions pale when compared to the fiery sun that is Mut. Being a daughter has not dimmed Mut's power. That would come later.

MISTRESS OF TERROR

The Twenty-first Dynasty was a changed world. The Thebaid was removed from the political center, now concentrated in the northern part of the country where the kings not only ruled but also were buried at newly aggrandized cities such as Tanis in the Delta. To the south, in Upper Egypt, the family of the high priests at Karnak controlled temples up and down the Nile, and their wives held many offices with which women do not seem to have been associated earlier, for example, prophets of Mut.[44] It is possible that records are simply more plentiful for this period, but it is also likely that the priestly families of Upper Egypt, although intermarried with the royal family, were fairly autonomous and arrogated to themselves, regardless of sex, as many offices as possible. It has also been suggested that the records hint of the participation of the women of the high priest's family in the editing of religious books at this time.[45]

Perhaps for this reason we now find the most powerful depiction of Mut on a religious papyrus. Like no other goddess, Mut was portrayed in more than one illustrated version of the Book of the Dead beginning in the Twenty-first Dynasty as possessing three heads and a male's phallus. An accompanying vignette shows the goddess this way, standing with outstretched wings. Chapter 164's rubric for the accompanying text states: "To be recited over [a figure of] Mut which has three heads, the first shall be like that of Pakhet, and shall have plumes, the second shall be like a human and shall have the crowns of the south and the north, and the third shall be like that of a vulture and have plumes. The figure shall have a phallus and a pair of wings and the claws of a lion."[46]

A horrific image perhaps, but one that expresses far-ranging, perhaps absolute, powers. The text of the chapter itself makes reference to the lady who is "mightier than the gods" and who "makes souls strong and makes sound bodies and delivers them from the abode of the fiends which are in the evil chamber." Mut then was able to rescue and protect the deceased Egyptians who called on her. Thus, at least by the post-Empire or Third Intermediate Period, her power could extend beyond the world of the living and save souls fettered in the Netherworld. This was a goddess to be contended with, even if her monuments and cult places were not as extensive as Hathor's or Isis's.

There is a darker side of Mut that has received little attention thus far in scholarly literature. As protector of the pharaoh in particular she had responsibility for quelling opposition to his rule. Dissension is not tolerated in a totalitarian state; it is branded as treason. Already in the Middle Kingdom we can see this attitude clearly enunciated in the didactic literature: suppress the rebel, destroy the traitor. By the latter part of the New Kingdom those who resisted the king were destroyed

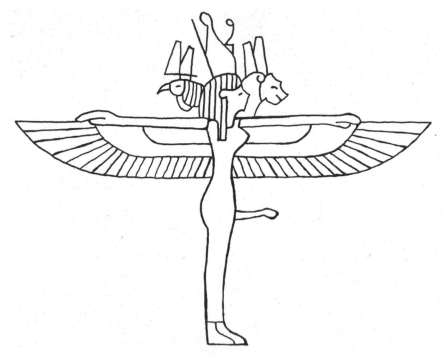

Figure 24. Mut as all-powerful, from a late Book of the Dead. Drawing by Lee Payne.

by fire—on the great brazier of Mut. That this is not metaphoric is clear from a number of references, both in Egyptian and in later classical period historical texts reflecting political events in Egypt in the last millennium B.C.[47] The body of a criminal could not be buried. Since early times death by fire was the possible punishment of the adulterous wife and the political traitor. However, capital punishment could only be decreed by the Crown, not by a local jurist or tribunal. The image of a large boxlike furnace into which were forced the enemies of the state has survived. Why a goddess was deemed the one deity responsible for this cruel and unusual punishment is not known, and may involve more than simply Mut's traditional role as protector of the ruler. The connection between Mut and horrible punishment may be limited to the north, where at the old political capital of Memphis, still the major city of the land, her divine spouse was Ptah, god of craftsmen, which included metal smelters. Why a goddess rather than a god? Perhaps this emphasizes the fierceness of the goddess who is the Eye of Re and

Mut's protective role vis-à-vis the king and the sovereignty of his state. Most significantly, it demonstrates that Mut was the divine manifestation of the state. Thus, sadly, we find the once-benevolent mother goddess presiding over early episodes in the history of holocaust, proving that over the centuries all peoples have had the capacity for excessive cruelty to fellow human beings.

With the passage of time, Egypt's fortunes faded. She suffered foreign invasions that were cruel and rapacious, and her people may have lost heart. Insecure men tend to take a more dominant position with respect to women, and one finds in the literature and monuments now that Mut, once Mistress of Heaven and divine wife of the King of the Gods, began to take on a different and perhaps more subservient role. Mut is encountered more frequently in the first millennium B.C. (Late Period) as the daughter of Amun. Their marital union was not one of equals, as it had been originally or as in the case of Isis and Osiris. Rather Mut now became the attractive daughter who propitiated her father by presenting to him the menat cultic instrument.[48] This change may be seen in the case of Hathor as well. Although Mut and Hathor are understood as the mother, wife, and daughter of Re the sun god and thus, as some Egyptologists have argued, personify the eternal cycle of birth and rebirth, it is also obvious that a daughter is subservient to a father and that neither Mut nor Hathor began her illustrious career in this position. The Empire Period had experienced regent queens and female pharaohs, but such powerful women are not found later in Egypt's history, at least not until the Ptolemaic (Macedonian) Dynasty. It is possible that male theologians wanted to supply no theological basis or comparison on which an ambitious royal woman could stake her claim to the throne, or that in general independent women were now less likely to be tolerated by society. Thus great goddesses are no longer presented as wise elder ladies, capable of administering the state, but as coquettish daughters involved in incestuous relationships with their fathers. The first inkling of this may be in the ribald episode in the Ramesside text known as "The Contendings of Horus and Seth."[49] It can be argued, however, that the gods, both male and female, are made to look childish and petulant in that text, which may have been political satire or just a literary farce written by a nonbeliever. That the distinguished Hathor of the Old Kingdom, a true divine mother of the king and the power of the sun, could be associated by a Late Period author with a woman who brings bad fortune is also disturbing,[50] and very possibly is indicative of a decline in the status of women during the first millennium, or a general bitterness and depression among the male intellectuals of an Egypt that had become, as it is characterized in the Bible, a "broken reed."

The title God's Wife, once held by a royal princess, had been taken by the wife of the high priest of Amun in the post-Empire's Twenty-first Dynasty. This lady was usually a princess of the royal house in the north who was given to the most influential leader at Thebes in a political marriage meant to ensure the loyalty of the southern pontiff at Karnak. Later, in the Twenty-second Dynasty, King Osorkon III, who was of Libyan heritage, saw to it that his daughter was consecrated as God's Wife, but now it seems the princess was expected to remain celibate throughout her life.[51] This would stay the rule for centuries, each God's Wife or Divine Wife of Amun adopting her successor. Because they themselves were daughters of the royal house, these sacred women saw the goddess with whom they closely identified as a daughter goddess, even the primeval female Tefnut, rather than a crone who was mistress of the royal crowns. Like royalty, the God's Wives wrote their names inside royal cartouches and had a prenomen as well as a given name. The prenomen often contained the name Mut, which emphasizes their association with that goddess. Indeed, just as earlier the queen of Egypt had been the earthly manifestation of the goddess Hathor, the Divine Wife at Karnak may very well have been thought of as the earthly manifestation of Mut. However, the goddess now had a role otherwise associated with Hathor, for example, propitiating her father with her singing and menat shaking. This allowed Mut to also be regarded as the daughter of Re. Tefnut, often shown as a lioness-headed goddess, was also a daughter goddess, having been sired by the creator Atum in the Heliopolitan cosmogony. Mut-Tefnut is found as a syncretistic combination of the Late Period. Possibly this change in the interpretation of the goddess's role may reflect some sociological change in the role of the queen in Egypt's Late Period (ca. 800–300 B.C.). Certainly in Upper Egypt by this time it is not the queen but the king's sister or daughter who occupied the most important sacerdotal position at the Temple of Karnak in the realm of Amun-Re, while the seat of royal political power was in the north. The daughter role was not the only one Mut played, however, even in the later periods. She was then called "the daughter who became a mother, who brought forth the light anew," this light being the moon, or her son Khonsu. She also is spoken of as a supreme mother. She was believed to lend her strength to pregnant women and to ensure the safe delivery of their children.[52] Mut's cult was well attended throughout her later history. On his statue, now in Berlin, Mentuemet, the Fourth Prophet of Amun at Karnak during the Twenty-sixth Dynasty, stated:

> I have renewed the temple of Mut-the-Great, Isheru's
>   mistress,
> so that it is more beautiful than before
> I adorned her bark with electrum
> all its images with genuine stone."[53]

This priest of Amun left more than one fine statue of himself in the Mut temple as well.

HOLY CATS

While much more of our documentation survives from Upper Egypt, very early in Egypt's history a major city in the delta was home to the cat goddess Bastet of Bubastis, who is prominent at the height of the Old Kingdom. She perhaps became even more widely revered in the Twenty-second Dynasty when her city was more influential politically, its ruling family having ascended to the kingship of Egypt. In this later period (ca. 900 B.C.) Bastet took the form of a domesticated cat, often of a woman with a cat's head. Bastet came to be called the mother of the king but was approached by human supplicants for help in their daily lives.

Numerous bronze images of the cat goddess survive from the last dynasties. Sometimes she holds a sistrum and sometimes a basket filled with kittens. Bastet was generally thought of as friendly and concerned with childbearing and nurturing and thus the opposite of the ferocious Sekhmet. Domesticity for female deities was now the order of the day.

Approximately forty feline and lioness goddesses appear throughout the history of Egyptian religion. One was Pakhet (She Who Scratches), who enjoyed long popularity in Middle Egypt. Mafdet, the female panther deity, shows up in vignettes of the Book of the Dead and mythological papyri of the Ramesside period. Undoubtedly, the Egyptians saw the cat family as feminine. By the New Kingdom the cat was a popular household pet, probably for its skill in ridding houses and granaries of rodents, and it has been suggested by Jaromir Malek that thus even the humble could have a manifestation of the goddess Bastet among them.[54] Bastet was protectress of women, and the cat's fertility and nurturing instincts related Bastet to the concerns of human mothers. Herodotus reported on the devotion of the Egyptians to their house cats, and in the Late Period extensive cat cemeteries began to appear in Egypt at places with cat goddess cults. The faithful paid for proper burials of the sacred cats that must have overrun these shrines. Archaeologists have found vast catacombs of little mummies dating to the Late Period. However, many household pets also received fine burials. Prince Thutmose, son and original heir of Amunhotep III and Queen Tiy, had a fine stone sarcophagus created to receive the burial of his pet cat.

When Herodotus visited Egypt in the mid-fifth century B.C., he reported on the great festival celebrating the goddess Bastet, whom he called Artemis after the popular fertility goddess of his native land in Asia Minor. He estimated that more than half a million pilgrims flocked to Bubastis and described the bawdy merriment and drunkenness that characterized the festivities. Thousands of bronze statuettes of Bastet survive from the Late Period. Sometimes the cat is dressed as a woman, standing or seated, holding ritual objects such as the menat. Sometimes the full cat form is shown, but the large ears may be pierced and fitted with golden rings. The plentiful bronze and faience images of house cats and their kittens indicate the wide favor of this smallest and friendliest of the cat goddesses.

This was an era of political setbacks (Egypt experienced the brutal Assyrian invasions followed by the Persian invasion, for instance), and religious hysteria may be an indication that great insecurity was felt by the populace of a country that had been immune to such misfortune for most of its history. Herodotus reported that anyone who killed a sacred animal was punished with death, and if a house caught fire, all the neighborhood would try to rescue the household's cats, even giving this priority over fighting the fire.[55] During the reign of Ptolemy XI, an angry mob is said to have lynched a Roman who accidentally killed a cat.[56]

MUT'S FINAL CENTURIES

The Mut precinct is seldom visited by tourists because of its remote location to the south of the great Temple of Amun at Karnak, but it is worth the extra walk. As one nears the site there is an ancient and impressive avenue of ram-headed sphinxes that connected the two temple precincts. The Mut precinct represents the last building phases and boasts three major temples (in ruins) and several smaller structures. There is a certain charm in the quiet of the place, in the several large Sekhmet statues that still stand, askew, scattered about the edge of a mostly dry pond, and in the weedy, uneven terrain that hints at more to be found just below the surface. A woman, Margaret Benson, daughter of the Archbishop of Canterbury, excavated here at the end of the nineteenth century. She found many splendid statues, dedicated

Figure 25. Author with Sekhmet statues at the Metropolitan Museum of Art. Photo by L. H. Lesko.

by the faithful from many different periods in Egypt's ancient history.[57] The Brooklyn Museum has recently returned to the site to seek out even more of its mysteries.

The Mut temple at Karnak was maintained throughout Egypt's final dynasties and was added to in the Ptolemaic Period, the final, foreign dynasty that concluded with the famous Cleopatra. The propylon seen today in the enclosure wall is Ptolemaic (erected under Ptolemy II Philadelphus and Euergetes I). Here the relationship between Amun and Mut is that of father and daughter. Reliefs and inscriptions on its portico indicate that the return and reconciliation of the Eye of Re, the sun, was celebrated then, with much music and dancing, just as it had been one thousand years earlier in the Nineteenth Dynasty. Thus it portrays a religious tradition that reaches back to the New Kingdom.[58] This myth and cult of what came to be understood as the "first feminine being" continued to be celebrated into the Roman Period as the welcoming of a beneficial force for all of Egypt. Keeping the goddess in Egypt and keeping Egypt in her heart, promoting a happy relationship between the two for the good of all, was the primary object of Mut's cult and her clergy, one of whom recorded the following on the wall of the Ptolemaic portico of Mut's temple at Karnak: "I am the perfect sistrum player for the Golden Lady, who pacifies the heart of my mistress every day."[59] This apparent hearkening back to a stronger, more traditional image of Mut occurs in a dynasty known for its strong queens, some of whom shared the rule with their husbands and were deified on death. It coincides as well with the increased status of the goddess Isis, whose story will be told next.

CHAPTER 7

ℐSIS, GREAT OF MAGIC

Because Egyptian religion embraced competing cults, even foreign gods, and saw value in a multiplicity of possibilities rather than dogmatically insist on only One Way, the syncretistic merging of deities was quite common. It is not surprising that the goddess Isis, model wife and mother deified, became closely associated with Mut and especially Hathor. She appears with increasing frequency in funerary art from the New Kingdom onward and often preempts Hathor, although Hathor remained the more important goddess for the next three hundred years and continued until the last as Welcomer to the West for all good deceased believers. But increasingly, evidence shows, Isis moved into greater prominence, especially during the last millennium before Cleopatra.

Older than Hathor, Isis can be traced back to the Pyramid Texts. Her popularity, along with her husband's, burgeoned among the common people during the Middle Kingdom, and rulers paid homage to her in temples built since then. There are many signs that her cult continued to develop throughout the New Kingdom, Third Intermediate Period, and Late Period, and was embraced by foreign settlers in Egypt as well. As time passed, Isis absorbed the attributes of most other goddesses and some gods and became a supreme deity, famous for her curing and redemptive powers. Her cult was widespread in the greater Hellenistic world. She was the longest enduring of Egypt's goddesses.

ISIS, GREAT OF MAGIC

Trust in Isis.
She is more effective than millions of soldiers.
CLEOPATRA II

She is the brightest stationary star in the night sky, visible at the heel of the constellation Orion. Today we call her Sirius, or the Dog Star, but the Egyptians knew her as Soped or Sothis, as the Greeks named her. This star was equated with Isis, and she was a most remarkable star, mysterious in her disappearances and reappearances. Every year she emerged from behind the sun in the middle of summer to mark the start of the Egyptians' New Year on the agricultural calendar. Most important, she heralded the first rising waters of the anticipated and vital annual inundation of the Nile. When the Nile sank and the heat of summer engulfed the land, like a blast from the desert, Egypt was on the verge of death. Only the rising Nile could bring the land to life again, and Isis/Sothis, appearing after an absence of seventy days, would cause the waters to rise.

Always identified with the reviving of a parched land, Isis would also revive her murdered husband, to ensure the continuance of his line. The story of Isis and Osiris is Egypt's first love story. Eventually they won out over all other deities, promising everlasting life to all humanity. But first they existed as gods of fertility and of the sky. Their stories are thus multiform.

The prehistoric culture of Upper Egypt, the southern two-thirds of the country, cannot be distinguished from the prehistoric cultures of the Sudan. Among African tribes, even in our time, the throne of a chieftain is known as the mother of the king and is endowed with the magical ability to turn a prince into a king. The word for throne in ancient Egyptian is *aset*, which is transliterated as Ese or Isis. The goddess Isis, shown with the hieroglyph for "throne" on her head, was the Egyptian throne personified and deified (see fig. 26). Isis the throne made the king of Egypt.

Figure 26. Statuette of Isis as a mourner (throne on her head), Egyptian Late Period. Hay Collection, Gift of Granville Way. Courtesy of the Museum of Fine Arts, Boston.

Because this identity has its origins in prehistoric times, it may well reflect a powerful role for queen mothers, perhaps once understood as the carriers of legitimate rulership from one generation to another, an importance that some scholars consider lost soon after the formation of the historical state. The later Osiris myth and the different role it gave Isis has been suggested as historical evidence for the transition from a matrilineal to a patriarchal succession in which a son inherits from his father. That is perhaps why tombs of queens of the First Dynasty are as large as those of kings and why in the Second Dynasty a decision is said to have ensured the right of a woman to rule the country.[1] This is interpreted as the right to rule on behalf of a prince before he came of age to govern. By allowing his mother the regency, the throne was kept safe for the youth and could not be wrested away by other claimants, such as his father's brother.[2] Indeed, in ancient Egypt the role of mother, whether in the royal family or among commoners, was an honored and influential one. It was Isis in her role as mother of Horus who is encountered in the earliest Pyramid Texts, while Isis and Osiris are not clearly associated as husband and wife until the Sixth Dynasty's editing of that royal funerary literature.[3] In historical mythology, as we have seen, theologians drew up family trees regularizing the age-old myths and trying to put them in order but also trying to use all valuable stories, attributes, and epithets. The theologians were also motivated by the need to explain how and why the king of Egypt was to be regarded as divine, because the divinity of the king was the cornerstone of their centralized state—the first large unified state in the history of the world. In the Heliopolitan cosmogony, Isis and Osiris, along with Seth and Nepthys, were the children of Geb and Nut. The offspring of Osiris and Isis was their only son Horus, and Horus was the god with whom the king of Egypt would be identified, the living manifestation of this divinity on earth.

Although Pyramid Texts predated the pyramids, they reflect developments and adaptations over a long period. More than one myth concerning Isis and her son Horus can be discerned in this vast collection of spells. We can see an unresolved confusion between characteristics and activities of the divinities of the sky and of the earth. However, a strong theme is the story of Horus's struggle for the kingship. Unlike later versions, it originally presented Horus as a mature, if young, man at the time of his father's death. Thus he is fully capable of taking immediate action to avenge his father's murder at the hands of Osiris's jealous brother. This suggests that until the latest editions of the Pyramid Texts (found inscribed inside tombs of Sixth Dynasty kings and principal queens) it was Hathor and Neith who held preeminent positions as goddesses in the state religion, and Isis played a more minor role in the royal funerary literature as protector of the dead king and mother of his heir, Horus, the living king. Thus her original identity as the personification of the throne is preeminent. Isis may not have been linked with the star Sirius from the start either, as Hornung has found that in the early dynastic period Sirius was worshiped in cow form but soon thereafter became a manifestation of Isis.[4]

In the later Pyramid Texts, however, Isis does play a vital and dramatic role, with her sister, in finding Osiris's corpse and remembering or revivifying him: "Isis has reassembled you, the heart of Horus is glad about you in your name of Foremost of the Westerners, and it is Horus who will avenge what Seth has done against you" (PT Utt. 357). "Foremost of the Westerners" refers to a very ancient guardian of the cemetery of Abydos, Khentiamentiu, with whom Osiris later became identified when he claimed the great burial ground of the earliest Egyptian kings for his own cult place. It is still possible to find the little foxlike animal, this most ancient of Abydene gods, as one explores the extensive and fascinating archaeological site of Abydos.

It is believed that the religion of Osiris, Isis's husband, was not well established until the second half of the Sixth Dynasty. At this time the holy family of Isis, Osiris, and Horus became firmly fixed as well in the royal liturgy and in royal art. When the Osiris legend took hold among the people, the story of the death and resurrection of a good king was elaborated and Isis took on a more powerful and sympathetic role as the one responsible for the revivification of her husband. Through this she was related to the annual beneficial flooding of the Nile. Isis became renowned for her magical powers, not only in funerary literature but also in popular thought.

Just as storytellers were in demand in Egypt in the nineteenth century A.D., many of them were women,[5] the same was probably true in antiquity. Their stories concerned the living, those who sowed and reaped with their eyes on the stars and on the Nile flood. Thus the story of the dead king who was revived before burial was linked to the god of vegetation: his death could be seen everywhere in the wilting and dying off of the fields during the hottest months of late spring and early summer. If Osiris was an ancient vegetation god, his resurrection was apparent with the coming of the inundation, caused by the widow who shed many tears over her loss. Isis became synonymous with fertility and plenty, the increase of herds and the bounty of the harvest.

Although it is only alluded to briefly, perhaps because it was felt that such an unfortunate story should not be dwelled on, the tale of Osiris's murder is acknowledged in the Pyramid Texts. Why did this story of the dying vegetation god take such a criminal turn in Egypt? Here we must refer to the distinction in Egypt that is still seen so clearly today between the fertile Nile valley, the Black Land (which gave Egypt's its ancient name of Kemet = Black) and the Red Land, Deshret, the desert. It is possible to stand with one foot in each. The open desert is formidable, even frightening in its seemingly boundless sterility, and it can fill one with a sense of hopelessness and despair. In Egypt it is also known as an aggressor, for it has often devoured once-fertile fields and even occasionally swallowed entire towns.[6]

A sandstorm can engulf planted fields, resulting in lost harvests and famine. Thus a terrible tension exists between fertile land and desert, between the possibility of life and the threat of death, between Osiris and his brother Seth. As Herodotus commented, Egypt was the gift of the Nile. Without its life-giving water, without Osiris, the deified flood and its fertile silt, there would be no inhabitable cultivated land, no life possible at all. Seth must not win in this desperate battle. Osiris and justice, life itself, must triumph, and this Isis would ensure. She is the female principle, the female role in the act of reviving life, sustaining life and defying death. If Osiris is the deified floodwaters, Isis is the star that calls forth the inundation.

The Red Land and the Black Land can live in harmony next to each other, but this harmony must be maintained carefully. The perfect state of nature, exemplified by the goddess Ma'at and the responsibility of the king of Egypt, included for Egyptians this harmony between desert and fertile land. But the ancients needed to explain occasional natural calamities. They believed these events took place in the realm of the gods, and thus a great drama was imagined and enacted: the good god Osiris might be killed by his brother Seth. This could have been the meaning behind the dreaded Khamsim (sandstorm) that would blow for fifty days and coat everything with sand and dust and threaten the young crops in the fields. But there is another possible explanation.

Historical Egyptian art and texts provide us with vignettes of a ceremony of renewal called *heb sed* that was undergone by kings who had ruled for a long time. This festival had its origins in the ancient African custom of slaying an aged chief who was no longer able to lead his tribe. There may be some hint of this ritual in the murder of Osiris. At the very least Seth, representing the opposite of fertile land and the political opposition to a reigning king, was the challenge the dead king's son had to meet head on. Seth alone of all the gods does not take on a recognizable animal or human form but seems to have been depicted nightmarishly, like other mythical animals of the desert as they were portrayed in historic Egyptian art.[7]

In the story of Osiris and Isis, which has come down to us from Plutarch, who wrote thousands of years after it was first conceived by the Egyptians, we are told that Osiris was a good and popular king.[8] His evil brother Seth became jealous and plotted his murder. He threw a party and as an amusement offered his guests, among them Osiris, a beautiful coffin if they could fit it exactly. Each guest tried it out, but it was intended for Osiris. When the king climbed inside, Seth's henchmen closed the lid and nailed it shut. Then Osiris was thrown into the river to drown. Instead the Nile carried the coffin far out to sea and beyond. Some versions of the myth have it beached on the Levantine coast at Byblos. Isis, Osiris's wife, set out to find her husband's body. A tree, which later became a pillar in the royal palace, had grown around the coffin before Isis arrived at Byblos. That is where Isis finally located the coffin and recovered Osiris's body. At the Hathoric Temple of Dendera a relief depicts the coffin of Osiris enclosed in the branches of a tree.

After returning to Egypt with her husband's body, Isis was joined by her sister Nephthys. In the Pyramid Texts the two sisters are described as mourning the deceased king and causing him to live again. They both suckle the king, their brother, like a babe, thus assisting his rebirth and preparing him for eternal life. Indeed, the milk of Isis is mentioned in the Pyramid Texts as being an essential ingredient for the resuscitation of the deceased. In funerary art the wailing women are depicted with a white sash tied around their brows to denote their status as mourners, usually kneeling, one at the head and one at the feet of the corpse. They often are shown accompanying the corpse on the funerary boat on its final voyage to the tomb or on the pilgrimage to the great national cemetery at Abydos.

Later in Egypt's history Isis was portrayed in sculpture in human form with large wings embracing Osiris, who is smaller in stature, more like a son than a husband. However, drawings on contemporary funerary papyri show her as a kite hovering above Osiris, who is revived enough to have an erection and impregnate his wife. Interestingly, in the earlier Coffin Texts of the Middle Kingdom a more dramatic, perhaps more refined, event occurs: Isis is impregnated by a lightning flash.[9]

> The lightning flash strikes, the gods are afraid, Isis wakes pregnant with the seed of her brother Osiris. . . . She says: O you gods, I am Isis, the sister of Osiris, who wept for the father of the gods. . . . His seed is within my womb, I have molded the shape of the god within the egg as my son who is at the head of the Ennead. What he shall rule is this land, the heritage of his father Geb. . . . Come, you gods, protect him within my womb for he is known in your hearts. He is your lord, this god who is in his egg, blue-haired of form, lord of the gods. . . . I am Isis, one more spiritlike and august than the gods; the god is within this womb of mine and he is the seed of Osiris. (CT Sp. 148)

Thus Isis became pregnant and carried Osiris's son Horus to term. Meanwhile Osiris's body was discovered by the enraged Seth who pulled it from its mummy wrappings and tore it to pieces—fourteen to be exact—that he then scattered throughout Egypt. Now again Isis needed to search for the remnants of her spouse. Wherever she found a body part, she buried it on the spot. This is the version preserved by Plutarch, but it must also be of earlier date, as over each body part the ancients erected a holy shrine. Towns all over Egypt were honored for hosting a sacred part of the god's body. These burial places of Osiris dotted the countryside and were maintained as sacred places for centuries.

Isis and Nephthys are often depicted wearing a baglike kerchief tied at the nape of the neck. This is seen also in ancient paintings of women working with the grain harvest and thus may be relevant to the Osiris imagery of sprouting grain. Often an earthen and seeded silhouette of

Osiris was placed within a tomb and watered so that it might sprout and symbolize the resurrection of the god and of the deceased person who identified with him. The sisters were also portrayed in art and in religious texts as female falcons or kites, probably a reference to birds of prey and to the sound the birds make, reminiscent of the cries of distraught women. The two sisters did not merely mourn the dead king; using their magical powers, they preserved his flesh from decay: "Your libation was poured out by Isis, [Nephthys has cleansed you, these your two] great and mighty ones who gathered your flesh together, who raised up your members, and who caused your two eyes to appear in your head" (PT Utt. 670). Even the cloths in which the women wrapped the corpse of Osiris had magical powers that ensured its resurrection. It was Isis who was expected to loosen the wrappings that transformed the deceased. By freeing the mummy she made it possible for Osiris to pass into eternal life.[10]

Isis and Nephthys led the deceased triumphantly from his earthly abode into the sky to join the greatest gods, including the grandmother goddess Nut:

> Isis will converse with you. Nephthys will speak to you. The glorified spirits will come to you, bowing down, and kiss the earth at your feet because of the terror of you. . . . You will go forth to your mother Nut, and she will take your hand and give you a road to the horizon, to the place where Re is. The double doors of the sky will be opened for you. (PT Utt. 422)

The sisters then help the dead but revivified king into heaven with this amusing burlesque of a king mounting the proffered backs of two women:

> I will go forth on the hips of Isis
> I will climb up upon the hips of Nephthys. (PT Utt. 269)

The deceased king or queen, for whom this religious literature was originally intended, was meant to cross the heavens in the solar bark. Today, at the pyramids of Giza, one may see the one-hundred-twenty-foot wooden craft of King Khufu that is still marvelously preserved after

Figure 27. Nephthys and Isis as kites, Tomb of Queen Nefertari. Photo by L. H. Lesko, 1965.

forty-five hundred years.[11] Buried on the south side of the Great Pyramid, this boat and its mate may have been intended to be the two polar barks necessary to cross the day and night sky:[12]

> You will go forth and you will go down, going down with Nephthys, becoming dark with the night bark of the sun.
> You will go forth and you will go down, going forth with Isis, arising with the morning bark of the sun. (PT Utt. 222).

Later were imposed on this identification of Isis and her sister, as vital for the rebirth and eternal life of the deceased, more episodes elaborating on the Osiris myth that explained and justified the process of royal succession among the Egyptians. That this episode of the Osiris myth was designed in the historic period, once the nation was unified and functioning as a powerful centralized state, is obvious from its slight reference in the Pyramid Texts. In the earliest literature Horus is usually presented as a powerful figure, a mature son who participates with Isis and Nephthys, sometimes identified as his two sisters, in the reassembling of his father's corpse and becomes his avenger. Thus the magical revivification story by Isis alone was a later addition.

We learn from Plutarch that after she was impregnated by her dead husband, Isis's confinement and nurturing of her infant son took place in the marshes of the delta, where they could not be found by the wicked Seth. Isis needed all the magic at her command to raise Horus in hiding, and she lovingly protected the child from all threats until he grew strong enough to take on Seth in a struggle to regain the throne that had been his father's. There is but sparse reference to a young Horus being raised in the swamps of the delta in the Pyramid Texts. Utterance 519 tells of Isis burning incense before "the young child that he might cross the earth on his white sandals and . . . see his father Osiris." This must be a late version, added in the Sixth Dynasty, as the great majority of references to Horus, the son of Osiris, present him as mature. In the Coffin Texts of the Middle Kingdom one spell (286) has Horus commenting that he was conceived in Pe and born in Chemnis, so the details of Plutarch's story seem to have ancient origins.

Because Horus was ultimately successful in inheriting the kingship, as early as the First Dynasty the Egyptian kings' names are recorded with the symbol of the Horus falcon above them. These Horus kings ruled from a new capital city at the apex of the delta—Memphis—but returned to their home region in the south to be buried. One of these cemeteries on the west bank at Abydos, considered Osiris's burial place, later became a holy shrine. The private memorials erected by wealthy Egyptians of the Middle Kingdom (early second millennium) at Abydos express their wish to spend eternity in the presence of Osiris, inhaling his incense and enjoying the offerings that were first presented to him.[13] By the reign of Senusert III of the late Twelfth Dynasty, the deceased express a desire to be "powerful in heaven, a blessed spirit on earth, and justified in the Netherworld."[14] There are references to resurrection in the epithet "repeating life." Thus, although the explicit portrayals of Osiris's hall of judgment in the Netherworld would not appear for centuries yet, and details of the hoped-for life beyond the grave are sparse compared to those found in the New Kingdom, by the Twelfth Dynasty there must have been the beginnings of thoughts about what it would be like to die and yet remain in the realm of this victorious god, indeed, to become a god like him.

In the late Middle Kingdom we find the dead imagined in the guise of Osiris. Kurt Pflüger, who studied the funerary stelae of the Middle Kingdom excavated at Abydos, was convinced that "any commoner, even of the humblest position, established contact with deity to a much greater extent than had already been done by the mentioning of divine names."[15] However, it was only Osiris and another funerary deity, the doglike Wep-wawet (Opener of the Ways), who are portrayed on Twelfth Dynasty stelae. Isis is not seen here but is ubiquitous in the funerary texts inscribed on coffins of the period. It is also clear that she had a cult of her own by the end of the Old Kingdom at Kusae, in the company of Hathor, who figured importantly in rites at the time of burial.[16]

By the Middle Kingdom, the annual religious pageant at Abydos involved a great procession that followed the image of the god Osiris from his temple to his tomb amid scenes of combat. Ikhernofret of the Twelfth Dynasty has left an account of his responsibility in organizing this annual festival, which included dramatic events and elaborately decorated bark shrines for the god: "I conducted the Procession of Wep-wawet, when he went forth to avenge his father. I repulsed the attackers of the *neshmet*-bark, I overthrew the foes of Osiris. . . . I cleared the god's path to his tomb in Peqer. I protected Wen-nofer on that day of great combat. I felled all his foes on the shore of Nedit."[17]

The great age of the pyramid-building Old Kingdom had been followed by one of social unrest and short reigns, competing political centers, and even perhaps famines, earthquakes, plagues, and social revolutions. The instability and the numerous ephemeral kings shook the people's faith in an invincible god-king on earth and forced them to look elsewhere for salvation, toward the true gods of their ancestors, the deities they could see in the sun and the stars. They looked with hope to the deities concerned with the West, the world beyond this one, for reassurance of better things to come. Thus by the Middle Kingdom Osiris's popularity had soared among the people, and the story of the death and resurrection of a good king was elaborated. The Pyramid Texts had already recorded the mourning of Isis and Nepthys (PT Utt. 701), but Isis had not always received recognition along with Osiris. One hymn to Osiris from the Middle Kingdom does not even mention his wife. It would seem that during the Middle Kingdom, a feudal age with a decidedly patriarchal slant, Osiris was more likely to be credited with the powers of resurrection, even though earlier the

Pyramid Texts had credited Isis with these powers in regard to the dead king. However, it may be assumed that Isis and Nephthys did have a role in the dramas enacted at Abydos even in the Middle Kingdom.

By the Middle Kingdom the old religious literature of royalty was in large part taken over by commoners and, edited to reflect the changes, was written on the inside of their rectangular wooden coffins. Osiris was rewarded with kingship over all the dead who were deemed just and thus deserving of eternal life with him. Now the right to reach and live in Osiris's kingdom in the Beyond became the goal of Egyptians of both sexes and, theoretically, of all social classes. Osiris's hall of justice, where moral behavior was proclaimed by the deceased and judged by a tribunal of deities, was not yet described in the Coffin Texts, but good deeds and responsible behavior, such as helping one's neighbor and showing loyalty to one's king, is often cited in Middle Kingdom texts as the attributes of those who could expect to be granted eternal life.

Decades ago, Breasted was struck by this democratic development of the Egyptian religion. Now all people were given deities of a human and sympathetic nature.[18] Hathor, in the funeral context especially, was still associated with royalty and the funerals of the rich and powerful who took to themselves many royal prerogatives whenever possible. Isis and Osiris may have been gods of the people, but it must be remembered that not everyone could afford a wooden coffin inscribed by professional scribes and painters.[19] Thus even the Coffin Text spells were not within reach of everyone.

Eventually the funerary literature was written on papyrus scrolls, which may have been more easily attainable. These Books of the Dead begin to appear after the Second Intermediate Period. The New Kingdom which followed, with the Eighteenth Dynasty as its founding family (1554–1304), saw a considerable effort to compose detailed texts for royal tombs that described the rulers' expectations for eternal life in solar terms, but in which Osirian elements appear as well. Elaborate portrayals of the Egyptian's conception of the Osirian tribunal now appear on the illustrated Books of the Dead in its chapter 125.[20]

The important innovation of this age was the demand that everyone justify his life before Osiris before he or she could hope to attain eternal life in his kingdom. The deceased had to swear that he had not committed a long list of offenses. This testimony took place before an enthroned Osiris and a tribunal of major deities, in his subterranean realm. Now the heart of the deceased was weighed by Thoth, the divine scribe, on a scale that, it was hoped, would balance with the feather of Truth. Isis stands alongside her husband at his throne; sometimes she is joined by her sister Nephthys. Isis also sits on councils who judge the deceased.[21] She is part of the Councils of Busiris, Pe and Dep, Wepwawet, and Rosetau, where there was an important cemetery and cult place of Osiris. Indeed, it was identified as a possible location for his tribunal, for the final judgment of the dead. All these cult places actually refer to other traditions, other deities involved in funeral cults, such as the dog Wep-wawet or Sokar of Rosetau. Isis's significant role in the funerary cult, after the possible hiatus of the Middle Kingdom, may well reflect the elevated power of women in the ruling family of the Eighteenth Dynasty and their patronage of this and other goddesses, marking a clear distinction between their attitude and that which prevailed during the Eleventh and Twelfth dynasties.

The Book of the Dead contains numerous chapters with spells that allow the deceased to see Osiris and Re and that offer protection against the many traps and demons that might threaten the deceased in the afterlife. Chapter 15 contains a hymn to Osiris that acknowledges an important role for Isis as a protector:

> Isis will embrace you in peace and
> she will drive away the opponent from your path.
> Place your face to the West
> that you may illumine the Two Lands with electrum.
> The sleepers have stood up to look at you,
> breathing the air and seeing your face
> like the rising of the sun-disk in its horizon,
> Their hearts are pleased with what you have done,
> To you belong eternity and everlastingness.[22]

Isis had a life of her own outside Osiris's subterranean realm. Indeed, early in the Twelfth Dynasty, during the reign of Senusert I, both Isis and Bastet are referred to as the two main deities of the Heliopolitan nome on a shrine that king erected at Karnak.[23] This surely indicates that the mother goddess cults were still very much needed by the living. Isis's cult is attested at Hierakonpolis, Edfu, Akhmim, and Koptos during the Middle Kingdom, but it is obvious that the formal cult's emphasis was on her role in the earth's fertility, occasioned by the Nile flood that she announced. This is clear because the towns of Akhmim and Koptos were long associated with the cult of the fertility god Min. Throughout history Isis would have her own priesthood and temples in these towns.[24] Isis's identification as a "living" goddess concerned with fertility made her popular, and her cult was probably widespread among the common people by the Middle Kingdom. This identification caused her to become linked with the very ancient fertility god Min.

> Hail to you, Min in his procession!
> Tall-plumed, son of Osiris,
> Born of divine Isis.[25]

Min had a longer history than the above Middle Kingdom hymn indicates. He may, in fact, be traced back to the prehistoric age: his "doorbolt," "thunderbolt," or phallic totem is found drawn on numerous pots of the prehistoric Gerzean period. Two very large stone statues of this ithyphallic god dating to the First Dynasty were discovered by Flinders Petrie at Min's cult temple in Koptos.[26] This god's images were usually painted black to link him with the fertile soil of the Nile valley, but he was also worshiped in the form of a white bull. His sacred plant was the long lettuce, whose juice, it is said, reminded the ancients of semen, and it was apparently eaten as an aphrodisiac.

Isis was worshiped at Min's town of Gebtu (Greek Koptos), forty kilometers north of Luxor, for much of her history, but she was also worshiped farther afield. For instance, she was represented with Min at a temple of Horus in Buhen in Nubia in the early Eighteenth Dynasty[27] and was known as Mistress of Nubia during the Nineteenth Dynasty, when her cult was maintained at several temples created during the reign of Ramses II in that southern region. Few temples from the Middle Kingdom and the New Kingdom have survived or been excavated outside the area of Luxor—the domain of Amun, Mut, and Khonsu—so Isis's cult may actually have been celebrated far more widely in these periods than archaeology has yet indicated. Certainly her reputation as a devoted wife and tender mother (which won Isis so many adherents in later centuries) was already making her appealing to the Egyptian masses by the Middle Kingdom. People were drawn to a divinity who had known suffering and who thus was bound to be sympathetic to their personal tragedies. Isis was the most humane of deities, not only in concerns but also in appearance as she was not generally associated with an animal. She was also known for her sympathetic magic. She could cure as well as protect, and the major medical papyrus of the New Kingdom, dating from the very beginning of the glorious Eighteenth Dynasty, if not earlier, hails Isis as the divinity of cures:

> O Isis, Great of Magic,
> Heal Me,
> Release me from all things bad and evil.[28]

It is perhaps not surprising that Isis enjoyed an official surge in popularity—perhaps was rediscovered—by the Eighteenth Dynasty, which is renowned for its powerful queens and even a female pharaoh. Now, in the tomb of the great king Thutmose III, the age-old symbol of Hathor—the sycamore tree goddess shown suckling the king—is called Isis (see fig. 28). Isis was the name of Thutmose's natural mother, so the nurturing and protecting by Isis of her son Horus, equated with the living king, is graphically portrayed. Thutmose III, otherwise known as the Napoleon of ancient Egypt, was honored and recalled for centuries as a truly great king, an empire builder who through his conquests brought increased power and wealth to Egypt. If his family chose to honor Isis, the goddess's fame would indeed have soared. Hatshepsut, his predecessor and early nemesis, had honored Hathor in her elaborate temple at Deir el-Bahri and had also actively promoted Mut, so that Thutmose III's sponsorship of Isis may well have been a deliberate attempt to evoke notable changes in his realm. Isis's name remained used by the royal family of the Eighteenth and later dynasties, further indicating the importance of this goddess.

Isis appears in an Eighteenth Dynasty hymn dedicated by an offical named Amunmose and his wife, Nefertari, and the goddess is credited with the power of speech: "the excellent of tongue whose speech cannot fail." The long hymn of twenty-eight lines contains the fullest accounting of the Osiris myth that survives from pharaonic literature, and although it avoids details of Osiris's assassination, it clearly describes Isis's ability to revive her spouse and conceive his heir:

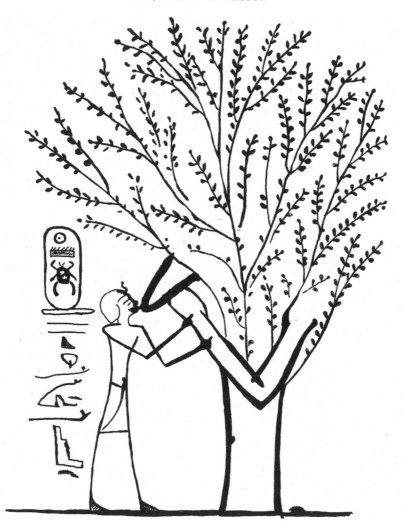

Figure 28. Isis as a tree goddess, nursing Thutmose III, from his tomb. Drawing by Lee Payne.

His sister provided his protection
driving away the enemies
putting a stop to the misdeeds of the disturber
by the power of her mouth
the excellent of tongue whose speech cannot fail
effective in command

Beneficial Isis who protected her brother
Who sought for him without wearying,
Who traveled around this land in mourning
she cannot rest before she finds him
who made a shade [*shwyt*] with her plumage [*shwt*]
who created a breeze with her wings
who jubilated, having revived her brother
who lifted up the inertness of the weary one
who received his seed, who produced an heir
who suckled the child in private,
the place where he was was unknown.[29]

The pilgrimages to Osiris's great shrine at Abydos continued, of course. The wealthier Egyptians had their mummies taken there by boat before interment to share in, if only briefly, the sacred reversion of offerings and come directly into the presence of Osiris. The pageants honoring the god and recalling his triumph over his enemies were still acted out, and now Isis and Nephthys were definitely present, taking leading roles in the public mourning of the Lord of the Dead. Texts from later periods describe the commemoration of Osiris's death and resurrection at Abydos with lamentations for Osiris and jubilation at his resurrection. Two women were selected to portray the goddesses— maidens whose bodies were shorn of all hair and whose arms were marked with the names of the goddesses—and lead the mourning. Two papyri from a later period preserve texts purporting to be the lamentations of these goddesses. In the Lamentations of Isis and Nephthys the women speak alternately, whereas in the songs, Isis takes a leading role. The Ptolemaic Period papyrus that preserves the text of the lamentations[30] was appended to a Book of the Dead manuscript of a woman. It is illustrated with a sketch showing two female priestesses seated on the ground, each holding a vase of water and a loaf of bread, offerings traditionally left at the tomb for the ka of the deceased, who is associated with the god Osiris. This text was used in the funeral service, while the longer Songs of Isis were recited during a four-day ritual in an Osiris temple. Isis speaks:

O good youth, come to your house!
It is long, long ago and I have not seen you!

My heart mourns for you, my eyes search for you,
I am seeking you in order to see you!. . .
Come to your beloved, come to your beloved!
Wennofer, justified, come to your sister!
Come to your wife, come to your wife,
Weary at heart, come to the lady of your house!
I am your sister by your mother.
You shall not depart from me!
Gods and men, their faces are toward you.
Weeping for you together!

Nephthys speaks:

O good Sovereign, come to your house!
Make glad your heart, all your enemies are nonexistent!
Your Two Sisters are beside you as protection for your bier,
Summoning you in tears!. . .
I am Nephthys, your sister, your beloved!
Your rebel is fallen, he shall not exist!
I will be with you, as protection for your body,
Forever and ever!

Isis continues:

. . . Your sacred image, Orion in heaven,
Rises and sets;
I am Sothis following him,
I will not depart from him! . . .
Oh my lord! There is no god like you!
The sky has your *ba*, the earth has your image,
The Netherworld is equipped with your secrets,
your wife is your protection,
Your son Horus is ruler of the lands!

The songs similarly call to Osiris to come home and make numerous references to episodes of the Osiris myth that has not survived in a complete and connected version from Egyptian sources but was collected and published as a complete story by Plutarch. While Isis and

Nepthys act equal parts in the lamentations, the songs are mainly sung by Isis. The following are a few excerpts from this very long text.[31]

> May you come to your house, O Osiris, your place where
>   one seeks to see you;   5.18
> May you hear thou the complaint of Horus in the arms of
>   his mother Isis.
> You were opposed, having been placed throughout all
>   lands, but he who reunites your body, shall receive your
>   house document [inheritance] . . .
> O great Bull, lord of passion,   5.24
> Your bird is your sister Isis . . .

Isis sings:

> I hid myself in the rushes to conceal your son in order
>   to answer for you.   7.14

Lector:

> To you belongs those who go forth to the gods   9.25
> Happy (the Nile) is the efflux of his body, to nourish the
>   nobility and the common folk,
> Lord of provision, ruler of vegetation,
> . . . tree of life which gives divine offerings.   9.28

Isis sings:

> I am a daughter of Geb . . . but you avoid me,   13.2
> O youthful one, outside his proper time.
> I walk the roads since love of you came to me,
> I tread the earth, without my wearying from seeking
>   you,   13.5
> Flame is against me because of the love of you. . .
> May you come to me in haste since my desire is to see
>   you   15.9
> Isis comes to you, O Lord of the Horizon, according as she
>   begat the Unique One, the leader of the gods;   17.3

She will protect you,
she will protect your face,
She will protect the face of Horus,
Even the woman who created a male for her father,
Mistress of the Universe, who came forth from the Eye of
   Horus,
Noble Serpent which flamed forth from Re,
and which came forth from the pupil in the eye of Atum
When Re arose on the First Occasion.

This is a late text but may very well reflect the libretti of the music-enriched festivals at Osiris temples of earlier periods. From the New Kingdom on, Isis appears wearing the sun disk and cow's horns head-dress familiar from images of Hathor. This has been taken as signifying her move into Hathor's domain as a solar goddess, but it may just as easily have been a way the ancients had of honoring Isis, emphasizing her universality but also rewarding her with the age-old sacred symbols reflecting the power of the other great goddess. The importance of the cow to the Egyptian was never forgotten but lay deep at the heart of their culture.[32] The most venerated beings were marked for honor with this association. In their tomb art nobles are promised that they will be enduring as the stars in the afterlife and be fed by the milk of Isis.[33] Records found in the great Memphite cemetery of Saqqara dating from the end of the Eighteenth Dynasty show that Isis has assumed the Hathoric title, known from Thebes, Lady of the Beautiful West.[34] Thus the traditional story of Isis and Osiris continued throughout the New Kingdom (Dynasties 18–20) and beyond, but it is clear that Isis was such a popular figure in the Egyptian imagination that by the New Kingdom additional stories about Isis and her son were written down. In this way Isis's personality becomes more developed than that of any other goddess. She is well rounded: a woman of maternal feeling and loyalty but also clever and forceful. It is not possible to know whether Hathor had lost some standing because of her own aggressive images, the snake and the cow. Isis was more humane than any other goddess and for this reason won, and never again lost, the hearts of her people. Surely she reflects the values of her time, what women themselves would find admirable in women, in mothers in particular. Thus these commendable attributes were projected onto a beloved goddess.

In the "Contendings of Horus and Seth," a tale that survives on a papyrus from the New Kingdom (late second millennium) but may reflect a story of earlier origins, Isis is a determined supporter of her son Horus's claim to the throne of his father.[35] The story, however, shows that his accession was not a sure thing and that Seth, his evil uncle, murderer of Osiris, had the support of some of the greatest gods. The action centers on the great divine tribunal before which Horus had to appear to make his claim on his father's title. Seth had strong support in his claim from the old gods Atum and Re-Harakhty, but Thoth, the scribe of the gods, was instructed by other gods present to write a letter to the senior goddess, Neith, asking her opinion. She answered favoring Horus, saying giving the kingship to anyone else would be an injustice. When Seth was allowed to argue his case (that he was the strongest of all the gods and the protector of the sun god against his enemies) he won many hearts. This angered Isis, who protested vigorously. Re-Harakhty decided to remove the trial to an island from which Isis would be barred.

Always resourceful, however, Isis disguised herself as an old woman and bribed the ferryman to take her across. Once there she transformed herself into a beautiful young girl to whom Seth was strongly attracted. Engaging her in conversation, Seth heard her story of how she was the widow of a cattle herder by whom she had a son. Recently, she told him, a stranger had come and threatened to beat her son and carry off the cattle. Isis asked Seth to help her against this rapacious man, and he replied indignantly in her support: "Shall the cattle be given to strangers while the son of the farmer lives?" Here the fun-loving Egyptians were enjoying a chance to pun: their word for "cattle" was pronounced similarly to the word for "office." Thus Isis had tricked Seth into admitting that the office of the father should indeed stay with his son! Seth then realized he had been tricked by Isis and related the whole story to the tribunal. Even Re-Harakhty had to admit that Seth had passed judgment on himself.

Seth did not give up on his struggle with Horus, however, and a series of fights and contests ensued, with no definite resolution until Osiris himself was asked his opinion of the whole matter. He threatened to unleash the dogs of the Underworld against the gods if they did not settle the dispute in favor of his son. Frightened by this prospect, they all agreed. Thus Horus became forever more the king of

Egypt. It has been noted that the image of Isis as an old woman stressed not only her widowhood but her wisdom.[36] Isis's quick changes reveal her cleverness and her magical powers. In the end, thanks to the intervention of both of his parents, Horus was successful. From the First Dynasty on, the Egyptian king's names are recorded with the symbol of the Horus falcon above them.

Egyptologists frequently define Isis as a mother goddess, the sister and wife of Osiris, and the mother of the young Horus. Period. However, it is obvious that Isis played other roles exceeding this domestic one in the funerary religion and royal mythology, roles that extended beyond the circle of deities and the king and had a profound impact on the lives of her common-born followers. Else why would her cult have endured longer than any other Egyptian deity's? Her later supreme power should not be ascribed to the embellishments of only a European cult following. Already in Egypt her magic was proverbial, and one of the myths that has survived has to do with Isis's power over even the supreme god Re. Isis was clever and knew that one way in which she might have power over Re was to learn his most secret of names.

It seems that Re was out strolling one night. As he was already aged, he drooled, and from the spittle of his mouth wetting the ground, Isis scooped up and formed a little mud into a snake. This snake then bit old Re, who in great pain begged his daughter Isis to use her magic to dispense with the fiery venom afflicting him. However, Isis told her father that she could do nothing for him unless she knew his secret name. This Re refused to divulge. In his agony he finally relented and told his secret name to Isis, who then was able to work her magic and quell his suffering. Thus Isis truly became Great of Magic or as some texts call her, The Greatest, for in gaining knowledge of Re's real name she knew everything.[37]

Isis's New Kingdom statues show her as a protector of the dead pharaoh and his remains. In this role, which she shared with her sister Nephthys as well as with Neith, with her arrows, and Selket, with her scorpion sting, she appears as a guardian on the corners of royal sarcophagi and canopic chests. The most famous expression of their roles is seen in the graceful girl-like freestanding figures guarding the gold-covered canopic shrine of Tutankhamun. With their outstretched arms these goddesses can be imagined saying: "I have come, I encircle my son (with my arms), Lord of the Two Lands Neb-Kheperu-Re, the justified one. I shall be his protection eternally as I have done for Osiris."[38]

A cult of Isis and of Osiris existed in the vicinity of the Great Sphinx of Giza, where he was known as Osiris, Lord of Rosetau, the vast Memphite cemetery extending from Giza to Saqqara that rivaled Abydos as his cult place from the beginning of the New Kingdom. Rosetau, serving the largest city in the country, constituted the preeminent cemeteries of the Egyptian Empire period, and were far more extensive than the now better known private cemeteries at Thebes. A temple to Osiris stood south of the Sphinx by the Eighteenth Dynasty, and inscriptions of this time include Isis as his wife, just as the Books of the Dead depict her at his side. Stelae from here now show her wearing the headdress of Hathor, and one depicts her seated within a kiosk supported by columns with Hathor head capitals. Thus Isis's followers borrowed the iconography of the other powerful goddess to give Isis extra prestige. Isis is named in the inscriptions as the Great One and Divine Mother.[39] Perhaps it was because of her well-known role as protective guardian of the dead that a temple to Isis came to be constructed in the Twenty-first Dynasty near the base of the Great Pyramid of Giza, using the site of the mortuary temple of one of smaller pyramids built for one of King Khufu's queens in an area that had grown to become a well-used cemetery for all classes of people. By the Late Period Isis is known at Giza as the Mistress of the Pyramid and thus is associated with the grandest edifice in the land.[40]

The primary cult temple to Osiris had stood at the sacred old royal burial ground of Abydos since at least the Middle Kingdom, and to this great pilgrimage area Seti I of the Nineteenth Dynasty added a magnificent temple with seven large vaulted shrines dedicated to major gods of his empire.[41] Among these were two goddesses, Mut and Isis, each present as members of their great triads. Isis is here called The Great, Mother of God, and Mistress of Heaven. The cult of Isis and Osiris continued at Abydos for another thousand years at least. This same king supplied the route to the goldfields in the eastern desert with wells and a temple, which was known as the Well of Seti. Here Isis, along with other great gods, had a cult statue in the inner sanctum.

Isis's inclusion in the Heliopolitan Ennead and her presence in temples outside Amun cult centers are testimony to her importance during the New Kingdom, which saw her as a source of strength, good health, and solace for the living as well. She also appears more and more frequently in the sun bark instead of Hathor and in roles such as the official Welcomer to the West of deceased worthies in the tombs of the later New Kingdom, thus again encroaching on Hathor's domain, even though both goddesses remain associated with funeral rites.

Isis had cult places at several other Egyptian towns as well. Private monuments attest to women serving as songstresses in her cult at the capital city of Memphis and at the village of artisans near the Valley of the Kings in Thebes during the Nineteenth Dynasty.[42] Isis also merged with other prominent goddesses such as Hathor, Mut, and the primeval Nekhbet of El-Kab as well as Neith at Sais. During the last millennium B.C. the city of Busiris was an important cult center for the Osiris-Isis religion, as it had been for Neith. It was one of the mythological sites of Osiris's tribunal, and here a great festival of Isis was held during which animals were sacrificed and crowds of worshipers beat their breasts in mourning rites.[43]

Isis's popularity can also be seen in love charms of the period, which relate her to the typical woman. For instance, charms have survived which promise to make a woman love a man as much as Isis loved Osiris, or, if the pursued lady in question was already married, to hate her husband like Isis hated Seth.[44] There were magical amulets connected with Isis as well. One, called the knot of Isis, or *tyet,* is invariably produced in a reddish semiprecious stone, jasper, and may actually be meant to represent a sanitary towel: it is a folded cloth that perhaps is meant to appear soaked with the goddess's blood. Feminist spiritualists credit menstruation with female creativity and power, and Spell 156 in the Book of the Dead speaks of the power of Isis's blood, which can provide general protection for the deceased, and the *tyet* is usually found among the mummy's wrappings, often at the deceased's throat:[45]

> Spell for a *tyet*-amulet of red jasper:
> Words to be said by [name]
> You have [your] blood, Isis.
> You have [your] effectiveness, Isis.
> You have [your] magic, Isis.
> The amulet is a protection of this Great One,
> guarding against the one who would do him harm.

Jan Bergman has drawn attention to Isis's role in relation to the concept of destiny, both for individuals and, perhaps originally, for Egypt.[46] This relates to Isis as Sothis-Sirius, the Dog Star, who announced the rise of the Nile and thereby the beginning of the new year. New Year's Day, which was called the birthday of Isis, is always a time of predicting what lies ahead, and Isis is actually called Year in some late texts. From at least the Middle Kingdom, gods were understood by the Egyptians to have an active role in people's destinies. The Seven Hathors proclaimed the fortunes of newborns in later tales, but one story from the Middle Kingdom that reflects on a historical event of the late Old Kingdom shows that Isis, too, pronounced the destiny of the new born.

The famous tale is found in the anthology of Papyrus Westcar from the Middle Kingdom.[47] In this tale, Isis and Nephthys, along with Heket, the goddess of childbirth, act as emergency midwives while disguised as a traveling band of entertainers. The children (triplets) who they help to deliver are future kings of Egypt, although the parents are not of royal blood. Isis calls out the names of each child as he emerges into her arms. Thus she seems responsible for predicting what was entirely unexpected, and perhaps she should be understood as decreeing this turn of events. In the famous Tale of Sinuhe, an Egyptian courtier of the early Twelfth Dynasty blames his precipitous flight from Egypt on fate decreed by a god.[48] Wen-Amun of the Twenty-first Dynasty prayed to Amun, whose cult he served, for a fifty years' addition to his fate. Thus, as Bergman suggests, Isis may early have shared this divine ability to prolong human life just as she received special powers when she tricked Re into divulging his secret name.[49] Thus it is not surprising to find later texts calling Isis "Mistress of life, ruler of fate and destiny." Isis's magic and its effectiveness in protecting the worthy deceased who owned a copy of the Book of the Dead is recalled in its chapter 69: "My son and his mother Isis protected me from my male enemies and my female enemies who were doing all kinds of evil and bad things against me." In Spell 151, Isis herself speaks to reassure the deceased:

> I have come that I may be your magical protection.
> I give breath to your nose, even the north wind that came
>   forth from Atum to your nose.
> I have caused that you exist as a god with your enemies
>   having fallen under your sandals.

You have been vindicated in the sky, so your limbs might
    be powerful among the gods.

Later we will see that this ability to overcome destiny made Isis especially appealing to people in the larger world.

Isis's power to protect the living, indeed all of Egypt itself, is probably signified by having her major shrine on the island of Philae at Egypt's southern border. In this way she protected Egypt from invasion from the south. Isis's cult buildings cover one quarter of the island and can be traced back to the Twenty-fifth Dynasty (reign of Taharqa, 690–664), but most likely her cult was established there at an earlier date. Nearby, the smaller island of Biggeh was dedicated to Osiris, and one tradition at least considered it his burial place. Low-lying, this island was often covered by the inundation and then reemerged, like the first hillock from the waters of chaos at the first moment of creation. Her size, more than twice that of Osiris, in surviving statues of the Egyptian Late period, where she enfolds her mummified spouse with her giant wings, can leave no doubt, however, who has become the stronger, more impressive deity.

Spell 142 in a late version of the Book of the Dead enumerates Isis's many identities, calling her The Great, Mother of the God, the Divine, Daughter of Nut, Great of Magic, and Possessor of Magical Protection. She is linked with many towns: Assiut, Koptos, Akhmim, Abydos, Pe, and Dep and all the cardinal points: "Isis in all her Manifestations, . . . Isis in all her Aspects." Similarly, the hymns written to honor her at Philae identify her with other major goddesses, whose powers she had absorbed to become one "whose power is unequaled in Heaven and on earth."[50]

Scorpions and their venom were a constant nuisance in ancient Egypt. A famous stela dating to the Late Period contains the story of Isis and the Seven Scorpions. These feared creatures guarded Isis when she was hiding in the delta marshlands with her small son. After traveling many miles one day, this odd entourage stopped at a house to find rest but was refused by the housewife, who did not take kindly to letting into her domicile seven scorpions. So Isis traveled into the town and found another home whose mistress did receive her in a friendly manner. Her scorpion friends were annoyed with the first woman, however, and decided to collect all their venom on the sting of one of them to give him sevenfold power. This scorpion then returned to the first house, crawled under the door, and stung the son of the family, who became very ill. His frantic mother desperately ran around the town asking for help for her sick child. Isis decided to help her and laid her hands on the stricken child, calling on the poison to leave him. Predictably, that child lived, and because of her success, for centuries after Egyptians who were stung by scorpions made a poultice of barley bread to draw the poison from the wound and uttered the name of Isis, Mistress of Magic and Speaker of Spells.[51]

Isis's magical ability to rescue the afflicted is one example of her important role as a savior goddess. This totally human-appearing deity successfully bridges the gulf between divine and human beings. She is much more personable and sympathetic than most Egyptian deities and obviously was concerned for the welfare, not only of her husband and son, but also of other people. From what classical authors such as Plutarch have written, concern for consoling people and holding out hope to those who had suffered trials and misfortunes was one of this goddess's characteristics. The popular understanding of her as a deity who cared and did not stand aloof from human suffering, a goddess who extended her hand and her power to save humans from ill, a "savior goddess," as Bleeker has termed her, probably helped in large part to increase the number of her adherents.[52]

There is no doubt that Isis became a major deity for the Egyptians of the last millennium B.C. Under the Thirtieth and last native dynasty (the Nectanebos), a great Iseum was built in the delta at a site now known as Behbeit el-Hagar. This was a huge granite temple, beautifully engraved with fine relief art, which today is a sad toppled ruin, stripped of much of its wall scenes. This last dynasty also built for Isis on Philae at the southern border, near the first cataract of the Nile, one of the most delightful of ancient sites in Egypt, so that at both ends of Egypt's Nile valley the great goddess could extend protection and receive worship.

King Nectanebo of the Thirtieth Dynasty left a temple on Philae, but most of the buildings still standing there were constructed by the Ptolemaic Dynasty (Cleopatra's family). Because each of these huge temples took centuries to build and decorate, they were finished under the Roman emperors, who seized Egypt on the death of Cleopatra, last of the Ptolemies and seventh of her name, in 30 B.C.

Figure 29. Isis's Temple of Philae. Photo by L. H. Lesko.

While the largest temple on Philae is dedicated to Isis, there are also shrines to Imhotep, the healing god, and to Hathor, and there are chapels to some local Nubian deities as well. Today this sacred island is forever submerged under the waters of Lake Nasser. Indeed, Philae was half-submerged for most of the twentieth century, due to the building of the first Aswan Dam. Faced with its total disappearance once the new High Dam at Aswan was completed, modern technology and UNESCO funding rescued the site by removing all of the ancient buildings, almost magically, and reassembling them on higher ground, on the island of Agilqiyya near their original setting. In time, perhaps, the landscape here will resemble the original Philae, but when we read the descriptions of Amelia B. Edwards or Pierre Loti, who visited the site in the nineteenth century, we cannot but feel that some of the ancient mystique has been forever lost:

> The approach from the water is quite the most beautiful. Seen from the level of a small boat, the island, with its palms, its colonnades, its pylons, seems to rise out of the river like a mirage. Piled rocks frame it on either side, and purple

mountains close up the distance. As the boat glides nearer between glistening boulders, those sculptured towers rise higher and ever higher against the sky.[53]

The visitor ascends a steep bank to find herself at the lower end of a long and unusual courtyard flanked on the east and west by covered colonnades of differing length. On the west thirty-one columns display varied capitals of rich ornamentation, and on the east a smaller number serve as an arcade to cell-like rooms.

> The twin towers of the propylon, standing out in sharp unbroken lines against the sky and covered with colossal sculptures, are as perfect, or very nearly as perfect, as in the days of the Ptolemies who built them. And now we catch glimpses of an inner court, of a second propylon, of a pillared portico beyond; while, looking up to the colossal bas-reliefs above our heads, we see the usual mystic forms of kings and deities, crowned, enthroned, worshipping and worshipped.[54]

Today's visitor has an advantage over Miss Edwards, however, if she goes at night and visits the temple lit so sensitively for the *son et lumière*. Now each carved detail of cornice, capital, and relief stands boldly forth to win one's admiration. The intricacy of the carving and the architectural design thus revealed is breathtaking. The pattern, richer here than at earlier pharaonic temples, amazes and delights the eye. From the distance, over the dark, placid waters of the lake, the island glows in its floodlights and seems, again, a mirage—a fantasy, or the primeval islet risen from the waters of Nun. Aswan, drenched in sun, bougainvillea, and roses, is the most charming region of Egypt, and nearby Isis's Philae remains the most enchanted isle of the Nile.

As mentioned, the ancients believed that Osiris's tomb was located on the nearby island of Biggeh, and texts tell of the journeys that Isis made to look after his tomb. Every tenth day, which concluded the Egyptian week, was a holy day of obligation, a day to honor one's ancestors and visit the burial places of one's family members. Thus every tenth day Isis conducted rites at Osiris's tomb and supplied him with offerings. It was also on this island of Biggeh, where Isis was said to live in a sacred mound, that she poured out the inundation that revived Egypt, "making all people and green plants grow," and it was here that Osiris became rejuvenated.[55] It would seem the ancients took pity on Isis, the widow, and to assuage her loneliness gave her here at Philae, late in her story, a companion in the form of Arensnuphis, an obscure god who also has a temple on the island's south end.

This great mother goddess seems to have entranced immigrants to Egypt. When the merchant princes of the delta city of Sais came to rule over the land of Egypt in the sixth century B.C., they opened up large fertile areas of the country to foreign investment and to settlement by desirable foreigners, namely Greeks, who founded many cities in the Fayum district and in the delta. The Greeks found the image of the divine mother Isis very similar to their own Demeter, who also lost, searched for, and mourned a family member and was closely associated with the fertility of the earth. They associated Osiris with their Dionysus. However, the Egyptian divinities seem to have had even more appeal to these immigrant Greeks than their own Hellenic cults, probably because the Egyptians believed so strongly in a life after death. Greek religions were vague on this subject and, at best, did not hold out anything too appealing as the fate of the dead. The Greeks probably saw that their Egyptian neighbors were happily confident of eternal life, and thus they too came flocking to the Egyptian religious shrines and were able to embrace Isis and Osiris easily because they were always depicted in human form. Greeks still in their homeland heard about Isis too, of course.

Egyptian merchant traders carried her cult abroad wherever they went, just as centuries before Egyptians trading with Lebanon had brought along Hathor and built a shrine for her at Byblos. The transplanted cults were led by Egyptian priests who introduced Egyptian books and the trappings so familiar from the ritual and cults in their homelands: shaven heads, white linen robes, incense, the sistrum, and sacred water from the Nile.

The appeal of Isis to foreigners was evident in her following, not only among the Greek communities in Egypt, but in the acceptance of her cult in Greece itself. In the fourth century B.C. Isis had a cult place at Piraeus, Athens' harbor city, whence it spread to the Greek islands as well.

Alexander the Great conquered Egypt in 332 B.C. in his quest for world empire. Although he died prematurely, his success had a major impact on society: now people of the ancient Mediterranean world belonged to something greater than the sum of its parts, as old city-states vanished, swept up in the tide of internationalism that characterized this new age. Meanwhile, in Egypt, Alexander the Great's conquest was followed by three hundred years of rule by a foreign dynasty, the Ptolemies, descended from one of his Macedonian generals who divided Alexander's vast empire among themselves. The empire that Alexander had forged (it spread from Macedonia in today's northern Greece east to India) transcended national states and induced in its people a sense of cohesion, a role in a greater entity that transcended the old boundaries of their homelands. Along with the idea of being citizens in this new world, the concept of a ruling divine reason and a universal spiritual heritage was introduced. Later this view led Plutarch to argue that the gods of Egypt should be preserved, as they did not serve the Egyptians only but were part of the common heritage of mankind.

The military and the merchants now crossed geographic boundaries as never before, and migrations of individuals and private families was common too in the Hellenistic age. Separated from their homes, such people found themselves quite alone. Old social ties were lost, and the restraints of tradition vanished. *Individualism* was the keyword of the age; the nuclear family rather than the extended family of the old country had come to the fore.[56] New anxieties undoubtedly attended this "aloneness," and subsequently Oriental cults came to Europe and were well received because they seemed to be more sympathetic and comforting to those who needed protection and help.

Chief among these "new" deities for Europeans was Isis. Her cult spread dramatically and was especially attractive to women. She was a goddess who befriended women, who promoted marriage (she is credited with the very idea of the institution of marriage), and who preached the gospel of close family ties and respect among members of the new nuclear family. Women could identify with her struggle to raise her son alone and admired her eternal love for her husband. Many people in antiquity lost their mothers at a young age from disease or the complications of childbirth. Thus an emptiness, a longing for a mother figure in their lives, was fulfilled by contact with beneficent deities like Isis.[57]

Under the Ptolemies, whose political influence and trading depots were widespread in the eastern Mediterranean, Isis cults sprang up at important ports from Rhodes to Corinth, and even, some say, over a wider area from Bactria to Thessaly. The earliest Hellenistic coins from Halicarnassus, Rhodes, and Myndos bear the likeness of Isis, as do those of Egypt's Alexandria. As Isis traveled she took on attributes of other goddesses native in these lands, and the Europeans in Egypt were quick to identify the prominent Egyptian gods they encountered with ones they and their ancestors had worshiped in their homelands. Thus both Herodotus and Diodorus Siculus, who wrote more than three hundred years later, in the first century B.C., identified Isis with Demeter, the Greek goddess of the harvest. Indeed, texts of this Ptolemaic period refer to Isis's discovery of grain, and one festival in her honor saw her faithful marching in procession holding sheaves of grain.

Isis became responsive to the concerns of the locals in her new cult places. For instance, in many waterfront communities around the Mediterranean Isis was hailed as Mistress of the Seas, and an important public festival of hers took place in March, at the beginning of each year's sailing season. A beautifully painted boat, loaded with offerings for the goddess, was launched crewless on the water and watched by crowds of faithful until it disappeared from view.[58]

Phoenician merchants carried the image of Isis and her cult westward to Carthage in North Africa (modern Tunisia), and in due course Spain received her too. From Greece and the Iberian Peninsula Isis's progress continued on the European continent with the expansion of Roman arms. The next six hundred years would take her as far north as the Rhine valley and even to Britain.

Along with her fusion with Demeter and even with the Asiatic Artemis, Isis's cult was brought into the realm of a mystery religion. This was not, as far as is known, originally part of her cult in Egypt; some would disagree, but there has not been enough earlier Egyptian evidence to settle the matter.[59] Because the Hellenistic rites were secret, little is known about the mysteries of initiation and acts of abstention and purification that the devout practiced. However, the Hellenistic mystery cult did build on some fundamental characteristics in place in Egypt at least one thousand years before: a professional priesthood, a regular ritual with music and dance, cult dramas, the use of sacred water from the Nile, shaved heads of priests, and pure white linen vestments, elaborate public processions, and incubation (sleeping overnight) on the temple's grounds, as well as the interpretation of one's dreams by temple personnel. It was hoped that the deity would appear to the incumbent who was seeking a cure from physical or psychological distress. Isis's ability to cure was no doubt tied to her reputed great magical powers.

Back in Egypt, the Ptolemies, ruling from their new seacoast capital of Alexandria, tried to placate the subjected native population with a building program throughout the country, begun under Ptolemy II (284–246 B.C.), of enormous temples to local Egyptian deities intricately decorated with texts and relief scenes. The immense majesty of Isis was clearly reflected in a colossal statue of her that was erected at Alexandria under the Ptolemies and fished out of the waters off Fort Kait Bey in the 1960s. It must have stood in the royal quarter, which today is underwater. A major temple to Isis and Serapis was, of course, located in this new capital city. Isis, patron of Alexandria, was named Isis Pelagia or Isis Pharos, in connection with its famous lighthouse and her concern for sailors. Queen Arsinoe II, called Philadelphia because she married her brother Ptolemy II, identified herself with this goddess (Isis was married to *her* brother, Osiris) and did much to increase devotion to her cult.

The Ptolemaic building program included the magnificent Temple of Dendera, the old cult place of Hathor, where Hathor shares the iconography with Nut and some inscribed dedications with Isis, who has a smaller temple of her own in the precinct. The god Horus received a lavish new temple at Edfu, and Isis herself had several important temples scattered throughout Egypt, from Alexandria to Philae.

The hymns to Isis that were inscribed on the walls of the sanctuary of her temple at Philae are extremely important as very few earlier hymns to Isis have survived. For five hundred years Philae remained one of the major religious centers of Egypt and, indeed, the entire eastern Mediterranean, to which people made pilgrimages from as far away as Rome. It is clear from these Philae hymns, written so late in Egypt's ancient history, that typical, well-known, and age-old royal Egyptian phraseology is used to celebrate Isis, and thus the priestly composer was probably an Egyptian. Their publisher points out that these hymns were part of a long religious literary tradition that was even this late, and under foreign domination, still remarkably vital.[60]

Phrases in some of the hymns are familiar from much earlier epithets used for the chief queens of Egypt. Isis is addressed in one:

O Isis, the great, God's Mother, Lady of Philae
God's Wife, God's Adorer, and God's Hand
God's Mother and Great Royal Wife
Adornment and Lady of the Ornaments of the Palace
. . . who fills the palace with her beauty
Fragrance of the palace, Mistress of Joy
Who completes her course in the Divine Place . . .
Princess, great of praise, Lady of Charm
Whose face enjoys the trickling of fresh myrrh.[61]

All the above titles were used for the Great Royal Wife and the King's Daughter at least as early as the New Kingdom, fifteen hundred years before this hymn was written. Other hymns extol the roles of Isis:

Isis, giver of life, residing in the Sacred Mound, Satis, Lady
    of Biggeh,
She is the one who pours out
the inundation
That makes all people live and green plants grow,
Who provides divine offerings for the gods,
And invocation-offerings for the Transfigured Ones
(the dead) . . .
She is the Lady of Heaven, Earth, and the Netherworld
Having brought them into existence through what
her heart conceived and her hands created
She is the Ba that is in every city,
Watching over her son Horus and her brother Osiris.[62]

Here Isis is credited with being the Creator of All—heaven, earth, and the hereafter. Again, as we saw with the goddess Neith, the Egyptian priests of a goddess had no hesitation in claiming preeminence for her and saw no difficulty in having a female take on the role of Creator.

Hymn 5 calls Isis "Mightier than the mighty, stronger than the strong," and another evocation, carved during the Roman period at Philae on a wall of the hypostyle hall there spells out the goddess's powers even further:

Mighty one, foremost of the goddesses
Ruler in Heaven, Queen on Earth
Sun-goddess in the circuit of the sun-disc;
Mistress of battle, Montu (war god) of combat,
One to whom one cries out on the day of encounter;
Mighty protectress without her equal,
Who saves all those she loves on the battlefield;
Whatever comes forth from her mouth is accomplished
    immediately
All the gods are under her command;
Great of Magic when she is in the palace,
Great one upon whose command the King gloriously
    appears
on the throne.[63]

Here, as this hymn's publisher, Louis V. Žabkar, pointed out, the mythological and "historical" roles of the goddess are combined. From the start, Isis is given precedence. Isis is "described as a supreme deity, who gives orders to the gods and decides the destinies of the kingly office." She is given precedence by being proclaimed, in Hymn 8, the First Born of Nut. In Hymn 5 she is equated with Sekhmet and even the old male war god of Thebes, Montu, but if she is a war goddess she is one "who saves all those she loves on the battlefield." Žabkar pointed out that to save those she loves, "Isis does not hesitate to step into the thickness of the battle itself."[64] This was also a role associated with her "living spouse," Serapis, provided her by the Ptolemies, so it is surprising to find Isis active on the field of battle.

Isis had reached Italy through Italian merchants who carried her cult from Delos to Compania some time during the Republic. Her cult began modestly, but her attraction was significant, and participants in her cult came from all walks of life and levels of society: women, slaves, and soldiers as well as high municipal officials and members of the imperial family.[65] Even without official imperial sanction, Romans carried her cults with them as they expanded their empire and settled along major rivers and trade routes throughout Europe. Thus the ruins of major temples to Isis are found from Hungary to northern England. The archaeological maps of Spain, Italy, Germany, France, and England are sprinkled with artifacts of the Egyptian cults.[66] In her wanderings far from Egypt, Isis was not alone. Accompanying her during the Roman period were a form of her child, Horus, then called Harpocrates; Anubis, the dog-headed guardian of the dead; Osiris, her brother, sometimes even her ancestor, the god Atum; and a new syncretistic deity invented by the Ptolemies, Serapis, a combination of Osiris and Zeus. In the company of Serapis, Isis entered the Greek pantheon and received a place beside the Olympians.

Serapis also was touted as a god of healing, and it was further claimed that he would protect soldiers from death on the battlefield. However, he seems to have failed the Ptolemaic Egyptian fleet, which was defeated by the Romans, and he slipped from favor in Egypt, where his cult had not had the wide appeal of Isis's. He had been created for export as another attempt to provide the widely dispersed realm of the Ptolemies an omnipotent male god with the appeal of Isis. However, Serapis, though he had cult priests in Greece, shared these with Isis, and he certainly never eclipsed his consort in popularity. Hers grew steadily; Isis became a truly universal goddess and the *only* deity to many of her faithful.

The best-preserved Roman temple to Isis is, as one might expect, at Pompeii. This is not a large structure, although scholars estimate that at least two thousand people in this town worshiped the goddess. Surrounded by a high wall, to keep it from the eyes of the uninitiated, the little temple was built on a high platform approached by a flight of steps, which are flanked by at least one pair of sphinxes. Palm trees grew nearby, and the sacred ibis had free run of the grounds. On the property was a cistern holding Nile water, and there were also cells for the priests, who are portrayed wearing white garments. The paintings that once decorated the cult place are now on display in the Naples Museum of Archaeology, and a fresco from the nearby town of Herculaneum portrays a sanctuary of Isis in which both male and female priests officiate. The paintings and surviving statues from the towns buried by Vesuvius depict Isis clothed in the flowing dress of the first century with a noticeable knot just under her breast. Her hair is curled, covered partly by a veil, and she sometimes wears dangling earrings, just like any well-dressed Roman matron. In one hand might be a jug for sacred Nile water or, as sometimes indicated by its shape, for her own milk, and in the other the ancient cult instrument of the bronze sistrum rattle. Isis is depicted with either a small crescent moon or a lotus on her brow, and one painting presents her with the sacred cobra in her hands.[67] A surviving relief sculpture shows her priestess managing a cobra as she walks in a procession.[68]

The best opportunity to gain some insight into the mysteries of Isis, which may not predate the Ptolemaic dynasty, comes through *The Metamorphoses, or The Golden Ass,* by Apuleius, a Roman born in North Africa (ca. 125 A.D.) and educated at Carthage and Athens. The novel relates the adventures of Lucius, who through the misuse of a magical unguent was changed into a donkey.[69] In such a form he suffered indignities and hardships but finally was released from his torments by Isis, who appears to him as a vision of great beauty and power. At her direction he attended her festival in Corinth's port Cenchrae, where Isis's temple is now underwater. There Lucius, as instructed by Isis, gobbled up a wreath of roses carried by a priest in her sacred procession which promptly transformed him back into his human form. Consequently, he became devoted to Isis and eventually was initiated into the mysteries of her cult. Although he could not divulge the wisdom acquired by initiation, Lucius explains that the initiation took place at night and was "like a voluntary death and a difficult restoration to health."[70] An initiate had to be called by the goddess, and Isis demanded abstinence from Lucius. He had to fast ten days, rejecting meat and wine, before he could undergo his first initiation. As a result of their new status, the initiated would be "reborn" and brought by Isis into salvation in a realm where beauty and goodness prevail.

Isis, Serapis, and their entourage had became popular with the Romans, probably because of the following Isis had among the Greeks. Their cults had come to Rome already during the Republic. The dictator Sulla (138–78 B.C.) is credited with repairs to the temple of Isis Fortuna. In the time of Julius Caesar, Cleopatra's presence at Rome excited anti-Egyptian sentiments, which were exacerbated when the Roman knight Decius Mundus masqueraded as the god Anubis and raped a respectable and gullible noble Roman matron in the Isis temple on the Capitoline Hill.[71] The closing of that temple and the crucifixion of Isis's priests was the result, but soon this cult, which was actually quite puritanical, proved too popular and appealing to be denied, and it appeared again in Rome, where it lasted for at least four more centuries. Some emperors found excuses for persecuting the cult because it was not in their interest to let their people be diverted from the imperial cult, which called on everyone to swear absolute allegiance to the emperor. However, these times of persecution were short compared to the long tenure Isis enjoyed at Rome, where even some emperors, such as Otho, were among her initiates. Later, Hadrian, who had visited Egypt and who is credited with buildings on Philae, had constructed at his palace at Tivoli outside of Rome a miniature Egypt in an extensive garden with many sculptures depicting Isis. Today there is a remarkable statue in the Vatican's collection, a Janus-like sculptured head found at Tivoli, where a goddess has the face of Isis backed by a cow's head, presumably showing the syncretism between Hathor and Isis that had become well established by this time.[72]

It seems likely that the emperors were attracted to the idea of divine kingship, always associated with Egypt's pharaohs. Now the Caesars had themselves portrayed in the traditional *nemes* headdress and short kilt of Egypt's kings, and the imperial cult of the Caesars could easily assimilate Egyptian features too. For instance, the more eccentric emperors, such as Caligula, who dedicated a large temple to Isis, claimed divinity for their own persons. To Rome were even brought soaring obelisks, plucked by the Caesars from Egypt's temples, to adorn the Iseum Campetre. In the second century A.D., the emperor Hadrian still recalled Isis's early Egyptian equation with the star Sothis by commissioning a sculpture of Isis-Sothis-Demeter with the goddess wearing a lotus lily on her brow, recalling her power over the Nile flood.[73]

The later Roman emperors seem to have become convinced of the value of Isis's partner Serapis to their armies, and from Antoninus Pius onward, the emperors adopted the concept of a god who not only protected their soldiers but also brought them victories. As a reflection of this, there survive thousands of coins minted by the later emperors bearing the images of Serapis and other Egyptian deities until late into the fourth century.

Isis probably represented many things to her followers, but one still must ask just what it was that made Isis so universally acceptable, so enthusiastically received by a world that knew many deities and other mother goddesses. Certainly Isis's ability to promise everlasting life to all who lived out their lives following the tenets of her religion would have drawn many, both men and women and people of all classes, to her cult, just as the afflicted flocked to her sanctuaries for cures.

Sharon Heyob believed women "sought Isis out most eagerly to fill a need which the Greek and Roman religions failed to fill."[74] The "humanity" and goodness of Isis was, if anything, embellished in her last centuries. For instance, in the Roman period Isis's story had become embellished with tales of Osiris's infidelity with her sister Nepthys and Isis's adoption of their love child, Anubis. Thus Isis demonstrated forgiveness, generosity of heart, and deep family loyalty. Certainly, Isis of Roman times was extremely appealing to women and to men of all levels of society. Her greatest attraction, however, was probably her promise of salvation, both in this life and in the life beyond the grave.

It has also been argued that Isis's followers were most impressed by her ability to rise up against awesome, all-powerful, frightening Destiny, much feared by the Greeks and Romans, and to assure her people that she had conquered it.[75] Isis subjugated the force that had kept other deities and certainly human beings powerless in its grasp as long as anyone could remember. Now, at last, a goddess came forth who proclaimed, "I have conquered Destiny," as Isis does in the famous Aretalogy (or praise text) from Kyme (see below). Isis was victorious over fate and herself assumed the role of Destiny. Thus in the *Golden Ass*, Isis is characterized as "Providence who supplants blind Fortune." And she was also understood as victorious over fate when she is called Isis Victrix by the Romans.

Through initiation into her mysteries, such as Lucius endured, the initiate was saved, would begin a new life in which he or she shared the fate of this goddess and, even in death, would be spared from the nothingness for which other mortals were destined. The sacred rites of Isis meant peace for the deceased, but more than this, Isis's ability to initiate and liberate the *living* person was probably a new feature of the Hellenistic age, an aspect unknown, or at least undocumented, for earlier ages in pharaonic Egypt. Isis, as exemplified by those few lines in the Eber's Medical Papyrus of the New Kingdom, was long before acknowledged to have had the ability to alter people's "destiny": "You should know that I and I alone have the power to prolong your life beyond the bounds appointed as your fate."[76] It surely was this power over bleak and frightening Destiny, this hope in a new and more blissful life to come, or a prolonged life, as well as a blessed hereafter, that Isis could ensure to those who believed in her and endured her prescribed initiations. Such powers called many from all over the ancient world to her.[77]

There are a number of pieces of Roman literature that reflect the devotion of her followers. Besides *The Metamorphosis* by Apuleius, another famous novel, Xenophon of Ephesus's *Ephesian Tale*, which is something of an ancient *Perils of Pauline*, describes the ideal of chastity and marital fidelity and loyalty to children that Isis inspired in her flock.[78] Indeed, the Isis aretalogies credit Isis with the creation of the institution of marriage. Isis probably injected a new morality into the Roman Empire. Apparently betrothals were celebrated in the Temple of Isis and a Roman couple who wished to be married would often go before her altar to plight their troth.[79] Women held the positions of priestess and basket carrier in her cult, even if high priests were generally men. Wealthy Roman matrons traveled all the way to Aswan on Egypt's southern border, an incredibly long and difficult pilgrimage in that time, to visit Isis's sacred shrine on the island of Philae whence they brought back holy water of the Nile, so profound was their reverence for this goddess.[80]

In the Greek tradition, there are texts, called aretalogies, that are not much more than lists proclaiming the virtues of deities, usually put in the first person, that is, written as if the deity is speaking about herself. This speech may have had Egyptian origins, as such brief statements are encountered as early as the Coffin Texts, where Isis, in Spell 148, says of herself: "I am Isis, one more spirit-like and august than the gods."

The most complete body of late aretalogics of Isis comes from Kyme but makes the claim that its text was copied from a stela in Egypt's ancient city of Memphis which had stood before its temple of Hephaestus, the Egyptian god Ptah. This would have been a major temple, as Memphis was the ancient capital city and chief cult place of Ptah. In book 2, line 176, of his *Histories* Herodotus mentions a temple to Isis at this ancient capital city. It would have been odd had she not had a cult there, but Žabkar was suspicious of this claim. He thought that no Egyptian original would have existed; that the Aretalogy of Kyme was originally composed in Greek.[81] However, because the entire corpus of the Isis hymns was engraved on the walls of Philae before the Greek composition of the Aretalogy, he felt that Philae provided the source or inspiration for the Greek writer of the Aretalogy, which borrows some Egyptian elements.

Certainly, there are Greek allusions too, as in using Greek rather than Egyptian names for some of the gods and perhaps in the emphasis on seamanship and in the allusion to the beneficial properties of rain. In Egypt rain is often destructive, but it also causes the land to become fertile. The great Nile is not alluded to, although the ancient association of Isis with Sothis is made. The two types of Egyptian scripts, sacred and secular, are mentioned, and the Hathoric role of the goddess in the sun's bark is certainly Egyptian. Like the Egyptian goddess Maat, Isis is credited as a lawgiver, and the importance of the oath is expounded—all hearkening back to traditional Egyptian values epitomized by Maat, whose role Isis is assuming, as she has assumed Hathor's. Certainly Isis's concerns for marriage, love between husband and wife, and closeness between parents and children would have been hers for millennia.

The Greek authorship of the Aretology is hinted at also by the concern shown Greeks and barbarians (Egyptian texts rarely acknowledged any other peoples except as enemies). It is interesting to note that Isis is called Mistress of War, an unusual epithet for her but also found in one of the Philae hymns, where she is equated with Montu, the Egyptian war god. Does this suggest that Isis has been credited with attributes of foreign goddesses like Athena, or is she assuming one of the identities of the Egyptian Neith or Sekhmet in the Aretalogy?

The Isis Aretalogy has been known much longer than her hymns at Philae and thus remains the major piece of literature associated with her. The version that follows here dates to the Ptolemaic period. It is the standard version and the only complete one of the so-called M-text.

> I am Isis, ruler of every land
> I was taught by Hermes (Thoth), and with Hermes devised
> letters, both hieroglyphic and demotic, that all might not
> be written with the same.
> I gave laws to mankind and ordained what no one can
> change
> I am the eldest daughter of Kronos
> I am the wife and sister of King Osiris
> I am the one who discovered wheat for mankind

I am the mother of King Horus
I am the one who rises in the Dog-star
I am the one called Goddess by women
For me was built the city of Bubastis
I separated the earth from the Heaven
I showed the paths of the stars
I regulated the course of the sun and the moon
I devised the activities of seamanship
I made what is right strong
I brought together woman and man
I assigned to women to bring into light of day their infants
  in the tenth month
I ordained that parents should be loved by children
I imposed punishment upon those unkindly disposed
  toward their parents
I with my brother Osiris put an end to cannibalism
I taught men the initiation into mysteries
I instructed them to revere images of the gods
I established the sacred cult places of the gods
I abolished the rules of the tyrants
I put an end to murders
I compelled women to be loved by men
I made the right stronger than gold and silver
I ordained that the true should be considered good
I devised marriage contracts
I assigned to Greeks and barbarians their languages
I made the good and the bad to be distinguished by nature
I made that nothing should be more fearful than an oath
I have delivered him who unjustly plots against others into
  the hands of the one against whom he plotted
I impose retribution upon those who do injustice
I decreed that mercy be shown to suppliants
I honor those who justly defend themselves
With me the right has power
I am the mistress of rivers and winds and sea
No one is honored without my consent
I am the Mistress of War
I am the Mistress of the thunderbolt

I calm the sea and make it surge
I am in the rays of the sun
I attend the sun in its journey
What I decree, that is also accomplished
All yield to me
I set free those who are in bonds
I am the Mistress of seamanship
I make the navigable un-navigable, whenever I so decide
I founded enclosure walls of the cities
I am called the Lawgiver
I brought up islands out of the depths into the light
I am the Mistress of rain
I conquer Destiny
Destiny obeys me
Hail, O Egypt, that nourished me![82]

Isis here claims sovereignty over the entire world but does not forget her Egyptian roots. She clearly identifies herself as a deity for women ("I am the one called Goddess by women"), and she pays special attention to the concerns of women, taking credit for promoting the institution of marriage and love between women and men; setting the gestation period of pregnancy; and demanding love and respect in children for their parents. In another aretalogy she goes so far as to say she has made the power of women equal to that of men.[83] Surely Ross Kraemer is correct to believe that Isis's religion was "more favorable to women than any other."[84]

Isis's references to delivering justice and attending the sun in its journey reflect ancient roles of major Egyptian goddesses, but to these are added explicit claims of power that go beyond the vaguer "Mistress of Heaven, Mistress of All the Gods" titles known from earlier history. With the sparse preservation of earlier Egyptian documents, however, it is difficult to know just what attributes were a late addition.

Plutarch, whose mistress was a priestess of Isis, described Isis as the fruit-bearing power in both the earth and the moon. Thus, toward the end of her story, Isis assumed the capacities not only of other goddesses but also of venerable Egyptian gods such as Geb and Thoth. She outlasted once-mighty Amun and Re. At the end of their history, the

Egyptians were willing to restore to the mother goddess the powers that the Old Kingdom and later theologians had denied her.

Known now as She of Many Names and Many Forms, Isis might be said to have crossed all boundaries and embraced devout people from many lands and many faiths whose goddesses merged with her, now making Isis the supreme saving goddess of all humanity. The most significant statements are those surely in which Isis expresses her control of Destiny. Her ability to affect fortune, to alter fate, was highly regarded and is believed to have been of most importance in attracting a following. These claims in the Aretalogy match Isis's proclamation in the *Metamorphoses* when the goddess says to Lucius: "I am here taking pity on your ills; I am here to give aid and solace. Cease then from fears and wailings, set aside your sadness; there is now dawning for you, through my providence, the day of salvation" (11.5). And later Lucius responds: "Thou in truth art the holy and eternal savior of the human race, ever beneficent in helping mortal men, and thou bringest the sweet love of a mother to the trials of the unfortunate" (11.25).[85]

Although Isis's cult appealed to people from all walks of life, including slaves, it required an outlay of funds to be an initiate. Thus slaves and freed persons had to have some income to join, and indeed Lucius seems to have become impoverished, although the sense is more in keeping with Jesus Christ's admonition: "Leave all you have and come follow me." Charity was also promoted by the Isis cults in the Roman Empire. Associations attached to her temple were formed to help needy parishioners but doubled as social clubs that held banquets and promoted good cheer among her celebrants. This concern for the needs of the individual in Isis's religion was shared by other popular Hellenistic cults.

Isis's powers of salvation was Egyptian in origin but carried over into the Hellenistic European world and won hearts far and wide. Isis was also a specialist in cures, a feature for which she was already famous in Egypt, where her temples, like those of Hathor and other deities, contained sanitoriums. She was later known as Isis Hygieia, or health personified and deified. At Athens Isis shared a temple with Asclepius, and incubation was practiced in both of their cults.[86] Serapis shared this concern with health and curing the infirm, and the two gods became renowned for their successes and earned good incomes for their sanctuaries through their healing fees.[87]

There is another feature of Isis, acknowledged in the Aretalogy of Kyme but not always given the credit it deserves. The eminent scholar of Egyptian religion J. Gwyn Griffiths draws attention to Isis's kindness and love. She is credited with bringing together men and women in sexual relationships that are the basis of family life, and as Griffith points out, she made sexual love "socially acceptable within the divinely ordained context of the family. . . . One might paraphrase this doctrine by saying that Isis is the goddess who shows to mankind that God is love." In allowing Eros to be part of the concept of divine love, the Isis theology hearkened back to ancient Egypt and the involvement not only of Isis but also of Hathor and other deities who offered erotic love as the means to immortality. Herein, as Griffith notes, "lies the main difference between the Isiac and Christian use of the term."[88]

From its beginning century, Christianity would have vied with this popular cult of Isis for the hearts and minds of men and women, and many scholars have suggested that the veneration of the Virgin Mary was a direct response to the competition from Holy Mother Isis.[89] Early Roman churches, such as Santa Maria Magiore, are built adjacent to the sites of Isis temples. Isis Bringer of the Crops has been identified at the Church of the Ara Coeli in Rome, and the Church of Santa Maria Navicella on top of the Caelian Hill marks the site of an earlier Iseum Metellinum.[90] Well-known festivals for the Madonna, still popular in Europe, doubtless replaced the public outpourings of devotion exhibited by Isis's ancient devotees, just as her image came to be worshiped as the Black Madonna.[91] It was not an easy transition, however. An emperor might convert to Christianity and decree, as Constantine did in 331, that all pagan temples be forever shut, but the popularity and power of this goddess is evidenced in the violence that attended her end. Her temples had to be destroyed, her statues smashed, her priests executed. And yet Isis survived in the hearts of many who could not easily be persuaded to give up on their beloved Divine Mother, Protector of the Family, Dispenser of Destiny, and Mistress of the World. All her many powers, over the seas, over the fields, and as promiser of eternal life for her faithful, had to be taken over by the Mother of Christ.

While many Roman portrayals of Isis show her with holy babe in arms, she is as also shown holding the cornucopia, or horn of plenty. Here too there are survivals. An image of a woman enthroned on an island of flowers, surrounded by trees and water and holding a

Figure 30. Statue of Isis and Osiris, Twenty-sixth Dynasty or later. Courtesy of the Walters Art Gallery, Baltimore.

cornucopia, appears on faience plates produced in Delft in the early eighteenth century. Perhaps the artist was portraying Mother Nature, but the origin of the image is surely an ancient goddess, whether Demeter or Isis (and these two did combine in the Roman world). Whether or not this figure of later European folk art is a direct descendant of the goddess of ancient Egypt,[92] we have seen that the Egyptian goddesses were worshiped for two-thirds of human history. They commanded the loyalty and devotion of kings and commoners alike, and men and women all over the civilized world looked to them for salvation. Both sexes served in their priesthoods and filled the ranks of the faithful. The goddesses Hathor and Isis represented the great natural phenomena—sun, moon, and stars, the fertility of the earth and mankind, the pleasures of love and family life—and worked the power of magic against gods and humans alike. They interceded in daily lives, found people mates, punished and cured, nourished the newborn and protected the dead, and brought about a blissful existence for those who deserved eternal life. They were always present, playing an important, decisive role in every stage of human life. Isis, however, went beyond all in her compassion and love. She was not aloof but both caring and powerful. She understood and she was needed. She was salvation.

$\mathcal{T}$EMPLES, THEIR RITUALS, AND THEIR CLERGY

When the stone towers and columned halls of the temples of Upper Egypt were first seen again by Western eyes in the eighteenth century, they were interpreted as palaces of the pharaohs. However, the ancient monarchs, like their subjects, lived in mud brick buildings with mostly wooden architectural elements. It was only the gods who were worthy of constructions that would last for eternity. There was thus a strict demarcation between the worlds of the sacred and profane, expressed by high walls and enduring stone edifices.

TEMPLES

The Egyptians customarily recycled materials, and their earlier temples were often used as quarries. Therefore, the temples that remain today are generally those built in the New Kingdom and later. Unlike the houses and palaces of the living, which have disintegrated down to their foundations, the temples of the later ages and the tombs (stone pyramids or rock-hewn sepulchers) are what dominate the ancient landscape today. Temples and tombs were meant to endure throughout eternity, and their names, for example, Mansion of Millions of Years, reflect this.

Large-scale architecture was a challenge embraced by the ancient Egyptians, and the magnitude of their constructions never fails to amaze the visitor, just as it was meant to impress the ancient devotee. Today the stone walls present a yellow or gray monotone to the viewer, but in antiquity they were much more colorful. Whitewashed walls emblazoned with scenes and inscriptions of hieroglyphs, all painted in primary colors, must have been dazzling, if not garish, when produced on such a large scale.

There were two types of temples, the cult center for a divinity that was usually located in or near a town and those connected with the tomb of the pharaoh and dedicated to his cult. These types of "funerary," or royal cult, temples survive from the Old Kingdom not only because they were built in stone like the pyramids to which they are adjacent but also because of their location in the desert, removed from the towns of the living and thus somewhat protected. While the structures affiliated with the royal cult have survived from the Old Kingdom, at least their foundations but sometimes almost in their entirety, as in the Valley Temple of Khafre at Giza, records survive for that early time also documenting cult temples of Ptah, Neith, Hathor, and Thoth, to name but a few deities. Temples in towns were likely torn down and rebuilt several times over the millennium, so the actual appearance of the Old Kingdom cult temple is not well understood. However, there is a good chance that most were not built in stone but in brick. Stone is not attested for town cult temples until the Middle Kingdom, even though it was the preferred building material for temples associated with the royal burial sites.

The Egyptian word for *temple* may be literally translated "divine hut," and the Egyptians of the archaic age (3100–2800) seem deliberately to have hearkened back to remote prehistory when contemplating the proper appearance of a house of god. While brick architecture was used on a large scale in Egypt since the First Dynasty, and this included temple building, some early representations, drawn on small objects, and some later interpretations, such as the stone funerary buildings at Zoser's step pyramid, suggest features of the most primitive architecture—the reed or palm leaf booth, which since time immemorial had served to shelter human and beast. Although these apparently do not actually portray correctly the temples of gods in the protodynastic and early dynastic period, the lightweight shelter came to be thought of as the first, and thus the best, way to house a deity, commemorated forever more in the form of the naos, or tabernacle, that actually enclosed the divine image within the sanctuary.[1] Today in the countryside of Egypt one still can see the original type of reed fence plastered with mud forming walls and gateways. The loose frond ends were later interpreted in stone as the cavetto cornice topping the pure and sophisticated lines of imposing stone architecture. By the Middle Kingdom, if not before, this early architectural form was commonplace among the stone cult temples of Egypt.

First, however, came the grand but simply designed constructions of the kings and royal family of the Fourth Dynasty. Gigantic stones, great ashlar blocks of granite, perfectly finished and fitted, were used to create mammoth walls that could stand forever. The Valley Temple of Khafre is the best-preserved example, revealing walls devoid of ornamentation, the only inscriptions being on the door frames. Its floor was of alabaster, which can take a luminescent polish, and inside sat twenty-three identical stone statues of the king. The earliest stone temples of any size to be dedicated to gods survive today as ruins of the sun temples built near the royal pyramids of the Fifth Dynasty at Abu Sir. However, the Temple of Re at Heliopolis should have preceded these, and may actually be imitated by those at Abu Gurob in the desert west of Memphis. The sun temple, by its very nature, had to consist mainly of an open court, surrounded by a shadowy colonnade. A very large, flat altar stone in the form of four *hetep* ⌐▲⌐ hieroglyphs around a sun disk sat in the courtyard at the base of the gigantic sun icon, or benben—a squat obelisk on a podium.[2]

It is believed that major state cult temples at Memphis, the capital city, had already been built there in stone since the beginning of the historic age and would have been constantly enlarged and improved on by each king, just as was done (and clearly traceable) later in the Middle and New kingdoms at Thebes in the south. Certainly the stone chapels that were erected at provincial sites such as Dendera, Tod, and Thebes in the Eleventh and early Twelfth dynasties are elegantly decorated with refined reliefs (showing the king in the company of the gods) and thus suggest they are the heirs of some sophisticated tradition of stone buildings beyond that of the funerary complex.

Indeed, the sun temples of the Fifth Dynasty had interior walls—unfortunately now fragmented and mostly lost—decorated with carved and painted scenes depicting nature and the seasons.[3]

That the rulers of the Middle Kingdom produced major stone temples of gigantic dimensions is indicated by the megalithic granite architectural elements at Bubastis which survive usurped by Ramses II of the Nineteenth Dynasty.[4] Otherwise very little is left of any large-scale stone constructions from this period, because later rulers used the building blocks of earlier structures to construct their own monumental temples. Perhaps the fact that the stones came from consecrated temples gave them a special sacrosanct quality that rendered them all the more appropriate to be used in constructing a new house for a deity.

A well-preserved early stone cult temple is at Medinet Maadi at the southern rim of the fertile Fayum district. Built by Amunemhet III, of the Twelfth Dynasty, it was appropriately dedicated to the harvest goddess Renenutet and the local god of the Fayum, Sobek (the crocodile god). This small temple had a rectangular plan with a recessed portico of just two columns (in the form of papyrus bundles) in the main facade. Inside a small transverse hall precedes three chapels for the cult statues of the temple's deities. Amunemhet II's temple at Tod is the classic temple plan that would be repeated for the next two thousand years. Encountered for the first time here are a pyloned gate, a columned hall, and a central axis leading to a sanctuary. The earliest columns in these sacred buildings were clearly meant to imitate bundles of reeds (as seen already in the Third Dynasty Zoser complex at Sakkara) and then palm trees (as found from the Fifth Dynasty at Abusir), but the Middle Kingdom introduced a new style of capital, the head of Hathor, full faced, blue haired, and often with a cow's ears, a style that would remain in use in many temples to goddesses for the next two thousand years.

The earliest Hathor shrine at Sinai's Serabit el-Khadim dates from the Middle Kingdom's Twelfth Dynasty (ca. 1900 B.C.) and included a rock-cut grotto preceded by a built portico and court. This "cave of Hathor" was probably also present at Deir el-Bahri in the Eleventh Dynasty and certainly was created there for the goddess during Hatshepsut's reign, but Hathor's most famous temple is, of course, the gigantic jewel now seen at Dendera. Begun in the second century B.C., this temple followed the classic single axis plan and has two enormous hypostyle halls. Throughout, the lofty columns have Hathor head capitals above which are sistrum-shaped architraves. There were innovations here in the form of crypts, whole suites of rooms in three stories set in the thickness of the outside walls and staircases that lead up to the roof, with the walls of the stairwells carved with the figures of priests ascending and descending the stairs. On the roof are further indications of sacred rituals. There are two shrines to Osiris, one with a ceiling carved with the zodiac. There was also a kiosk on the roof in which the ritual of Hathor's union with the sun disk was performed. Carved in the center of the rear outside wall of the temple was a huge face of Hathor, in the form of her sacred sistrum. The condition of the face today indicates this was once covered with gold, understandable since Hathor was known for millennia as the Golden One. The visage lies immediately outside of the holy of holies, elevated above the floor, in which the goddess's sacred image was probably kept.

Outside, a temple was usually approached by a processional way, called the Way of God. At Luxor today one sees these stone-paved broad avenues lined (and protected) on both sides with inward-facing sphinxes leading up to the great pyloned gates of temples such as those of Amun, Mut, and Khonsu at Karnak and the Temple of Luxor. Those sphinxes lining the processional way to Amun's Karnak have the head of a ram, Amun's sacred animal; those before Luxor have the head of the king, for Luxor is the place where the divinity of the pharaoh was ensured and proclaimed. How far back in time the sphinx alley can be traced is problematic, but massive sphinxes in duplicate date from at least the Middle Kingdom. The main outer door of the temple stood in the center of the twin pylons, lofty truncated pyramids with rectangular bases, meant to portray the horizon's hills between which the sun would rise. Some ancient theologians identified the pylons with the goddesses Isis and Nephthys, who between them supported the sun as it rose, proclaiming the entire temple as the "horizon" wherein the sun rose and set. In front of the pylons were fitted pairs of flagpoles. The flag was the hieroglyph for "divinity," and thus the flags announced the presence of the deity within the gates. Behind the pylons was an open courtyard called the *uba* where a shadowy portico of columns stretched at least along the rear wall of the court, if not sometimes on all sides of it. By the New

Kingdom, the standard temple design had come to be a single axis series of courtyard, columned hall, and sanctuary.

Preceding the inner sanctum and its adjacent rooms in the temple was the hypostyle hall, or *wadjit*. This name expresses the idea that the hall was a primeval swamp of papyrus reeds, albeit cast large in stone. The shrines for the gods, opening off the hypostyle hall, might have been regarded as primeval hillocks. If so, it was appropriate that the shrine of a god could be reached only by first crossing the waters of chaos from which the primeval hill arose on the day of creation.[5] The roofed and columned hall was set transversely on the longitudinal axis of the building and covered the temple's entire width. The columns were stylized papyri, arranged in straight rows. The central nave at most temples is lined by taller columns with open papyrus flowers as capitals; the side aisles have somewhat shorter columns with closed bud capitals. In temples of goddesses, however, these flower capitals are often replaced by the head of Hathor supporting a sistrumlike architrave. The difference between the roof elevations of central and side aisles seen in some temples was filled with stone grates—clerestory windows—that let in only dim light.

Ptolemaic temples still have their roofs and show us that the ceilings of the great halls were decorated with celestial images—the goddess Nut and the disk of the sun (as seen in Hathor's temple at Dendera) or even maps of stars and decans. Thus a sky was provided above the primeval swamp of the hypostyle hall. Repeatedly shown over the central aisle, as can be seen today inside the enduring rock-cut temples of Ramses II at Abu Simbel, hovered the vulture goddess, wings outstretched protectively over the select few who proceeded up and down the holy way.

Clearly the temple was regarded as the home of the divinity and was not a gathering place for the faithful. The masses did not crowd into pharaoh's palaces, and, similarly, the people did not generally enter the houses of divinities. Important laity such as government officials, priests and their acolytes, and choirs were admitted through the pyloned gates into the outer courts, possibly at times even into the dimly lit hypostyle hall that preceded the sanctuary within the temple proper, but it is very likely that only those directly concerned with the cult and its rituals and regarded as purified ones penetrated further to stand in near-darkness before the tabernacle itself. The pharaoh was understood to be the high priest in each major, state-financed temple. The prophet would speak always in the name of the king. The ruler standing before the god of the temple is one of the most frequently depicted scenes on a temple's walls.

Some temples, such as the royal temples, dating to the New Kingdom, on the west bank at Luxor had two open courtyards, the first being the most public as it served a small rest palace of the king located immediately to its south. Here, as shown in the reliefs surviving at Ramses III's temple (Medinet Habu), all types of festivities, including athletic contests, jousting and musical programs, and reward cere-monies, would have taken place for the delight of the royal family and courtiers. Beyond the second pylon was the true first court of the temple proper which was itself fronted by a terrace supporting a portico. On the walls of the first court was sometimes inscribed infor-mation on the daily routine as well, how the offerings for the morning were placed on a "great jar-stand of gold" in the forecourt of the temple each day and the rising sun was adored.

The temple proper, or core temple, was approached by a ramp, and the floor of the temple inside continued to rise as one penetrated its central aisle to the holy of holies with its naos of the resident deity. First one crossed the "swamp" of stone papyrus reeds, the hypostyle hall, however. The inner sanctum was located at a higher level and was meant to be thought of as the primeval hillock where the god began all creation. The roof line also was lowered toward the temple's rear so, as Alexander Badawy expressed it, the god dwelled where heaven and earth met.[6] A stone naos at the center sheltered the tabernacle, inside of which was the small figure that is never portrayed in the temple scenes depicting holy processions. Nearby stood the stone pedestal supporting the portable bark shrine in which the tabernacle of the divinity would ride whenever it emerged from the temple. This was a golden boat carried on poles shouldered by white-robed, shaven priests. The naos was set on the boat under a light frame covered with a curtain. No impious eyes could view the divine figure or even its shrine. Lofty ostrich feather fans, holy standards, and incense burners surrounded the sacred boat shrine at such appearances.

To the sides of the central sanctum were other chapels devoted to the cults of secondary deities and deities related to the god of the temple. Their chapels as well had wide doors that permited entrance

and exit by a large boat shrine. Various storerooms and offering preparation rooms, including sometimes perfume laboratories, sacristies, and
a library filled the remaining space of the temple proper. Outside in the
cult temples built for goddesses in the Late period one finds a birth
house, or Mammisi, as well as houses for the staff, granaries and store-
houses, and often a sanitarium.

Due to the doors and windowless walls, little light penetrated the
interior of an Egyptian temple. No doubt the darkness, the clouds of
incense, and the chanting of the god's servants created a very spiritual
if not intimidating atmosphere. A priest of the Late period recalled in
his autobiographical inscription, "I entered into the presence of the
god in the holy place while I was afraid and in awe of him."[7]

Today, with the temples in ruin, there is more light, and the songs
of birds and the chatter of tourists dispel the original ambience.
However, the spirituality of these ponderous, shadowy buildings can
still affect one. Florence Nightingale recorded a profound spiritual
experience in the temple Seti I built on the west bank at Luxor at
Gurna,[8] and a sense of spirituality still fills the shadowy colossal halls of
the well-preserved temples of Upper Egypt. It is very easy to visualize
the white-robed clergy and the gilded bark shrines and hear the tinkling
of the sistra and the rustling of the beaded menats shaken by the women
musicians as accompaniment to the intonations of the lector priest.

As Lanny Bell has stated, "The temple circumscribed and architecturally delimited a site whose sacredness distinguished it from the
mundane populated space around it. The temple was set apart—both
ritually, by consecrating the ground on which it was erected and out of
which it seemed organically to grow, and architecturally, by building an
imposing series of progressively more restrictive walls to surround and
protect it. The temple's ritual and architectural barriers repulsed the
chaotic forces that continually threatened the ordered world within."[9]

The house of the god also bore markers of special adornment and
significance. When Egypt possessed the gold mines of Nubia, there was
so much of the precious metal available that sheets of gold, presumably
often decorated with hammered relief scenes, were attached to door
jambs and used as wainscoting. This was still sometimes the practice in
the latest period of temple building, as the series of holes that once
held wooden pegs are visible at the Isis temple on Philae where sheets
of gold once covered the holy figure of Isis.[10]

Lofty obelisks were covered, at least their pointed tops but some-times completely, by precious metal. The female pharaoh Hatshepsut left this description of her dedication of truly splendid obelisks at the Temple of Karnak:

> My heart directed me to make for him
> Two obelisks of electrum
> whose pyramidions would join the sky
> In the august columned hall
> Between the two great pylons of the King.[11]

This lavish display did not cease, and from a much later period there is a famous quote from the *Paedagogus* (3.2:4) of Clement of Alexandria: "The temples sparkle with gold, silver and mat gold and flash with colored stones from India and Ethiopia. The sanctuaries are over-shadowed by cloths studded with gold."

The cedar doors of the temple were also decorated with precious metal, and those on the main aisle were fitted into door frames that, by necessity, were shorter than the lofty central aisle of the temple. To permit the procession of the tall fans and standards typically carried along with the boat-shaped shrine containing the deity by the priests, the door frames had open or broken pediments but could still service an actual door on pivots.

This enclosed temple structure was further protected from floods and kept from impious eyes or threats by a great wall, which, for-tresslike, was topped with crenellations and could even have watch towers at regular intervals. Thus, instead of being a welcoming holy sanctuary, the Egyptian temple was a fortress constructed to keep the uninitiated at bay and the deities and treasure within protected from any threat.

RITUALS

Promptly at first light of dawn, the god was awakened in his or her inner sanctum. The ritual that followed has fortunately been preserved in records from more than one temple and from more than one reign. There are striking resemblances between the daily temple ritual and that conducted at private tombs for those who could afford to leave endowments for perpetual offerings. The lighting of lamps on certain mornings of the year, for example, New Year's day, at the Wag feast, on the eighteenth day of the month of Thoth, and at the Feast of the Valley in the tenth month of the year, is documented for private tombs as well. In the early Twelfth Dynasty, the governor of Assiut, Hapzefa, commissioned ten contracts to ensure that services on festival days would be carried out before the statues in his private tomb chapel.[12]

Every day there were three main services in the temple—dawn, midday and evening, with the morning service being the most important. That service would have started at the first light of dawn, which was watched for by at least one priest on the temple roof. He had probably been there throughout the night measuring the hours to keep track of time so that the rituals of the temple might be carried out at precisely the right hour. Meanwhile two priests carried into the temple a libation vessel filled at the sacred well, censing the water with incense in the process. Already before dawn, in the kitchens to the east of the temple the food offerings that were to be laid before the gods of the temple had been prepared. Finally all was ready to be carried into the temple escorted and censed by the priests. At the signal from the watcher on the roof, the officiating prophets would enter the main door of the Pronaos. On the thickness of each jamb of this door was an inscription of a Declaration of Innocence, which presumably was to be recited during entrance. The prophet who would approach the god would be purified, properly dressed, and invested. Then, while hymns were sung by the women of the hener (musical troop), he proceeded solemnly toward the sanctuary and the god's naos whose doors were sealed.

Before they could enter the temple, however, all the priests and singers had to be in a purified state. They had shaved all body hair and washed themselves in either the sacred lake of the temple or at a stone basin outside its door. Fairman believed that at the temple at Edfu the libations were drawn from a well dug under the east wall of that temple, to ensure its extreme purity because the sacred lake, lying as it did outside the temple's wall, would not have been deemed pure enough.[13] The temple staff then purified their mouths with salt water. The spray of water poured over a priest is depicted as a stream of ankh signs (the hieroglyph for "life"), and the water was regarded as more than a cleansing agent: it was the primordial water from Nun, the most sacred substance that preexisted all else, the water from which all life had emerged. Contact with this holy water bestowed a special sanctity on the clergy: "After I came from Nun, had rid myself from all that was evil in me, had exchanged evil with purity, and had loosened clothes and ointments according to the purification of Horus and Seth, I entered into the presence of the god in the holy place."[14]

Holy water was not the only liquid associated with purification rituals. Wine too was used as a libation, often offered to deities because of its power to gladden their hearts. Pharaoh Seti I of the Nineteenth Dynasty is portrayed in his beautifully decorated temple at Abydos holding a large jar without handles as he kneels in front of the god Ptah-Sokar. He pours wine from this vessel into a rectangular basin. Such stone offering tables, actually slabs, which had shallow troughs, are among the most commonly found furnishings from temple sites. Wine was the drink of the gods (as well as of the wealthier classes of humans), and small round jars of wine are often depicted being offered to deities by the king.[15] Wine in lotus-shaped chalices sits beside the altar at Edfu in the portrayal of the enormous offerings presented there during the New Year Festival. Besides meat offerings of cattle, oryx, gazelle, ibex, and geese, which would be burned, vegetables, flowers, and fruits were offered. Portrayals of such a menu reach far back in Egypt's history and were deemed necessary to keep the deities pleased with the king and partial to Egypt.[16] If Herodotus is correct in his report (2.39), wine was poured over the sacrificial animals at the altar before they were slaughtered. Thus wine should have been regarded as having the power of purification or consecration.

For illumination in the holy of holies, a torch was lit (perhaps it was an oil lamp as elaborate as those found in Tutankhamun's tomb), and some have interpreted this to signify the victory of light and the day over the powers of darkness; indeed, it has been suggested that by lighting the torch, the priest helped to bring about the sunrise itself and with it victory over death and enemies.[17] However, there was little if any light otherwise in the inner temple, and thus artificial light was mandatory. Incense was burned while appropriate spells were recited and the inner sanctum was approached. The seal of the god's shrine was broken.

Presumably all humans approached the divine presence similarly. Kissing the earth before the deity (or king) has been portrayed in art with the worshiper down on all fours and forehead to the ground. Next, one either knelt or stood with arms raised in adoration of the deity with the appropriate words spoken or sung.

Texts on papyri and temple walls have survived which have helped scholars, such as Harold Nelson of Chicago and H. W. Fairman of Liverpool, to reconstruct the many episodes of the daily ritual.[18] The first, as described on the eastern wall of Karnak's hypostyle hall, was the burning of incense to appease the uraeus goddess, who protected the god's shrine. As the doors of the sanctuary were opened, the Morning Hymn was sung. In it the deity of the temple and other resident gods and goddesses and the individual parts of the temple itself were addressed and bidden to rouse themselves from slumber.

After the seal on the bolted door was broken, the bolts were withdrawn. Every ritual act was accompanied by an intoned statement and had a supernatural, magical effect. The priest first exorcised any evil spirits that might linger to threaten the inhabitant of the shrine. Then the two bolts were pulled back one by one. The double-leafed door was opened to reveal the sacred statue. The head of the deity was uncovered and the veil taken away, revealing the deity in all her awful majesty. The priest recited:

> I have seen the god, the Power sees me.
> The god rejoices at seeing me.

Holy water was sprinkled, followed by a second libation:

> Rise, great god, in peace! Rise, you are in peace!

The singers responded:

> You are risen, in peace.[19]

Recorded hymns were often very long, and the musical accompaniment was probably in progress throughout the temple ritual. Lisa Manniche suggests that the temple songstress shook her sistra instrument "to divide the phrases of recitation. The sound of the sistrum could be complemented by the rattliing of the *menat*, a heavy necklace made of rows of faience beads, usually carried by the women in their free hands rather than worn."[20] Other deities housed in the temple would also receive sung morning greetings and praises. The temple musicians consisted of percussionists, harpists, and lutenists as well as dancers and singers, at least in the cult of Hathor. Tambourine playing seems to have been very prominent in religious services of the Greco-Roman period. On the walls of the Temple of Dendera are depicted no less than twenty-four female tambourine players in a row.

The presentation of Ma'at, an image of the goddess, with an ostrich feather standing straight up on her head, who symbolized justice and the proper order of the universe, was presented as a part of the morning ritual—again with appropriate hymns praising divine order and justice. There was a laying on of hands performed with the god's image to lift it out of the tabernacle, better to serve the deity. The priest impersonating the king of Egypt knelt before the god in a salutation with a *nemset*-jar: "Comes the incense, comes the perfume of the god, its perfume comes to you, the perfume of the Eye of Horus is to you, the perfume of Nekhbet which comes forth from Nekheb. It washes you, it adorns you, it takes its place upon your two hands."[21]

Thus, just as the ancient Egyptians washed their hands before eating when attended by servants at a banquet, the nemset-jar of perfumed water cleansed the god before he received his repast. Wine, bread, cakes, and honey, but also onions and meat and beer, six different fruits, including grapes, often made up the offering. The priests recited the menu, and then the lector priest called on the sem-priest to pronounce the "boon-which-the-king-gives" spell for the god in his three forms: "An offering which the king gives of a thousand of bread and beer, oxen and fowl, ointment and clothing and every pleasant thing."

Special spells have been identified for the presentation of beer, white bread, cake, wine, and milk. Spells exist for the cooking of the meat, which may have been done for small portions immediately at the shrine of the god, if these scenes and spells are to be believed. A small offering stand was affixed over a burner. Incense and fat were put on the fire. Next a piece of meat was placed on it, having first been spitted. A fan was used to increase the intensity of the fire. Spells were recited for each of these steps. The priest then arranged the offerings on a table, spreading out the meal for the god. A representative amount was placed on a tray that was "elevated" before the divine image. A wall scene depicts the assembling of offerings to elevate offerings, in which the king gathers together samples of various items of the god's repast preparatory to elevating them before the deity:

Elevate offering to Amun Re, Lord of the Thrones of the
Two Lands.

All life emanates from him, all health emanates from him,
all stability emanates from him, all good fortune emanates
from him, like Re forever.[22]

The offerings were considered the Eye of Horus, "the symbol of all
that is good and holy restored to sound and undamaged condition.
The Eye signified the salvation of cosmos, society, and individual." The
act of sacrifice was "not so much a gift from men to the gods as a sacred
act through which men could contribute to restoring and maintaining
cosmic harmony. The priest could do this because he took on a divine
role."[23]

At this time of sacrifice, myrrh was burned before the god. The king
(priest) extended both his hands, holding in one a censer while with
the other he conferred a blessing or salutation. Next spells were recited
for the conferring of offerings:

Bring your honor to this your bread which is warm,
to this your beer which is warm,
to this your roast which is warm.[24]

After the deity had presumably consumed the food offerings, there
were still six steps to be performed before the regular daily ritual could
be concluded. These rites were to be introduced by calling out "hail to
you" at the side of the door, while a priest sprinkled water on the four
walls of the god's shrine to purify it.

At certain times, but possibly not every day, the god's image was
dressed in fresh linen of the finest cambric:

I clothed the god with his regalia
in my rank of master of secrets
in my function of stolist
I was pure of hands in waiting on the god
a priest whose fingers are clean.[25]

The weaving and presentation of cloth was part of the ritual in the
cults of goddesses like Hathor. An inscription at the Temple of Dendera

refers to a woman of priestly rank as "she who unites with the Red Cloth," a remembrance in text of a very early rite, even though the art of intervening periods does not record the scarf; the Middle Kingdom Coffin Texts, however, do have the deceased state that she has woven a dress for Hathor (CT Sp. 486), while in the preceding spell it is four gods—Horus, Thoth, Osiris, and Atum—who have woven the dress. Very likely presentation of clothing was a part of the daily ritual for Hathor, as it has been documented in the case of other deities. This Spell 484 suggests that the donning of certain robes by the Great Lady's followers was also part of her cult's rituals.

The food offerings were removed from the presumably sated god and presented to the other deities in the temple, followed by the deceased kings and other officials who had statues there. Finally they would be removed for consumption by the clergy. A Late Period cult book on Papyrus Jumilhac states, "If the quantity of offerings on its altars is poor, the same will happen in the entire country; the life of the living will be poor. If there is a large quantity of offerings in this place, abundance will occur in the entire country and every belly will be filled with the tree-of-life (grain)."[26] If this had always been the reasoning behind food offerings, it is easy to understand why temple scenes depict huge quantities of every type of food.

Finally the divine image was replaced in its tabernacle, its face was once again covered with a veil, more purification with water and incense was performed, and then the double doors were closed: "The door is closed by Ptah / the door is made fast by Thoth."[27] The closing of the doors and the replacing of the bolt and the seal were all steps accompanied by the appropriate chants. The enclosure of the god by his tabernacle was likened to the embrace by a senior god:

> Your father, Osiris, has placed you within his two arms in
>   his name of "Horizon in which Re circles around"
> Life is given to you in the presence of your father, Osiris
> that you may have power through it,
> that you may be content with it
> and you shall be a living one, the foremost of the gods.[28]

The shrine was ritually freed of evil spirits, and the servants closed the doors of the tabernacle, leaving the god in darkness. The reversion of offerings left from the previous day could then take place for the benefit of the temple staff. Of course, the reversion of offerings was accompanied by its special ritual and magical spells too, for example: "Your enemy withdraws himself for you. Horus turns himself to his two eyes in this its name of reversion-of-offerings. Your perfume is to you, gods and goddesses, your sweat is to you, O gods. I am the priest I have come to perform the rites for (the deity) and for his son, King N. Your divine offerings revert to you. Receive them upon the hands of the King of Upper and Lower Egypt, son of Re, his beloved."[29]

After the reversion ceremony more libations and incense were offered: "Take to yourself this your libation, which is in this land, which produces all living things. Everything, indeed, comes forth from it, upon which you live, upon which you exist."[30]

On certain holy days other rites could be added to the usual daily scenario. For instance, at the First Day and Sixth Day festivals a bouquet of flowers was presented to the god. There were special spells for chanting on the morning of New Year's Day, including one for burning a special torch and a special salutation with the *nemset*-jar.

Details on the midday service are meager but indicate it was regarded as much less important and thus was shorter in duration than the morning service. Apparently no more offerings were brought into the sanctuary and it remained closed. The evening service seems to have been concerned with the setting of the sun, honoring Re, who was retiring for the night. Some texts suggest that a watch was maintained during the twelve hours of the night by some priests. They prompted Fairman to suggest that "certain rites were celebrated in the temple each hour of the day and night, but of the nature of these ceremonies we know nothing."[31]

Great temples bore carvings of calendars of holy feasts, which indicate that more than forty special festivals might be celebrated in a major temple in the course of a year. Festivals varied in length from one to fifteen days, sometimes even more. There was of course the New Year Festival, which was supposed to coincide with the rising of the Nile, beginning on the thirtieth day of the fourth month (end) of the summer season, ending on the fourth day of the first month of inundation. Special festivals for Osiris were celebrated in all the temples of Egypt during the Fourth Month of Inundation. Important festivals such as that which welcomed the Eye of the Sun back to Egypt, are known best from rather late texts, which may describe proceedings differently than they would have appeared centuries earlier. Hathor (or her form as Sekhmet, or even Tefnut) was believed to have traveled as far southeast as the land of Punt, the region out of which the sun rose in the winter months.

Such a wandering can be seen by all of us who live in the Northern Hemisphere in the wintertime, when at the winter solstice the sun is indeed farthest south and from which she returns to bring back the warm spring and summer. The arrival of the goddess in Thebes (on her way back to Memphis) was cause for much celebration. If the text near the entrance of the Temple of Medamud, carved during the Ptolemaic period, is to be believed, the greater part of the festival took place at night by torchlight. The celebration entailed the consumption of great quantities of beer:

> Come, O Golden One, who consumes praise
> because the food of her desire is dancing,
> who shines on the festival at the time of illumination
> who is content with the dancing at night
> Come! the procession is in the place of inebriation
> that hall of traveling through the marshes.
> The drunken celebrants drum for you during the cool of
> the night.[32]

John Darnell, who has studied the lengthy text from which I have quoted sparingly here, has suggested that the Egyptian celebrants welcomed the goddess with festival booths placed on the bank of the Nile. That inebriation was often a part of temple festivals is suggested by a much earlier, New Kingdom text quoted by Darnell: "she is like a drunken woman, seated outside the dwelling place [of the god]."[33] Perhaps the momentary alleviation of suffering from life's torments both physical and psychological that the intoxicating beverage can provide gave a somewhat magical aura. Transported into a happy state, the Egyptian was in a better frame of mind to rejoice over the epiphany of her favorite goddess.[34]

Ecstatic dances by Egyptians, but also Libyans and Nubians, were seen at such religious festivals. In scenes of the Opet procession at the Temple of Luxor, Libyan club dancers are in evidence, as are stick fighters on the reliefs at Ramses III's temple at Medinet Habu (this dance is still performed in Upper Egypt), and "Libyan-attired girls hanging their heads over and waggling their hair"[35] are seen in earlier renditions of Hathoric rites. The farthest destination of the sun's eye had been the near-mythical but actual land of Punt (modern Eritrea) on the Red Sea coast. Here the monkeys did a jumping dance to express their delight in the appearance of the goddess. Back in Egypt, men and women performed this dance. "These reversals of roles between the humans and apes [was] an expression of the reversed world appropriate for the drunken revelry accompanying the return of the far-traveled goddess near the beginning of the year."[36]

> The whole world rejoices for you
> the animals dance for you in joy
> The Two Lands and the foreign countries praise you.[37]

CLERGY

Direct contact with the deity, whereby it could partake of the food necessary for its sustenance, has been taken by some scholars as "the chief end and purpose of the daily temple service."[38] Thus the Egyptian priest can be considered a caregiver for the goddess, serving the deity to keep her pleased with humanity and present on the earth, where harmony would then reign. As one priest reminisced, "I was given access to the god when an excellent youth. I was introduced into the horizon of heaven (the temple) to sanctify the mysterious image of the god who is in Thebes, to satisfy him with his offerings."[39]

While Amun-Re, the king of the gods, was master of Karnak and celebrated in the endless vignettes carved on the walls of this gigantic temple, he was often depicted accompanied by his consort, Mut, and other great goddesses, such as Isis and Hathor, as well as by his son, Khonsu. When the king offers incense or wine to Amun or his bark shrine, Mut and Khonsu and their bark shrines are usually present as well and receive their due.

Besides the prophets, the leading priests of which there were probably usually several in ranking First, Second, Third, and Fourth, a number of other people were involved with the service. The temple's hener, musicians and singers, were led by a lector priest who intoned hymns as well or read from a ritual book. Others were responsible for preparing offerings, and officials and members of the royal family, if they wished, could also participate in the ceremonies, particularly consecrating offerings. The following was written of a service for Hathor:

When the royal children pacify you with what is desired,
the officials consecrate offerings to you.
When the lector exalts you in intoning a hymn,
the magician reads the rituals.
when the organizer praises you with his lotus blooms,
the percussionists take up the tambourine,
the maidens rejoice for you with garlands,
the women with the wreath-crown.[40]

Droughts, earthquakes, plagues, and armed attacks could be explained by deities turning their backs on Egypt, showing displeasure for a lack of care. Thus a wise king made sure his temples were well established, his priesthood dedicated, and his gods content.

Egyptian priests did not preach to the populace to convince them to embrace a particular god or goddess. Indeed, the Egyptians, like other polytheists, were tolerant of other religions and welcomed and adopted foreign deities if they were well regarded for their powers in other lands. Deities did not teach or lead their devotees into a virtuous life. Contact between deity and devotee was not that intimate, and the relationship was not one of teacher and pupil. Moral teaching was certainly carried out in Egypt, not necessarily in the temple but in schools, which could have been associated with temples or palaces, or in government bureaus. Presumably society's standards and morals were taught in the home as well. The precepts that have survived are of a practical, commonsense nature rather than philosophical musings on the good spiritual life. However, behavior fitting a moral code was expected, and no deceased person could hope for eternal life in Osiris's realm if he or she did not pass the final judgment, which involved denials of what was then considered improper and immoral behavior.

There was no delineation between temple and state in this ancient society; the two intermeshed in theory, if not always in practice. A strong ruler would appoint priests he could trust or control, even though the priesthood hoped to keep positions within the same families for generations and thus hold on to some independence as well as power, wealth, and social prestige. Mobility in the careers of some priests has been documented. For example, Nebwenenef, a high priest of Hathor at Dendera later became the first prophet of Amun at Thebes, having been chosen by an oracle for that position during the reign of Ramses II. Undoubtedly Nebwenenef was considered a prime candidate for this exalted position because he had first been chief of prophets of all the gods between Gurna and This. As such, he was supervisor for the temples of Abydos, where Ramses II and his father both had built extensively. His sons and theirs continued to serve Hathor in the priestly positions at Dendera for many generations.[41]

While H. H. Nelson saw the temple ritual as immediately practical—designed to meet the needs of the resident deity—its purpose has also been interpreted by the French Egyptologist Serge Sauneron and many others as cosmic, conceived to preserve the perfect status of the world, to establish righteousness, to conquer evil. Certainly early societies were very vulnerable; theirs was a precarious existence in an unstable world, a world barely controllable except by elaborate magical ritual. It was only the gods who could ensure the continued existence of this essentially dangerous universe, and much depended on the priests and king to keep the divinities inclined toward helping and protecting Egypt and its people. The function of the house of god and its personnel, then, "was to protect the gods from attacks by hostile forces, to nourish them, and keep them in perfect condition, in order to facilitate their cosmic task and to keep from them any influence which could impede their action."[42]

FESTIVALS

Documents show that by the late New Kingdom there were at least sixty-five feast days, almost one-sixth of the calendar. Among these were celebrations of the full moon, the beginning of spring, the harvest, and the coming of the inundation. This last, the life-giving waters rising to flood a parched land must have been an occasion of great rejoicing:

May you follow Thoth
on that beautiful day of the beginning of Inundation
May you hear the jubilation in the temple of Hermopolis
when the Golden One appears to show her love.[43]

The months of the Egyptian year were named for these important celebrations or for the deities, surely a good way to promote the knowledge and remembrance of such feasts among the people. There was a month of Hathor, another of Thoth, and one known for "the navigation of Mut."[44]

One of the most important feasts at the great religious center of Thebes—from which more records survive than for all the rest of Egypt—was the Beautiful Feast of the Valley. Hathor's sacred realm in the bay of cliffs on the west of Thebes, now named Deir el-Bahri, was the "valley" to which the holy family from Karnak, with Amun in the lead, sailed for a two-day visit every year in the second month of the summer season. Attested since the Eleventh Dynasty, when King Montuhotep incorporated a Hathoric shrine into his own funerary complex there, this may well have been the favorite holy event of the Egyptian religious calendar, at least in Upper Egypt. There all the populace turned out to accompany the sacred barks on their river voyage directly across the Nile.

What a sight this regatta must have been. The long, ornate barges of the gods, glittering as the sun caught their gold-covered decks and ornaments, were accompanied by two royal sailing vessels, and hundreds of river craft of all descriptions crowded in as close as they dared to catch sight of the holy family.[45] The relief scenes on New Kingdom temples reveal how elaborate the sacred boats were. Almost all open space was cluttered with sacred standards and statues, and the boat-shaped shrine containing the naos in which the sacred image of the deity stood was itself placed within an elaborate canopy, topped and also fenced in by rows of raised cobras bearing sun disks on their heads. The naos was flanked by feather fans and papyrus bouquets. Both the god's barge and the boat shrine were carved with the heads of the deity on stern and prow, heads that bore sun disks or elaborate crowns and were adorned by necklaces. All of this was worked in gold and set with semiprecious stones and colored glass. The baroque effect must have been one of amazing splendor for the ancient Egyptians.[46]

The land journey too, across the green fields following the dike road westward to the dramatic curtain of cliffs that marked the valley of the Mistress of the West, would have been a colorful procession, with white-robed wab-priests struggling to shoulder the heavy boat-shaped shrines on long poles. From scenes of this carved on the upper terrace of Hatshepsut's temple, it is clear that there were six rows of five wab-priests each, and the portable bark was provided with several supporting bars for them to shoulder. On both sides of the bark walked the prophets, leopard skins draped over their linen robes. They were accompanied by others carrying divine standards and incense burners. The royal throne was displayed in this procession, as were two cheetahs, who may have been royal mascots. The military contingents were selected from the royal navy and the body guard of the pharaoh. These last were especially heavily armed, possibly to protect the royal family. More likely, however, they were there to symbolically protect the gods who had left the security of the Temple of Karnak to cross unknown territory, potentially full of dangers, before they reached safety again within the holy complex of the royal cult temple. The presence of priests carrying vases of water, braziers, and censers as they accompanied the bark shrines of the gods further suggests they are taking measures to preserve the ritual purity of the divine barks during this journey.[47] Along with the procession of dignitaries, priests, and soldiers were musical bands, troops of singers, and dancers, whose acrobatic postures in the artistic portrayals hint at ecstatic dancing and wild celebrations. Most likely the whole colorful parade was greeted by the cheers of vast crowds hailing the gods. Indeed, so impressive was the spectacle that people left engraved on their tomb walls their wish to be present to witness this annual event.

In the New Kingdom, the Karnak triad took up residence at the temples of Deir el-Bahri—Thutmose III had built his higher on the slope than Hatshepsut's—while the populace of the Thebaid flocked to the cemeteries to be with their families who were buried there. Those who could afford it purchased from the florists a floral collar in the shape of an *ankh* and brought along new clothing and hampers of food and wine as they sought out the burial places of their nearest and dearest kin. Then the people kept an all-night vigil. As dusk fell, torches and lamps were lit, and all across the bare slopes into which the tombs and graves were cut one could see the thousands of flickering lights and hear the din of songs and murmured conversations of those who hoped once again to commune with their departed loved ones. Alcohol was an integral part of the feasting that night, and drunkenness brought on the sentimental feelings and then the daze that led many to behold again and address again those they missed from this life.

Hathor's priestesses and her musicians visited the encampments of families and announced the presence of the Mistress of the West, the kindly goddess who welcomed the dead and comforted the living, and general camaraderie continued all night and into the following day. As has been pointed out by others, the Egyptian living and dead inhabited the same community; their society did not consist only of the living.[48] The dead could affect the lives of the living, and thus the gathering at the family tomb site was not just a sentimental journey but a sincere attempt to have contact with the dead and to honor the ancestors with offerings of food, drink, and clothing. Sometimes this communication with deceased family members could have a practical purpose—perhaps to win their support in a struggle with an opponent, or to persuade them to intervene with higher powers on behalf of the living. Visiting tombs with picnics is still practiced among the Egyptians of today.

The other major feast at Thebes was Opet, which took place at the Temple of Luxor and announced the rebirth of the world. It lasted for twenty-four days, from mid-August to early September, in the second month of the ancients' summer season, and was intended in part to encourage the life-sustaining Nile to rise again and flood a parched land. This festival also involved the traveling of Amun, Mut, and Khonsu from Karnak south two kilometers to Luxor, and in Hatshepsut's day the entire trip south was by land with a river return. Later the water route was used exclusively instead, possibly to keep some distance between the holy procession and the crowds that turned out to view it. The processional way and some of the earliest buildings at the Temple of Luxor were constructed under Hatshepsut, who also supplied way stations so that the priests might set down their burdens and perhaps cense the sacred shrines before proceeding to the temple. Today the citizens of Luxor celebrate a local Moslem holy man of the Middle Ages with an annual parade that includes festooned boats in a land procession. It is clear from the inscriptions there and from the human-headed sphinxes that line the avenue between the Temples of Karnak and Luxor that Luxor was dedicated to the king and that at the

Feast of Opet an important annual event took place which ensured that the land of Egypt would remain in the favor of the gods. Here the king was embraced by the divine ka and recharged with the divinity of kingship.[49] Under him the land would flourish and righteousness would prevail; that was the unquestioned power of the king. In attendance was Mut, Mistress of Crowns. She and her consort Amun in Opet are the subject of a gigantic dual statue that can still be seen in the Temple of Luxor. The bark shrines to accommodate the visiting triad from Karnak were built as three contiguous deep stone shrines at Luxor by Thutmose III of the Eighteenth Dynasty, but it is principally Amunhotep III of that dynasty and Ramses II of the next who are the architects and did the most to embellish its original plan, Amunhotep with a great court of appearances and Ramses with the pylon and six giant statues of himself, plus two obelisks flanking the front door.

A full calendar of temple festivals and feast days has survived, engraved in stone, on the side wall of Ramses III's temple at the southern end of the west bank at Luxor dating from the Twentieth Dynasty. This is the best preserved of the pharaonic temples, known today as Medinet Habu. Because of its fine state of preservation, this huge temple was chosen by James Henry Breasted as worthy of an intense effort at copying and publishing every inscription and relief scene on its walls— a work of some forty years duration.[50] From its great calendar of feasts, one can ascertain an idea of the religious year. For instance, there was a special festival on the first day of the year. It is very likely that on this occasion the holy family of the Temple of Karnak crossed the Nile to visit the temple of their "son," the reigning pharaoh. Bark shrines of Amun, Mut, and Khonsu could all be housed at his temple in the sanctuaries toward the back. Such religious festivals involving the divinities in their golden bark shrines probably took place in the second court of Medinet Habu, known as its festival hall. It was roofless but surrounded by shadowy colonnades, round columns on the north and south sides and square pillars fronted by attached Osiride figures of the king on the east and west. Two colossal freestanding statues of Ramses III once stood at the center of the western side at the terrace that lined that wall. The walls of this court are decorated with relief scenes of some of the great feasts held during a typical year under Ramses III.

Medinet Habu temple's calendar states that the feasts celebrated there included the Feast of the Valley, the Feast of Opet, the Feast of

Amun, and the Feast of Lifting Up the Sky. Why the calendar lists the Feast of Opet as occurring at the king's mortuary temple is unclear, as it has always been associated with the Temple of Luxor. However, the Feast of Opet is also portrayed on the walls of Hatshepsut's Deir el-Bahri temple, so it may have been such a vitally important event that it had to be preserved in these halls of eternity. Interestingly, the largest number of offerings for any feast that is recounted on the Medinet Habu calendar was that allotted to the Feast of Opet. It is possible, however, that because the king did not reside in the area, but far to the north in the delta, his arrival in the Thebaid to celebrate the annual Feast of Opet would have meant he would also visit the temple he had built on the west bank. He and his party could reside in the small palace on the south of the temple. The 11,341 loaves of bread and 385 jugs of beer laid out at Medinet Habu for the Feast of Opet may have been consumed by the royal visitors during that time at this residence.

On the eastern wall of Ramses III's Second Court, the goddesses Nekhbet and Wadjet, the protective deities of Upper and Lower Egypt, accompanied by three each of the souls of Pe and the souls of Hierakonpolis, are portrayed escorting Ramses III into the presence of Amun, who crowns the king, after which the god Atum hands him the crook and flail scepters, the insignia of kingship. The temple's calendar inscription shows that one of the major feasts there was the annual Coronation Feast, which lasted twenty days (as recorded for the twenty-second year of the king's reign).

The practice of carving reliefs and texts on the walls of temples illustrating the celebrations held there was continued in the Ptolemaic temples, and can be seen today at Philae and Dendera. Each of the goddess's temples contained a Mammisi wherein was celebrated the mystery of the divine birth of the goddess's child, who was also by equation the king of Egypt. Female members of the clergy at Philae, impersonating Isis and her sister Nephthys, read the decree proclaiming the son of Osiris the designated ruler on earth.

Scholars believe that a liturgical drama with priestly actors, including women, performed the annunciation of Isis's pregnancy, the forming of the divine offspring on the potter's wheel by the god Khnum, the goddess's safe delivery, the pronouncements by the Seven Hathors (the good fairies who pronounced fortunes for the newborn), and the suckling of the royal infant by divine wet nurses.

The Egyptians were aware of the cyclical events of nature and, as is clear from their deities, saw divinity in the flora and fauna around them. There were New Year's (Eve and Day) festivals, twice-monthly festivals, and royal occasions such as coronation commemorations and jubilees. There was a water festival for Mut, which was probably a splendid affair involving the goddess's golden barge, as it gave rise to the popular personal name in the New Kingdom, Mut-em-wia, literally "Mut in Her Bark." Annual celebrations to honor great deities could extend over many days and draw pilgrims to holy sites. Herodotus (2.60) describes the festivals of Bubastis, which, he claimed, attracted tens of thousands of people in a festive mood. The lengthy celebrations of the New Year's Festival, coinciding with the arrival of the Nile flood on about July 20, continued to be a major celebration for the entire nation through twenty days of festivities at major temples.

At Dendera and other Hathoric temples, the ceremony of the Union with the Sun's Disk occurred at the first of the year as well as at the days that marked the change of the season. Here, as very possibly in many temples of the land, the holy statue was carried by priests to the roof of the temple where it could be exposed to and could absorb the heat of the sun. Reliefs at Dendera show the queen of Egypt ringing the sistra while her husband burns incense preceding the tabernacle of the god up the stairway to the roof. There in the full light of day the procession would find a kiosk draped with curtains in which the unveiling of the divine image could occur. After the specified time spent on the roof, the holy procession could use another stairway that led down into the temple and its central sanctuary or holy of holies.[51]

A popular festival in Upper Egypt was the "sacred marriage" celebrated at Edfu, when Hathor sailed south from Dendera on a voyage of some fourteen days to visit Horus in his venerable abode. From the Late period also are attested the festivities of the annual festival when Hathor traveled from her temple at Dendera to the god Horus at Edfu, then understood as her husband. Along the way the populations of local towns turned out to greet and admire the glittering flotilla of the great goddess.[52] The two gods spent two weeks together, and Hathor's stay was probably the occasion of great merriment there.

A temple of Horus had stood at Edfu from time immemorial, and today is the best preserved of all the built temples of Egypt. Hathor in her golden barge had to be towed against the current to reach Edfu, and was no doubt accompanied by many other river craft bearing priestly delegations. She stopped at several towns along the river to visit other goddesses, for example, Mut at Isheru and Nekhbet at el-Kab. Because of all the stops and because much of the celebration took place outdoors, this religious festival must have attracted large numbers of lay people. The festivities at Edfu lasted fifteen days, beginning on the day of the new moon in the third month of summer and ending with the appearance of the full moon. When Hathor disembarked north of Edfu she was met and greeted by Horus, and the two holy statues received the ceremonial opening of the mouth ritual and food offerings. Together the two gods sailed still farther to the temple itself, where they entered the precinct by the eastern door of the high enclosure wall and spent the night together in the sanctuary. Each day there were food offerings, burned sacrifices, ritual slaughtering of especially marked animals. There was a visit to the necropolis in the area where the divine souls or ancestral gods of the Edfu region were thought to be buried.

Fairman, who studied the reliefs and texts of Edfu temple, believed he recognized numerous allusions to a harvest festival in the proceedings: the driving of calves, treading of the earth, offering of first fruits, and dispatching of geese to the four compass points are essentially aspects of a harvest festival, although the festival at Edfu did not correspond in time to the actual Egyptian harvest.[53] Fertility rites may be a better explanation, particularly because such rites are present at the sacred marriage between Hathor and Horus, who were manifested on earth by the king and queen of Egypt. As for the populace, an ancient writer described the city and the population that hosted a great religious festival thus: "[The city] is bestrewn with faience, gleaming with natron, garlanded with flowers and fresh herbs. The prophets and fathers-of-the-god are clad in fine linen, king's suite are arrayed in their regalia, its youths are drunk, its citizens are glad, its young maidens are beautiful to see, rejoicing is round about it, festivity is in all its quarters, there is no sleep in it until dawn."[54]

While lay people were not permitted to approach the deity directly and did not enter the great temples, throughout the year there were holy festivals that allowed participation by the public, and kiosks were apparently erected outside the temple to accommodate them. What went on at such festivals can be discerned from texts of the Greco-Roman period, and would not seem appropriate to those practicing today's major religions. Judaism, Christianity, and Islam, of course, developed in the Near East but sprang from cultures that taught moderation and modesty, valued virginity, and frowned on sex for recreation rather than for procreation exclusively. In Egypt, and it is likely this is true for earlier ages as well as those for which it is clearly documented, religious festivals were times of revelry. Drinking to excess was common, but so was sexual release for both men and women. Classical writers such as Strabo give us accounts of important Egyptian religious shrines of his time, such as that of Serapis at Canopus, which thronged with festivalgoers as well as those who sought cures or oracles: "Every day and every night Canopus is crowded with people on the boats who play the flute and dance unrestrainedly, with the greatest licentiousness, both men and women, and also with the people of Canopus itself, who have places to stay close to the canal for the purpose of the same kind of relaxation and merry-making."[55]

As Dominic Montserrat has pointed out, because Egyptians did not segregate the sexes, there was plenty of opportunity for men and women to meet outside the home, and religious festivals created a socially acceptable vehicle for this meeting and mingling.[56] The religion held out the hope for rebirth in a new and better world, but this would not be possible except through the tried-and-true human way of impregnation, gestation, and birth. Sexual activity thus was a natural, respectable, and necessary component of life on this earth and the means to eternal life as well. For this reason, the king of the gods was often shown unabashedly ithyphallic, and it was common to celebrate the nocturnal wedding nights of deities. Diodorus Siculus described the ritual involvement of women with the newly chosen Apis bull thus: "Only women may look at him. They stand facing him and, pulling up their clothes, display their genitals."[57]

This recalls, as Montserrat is quick to point out, the story of Hathor revealing her private parts to her father Re in the story "The Contendings of Horus and Seth."[58] There the goddess is attempting to restore the good disposition of the powerful and fearsome god. It is not impossible that Hathor's priestesses were prepared to go to any length to ensure the safety of the world. The bawdy scenes on the one obscene papyrus that has survived from pharaonic Egypt show women with the Hathoric sistrum in their hands.[59]

Women were supposed to have exposed themselves at the festival honoring Bastet, the cat goddess and deity of the city of Bubastis in the Egyptian delta. This was a major state festival attended by the cult images of other deities and throngs of people. Obviously, from the description of Herodotus, communal singing and drinking in mixed company plus "ritualized ribaldry" were part of this great national event. Montserrat suggests that the Bubasteia "inscribes female sexuality on the maintenance of cosmic order and the political status quo. . . . The sexuality of women was an integral part of the festival activity."[60] Unlike later religions that insist on celibacy for their priests and honor virgin martyrs, the ancient Egyptians felt that to die too young to have enjoyed the pleasures of sexual union was the worst of fates. Religious life and sexual experience were not inimical but were repeatedly linked by the Egyptians.

FOLK RELIGION

As we have seen, the resident divinity stood within a small boxlike tabernacle deep within the temple. A broad straight aisle approached the holy of holies, and before it was a space or a separate room that had a stone pedestal to hold the deity's portable boat shrine. The divinity is never portrayed in the temple scenes depicting holy processions. When he or she emerged from the temple it was within the tabernacle placed on the golden boat shrine that was shouldered by the wab-priests. The tabernacle was set on the boat under a light frame covered with a curtain. Thus no impious eyes could view the divine figure or its shrine. Petitioners seeking justice or help with problems might be presented on such public occasions. The god could take the role of an oracle. If it deigned to respond to a question, a "yes" answer was signified by bearing down with a forward weight on the lead priests of his entourage who proceeded forward. A negative response was signified by a withdrawal motion. While such oracular demonstrations occurred with the bark shrine of the King of the Gods at his temple in Karnak, they could also take place with local deities at provincial cult places.[61]

The deity emerged from the temple to visit other gods and goddesses at their shrines. Thus the major temples of Thebes, on the east

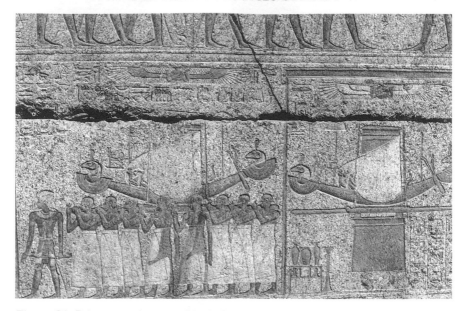

Figure 31. Priests carrying sacred bark shrine, Karnak. Photo by L. H. Lesko.

bank, were connected by the paved avenues of sphinxes that are such an impressive spectacle today. These were interrupted by way stations where the god's bark shrine could be set down, to alleviate the priests' burden but also, perhaps, to conduct special rites or to permit the presentation of offerings or petitions by the common folk. Such a station consisted of a stone platform supporting a stone pedestal, surrounded by columns or pillars, creating an open oblong chamber approached by ramps fore and aft. Thus the bearers of the god could easily walk up to the pedestal and set down the boat shrine within the shade of a roofed pavilion.

The gods might take to the river as well, sailing across on much larger splendidly decorated craft: "I made for him a festival shrine . . . of gold, silver, lapis lazuli, bronze, *senedjem*-wood and cedar." The small boat shrine and the larger golden barge both were decorated prow and stern with the heads of the divinity they bore. In the case of goddesses, it was the pleasant head of the holy woman, or two gazelles; in the case of Amun, it was the head of a ram. A boat in the form of an enormous goose, also sacred to Amun, is also described. Undoubtedly numerous other craft accompanied the sacred barges on their river journeys. The temples of Deir el-Bahri lay immediately across the Nile from Karnak. The sail across, by the Karnak triad for the Festival of the Valley and other events on the sacred calendar, was probably the oldest river regatta in that area. Originally the progression of Amun to the Temple of Luxor was made by land but also soon took place on the Nile. The temples on the east bank at Luxor are set parallel to the river, but were approached by a canal running perpendicular to it. Thus it was easy to have direct access to the river. Usually a small harbor basin sat below the temple which would have had a stone quay at the water's edge.

The populace must have felt as though they were separated from the holy families who dwelled within the fortresslike compounds. It has been suggested that the sign of the *rhyt*-birds (the hieroglyph for common people) with their praying human hands carved on the bases of some pillars within the great temples outer courts must indicate where members of the public were allowed to stand on certain occasions.[62] However, these chosen few were a distinct minority, and it must be assumed that most Egyptians never penetrated beyond the pylons of a major temple. It was to the rampart's external walls that people came to pray and leave petitions, just as is done today at the Wailing Wall in Jerusalem, a remnant of David's temple. The outer walls of Egyptian holy places often had ears engraved on them so that the gods could listen to the personal appeals of the illiterate masses. Some graven wall images of gods are titled in a way to indicate they too could listen to supplicants. At Karnak there was a cult place for Amun Who Listens to Prayers, designed for the common folk who could not enter the sacred space of the gods' houses. An image of Ptah Who Hears Prayers is identifiable at the High Gate to Ramses III's temple at Medinet Habu on Luxor's west bank.[63] Small stone stelae carved with human ears have been found which indicate, through their inscriptions, that people could leave their petitions as votives at holy places, in the hope that the deity appealed to would "hear" their pleas and respond in the desired way.[64] However, the living could also use intermediaries. Famous sages, priests, and officials were allowed to leave their own statues within the temple precincts, and in return for such a privilege these men engraved their monuments with texts in which they promise to intercede with the resident deity of the temple on behalf of anyone who honors the memory of the commemorated by a prescribed ritual: "I am the *is* of

the goddess, the messenger of his mistress. Anyone with petitions speak
. . . to my ear; then I will repeat them to my mistress in exchange for
offerings. Give to me *hnqt*-beer upon my hand and *srmt*-beer for my
mouth, sweet and pleasant oil for my shaven head, fresh garlands for
my neck. Pour out for me with wine and beer, [for] I am the *is* of the
Golden One."[65]

Some deities were undoubtedly deemed more approachable than
others, as attested by the numerous votives found around the Hathoric
shrines at Deir el-Bahri. Also, some deities were associated with curative
powers, and their temples accommodated overnight guests hoping for
a cure. The afflicted of soul or body were allowed to sleep on the
temple premises, sometimes for dream interpretation sessions with
certain priest or to be cured by a commiserating deity. One example of
this was the wise man Amunhotep son of Hapu who served Amunhotep
III, the Eighteenth Dynasty ruler. This sage was not the first of his class
to become deified after his death. His elaborate tomb on the west bank
at Thebes became the site of a pilgrimage, and his fame increased over
the centuries. One thousand years after his death, his cult was so popular
that it had to be removed to the ruins of the temple Hatshepsut had
built at Deir el-Bahri to accommodate the faithful. Here the infirm
came to sleep in the presence of the holy man in hope of a cure.[66] From
the late New Kingdom on comes proof that amuletic charms to ward
off misfortune, disease, and demons were inscribed on small bits of
papyrus to be worn around the neck. From such personal oracular
decrees we may turn to the public monuments, such as the large basalt
slab now in the British Museum and known as the Metternich Stela,
which is the grandest rendition of a magical *cippus* (pillar) of Horus.
Dating from the last or Thirtieth Egyptian dynasty, this stela must have
stood in a publicly accessible space. Featuring in high relief the figure
of young Horus standing on a crocodile and brandishing snakes and
scorpions in his hands, the spells of the lengthy inscription ward off
the devastating effects of bites. Thoth, the god of wisdom, is credited
with saving Horus from a scorpion sting, but another spell credits Re,
also portrayed in his sun disk at the center top of the stela, with con-
juring the poison to recede. It is believed that water poured over such a
stela transmitted its magical power to those in need. Many much smaller
"Horus on the Crocodile" stelae and statues have been unearthed, sometimes with no inscriptions and sometimes featuring other deities besides

Horus, such as Bes, the household god who looked after women and children in particular.

There are few settlement sites of the pharaonic period that have survived or been excavated by archaeologists, but one that has been identified and studied may be visited today immediately to the west of the line of royal temples on the west bank at Luxor. This is the community at Deir el-Medina, which was built in the Eighteenth Dynasty to house the civil servants who created the large tunnellike but highly decorated tombs of the royal family. Today one can see the stone foundations of a small walled village of row houses and visit the tombs of these royal artisans which have beautifully painted burial crypts below ground, the murals of which express the optimistic religious expectations of the owner concerning the Hereafter. It is clear from such painted scenes that these middle-class tomb owners believed they would enter the realm of the gods on death, that they would come face-to-face with the greatest gods and enjoy life in the elysian fields of the Great Beyond. Their tomb chapels, which were tiny offering places holding a stela portraying the pious family, were topped by small pyramids that evoke the solar religion. It is the burial crypts that were decorated. Today many preserve the brightly painted murals, some of which are vignettes inspired by the Book of the Dead cast large on the walls and vaulted ceiling. Here may be seen the primeval Mehet-Weret cow as well as Osiris, Isis, and Nepthys (the latter appearing as kites on the prow and stern of Osiris's boat). They and the western mountain, with the hands of Nut supporting the sun disk of Re, represent the alternative possibilities for eternal life with the great gods. Isis and Nephthys flank the jackal-headed (masked) priest of Anubis as he embalms the dead. The couple who own the tomb are shown worshiping before Anubis and Hathor, Mistress of the West. The goddesses Neith and Selket, long regarded as protectors of the dead, are present too, as seen in Tomb No. 2 of the workman Khabekhenet.[67] Thus it is apparent that the tomb owners were quite religious and optimistically spent much of their resources preparing their tombs and burial equipment so that they too could attain a state of blessedness on a par with their social betters.

Besides beautifully decorated tombs, the skilled artisans have also left us writings of numerous kinds, which show that they believed life's maladies and misfortunes were sometimes dispensed by gods and goddesses as punishments. They wore magical spells to ward off evils—attacks by dangerous animals, demons, or dead persons, for instance. On a happier note, love spells such as this one have been found too:

> Make x born of x run after me like a cow after grass,
> like a servant after her children
> like a drover after his herd.[68]

The villagers, plagued by problems, also had recourse to a local wise woman, or *rht*, who was perhaps clairvoyant and who may have been a fixture in many communities. People consulted this "wise woman" to help them find missing items and better understand puzzling events. Joris Borghouts has suggested that the village wise woman was a specialist in mythology "in order to determine which particular influence (*b'w*) of a god or goddess was responsible for a problem."[69] If he is correct, it follows that women were very much involved in handing down lore mythological or otherwise in this culture, perhaps in all early cultures, through an oral tradition.

Their village stood close to their own tombs but also was home to many chapels dedicated to favorite gods. Votive stelae—stone tablets carved with the images of whole families making obeisance before a favorite deity—were dedicated to expressing thanks or confidence in one or another deity, or winning the support of the powerful spirits who, it was hoped, would watch over the welfare of the devout both in this life and the next. The local villagers maintained cults of gods in modest chapels on the outskirts of their village, and both male and female villagers took on religious roles to service the local forms of the divinities. This community also embraced and deified their (alleged) founders, the great queen from the early Eighteenth Dynasty, Ahmose-Nefertari, and her son, Amunhotep I, for whom she had acted as regent for some years. The cult of this royal couple was maintained for the four hundred years of the village's existence and spread beyond its borders as well. They appear as living images in the private tombs with local priests burning incense before the royal figures. Several painted cult statues of the queen and her son have been found at this village.

There were about eighteen chapels built by this community on its outskirts.[70] One of the largest, at the north end of the village, was dedicated under King Seti I to the cult of Hathor. Long after the village was abandoned, the place remained sacred to the goddess and in the Ptolemaic period received a stone temple of even greater proportions. Many of the written texts that survive from this village (which has yielded thousands of private documents) refer to the worship of male gods, but judging from the size of Hathor's shrine, she was a very popular deity there. It could be that her following was mostly among the women of the village who were not educated enough to express their thoughts in writing. The artisans of course honored the deities, like Ptah, who were associated with crafts, while their literate administrators maintained shrines to Thoth, the god of wisdom and patron of scribes, and to Seshat, the goddess of writing. Alongside the great national deities, however, were local ones such as Meretseger, Lady of the Western Mountain, the divine spirit who inhabited the peak that loomed over their village.

Tomb scenes and secular texts alike indicate that divine processions with the gods' images were an important part of the religious activities of the village. There was probably no professional clergy here, but the workmen and their wives served as priests and chantresses on the feast days. As the wise Ani admonished:

> Celebrate the festival of your god,
> again at its season,
> When it is neglected, God is furious . . .
> The occurrence of singing, dancing, and censing is his
>   food,
> Receiving obeisance is beneficial to him.[71]

The deified founder Amunhotep I had many feast days through the year at which his statue was carried about the environs of the village by his wab-priests. He was called on to give oracular pronouncements with their help, to resolve disputes, and to identify perpetrators of crimes. Although there was a village tribunal, a plaintiff who was not satisfied with a decision could appeal to the divine Amunhotep for his opinion.

In his famous didactic text of the Nineteenth Dynasty, Ani instructs,

> Offer to your god
> Beware of wronging him
> You should not question his lead

Do not deal arbitrarily with him when he appears in glory.
do not approach him to lift him up.
You should not deface instruction,
Beware that he may give an abundance of favors.
Let your eye observe his furious conduct
And you should do obeisance in his name
He gives the power at a million forms
Those who magnify him are magnified.
Do not accost him when he appears
Do not jostle him in order to carry him
Do not disturb the oracles.
Be careful, help to protect him,
Let your eye watch out for his wrath,
And kiss the ground in his name.
He gives power in a million forms,
He who magnifies him is magnified.[72]

Several of the chapels had benches along two walls for seven people on one side and five on the other. The purpose of this arrangement is problematic, because it is not known whether the chapels served as meeting houses for work-related guilds or were cult places for families.[73] Found in the ruins of these chapels were libation basins and other cult objects and also ash from cooking. Animal pens have been identified close by, and it is likely that sacrifices with cooked meat offerings took place in the chapels, followed by the same type of Reversion of Offerings known from the principal temples' rituals.

These very religious workers also set up more than fifty small shrines dedicated to favorite deities along the path to the Valley of the Kings where they worked. They slept overnight at a camp near their worksite most days of the week, returning to their village and their families only on the weekend.

Literacy may have been higher in this village of skilled artisans, scribes, and administrators than it was in Egypt generally. Perhaps that is why organized religion flourished here: men could serve as reciter priests, reading from sacred scrolls, and the local artists could produce many shrines, cult figures, and votive statues and stelae for the inhabitants. At any rate numerous manuscripts have been recovered from Deir el-Medina that reflect on the spirituality of the inhabitants. For example:

Do not make noise in the abode of god,
Shouting is his abomination;
Pray you with a loving heart,
Whose every word has been hidden.
that he may provide your requirements,
When he knows what you say.
that he may accept your offerings.[74]

I praise the Golden One, I worship her majesty
I extol the Lady of Heaven
I give adoration to Hathor
Laudations to my Mistress!
I called to her, she heard my plea.[75]

From Deir el-Medina comes enough evidence to prove that ordinary men and women could serve the divinities in their local shrines, but the great temples of the land and their cults were administered by a more professional clergy, at least in the New Kingdom and later periods, when a true priestly class developed. It is time to study the exalted personnel that inhabited the special realm of the great temples of Egypt.

PROPHET, CHANTRESS, AND DIVINE WIFE

Earliest records reflect only the role of the royal family in religion and thus refer only to activities at the royal necropolis and the major cult centers of the Old Kingdom. We do not know what local village shrines might have existed. Just as the major governmental posts were held by king's sons and other male relatives in the Fourth Dynasty, the daughters and wives of kings were priests in the cults of major deities. At the height of the pyramid age, a time, it can be argued, that was the true pinnacle of Egyptian civilization, the queen acted as prophet of major gods such as Thoth and Wep-wawet and important goddesses such as Hathor and Neith and oversaw the cult of the deceased kings of her family as well. For instance, the first wife of King Khafre, Meresankh, was a priestess of the god Thoth and her mother, Queen Hetepheres, a prophetess of King Khufu, officiating in the mortuary cult of the predecessor of her husband, King Radedef, in what may have been the largest temple of her era.[76]

The Fifth Dynasty saw political and religious positions extended outside of the royal families, and thus common-born women appear in the records frequently as priestesses of the goddess Hathor, surely the most important goddess of the time, as she was the partner of Re in the recently expanded solar religion and thus regarded as the holy mother of the king of Egypt. Royal women still filled the roles of priestess of Hathor and other deities, but the numbers of temples probably expanded as records show that now there were hundreds of women involved in the cults. Women are found officiating, not only in Hathoric temples but also in the cults of Neith, Thoth, Khons, Wepwawet, and Ptah of Memphis.[77] The records are most plentiful for the great goddess Hathor, however, and they have been collected from the entire country and scrutinized by Marianne Galvin.[78]

Hathor's priesthood was predominately female until the end of the Old Kingdom. It is apparent that some women could be priestesses at more than one Hathoric temple and that positions in the temple hierarchy were not inherited. Thus the goddess's clergy formed through genuine devotion, not nepotism. By studying hundreds of documents, mainly tomb inscriptions, Galvin discovered that four hundred women held the rank of priestess or prophetess of Hathor; these women represented a cross-section of society and came from throughout Egypt. This indicates that the women were completely in charge of serving the goddess directly and of administering the revenues, mainly foodstuffs and linen, generated by lands and staffs belonging to the temple. Galvin also found mother-in-law/daughter-in-law connections among Hathor's clergy in the Old Kingdom.[79] Perhaps older women in her cult tried to find nice Hathor girls for their sons.

While prophetesses were full-time clerics, there were also lay women with the rank of *wabet*, or pure one, who served in the temple for one month at intervals spaced throughout the year and received the same payment for their services as did the men of this category. Another rank for Old Kingdom temple women was *meret* priestess; these served as members of the temple's troop of sacred musicians. Records suggest that the musical troops were first associated only with the goddess cults, like those of Bat, Isis, Nekhbet, Bastet, and Hathor.[80] They not only entertained the divinity, but also sang welcomes to the king in royal celebrations.

By the late Sixth Dynasty records begin to show a change: men were also attracted to the very popular and widespread cult of Hathor, and there was a decrease in the number of female clergy and an increase in the involvement of men. Most likely this important goddess, as divine mother of the king of Egypt, attracted so much material as well as personal support from the royal family that any official association with the cult automatically carried great prestige. Her temple's wealth was probably also a factor. At any rate, while the priestly posts remained, for a time, in the control of women, the men filled a new position, that of overseer of prophetesses, which hints at administrative responsibilities. This may have come about for the practical reason that few women were formally educated, and as the temples possessed land, tenant farmers, and other wealth, they required the services of professionally trained men to keep records and administer the endowments. Whether the women called in male help or had control wrested from them is unknown.

Soon men with leading positions in the provinces, such as governors, became chief priests in Hathor's cult while their womenfolk became members of the goddess's troop of musicians. Both males and females played cultic roles, as dance and music were very much a part of Hathor's religious observances, some of which, because of her role as welcomer of the dead into the West, took place in the cemetery.

Elite women are still found as prophets in the cult of Hathor during the first half of the Middle Kingdom (ca. 2000 B.C.). The burials of a number who were prophets in her cult are situated within the temple precinct surrounding the burial place of their royal husband, King Montuhotep II of the Eleventh Dynasty at Deir el-Bahri. The tomb of the wife of a vizier or prime minister of the pharaoh Senwosret II of the Twelfth Dynasty was in the adjacent necropolis, where inscriptions tell us she was an honored lady and prophetess of Hathor.[81] Three generations of the family of governors for the province of Kusae in Middle Egypt were leaders in the local Hathor temple, with the male governor being an overseer of prophetesses and the women of his family filling the clerical role.[82] However, by the late Middle Kingdom (ca. 1700 B.C.) the leading positions in the Hathor cult may have been exclusively held by *royal* women and, in the provincial cult centers, only by highly placed men, as female commoners in the rank of prophetess are no longer attested in the records that survive from that time.[83]

In other cults, such as that of Osiris, Lord of the Dead, at Abydos, women continued to play a major role in the mystery plays during the Middle Kingdom and later periods as well. There they impersonated Isis, the widow of Osiris, and her sister, Nephthys.

Abundant records indicate increased participation by lay people in the cults during the Middle Kingdom, and didactic texts designed to instruct the young in how to lead a good and successful life do not overlook religious obligations:

> A man should do what is beneficial for his soul.
> In the monthly service, take the white sandals,
> Enter the chapel and be discreet about the mysteries,
> Go into the shrine, and eat bread in the temple;
> Richly provide libations, increase the loaves,
> give more than the standing offerings,
> for it is beneficial for him who does it.[84]

It has long been recognized that the priesthood was limited in extent during the Middle Kingdom but grew in numbers and prestige under the New Kingdom. Now there were five degrees of rank held by men, the first, second, and third prophets, the divine father, and the *wab*-priests.

Although it dates to the Greco-Roman period, a text survives which probably reflects age-old standards for those who would enter the temple and the effort to keep the divine offices a mystery:

> O you prophets, senior *wab*-priests, chiefs of the mysteries, purifiers of the god, all who enter into the gods, lector priests who are in the temple. . . . Do not initiate wrongfully; do not enter when unclean; do not utter falsehood in his house; do not covet the property [of the temple]; do not tell lies; do not receive bribes; do not discriminate between a poor man and a great; do not add to the weight or the measuring-cord but (rather) reduce them; do not tamper with the corn-measure; . . . do no not reveal what you have seen in all the mysteries of the temples. . . . Beware, moreover, of harboring an [ungrateful] wish in the heart, for one lives on the bounty of the gods and bounty is what men call that which comes

forth from the altar after the reversion of the divine offerings upon them.[85]

The prohibitions, written in stone on the inside of door passages of the temple and passed by all who entered the sacred house, concern in part the fact that the temples could collect a tax, in the form of a portion of the harvest, from the tenant farmers who worked the land owned by the god's house. However, purity of soul was also important. The divine offices required people who were honest and just in their dealings with both divinities and people, and Egyptian ethics demanded equal treatment of both great and small, humble and rich.[86]

Anyone admitted within the sacred precincts of the temple who could approach the inner sanctum of the deity was regarded as a specially privileged person. This was not lost on earlier Egyptologists, who frequently translated as "priestess" the term *shmoyt*, a title for a female member of a hener troupe; a better translation is "chantress." The second half of the second millennium B.C., the Egyptian Empire period (New Kingdom), yields many private monuments on which the titles of Chantress and Musician often follow an elite lady's title, House Mistress. Upper-class women are often portrayed in sculpture or tomb paintings holding the menat-necklace and the sistrum rattle associated, particularly, with Hathoric rituals. The prestige of women who bore the title Chantress is indicated by the fact that in private letters from husbands, the men actually address their wives using their cultic titles.

Women who were chantresses of Amun in the Theban area seem to have participated at a number of different temples. In the New Kingdom the deities known to have had heners, were the goddesses Isis, Bastet, Nekhbet, and Hathor and the gods Montu, Khons, Thoth, Min, Sobek, and Amunhotep I, the deified king of the early Eighteenth Dynasty. The singers of Hathor seem to have impersonated that goddess, and the hener of Amun-Re also did so, as they participated in the great national festivals, like the Feast of the Valley, held in the necropolis annually. Like the male priests, the women of the temple were divided into phyles and served one month out of every three in the temple. This meant they had leave from their jobs should they be employed: "I your humble servant couldn't come myself owing to the fact that I, your humble servant, entered the temple on the twentieth day of the month to serve as *wab*-priestess for the month."[87] So wrote the House Mistress

Irer, in charge of a factory of women weavers in the Twelfth Dynasty, to her sovereign.

Documented at the Temple of Karnak from as early as Queen Hatshepsut's reign, the God's Wife of Amun, ostensibly a high priestess, had several cultic duties. Along with the highest-ranking male priests, she not only consecrated food offerings but also burned the names of enemies of Egypt over a brazier.[88] In a sense this was an official act of state in a state that was totally entwined with the religious establishment, and a magical way of protecting the sovereignty and security of the country. Thus these clerics acted in the name of the king and were, it is believed, highly esteemed for their impressive magical power. The God's Wife is also portrayed leading the other prophets into the purification tank, presumably for cleansing before entering into the presence of the god.[89]

Another high female religious title attested in the New Kingdom and later was that of Divine Votaress. In the Eighteenth Dynasty this was occasionally held by women of considerable status at court or by the wife of the First or Second Prophet at the Temple of Karnak.

The New Kingdom saw the professionalization of the priesthood. Literate men were positioned at the top of the hierarchy, and their sons often held important clerical posts in the major temples. However, their wives and daughters are found in important supportive roles in the same temple as their husbands or fathers. In this way priestly families became entrenched, intermarried with each other, and became a superior class. Such families came to control much of the wealth of the kingdom, which was bestowed generously by the pharaohs on the gods.

Usually the wife of the chief prophet of a temple was the leader of its hener and bore the title Chief of the Hener. In the Twentieth Dynasty, the Third Prophet of Amun was also the First Prophet of Mut, and his wife served as a chantress of Amun. These chantresses not only participated in temple services by providing the musical accompaniment, they also apparently helped administer the temple's estates. Records survive indicating that such women, at least those married to prophets in the temple, could receive and disburse commodities, particularly those destined for the temple's sacrificial altars.[90]

Heners associated with the cult of the goddess Hathor were involved in funeral rites in the cemeteries. Already in the Middle Kingdom tomb scenes portray the personnel of Hathor as including acrobatic bare-breasted women in short skirts dancing ecstatic dances while more fully clothed women clap accompaniment and sing. These performers are placed in front of the tomb or in the funeral procession. It may be that cultic celebrations of a sexual nature (psychologists have considered dance a sexual act) would have been believed to help the dead be reconceived and reborn in the next world. Throughout most of Egyptian history, both men and women are found together in such sacred troupes. These dances at graves may well have their origins in prehistory and be reflected in the figurines with raised arms discussed in the introduction.

Besides carrying out religious celebrations, the personnel of the goddess had many other concerns. A Third Prophet of Hathor, Lady of Dendera, has left a statue of himself that records his titles. He was "overseer of secrets of all the Gods and Goddesses of Dendera, pure one of hands, and stolist priest," as well as temple scribe. He was also "Overseer of providing all divine offerings . . . who pacifies the deity with necessities, overseer of the Great Plan of the Lady of Heaven, prophet and astrologer." This last position would surely have necessitated special training. There were administrative posts too under his charge: "overseer of *wab*-priests of Sekhmet, overseer of cattle, overseer of craftsmen." And besides being responsible for Hathor's cult, this same man claimed to be a prophet of many deities in their forms resident at Dendera: Re, Osiris, Ptah and Sekhmet, Min-Kamutef, and Amenemope.[91]

Royal women continued to play important religious roles during Egypt's Empire period of the New Kingdom. Indeed, the wife of the founder of its Eighteenth Dynasty, Queen Ahmose-Nefertari, held the title Second Prophet of Amun in the greatest temple of the land, that of Amun-Re, King of the Gods, at Karnak. Later records indicate that the Second Prophet was responsible for temple property: he was chief administrator of the estates, workshops, and treasuries and thus supervised the temple bureaucracy, the estate agents, scribes, shepherds, farmers, beekeepers, fishermen and guards, all who worked to provide the provisions and necessities for a smooth-running institution. However, Ahmose-Nefertari, who was distinguished later by deification after death and a cult that lasted for centuries, exchanged the post with her husband, the king, in exchange for enough lands and personnel to create an endowment to support a "college" of female temple musicians and singers.[92] These women may have lived celibate lives together, for they were apparently buried together in large tombs in the Theban necropolis, but we have no details, unfortunately, about this sisterhood.[93] From the Divine Birth inscription at the Temple of Luxor, however, comes a reference to Amun-Re, "pre-eminent in his harem." This suggests that at least some female temple personnel would be correctly considered as serving as concubines for the great god. However, there are numerous married women members in the hener of Karnak and other temples at this time, members of phyles serving only part-time, so that various levels of participation and intimacy with the deity are likely.

Although she was no longer Second Prophet in the Amun temple, Queen Ahmose-Nefertari took on the role of God's Wife of Amun, a title traceable to the Middle Kingdom. After her, it was bestowed on her daughter, Meritamun, and next on Hatshepsut, who was God's Wife until she became king, when her daughter Neferure assumed the cultic role. The mother of Hatshepsut's successor is also credited with this rank, and it can be traced through royal women until the "monotheistic" revolution of Akhenaten and Nefertiti, after which it was resurrected for the royal women of the Nineteenth Dynasty. Then the title was held by princesses, but queens, such as Ramses II's Nefertari, are shown sacrificing at the high altar, as in the brilliantly painted scenes inside her tomb.[94]

Like the king of Egypt, the principal queen and mother of the heir to the throne was also considered divine, equated with Hathor (daughter-wife of the sun god with whom the king was equated) or with Isis, the personified throne. Artistic portrayals of queens often depict them as the earthly manifestation of the goddess Hathor and later in the Ptolemaic period, as Isis. Royal women are frequently portrayed in temples in the company of the gods: Queen Nefertari is portrayed being crowned by Hathor in the queen's temple at Abu Simbel.[95] Queen Tiy was sculpted wearing the headdress of Hathor, the sun's disk and cow horns.[96] In comparison, the royal sons almost never appeared on the monuments. This has led to the suggestion that divine kingship was really an androgynous, or bipolar, concept, dependent on both the female and the male element that kept the cosmos functioning properly.[97]

Records pertaining to the various goddess cults are not as readily available as those pertaining to the clergy of Thebes and the vast temple complex at Karnak. From the end of Egypt's Empire period, when the country split politically between north and south and the First Prophet of Amun-Re at Karnak controlled the south and maintained the numerous great temples of the region, records show that the wife of the First Prophet became the Prophetess of Mut and her daughter became God's Wife of Amun. Before this there is no record of a female prophet for Mut; only males seem to have held this office. The surviving records are far from complete, however. Andrzej Niwinski believes that the title Divine Adoratrice of Amun was now a celibate office for a princess.[98] Maatkare, daughter of Pinudjem I, wrote her names on the monuments in cartouches, as if she were a queen, and in her funerary papyrus the princess receives offerings from priests, as if she were a god. She herself is not shown working in the elysian fields (BD Sp. 110) but has men doing the work for her. Women of this high priestly family also bore titles such as Divine Mother of Khons, sempriestess (presiding over the mortuary cult of the king) at the cult temple of Ramses III (Medinet Habu), and Prophetess of Amun and Mut. The first wife (later divorced) of the First Prophet of Amun Pinudjem as well as his second wife claimed titles such as Prophetess of Mut in Karnak, Prophetess of Khons in Karnak, Prophetess of Onuris-Shu, Prophetess of Min, Horus, and Isis in Apu, Prophetess of Nekhbet of Nekheb and of Horus in Per-Anty and Osiris, Horus and Isis in Abydos as well as of the cults of numerous other deities in Upper Egyptian towns. Niwinski interprets these titles as an indication that the wife of the high priest, parallel to her husband's supreme authority over the whole masculine priesthood, was "the superior chief of the whole feminine personnel in the territory subordinated to Upper Egyptian rule."[99] However, such a position had hitherto been indicated by the title Chief of the Hener of such and such a deity. The use of "prophet" now seems to give additional prestige and perhaps monetary rewards not known previously.

One of the products of the temple, and probably a source of revenue for them, was created in its House of Life, or scriptorium. These were the papyrus scrolls containing magical spells that allowed the justified deceased to enter before Osiris and his tribunal and gain access to a blessed afterlife. These Books of the Dead came in various editions, some with more spells than others and some illustrated in more detail or color than others. A case can be made for the participation of the daughters of the prophets at temples in the production of these books.[100] Not only illustrating but even possibly editing (choosing which spells should be included) may well have occupied young women of priestly families who were probably educated sufficiently, as elite women of the previous Empire period seem to have been.

The Twenty-first Dynasty has left a wealth of records reflecting on the family of high priests of Amun at Thebes and of Ptah at Memphis. It is obvious that prophets were succeeded by their sons and grandsons and that marriages were pursued between the families of the various grades of prophets at one temple and also the families of prophets at neighboring temples. This is found in the Twentieth Dynasty, if not earlier. The monuments of a priestly family of El-Kab, who served the vulture goddess Nekhbet in the reign of Ramses III, show that First Prophet Setau inherited his post from his father and that his father-in-law was a high priest of a deity in a neighboring town. Setau's wife had charge of the Hener of the goddess, and one of their daughters married the son of the First Prophet of Amun at Karnak. All but one of Setau's sons had priestly positions in their hometown.[101] Clearly the priesthoods of Egypt saw themselves as a select and superior class and attempted to hold on to the positions and revenues of their holy offices for generations. There are also marriages between priestly families and those of high officials, including mayors and taxing masters. Power, influence, and attendant fortune must have been the motivation (in the New Kingdom the temples are believed to have owned up to 15 percent of the arable land in Egypt), although similar levels of education, values, and culture would also have been considerations in such marriage alliances.

Most significant, however, were the marriage alliances during the Twenty-second and Twenty-third dynasties, when Egypt was under Libyan rule, between the royal family and the priesthood at Thebes; one involved a third prophet and a daughter of the royal house. The priest Nebneteru's handsome granite block statue in the Cairo museum expresses his satisfaction with a long life in the priesthood:

> I was an excellent unique one,
> An important one in his city, and
> greatly esteemed in the temple.

Amun was the one who appointed me to be door-keeper of
    heaven . . .
My concern was for the house of god
He gave me rewards in blessings
He favored [me] as he wished.
He rewarded me with a son . . .
I saw my sons as great prophets,
as one son after another came forth from me.
I attained ninety-six years,
Being healthy, without sickness.[102]

Marriages between the royal Libyan dynasty, ruling from the Egyptian delta, and the priests of Theban Karnak may have been an attempt on the part of kings of foreign extraction to gain greater acceptance in Upper, or southern, Egypt. It may also have been a means for the king to keep a political hold over the priests of Thebes, who were immensely rich and influential in that part of the country. There was still another way open to the ruling dynasts, however. The fourth king of that dynasty, Osorkon III (777–749) established his daughter, Shepenwepet I, as a celibate God's Wife who would live in Thebes and give all her attention to the Karnak temples and cults. She received all of the estates and property formerly possessed by the high priest there and in religious matters was very like a female pope, ruling by the word of Amun. Shepenwepet ensured her succession by adopting an heir, and this younger woman carried the venerable title Divine Votaress. As these women enjoyed long lives that spanned kingly reigns, they were a source of both moral and political stability and leadership in the southern half of the country. While the surviving records are sparse and haphazard, one tells of a Libyan lady Nebimauemhat, daughter of the chief of the Libu tribe and a contemporary of Shepenwepet and her successor, who belonged to the college of Theban temple women, apparently the same sisterhood that had been under the supervision of the Divine Votaress since the New Kingdom.[103]

This same Third Intermediate Period records the priestly post overseer of the nurses of Khonsu the child. Khonsu, of course, was the offspring (a moon god) of Amun and Mut. It would seem logical that his "nurses" were the ladies of his hener.

The Nubians of the south, who wrested Egypt from the Libyans, were also devoted to Amun. Their royal family installed a princess as God's Wife of Amun at Karnak, the first being Amunirdis. She in turn adopted her niece as her successor. The large pyloned funerary chapels of this line of women are still seen today at Medinet Habu on the west bank at Luxor. The mayor of Thebes at that time was also a priest at Karnak. He left many statues besides a gigantic tomb. On one statue now in Berlin he tells us,

> I renewed the temple of Mut the Great, Lady of Isheru
> So that it is more beautiful than before
> I embellished her bark with electrum and
> All its images with real stones.[104]

The Twenty-sixth dynasty was again a new royal house, and its Princess Nitocris was sent to Thebes from the delta palace of her father accompanied by a flotilla of boats containing a considerable "dowry" for her divine husband, Amun-Re.[105] This princess and God's Wife outlived her father and the administrators he had appointed for her. Before her reign of more than fifty years was finished, she was able to appoint her own administrators and also refused to adopt a successor so as to keep the kings in the north from having influence in the south. Finally in 594 B.C., when in her eighties, Nitocris adopted her great-niece Ankhnesneferibre, daughter of Psammetichus II, soon after he came to the throne of Egypt. This young woman was given the title First Prophet, or High Priest, of Amun, and is thus the only woman known to have held this high clerical office. It would seem that old Nitocris engineered this move deliberately to preserve the importance of women at Karnak.

From the seventh century B.C. comes evidence that the cult of Isis, at least in the north, was in the hands of a self-appointed and hereditary priestly family. "This would explain the lack of consistency in the portraits of Isis found in Egyptian art from this period and later. She does not have a typology familiar from the established images of her sometime partner Serapis, for instance. All the surviving examples of the Isis Aretalogies, or Praises, vary too, again showing independent sources."[106] Thus the cult of Isis was not under the control of a single high priest or one body of high clerics, and this was the case, most likely, for most of the Egyptian goddesses.

Figure 32. The God's Wife Shepenwepet from her tomb chapel at Medinet Habu. Photo by L. H. Lesko.

Herodotus, who visited Egypt in the fifth century B.C., lists in his *Histories,* book 2, the priestly class as the first of seven major occupations. It is clear that the priestly positions were still passed along in families and that the temples retained much of their power and importance.

From the last centuries before Egypt became a Roman possession in 30 B.C., the Ptolemaic dynasty of Macedonian origin ruled. The seacoast city of Alexandria was their brilliant new capital, but it had a largely foreign population. The major city for the Egyptians was still Memphis, and here in the cult of its own god Ptah women still played a role as musician priestesses in processions. A new title, Wife of Ptah, probably inspired by the earlier Theban Wife of Amun, was created by the famous Queen Cleopatra for the wife of the high priest of Ptah, and several funerary stelae record the lives and families of the high priests' wives.[107] The priests of Ptah may well have been singled out for royal favor because the south, rebellious throughout Egyptian history, may have been resisting Ptolemaic rule. Studies have shown, however, that the king reaped most of the tax wealth from the country now, and temples had to pay an annual tax from which they had been exempt in Pharaonic times. A royal subvention financed much of the costs associated with temple cults, although the Ptolemies appointed officials to represent their interests and thus controlled temple expenditures.

Evidence shows that women officiated in Isis's temples, although not necessarily in greater numbers or higher rank than men. Sarah Pomeroy has noted that women were "responsible for a very high proportion of dedications to this goddess in the Greco-Roman world" and that since women probably had less disposable income, this is noteworthy.[108]

The Ptolemaic queens of Egypt were identified with the major Egyptian goddesses, following an age-old Egyptian tradition. They were also, as certain earlier Egyptian queens, made divine on their deaths. Berenice I, the last wife of Ptolemy I, had more than one temple dedicated to her cult, which associated her with Aphrodite (Hathor). Ptolemy II lavished funds in celebration of the divinity of his late sister, who was also his wife, and on an extravagant temple at Alexandria to house her cult statue. Arsinoe Philadelphus was introduced as a *sunnaos theos* (shrine-sharing deity), to share the cult of many individual temples with their chief deity. As Dorothy J. Thompson has pointed out, this was "a bold and innovative move. An Egyptian-style cult of the new goddess, funded by a tax on orchards and vineyards known as the *apomoira*, was physically located in already existing temples, her close association with the well-established gods might serve to press her claim for acceptance among the population at large."[109] Later, in 238 B.C., the daughter of Euergetes I, Berenice, died during a national gathering of priests at Canopus and was promptly deified, assimilated with Tefnut, the daughter of Re, and her cult received another female priestly position, the office of *athlophore*. Indeed, Ptolemaic queens were identified with a number of different goddesses, both Greek and Egyptian, but foremost among them was Isis, who had now come to the fore both in Egypt and abroad.[110]

Deification of Ptolemaic queens, then, seems to have been quite common, and the deified queens had women priestesses who were daughters of leading families. Obviously, great social prestige was associated with serving the cult of the queen. The office could be held for life, and the officeholder could lead a normal life, that is, marry and have children, if she wished. In Alexandria, the Ptolemaic capital of Egypt, there was one female *canephore* (basket carrier) for the cult of the queen Arsinoe Philadelphus whose responsibilities included leading a grand procession of city officials and others while carrying a golden basket containing offerings. The monuments of this queen credit her with pharaonic titles and the epithets "daughter of Geb" and "image of Isis" in whose image she was often portrayed. A scene on Euergetes' Gate at Karnak depicts Ptolemy III burning incense before both Ptolemy III and Arsinoe II as the goddess Philadelphus.

Priestesses are recorded for the cults of Arsinoe II and Cleopatra I, II, and IV:

> I will make you a goddess at the head of the gods on
>   earth . . .
> I give you the breath of life that emanates from my nose
> to give life to your ba,
> to rejuvenate your body for ever and ever.[111]

There were still other sacred offices designated for women, and it would not be surprising if this stemmed from the strong tradition of female religious participation in Egypt of the pharaohs. The above mentioned Wife of Ptah became, once the Roman Augustus seized control of Egypt, a Prophetess of Caesar.[112] Certainly there continued to be groups of female religious singers in the temples.

This is seen for the cult of Isis in Europe too. There are a number of paintings surviving from Pompeii and Herculaneum, the towns that were buried by the eruption of Vesuvius in 79 A.D., which show the rituals of Isis in progress. A fresco from Herculaneum portrays a sanctuary in Campania complete with sphinxes and live ibises. A white-robed priest officiates, and a priestess holds the sistrum and situla (for holy water). Priestesses of Isis are documented from several sites, Ostia and Beneventum among them, and appear alongside male priests in the cult. There was also a choir, which recalls the ancient hener in Egypt.[113]

The cult of great Egyptian queens continued there in the Roman period, despite Roman rule and reductions in the power and wealth of the temples. Cleopatra VII, the most famous of all Ptolemaic rulers, was still celebrated at Philae, in the great Temple of Isis, during the early centuries of Christianity, enduring until 536 A.D. when the temple was finally closed by the Byzantine emperor Justinian.

TEMPLE WEALTH

"I filled its Treasury with the products of the lands of Egypt: gold, silver, every costly stone amounting to hundreds of thousands. Its Granary was overflowing with goodness and abundance; its lands, its herds, their multitudes were like the sand of the shore. I taxed for it Upper Egypt as well as the Delta. Nubia and Djaghi came to it bearing their tribute."[114]

Thus the wealth of his mortuary temple is described by a Twentieth Dynasty king whose reign actually saw poor economic times and a shrunken realm. The treasure and personnel, taken from captives of war, which Eighteenth Dynasty pharaohs presented to the Karnak triad, would have far exceeded the claims of Ramses III. However, his own temple, with its well-preserved suite of rooms that served as its vaultlike treasury, preserves graphically the endowments of such a religious institution. In the relief scenes that decorate the walls of the treasury, Ramses holds a tray of little bags that are labeled as containing "august precious stones," and Thoth, the "secretary of the gods," is depicted weighing gold of foreign lands while Ramses offers a pile of gold to

Amun-Re.[115] In a side room, the king is shown offering silver, gold, and temple furniture, including a harp, to Amun-Re and Mut.[116] Elaborate sacred vessels for myrrh and ointment are prominent in the relief scenes here. In another room the king is shown offering a chest of precious minerals before the shrine of Amun-Re and Khonsu.[117]

Elegant libation vessels of precious metals and intricately carved or painted chests were standard furnishings in the houses of deities. From the Medinet Habu relief scenes it is obvious that Amun-Re was also the recipient of raw materials—piles of gold and turquoise, blocks of lapis lazuli, and gums shaped into elaborate forms. Sacks of gold and ingots of copper are also pictured. Besides these, the inscription lists silver, royal linen, decorated garments, and resin. Papyrus Harris I, written to record Ramses III's munificence to the gods, lists many luxury items such as silver vases, silver caskets, silver weapons cases, and gold jewelry.[118] All these commodities were probably kept in the treasury of the temple. Gold mines in the Eastern Desert were owned by individual temples, such as Karnak and that built by Seti I at Abydos.[119] Great wealth continued to be expended on deities, and still under the Ptolemies, records tell of gold dust being poured out before the cult statues of goddesses, which are themselves covered in gold. The very walls of the sanctuary were quite possibly given a veneer of gold.[120]

Outside, the temple granaries were extensive, judging from those numerous brick-arched structures still standing at the Ramesseum, the temple built in western Thebes one hundred years earlier by Ramses II. The temples received the produce of numerous farms because extensive acreage of agricultural land belonging to the king, known as Khato-land, was administered by the temples. Because the farms could be scattered over much of Egypt, the boats of the temple tax masters plied the Nile north and south, collecting 30 percent of the harvest from tenant farmers. Great surpluses were protection against years of want when the Nile inundation was not at ideal levels and provided barter power, as wheat and barley were prime commodities of exchange. B. J. Kemp has observed that major Egyptian temples were "the reserve banks of the time."[121] Large parcels of acreage, grazing lands, and flax fields as well as numerous head of cattle also belonged to the temple. Ramses III boasted on his calendar that several thousand head of livestock had been captured during his campaigns against the Libyans. Most were turned over to Amun, the god of the empire. Meat was a luxury for the average Egyptian, whose diet consisted largely of fish and vegetables, but meat was certainly regarded as food fit for the gods and frequently is listed among the offerings made to them. Herodotus, who interviewed priests to learn about their life and customs when he visited Egypt in about 450 B.C., described the sacrifice of animals thus:

> They take the beast to the appropriate altar and light a fire. Then, after pouring a libation of wine and invoking the god by name, they slaughter it, cut off its head, and flay the carcass. The head is loaded with curses and taken away. . . . [T]he curses they pronounce take the form of a prayer that any disaster which threatens either themselves or their country may be diverted and fall upon the severed head of the beast. Both the libation and the practice of cutting off the heads of sacrificial beasts are common to all Egyptians in all their sacrifices, and the latter explains why it is that no Egyptian will use the head of any sort of animal for food. The methods of disemboweling and burning are various, and I will describe the one which is followed in the worship of the goddess whom they consider the greatest and honor with the most important festival. In this case, when they have flayed the bull, they first pray and then take its paunch out whole, leaving the intestines and fat inside the body; next they cut off the legs, shoulders, neck, and rump, and stuff the carcass with loaves of bread, honey, raisins, figs, frankincense, myrrh, and other aromatic substances; finally they pour a quantity of oil over the carcass and burn it. They always fast before a sacrifice and while the fire is consuming it they beat their breasts. That part of the ceremony done, they serve a meal out of the portions left over.[122]

The "father of history" goes on to state that Egyptians sacrificed only bulls and bull calves and never cows, on the grounds that they are sacred to Isis, who by this period was almost synonymous with Hathor. Nonetheless, the Saite rulers demonstrated their piety to Hathor with several outstanding artistic creations commemorating her, hoping thus to gain this goddess's protection for their rule.

It is recorded that when the Assyrians sacked Thebes in 664 B.C., they carted off two large solid gold-copper alloy obelisks from one of its temples.[123] Thus the wealth taken from Nubian gold mines was excessive indeed, and used lavishly by the pharaohs to demonstrate their devotion to the gods. Egypt rebounded after the Assyrian invasions and down into the early Roman Empire was a prosperous country. The amount of state revenues dedicated to the building and maintenance of temples under the Ptolemaic dynasty, which produced so many imposing edifices to assuage the native Egyptian population, must have been considerable.

$\mathscr{C}$ONCLUSION

Herodotus observed that "the Egyptians are religious to excess, beyond any other nation in the world,"[1] and surely this statement reflects not only the grand temples and lavish festivals he witnessed but also the general observances of the people to whom the great goddesses were very important and dear.

Neferabu, an artisan working in the royal cemetery at Thebes during the Nineteenth Dynasty, allows us an insight into his relationship with a favorite goddess:

> I summoned my Mistress
> having found her coming to me as a sweet breeze.
> She was gracious to me
> causing that I see her hand.
> She returned to me graciously
> Causing me to forget the pain that was in my heart
> For the Peak of the West is gracious
> when she is summoned.[2]

The favorite deity of a worshiper is always portrayed as supremely powerful. The multiplicity of goddesses that seem so bewildering to those of us who are products of a monotheistic world, it can be argued, were all manifestations of one Great Mother. That seems to explain most easily the syncretisms and cooperative borrowings and exchanges of the insignias and forms among the Egyptian goddesses. Certainly, they are mothers more clearly than they are wives, and, indeed, the mother figure carried considerable authority in Egyptian family life. But syncretism was used to make individual deities stand out as more powerful by combining and absorbing the attributes of one or more other divinities.

The Egyptian goddesses are strong personalities and, unlike the goddesses of Indo-European peoples, tend to be independent, not subservient to male gods. We do not find Egyptian goddesses forcibly married by male gods, and when married they still maintained a significant degree of independence and had in several cases multiple partners. They may have been associated with male partner gods but did not need these partners to display their formidable powers and work their magic.

Mut may have been the consort of Amun-Re, King of the Gods, but she was Mistress of the Crowns, Mistress of the Sky, Lady of the Two Lands, and also a consort to Ptah of Memphis. She had a career of her own but not much personality. She is the most artificial of goddesses because she was a figure that personified the state, a strongly masculine institution in which, other than queens, women did not play a role. It was Hathor and Isis who come across as appealing, genuinely female personalities to whom people could relate and turn with their personal problems. During life it was the goddesses to whom one turned for help in crises of body and mind; at death one could look forward to being embraced lovingly by the winged arms of Nut or Isis or being greeted by Hathor, who facilitated one's introduction to the Netherworld. Surely the religions of ancient Egypt could not have survived so many centuries had these deities not been approachable and believable. Surely it is significant too that while Re, the sun god, Amun-Re, King of the Gods, and Osiris, Lord of the Dead, are often thought of as the preeminent deities of ancient Egypt, in truth their cults were limited because they were removed from the life of the average person—the overwhelming majority of Egyptians. Re and Amun-Re eventually dropped into oblivion, and Osiris was overshadowed by his spouse. The cults of the great goddesses lived on.

The theologies of Egypt were replete with symbols of goddess power: the throne of Isis, the bow and arrows of Neith, the magical instruments (sistra and menat necklace) of Hathor, even the lionness head of Sekhmet and numerous other goddesses. The Egyptian artist portrayed all but the animal-headed deities as comely, svelte women, youthful and pleasing in appearance. In a rare statue Mut looks more mature, but she smiles amiably beneath the heavy weight of her crowns. None of the goddesses are meant to appear frightening except in their lionine form, and this aggressive and powerful image is generally put to good use on behalf of the people and the state.

It should be obvious that the ancient Egyptian goddesses in their strong images and many-sided personalities mirror the women who filled many roles in that society—public responsibilities as well as varied domestic concerns—but they also surpassed them in powers and activities, due to their divine nature. The goddesses were not only concerned with women's reproductive powers. They presided over the state, its safety and the monarchic succession. Their concern was for the abundance of crops and the health of the population. They decreed and also could alter people's fates, and ensured their deserving devotees a blessed life in the Hereafter. Even the lioness Sekhmet could be counted on to cure illnesses and protect against plagues, and this respect shown by the Egyptians for the lioness and the cow, the vulture and the cobra, indicates a sensitivity to and appreciation for the animal kingdom and the world of nature that has seldom if ever been equaled by any civilization.

Worshiped during two-thirds of human history, the Egyptian goddesses truly commanded the loyalty and devotion of royalty and commoners alike. Both sexes served in their priesthoods and filled the ranks of their faithful far beyond the borders of Egypt itself. Thus the claim of some spiritual feminists that men stand guilty of having tried to destroy powerful goddesses does not stand up against the Egyptian evidence. What might be said, rather, is that male gods were promoted by the state to a supreme position as creators (thus unrealistically stealing the process of producing future generations from divine females) or were put at the top of the pantheon as ruler of all the gods. However, the motivation was political: the Egyptian idea of divine kingship was the only way to unite what were once separate kingdoms under a leader who would not be seen as representing either but as descended to earth from the realm of the gods. Because most kings were male, the king was identified with male deities, and thus Horus, Re, and Osiris became prominent.

However, the female creator was still recognized, even promoted as late as Roman times in Egypt, as we saw with Neith at Edfu and Isis at Philae, and most of the great goddesses were termed Mistress (or Mother) of All the Gods and Mistress of Heaven. Thus diminution and denigration was not a sweeping and absolute fate of goddesses in ancient Egypt; far from it. Leading men of their towns and provinces were eager to serve in their cults already from the Middle Kingdom, and, as we saw in the New Kingdom, some were fanatic followers of their favorite goddess. Leading statesmen of the New Kingdom and the Late Period were proud to have their formal portraits depict them holding large insignias of a goddess like Hathor, even though some contemporary misogynist texts might, at the same time, try to cast her in a less than favorable light.

Although I have some awareness of their theories and claims, I have purposely read very little of the now-extensive literature of spiritual feminists in order not be influenced by them. This is not due to a lack of sympathy with their feelings and objectives but rather to the hope that I could gain as accurate and perceptive an understanding of what actually happened during humanity's earliest organized attempts to worship the Divine by looking at the original data, without being overly influenced by others' theories based on an assortment of data from various cultures and time periods.

It was clear to me that the very sparse and fragmentary documentation of early spiritual life in the Nile valley must be handled with care. Yes, there were goddesses from the beginning, but there were male partners as well, because a recognizable male god is depicted in the Gerzean paintings. Yes, warlords (call them patriarchs if you will) of the South, when they took command of the entire country, may well have forced their god Horus to the fore, to be understood as preeminent but identified with the king who controlled a newly united Nile valley and delta. But if Neith and her women followers were forced to recognize his supremacy, so were male gods beholden to Horus as well. This did not devastate the goddess cults of Egypt, nor did it prevent still more powerful divine females from being conceived in the historic periods that followed.

The goddesses Nut, Hathor, and Isis represented the great natural phenomena—the sun and the stars, fertility, the pleasures of life (love and music)—and along with many of their sister goddesses worked the power of magic for the good of humanity and on behalf of the gods. They interceded in daily lives, found people mates, punished and cured, nourished the newborn, and protected the dead. They offered hope in renewed and everlasting life for those who deserved salvation. They were always present, playing an important, decisive role in every stage of human life.

The religions of ancient Egypt and the literature they spawned show clearly that both men and women were able to relate to and love female divinities. The many forms these goddesses took—loving and nurturing, strong and aggressive, high-spirited and sexual—reflect the many moods of human females. That the Egyptians could recognize that there were so many sides to women and could celebrate these, make them respectable, by associating them with powerful deities in itself would lead one to the conclusion that women were not forced into repressed and limited roles by that society. The status of women of ancient Egypt as the most liberal known from the ancient world is something that I have argued for in several other publications and will not devote more space to here.[3]

Other cultures, other religions, have painted women in the darkest colors, have blamed Eve for all sin and suffering, have found woman impure and unfit for holy orders—even in some cases religious activity itself—and have proclaimed them lacking both mentally and physically. While the Egyptians distinguished between good and bad women and nurturing and angry goddesses, they obviously did not denigrate the female sex, and they celebrated the divine female in many forms. I have read Nut spells from the Pyramid Texts at the memorial services of colleagues, and the love and hope they epitomize struck listeners, including an Episcopal minister, most favorably.

Ancient Egypt was a positive, buoyant African culture in which music, dance, and alcohol were aids in the spiritual experience. This was a culture that portrayed elderly queen mothers as youthful, curvaceous sex goddesses in gigantic statuary in sacred places. Obviously women's bodies and sexuality were construed in highly positive ways by the Egyptians.

This was a society that appealed to Hathor for help in health, fertility, romance, and other personal matters, but also saw her and other goddesses as kindly receivers, indeed mothers, for their dead. The nurturing mother figure was extremely important, not only in religious contexts, but in the greater society.

This is a nation, the most powerful of its time for two thousand years, that created a goddess who wore the double crown of kingship and was credited with the careful administration of this world and the world of the gods; this was a people, the oldest of civilizations, who loved and spread the word about Isis, crediting her with the creation of all that is good and useful and giving her the power of bestowing eternal life.

From this people's earliest pinnacle of success, the Fourth Dynasty, come widespread female priesthoods; in their history's distinguished last millennium are found female prophets and pontifs in the greatest temple on earth. Certainly the Divine Adoratrices gained inner strength through their acknowledged cultic roles as earthly manifestations of goddesses as well as their practical responsibilities for their vast and historic domain. They are an impressive part of this civilization's record for appreciating and upholding the vital role of women in the spiritual life of the world.

I hope that this work, which has attempted to be merely an overview and an introduction to the "raw material"—the ancient art, artifacts, and writings that reflect the Egyptians' official and personal views of their greatest goddesses—will encourage more rational thinking and careful theorizing on the origins of goddess worship and the history of goddess cults. Egypt was one of the very earliest and most sophisticated and literate civilizations. It saw the need for several goddesses who all had individual strengths and responsibilities: the food supply, the administration of the land, the protection of the world, or welcomer of the dead. After thousands of years these female divinities combined to produce a super goddess known as Isis. With her compassion for human beings, she was the last obstacle to the "patriarchal religions" that succeeded her in influence and which required centuries to quell her. Only by the exultation of the Mother of Jesus, which began in the second century but increased in the fourth century, was Isis, the saving goddess and creatrix of all that is good and useful to humanity, finally defeated and abandoned to the ages. Today, like her marvelous Temple of Philae, she has come back (her cult has adherents in America and Europe)[4] and perhaps will find a place in the hearts of many more women who search for the female divinity, the Great Mother, to fulfill their personal longings. I hope women pilgrims will again find their way to beautiful sun-drenched Aswan and cross the waters of a specially formed lake to Isis's magical island, where one of the most beautiful temples in the world awaits.

$\mathcal{A}$ GLOSSARY OF GODDESSES

Although this list of goddesses is long, it is not complete. Many names attached to female divine figures are found in the ancient religious literature but without further identity.

Ahmose-Nefertari. Queen and consort of the founder of the Eighteenth Dynasty, she ruled the land as regent after his death on behalf of their son, Amunhotep I. She bore the title Female Chieftain of Upper and Lower Egypt and is credited with restoring temples throughout Egypt that had fallen into neglect during the previous reigns of the Second Intermediate period. Ahmose-Nefertari also held the priestly title God's Wife of Amun and founded a religious order, Divine Votaresses at Karnak. For her good works and her role at the birth of a new and brilliant stage in the life of her country, she was deified after death and enjoyed a cult for many centuries, popular among the common people.

Amunet or Amaunet, "the hidden one." Original female counterpart of Amun who was worshiped in Thebes at the beginning of the Middle Kingdom but who along with Amun was a member of the Ogdoad (the group of eight original deities) of Hermopolis that existed before creation. Amaunet was thus self-created. She was usually depicted as a woman wearing the crown of Lower Egypt and is the subject of a colossal statue at the Temple of Karnak dating to the reign of Tutankhamun.

While sometimes identified with Neith, she retained her own identity until the end of Egypt's ancient history.

Anath. A western Asiatic warrior goddess, originally from Ugarit on the Syrian coast, this goddess was probably introduced to Egypt by the Hyksos overlords but again promoted by the Ramessides, who saw her as a wife for Seth, although she sometimes accompanies Min, with the two sharing the role of fertility gods. The goddess is often depicted with weapons and wears the Atef crown, a high crown flanked with plumes. She is a protector of the king. Pharaohs sometimes named their dogs after her to stress ferocity. Ramses II even named a daughter after her. Anat was often termed Mistress of Heaven.

Anukis. The daughter and only child member of the triad of Elephantine, where her cult center was just upstream at Seheil, an island within the first cataract of the Nile. She was worshiped there together with her father, Khnum, and mother, Satis. Sometimes she is found worshiped independently, as at Komir. She is generally represented as a woman wearing a crown of tall feathers or as a gazelle. Her name means "to embrace," and as a water goddess she "embraced" the fields during the inundation period. Anukis's cult came to be associated with sexuality, and her cult center was considered to have obscene attributes.

Aritnefret. Lady of Heaven and Mistress of the Two Lands.

Arsinoe II. Ptolemaic queen of Egypt, wife of Ptolemy II. She died in 270 B.C. Her cult began then, if not before. She was regarded as a patroness of marriage.

Astarte. Western Asiatic warrior goddess who may have entered Egypt under the Hyksos domination in the Second Intermediate period and continued to be worshiped as far afield as Assyria and Mitanni. She was officially admitted to the Egyptian pantheon in the Eighteenth Dynasty and viewed as a consort of Seth. She sometimes wears a bull's horns and is known for her equestrian skill. She is shown fully human wearing the Atef crown and using the bow and arrow. Like other strong goddesses she is called a Daughter of Re.

Bastet. She of Baset (Bubastis) was a cat goddess, sometimes depicted as a lioness, known from Pyramid Texts. From the Middle Kingdom on, Bastet was sometimes depicted as a woman with a cat's head and was worshiped during the first millennium B.C. as the friendly domesticated cat, a gentle counterpart of the more dangerous lioness goddess Sekhmet. However, Bastet is one of the several goddesses known as

Daughter of Re and is thus identified with the sun's eye and its ferocity. She was also associated with the moon and protected women in their pregnancies. As she came from the eastern delta city of Bubastis, Bastet also represented the East. Herodotus visited the town in the fifth century B.C. and expressed his opinion that there was no temple in Egypt that was more attractive or whose festivals were better attended, so popular had this goddess become in the Late Period.

Bat. The full-faced female countenance and a primeval cow goddess of Upper Egypt. Bat is known for her two faces and is found thus on the early Narmer Palette and also on the bodies of sistrums. She was assimilated to Hathor by the New Kingdom.

Berenike II. Divinized Ptolemaic queen of Ptolemy III.

Beset. The female form of Bes, a lion-headed deity, known from Middle Kingdom sources, who was appealed to for protection of pregnant women and newborn children.

Cleopatra III (wife of Ptolemy IX), Cleopatra V (wife of Ptolemy XII), and Cleopatra VII (the great and last queen of Egypt). Identified with Aphrodite-Hathor.

Hathor. House, or Genealogy, of Horus. Personification of the Ennead, mother of the king, daughter/wife of the sun god Re, and thus a solar deity, but also the goddess of love and sexuality. As a promoter of fertility, she was very popular among the people. Because of her early royal associations with the necropolis, she was also identified with the desert, where cemeteries were located, and thus became the official welcomer of the dead. She could take many forms: woman, cow, lioness, or tree. Hathor, in her greatness, absorbed other goddesses throughout her history but in the end assimilated to Isis.

Hatmehyt. Fish goddess worshiped in the northeastern delta, as at Mendes from earliest times, shown as either a fish or a woman with the fish symbol on her head. Much later, she became the consort of the ram god Banebdjedet.

Hauhet. The female counterpart of Huh, boundlessness or infinity, one of the four pairs of gods in the Hermopolitan Ogdoad.

Hekat. A water goddess who helped Osiris in his resurrection from the dead and was present at the birth of royalty, hastening the last stages of labor, and thus a divine patroness of midwives. Hekat is usually shown in the form of a frog or a frog-headed woman, associated with Hermopolis. However, she was also the consort of Khnum, a creator god, and at his side breathed life into the beings he created. Cult places are known for her in Upper Egypt at Qus and in Middle Egypt at Hermopolis (Tuna el-Gebel).

Hepetethor. Coming into prominence in the Twenty-first Dynasty and known as Mistress of the West, this goddess seems more a demon, with the head of either a snake or a crocodile. Shown with knives in her hands, she could be a threat to the dead as well as their protector.

Hesat. Cow goddess and mother of the king, who appeared in the form of the golden calf whose milk quenched the thirst of humanity.

Imentet. Divinized West or necropolis region. This goddess of the dead is shown with the hieroglyph for "west" on her head and is a manifestation of both Hathor and Isis. She personified the western desert hills that received the burials of many kings and commoners.

Input. The bitch counterpart of Anubis, the jackal guardian of the cemeteries and god of embalming. She had her own cult in the seventeenth nome of Upper Egypt.

Isis. The personification of the royal throne and in myth the sister-wife of Osiris, who was revived through her magic long enough to impregnate her to conceive Horus, the divine king of Egypt. Identified with the star Sirius, she was associated with the renewal of the life-giving waters of the Nile. Later she came to be seen as a giver of eternal life to all who deserved it. Isis was more than a mother goddess and came to be seen also as responsible for the arts of civilization. Isis was worshiped extensively in the ancient Mediterranean world and then Europe after she was adopted by the Romans.

Ius-a'as. The scarab beetle on her head suggests that this goddess played a role in creation. She hailed from Heliopolis and can be seen as a counterpart to Atum, the creator god there. Late texts equate her with the hand of Atum with which he masturbated to begin his creative act.

Kauket. Counterpart of Kuk, darkness, one of the four pairs of primeval deities in the Hermopolitan Ogdoad.

Khefthernebes. Divine personification of the Theban necropolis in the New Kingdom.

Ma'at. Daughter of Re and the incarnation of cosmic order and social justice. Ma'at was always portrayed as a woman with an ostrich plume on her head and often in miniature as offered by the king during the holy services to demonstrate his role as upholder of order. It was said that the gods "lived on" Ma'at, as if partaking of her as their food. In that way they could maintain the cosmic order she represented. Ma'at is credited with giving mankind a code of ethics. She is among those goddesses regarded as the daughter of Re, and she also had a cult place of her own in the precinct of Montu at Karnak and perhaps other important places. Juridical matters may well have been decided in these "temples of Truth."

Mafdet. A cat goddess, regarded as a fierce panther who leaps at the necks of snakes. She also was lethal to scorpions, and her claws were associated with the barbs of the king's harpoon, which would attack the king's enemies in the Underworld.

Mehet-Weret. Goddess of the sky and the Great Flood who represented the watery heavens on which the sun god sailed and out of which the first land and life appeared. Usually depicted as a great cow with the sun's disk between her horns, she is sometimes called the mother of Re.

Mekhit. A lioness goddess, whose name means "She who has been completed." She was the mate of Onuris, who originated at This near Abydos. Possibly she is to be equated with the moon, or the injured eye of Horus.

Menhyt. One of the lioness goddesses, she also plays the role of a uraeus goddess on the head of Re and thus is extolled as a sun goddess. Although known early in the Esna region of Upper Egypt, Menhyt is associated with the Wadjet, the titulary goddess of Lower Egypt in Coffin Text Spell 952 but also is associated with Neith of Sais.

Merhyt. A water goddess, possibly representing the two parts of the Nile valley, north and south.

Merit. Goddess of music, who, by her song and gestures, helped to establish cosmic order. A director of singers known from his Fifth Dynasty tomb bore the title Priest of Merit.

Meretseger. Snake goddess who inhabited the Peak of the West, which overshadowed the royal burial grounds of the New Kingdom. "She who loves silence" could be shown as a coiled serpent or as a woman with a cobra's head. She was regarded by local people of the necropolis region as a punishing but also merciful deity.

Meskhenet. Presider over childbirth, she represented one of the magical bricks on which the ancient woman in labor squatted to give birth. Sometimes she is shown as a personified brick, but other times she is completely human with the symbol of a cow's uterus balanced on top of her head. After safely delivering a child, Meskhenet decided its destiny and thus was said to be the wife of Shay, god of fate. Her protective powers guarded the newborn, but she also had a role in the final judgment near the scale in Osiris's Hall of the Two Truths, where she could testify to the character of the deceased and perhaps facilitate in a symbolic rebirth in the Afterlife. She is found, assisting Isis and Nephthys, in the funerary rites.

Mut. The consort of Amun from the New Kingdom on and thus the goddess of Karnak and Thebes, she is a mother (of Khonsu and the king) but also the mature keeper of crowns, being portrayed always as a woman wearing the double crown of kingship. Mut was titled Mistress of the Nine Bows (the empire of Egypt), and she was associated with the fierce lioness Sekhmet and the cat Bastet. Her precinct at Karnak is known as Asher or Isheru.

Naunet. Female counterpart, in the Hermopolitan Ogdoad, of Nun, the primeval water, but she is actually the sky.

Nebet-hetepet. Goddess of Heliopolis associated with Hathor and Re; sometimes known as the hand, at other times, the penis of the creator god Atum. She is also known as Mistress of the Vulva and thus a manifestation of Hathor. She is also named as a mother goddess, or female counterpart of the male creative principle known in the sun god Atum.

Nefertiti. Mistress of All the Gods and Lady of Heaven were the titles bestowed on this chief royal wife of Pharaoh Akhenaton of the late Eighteenth Dynasty. With her husband, she would seem to have formed a holy family, or triad, with the god Aton, the solar disk, because prayers were addressed to all three. It seems that Nefertiti filled the vital role of mother goddess in her husband's "new" religion that has often been termed "monotheistic."

Neith. A primeval bisexual goddess and female creator associated with hunting and warfare (the work of men) and weaving (the work of women). Sometimes a consort of Seth or of Khnum and often called the mother of Sobek, Neith is usually portrayed as a woman wearing the Red Crown of Lower Egypt or as a totem with two crossed arrows, sometimes two crossed bows, or the coleoptera beetle. She was the preeminent goddess at the beginning of Egypt's history. Her original cult place at Sais, modern Sa el-Hagar, the capital of the fifth nome of

Lower Egypt, again came into great political prominence in the Twenty-fifth Dynasty. The Greeks identified her with Athena. Neith was one of the four traditional protectors of the king and of the virtuous dead, shown on the royal sarcophagus or encircling the canopic box. She represented the cardinal orientation West, as she was from the western delta city of Sais, but also the primeval waters and thus was considered a mother of the sun. At Khnum's Temple of Esna in Upper Egypt there is a creation legend that credits Neith as the first being and creator of the gods.

Nekhbet. Primeval mother goddess "She of Nekheb" (El-Kab), from one of the oldest towns in Egypt, this goddess was usually depicted as a vulture. Once the South conquered the North, she became the tutelary goddess of Upper Egypt and the embodiment of the White Crown of that kingdom. Some early texts name her the Great White Cow who dwells in Nekheb, perhaps because Nekheb was to be regarded as a divine nurse of the king in royal birth scenes. She stood for the cardinal orientation South, as she was from the southern city of Nekheb. With Wadjet she is a partner in the Two Ladies title of the king. Sharing the protection of the king, she appears on the brow of the ruler either as a second cobra or as a vulture head.

Nephthys. One of the children of Nut and thus loyal sister of Isis as well as sister to Osiris and Seth, of whom she was a consort, she does not appear to have had a cult of her own. She is frequently portrayed with Isis as mourning Osiris and thus is at times shown, like Isis, as or equipped with the wings of a kite. Her original role was to wail and mourn the deceased, but this was extended to the protection of the dead in general. She is found as one of the four protective goddesses around the corners of the royal sarcophagus and canopic jars chest. As spouse of Seth, she bore no children (Seth being linked to the sterile desert), but she was impregnated by Osiris with whom she had a brief liaison. Their son was Anubis, guardian of the cemeteries and god of embalming. Nephthys means "Lady of the Mansion," the hieroglyphic spelling of which was her headdress. Nephthys never seems to have been the object of her own cult as no temple or shrine is known for her alone.

Nut. Sky goddess, either the entire vault of heaven or, possibly, the Milky Way, personified as the nude woman arching over the earth god Geb her brother/husband (they are the children of Shu and Tefnut).

Nut bore the sun but also became known for receiving the dead into the sky; the worthy dead became the stars on her body. For centuries Nut was depicted inside coffins as the "mother" and protector of the deceased. She was the mother of the gods, the first generation who gave birth to Osiris, Isis, Seth, and Nephthys.

Pakhet. She Who Scratches, the local lioness goddess of Beni Hasan, where the monarchs of the Oryx Nome cut their tombs in the cliffs on the east bank during the Middle Kingdom. At this time she was also recorded in the Coffin Texts as a nighttime huntress. She is known from a temple built just to the south by Hatshepsut, the female pharaoh of the Eighteenth Dynasty. This came to be called Speos Artemidos, or the Cave of Artemis, by the Greeks, who identified Pakhet with Bastet, the Egyptian cat goddess, whom they equated with Artemis, goddess of the chase. At the temple Pakhet was worshiped as "the goddess at the mouth of the wadi," which refers to the lion's haunting of the watering places found at the desert edge.

Qadesh. A goddess from western Asia depicted as a totally nude female riding on the back of a lion. She entered Egypt with its New Kingdom empire and personified sexual pleasure. She formed a triad with the fertility god Min and the foreign god of war, Reshep, but is also known in Egypt as Eye of Re and Lady of Heaven.

Raettawy. Female counterpart of the sun god Re, she is depicted as a woman, who, like Hathor, wears a headdress of cow's horns and sun disk.

Renenet. Prosperity divinized, often found in the company of Shai, god of destiny. Her name means "nursing a child," and thus she was associated with the goddess Meskhenet in the birth of prominent people and in planning the destiny of the newborn. She is attested from the New Kingdom as a cobra goddess and at Deir el-Medina was associated with Meretseger.

Renenutet. Snake Who Nourishes, a harvest goddess usually depicted as a cobra or as a woman with a snake's head. Rather than venomous, however, Renenutet was nurturing and was an icon of divine mother-hood. She was a divine nurse, a birth goddess, and a fertility goddess as well as a harvest goddess. Originally Renenutet, who was the mother of the grain god Nepri, was protector of the ruler, but she is associated with his role of promoting plentiful harvests. In the Late Period, Renenutet became involved with controlling human destiny, deciding not only the length of a person's life but also its vicissitudes. She was a popular deity among the agricultural workers of the Fayum from the Middle Kingdom onward. Her festivals took place in the last month of the season of Peret, the time of sowing, and the following first month of the summer season when the crops began to ripen. Her cult at Medinet Madi in the Fayum combined her with Isis and itself survived the end of paganism. She became a Christian saint, Thermuthis.

Renpet. The goddess who personified the year.

Satis. Also known as Satet, consort of Khnum and goddess of the First Cataract region. Her cult center was on the island of Seheil just upstream from Elephantine. Usually shown as a woman wearing the crown of Upper Egypt flanked by two antelope horns, Satis was regarded as a water goddess and was associated with a crevice between the huge boulders of Elephantine where the Nile inundation was measured and traditionally thought to originate. Because of the inundation's life-giving waters, she is viewed as a goddess of fertility. As a giver of water, Satis is mentioned in purification rituals for the deceased (see PT Sp. 1116), bringing four jars of water from Elephantine. She was called the Queen of the Gods in the New Kingdom and was depicted as a goddess of hunting. However, she is also a national deity, a guardian of the southern frontier.

Sekhmet. Most distinguished of the lioness goddesses and consort of Ptah (or Ptah-Sokar) of Memphis, mother of Nefertem. An early reference in the Pyramid Texts credits her with conceiving the king of Egypt (who was often portrayed as a lion), and she is portrayed in the Fourth Dynasty as passing the life force to King Snefru. One of the many forms of the eye (or daughter) of Re and thus destructive and beneficent at the same time. She could spread as well as cure disease. She was present in a year of plague, but her priests were credited with the powers of curing; both magic and medicine were taught in her temples. Sekhmet protected the king by destroying his and Egypt's enemies. At the battle of Kadesh waged by Ramses II, her flames scorched the bodies of enemy soldiers. She was associated with the desert edge, such as where the usually dry riverbeds emerge into the region of the Nile valley. Such places were frequented by lions into Roman times.

Selket. Otherwise known as Serket, the scorpion goddess, and a protector of the deceased. Usually shown with a scorpion on her head, this goddess is otherwise human in appearance. Selket may have had her cult center in the western delta, but she joins Isis, Nephthys, and Neith at the foot of the coffin as guardians of Osiris, and any entombed person, and also their preserved internal organs. In particular, she guards the canopic jar of intestines and its god Qebehsenuef. Perhaps this responsibility is connected with her guardianship of a twist in the Two Ways traveled by the deceased, as portrayed on Middle Kingdom coffins. One myth credited her with protecting Horus the child when he took refuge in a papyrus thicket. While she is usually visualized as encompassing the scorpion and its venom, Selket is also among those goddesses who appear with a lionine head, as in the Twenty-first Dynasty Mythological Papyrus where she is armed with knives and has a double head (a crocodile projecting from her back).

Seshat. Goddess of writing and patron of libraries, she is the female counterpart (his wife or daughter) of Thoth, the god of wisdom who served as scribe-secretary to the gods. Depicted as a woman wearing a panther skin and with a seven-pointed starlike emblem on her head, Seshat was the keeper of the Royal Annals. In the Old Kingdom she recorded important royal triumphs such as the captives and tribute of a king; in the New Kingdom her duties included inscribing the name of the king on the leaves of the Persea tree, whose leaves represented years of the king's life, and recording his jubilees. Thus she is depicted holding a notched palm branch, the hieroglyph for "years." She was also a patroness of architecture and was shown present at the foundation of temples as early as the Second Dynasty, helping the king lay out their perimeters by "stretching the cord." Perhaps because literate people were in a distinct minority in ancient Egypt, Seshat seems never to have had a popular following or her own temples.

Shentayet. A cow-headed goddess whose name means "Widow." She was assimilated to Isis under the name Isis-Shentayit, incarnating the protective container in which Osiris was regenerated.

Shesmetet. Mother of the dead king and later of deceased persons in general, also known as Lady of Punt, the southern Red Sea port on the African coast. This is another lioness goddess who is invoked during the last days of the year as a protection against demons. Her name is also found as Smithis.

Sokaret. Female counterpart of the great cemetery god Sokar, she is found present at the burial ritual.

Ta-Bitjet. A scorpion goddess who is named in a number of spells against poisonous bites as the wife of Horus.

Taweret. Protector of women in childbirth was the chief role of this goddess who appears as a hippo but with the legs and arms of a lion and the tail of a crocodile and pendent human breasts. Apparently her ferocity was meant to deter any harm from women at their most vulnerable time. As a hippo goddess she can represent water, and this permitted her to preside in the domestic sphere with a role connected with women in labor and the breaking of their "bag of water." Taweret was enormously popular, as a great many charms in her shape or in the shape of the *sa* amulet that she usually carries attests. Taweret sometimes wears the solar disk and cow's horns and was one of the goddesses called Eye of Re. She was also known as Mistress of the Horizon because there was a Hippo constellation in the Northern Hemisphere, as is shown on the ceiling of the tomb of Seti I. Thus Taweret was a cosmic goddess and almost always visible to the many who sought her protection.

Tayet. Mummy bandages were called "wrappings from the hand of" due to this goddess being the patroness of weaving. She was exhorted in prayers to gather bones of the deceased and protect the body.

Tefnut. First woman, the daughter of Atum, who created her as moisture and consort-sister of the air god Shu. She is personified moisture and her name is onomatopoetic because the god spat her out together with Shu. With Sekhmet and Hathor she is referred to as Eye of Re and thus was a uraeus goddess, one who protects the king as well as the holy sun disk. Although sometimes portrayed as a woman wearing on her head a sun disk encircled by a cobra, or described as a serpent coiled around a staff, Tefnut appears often as a lioness goddess or as a woman with the head of a lioness wearing the sun disk and uraeus. She, along with her brother Shu, who could also be depicted in lion form, was worshipped for centuries at Leontopolis. She was the original "daughter" in the story of the enraged goddess who became estranged from her father and fled into Nubia, where she transformed herself into a lioness and devoured all living things. Re missed her and sent Shu and Thoth to bring his daughter back, in which they finally succeeded by promising her altars piled high with offerings of game.

Wadjit. Also spelled Edjo, or Uto, the Green One, referring to the serpent form she takes or the green of the delta's marshes and fields, which were her home. She is the tutelary goddess of the North, or Lower Egypt, and protector of the king. She is the (original) rearing cobra on his brow, the uraeus, also depicted as a cobra coiled around a papyrus stalk. Associated with the sovereignty of Lower Egypt and its Red Crown, it is Wadjit who crowns the king at his coronation. She is sometimes depicted as a lioness with a cobra on her head. Wadjit was worshiped at the twin towns of Pe and Dep in the delta, called Buto by the Greeks and known today as Tell el-Fara'in.

Wenut. The female divine hare known as "the swift one," who can also be found in snake form. She was particularly worshiped at Hermopolis in Middle Egypt.

Werethekau. Known as Great of Magic, she was a serpent goddess but was sometimes shown with the head of a lioness. She was a divine nurse for the king and a protector of Egypt.

Wosret. Goddess of Thebes whose name means "the powerful woman." This may well have been a local form of Hathor, however, for otherwise it is problematic why kings of the Twelfth Dynasty would incorporate this goddess's name in their own (i.e., Senusert), unless they were attracted to her martial associations. She often holds a mace and bow and arrows in her hands and has the hieroglyph for the Theban nome on her head.

$\mathcal{N}$OTES

CHAPTER 1

1. As seen at Çatal Hüyük in Anatolia (Turkey); see J. Mellaart, *The Neolithic in the Near East*, 106–10. For several photographs of Malta's goddess temples and colossus, see E. W. Gadon, *The Once and Future Goddess*, 57–68.

2. For a summary of current anthropological reasoning, see R. Miles, *Women's History of the World*, 8.

3. The role of women in the agricultural revolution has been recognized for at least thirty years. See W. H. McNeill, *Rise of the West*, 20–26; and more recently, M. Ehrenberg, *Women in Prehistory*, chap. 3.

4. E. J. Baumgartel, *Cultures of Prehistoric Egypt*, 2:143.

5. E. J. Baumgartel, "Predynastic Egypt," 469. Her data is from Upper Egypt, but similar finds have been made in the Lower Egyptian delta; see E. C. M. van den Brink, ed., *Nile Delta in Transition*, 252.

6. The Sumerians' great goddess Inanna was the star Venus and the goddess of the thunderstorm. From the body of their primeval goddess Tiamat, visualized as a great sea, the heavens and the earth were created. See T. Jacobsen, "Mesopotamian Religions," 458–59.

7. A. J. Arkell, *Shaheinab*, 5. M. A. Murray, "Burial Customs and Beliefs," 92–96, suggests that the divination of the vulture, jackal, and wild dog related to their presence in the areas where human carcasses were disposed of and that even in historical times it was only the elite who were given burial. However, recent excavations have found cemeteries of poorer folk, so burial would seem to have been general in historical times.

8. Baumgartel, "Predynastic Egypt," 492.

9. D. R. Hill, "Magic," 89–92.

10. Quoted by H. te Velde, "A Few Remarks on the Religious Signficance of Animals," 78.

11. Ibid.

12. Baumgartel, *Cultures of Prehistoric Egypt*, 1:18–19.

13. M. A. Hoffmann, *Egypt before the Pharaohs*, 152.

14. Baumgartel, "Predynastic Egypt," 492. Breasts decorate a jug found in the north at a prehistoric site, but a cultic connection was not considered by R. Friedman, "Imports and Influences," 334, fig. 16.

15. H. Frankfort, *Kingship and the Gods*, 162–80.

16. Baumgartel, "Predynastic Egypt," 494.

17. Baumgartel, *Cultures of Prehistoric Egypt*, 2:60–61.

18. Ibid., 61.

19. Ibid., 69 and pl. 5; P. J. Ucko, *Anthropomorphic Figurines*, 410–12.

20. Baumgartel, *Cultures of Prehistoric Egypt*, 65.

21. Ibid., 70–71. Baumgartel suggests that the donor (in this preliterate age) would have communicated this wish or prayer to the goddess by burying her own image with a deceased friend or relative, who would then convey the message to the deity. Baumgartel review of Ucko, *Anthropomorphic Figurines*, *JEA* 56 (1970): 201.

22. The Badarians were fully capable of producing much more detailed and well modeled human images in better materials. Surprisingly sophisticated ivory female nudes as well as some male figurines have turned up in settlement sites, even this early. See G. Brunton and G. Caton–Thompson, *Badarian Civilisation*, 46–47 and pl. 24.

23. Ucko, *Anthropomorphic Figurines*, 434.

24. F. Hassan, "Primeval Goddess to Divine King," 307–20.

25. B. Adams, "Predynastic Female Figurine," 53, fig. 31.

26. Hassan, "Primeval Goddess to Divine King," fig 2.

27. B. S. Lesko, *Remarkable Women of Ancient Egypt*, 29–35; S. Allam, "Women as Owners," 123–35.

28. E. B. Leacock, *Myths of Male Dominance*, 20.

29. Ibid.; H. Loth, *Woman in Ancient Africa*, 31–60.

30. Brunton and Caton-Thompson, *Badarian Civilisation*, 51.

31. Hassan, "Primeval Goddess to Divine King," 309.

32. E. O. James, *Cult of the Mother-Goddess*, 55.

33. B. J. Kemp, *Ancient Egypt*, 37–39.

34. Ibid., 32.

35. G. Lienhardt, *Divinity and Experience*, 115.

36. Ibid., 16–17, pls. 1 and 3.

37. Baumgartel, "Predynastic Egypt," 493, and *Cultures of Prehistoric Egypt*, 1:pl. 3, 2:pl. 6.

38. B. Fagan, "Sexist View of Prehistory," dismisses the idea of a widespread prehistoric mother goddess cult, as does L. Meskell, "Goddesses, Gimbutas and New Age Archaeology," 74–86, but thirty years ago W. H. McNeill pointed out that comparable male figurines do not survive from such early times and saw the possibility that the earth could have been thought of and represented as a fruitful goddess.

McNeill, *Rise of the West*, 8. The hundreds of "Venus" figurines found across Europe which have lent credence to a belief in a female divinity for Paleolithic society date, however, to a far earlier time (ca. 20,000 B.C.) than any Egyptian artifact. Badarian figurines are the first found in Egypt and date only to ca. 4000 B.C.

39. One of the earliest Sumerian goddesses was Ninhursag whose temple was located by archaeologists at the prehistoric site of Al-Ubaid in southern Iraq. A number of artistic renditions of cows and milking scenes have been found at this site too, which strongly suggests Ninhursag's sacred animal was a cow, but the importance of cattle in African Nilotic cultures is so well documented that no other parallels are necessary.

40. A. J. Weeramunda, "Milk Overflowing Ceremony," 252–61.

41. E. Hornung, *Conceptions of God in Ancient Egypt*, 103; Hassan, "Primeval Goddess to Divine King," fig. 4.

42. Baumgartel, *Cultures of Prehistoric Egypt*, 2:149.

43. D. P. Silverman, ed., *Searching for Ancient Egypt*, 207, pl. 63B.

44. J. Černý, *Ancient Egyptian Religion*, 27.

45. Baumgartel, "Predynastic Egypt," 493; Hassan, "Primeval Goddess to Divine King," 315; M. Raphael, *Prehistoric Pottery*; E. Neumann, *Great Mother*, 115–16.

46. Hassan, "Primeval Goddess to Divine King," 311, but he admits there would be more than one possible identification for such figures.

47. Ibid., 308.

48. Ibid.

49. Ibid., 319.

50. Ibid., 315.

CHAPTER 2

1. E. J. Baumgartel, "Scorpion and Rosette," 10–11.

2. H. G. Fischer, "Cult and Nome of the Goddess Bat," 7–23.

3. R. O. Faulkner, *Ancient Egyptian Pyramid Texts*, Utt. 497.

4. A. C. Mace and H. E. Winlock, *Tomb of Senebtisi*, 31–32.

5. R. O. Faulkner, *Ancient Egyptian Book of the Dead*.

6. A. Piankoff, *Shrines of Tut-Ankh-Amon*, fig. 46 and pl. 65 from Shrine 1.

7. Pyramid Text Sps. 825a, 1370, 1611. R. Anthes, "Egyptian Theology in the Third Millennium B.C.," 169–212.

8. F. Steegmuller, trans. and ed., *Flaubert in Egypt*, 150.

9. L. Duff Gordon, *Lady Duff Gordon's Letters from Egypt*, 169.

10. G. A. Wainwright, *Sky-Religion in Egypt*; R. O. Faulkner, "The King and the Star-Religion," 153–61.

11. In the much later Papyrus Carlsberg I, stars are described as traveling outside Nut's body in the night when they shine. R. Parker and O. Neugebauer, *Egyptian Astronomical Texts*, 1:67.

12. R. A. Wells, "The Mythology of Nut and the Birth of Ra," 305–21.

13. S. T. Hollis, "Ancient Egyptian Women and the Sky Goddess Nut," 210.

14. L. H. Lesko, "Ancient Egyptian Cosmogonies and Cosmology," 118–119. Twelve stations in the body of Nut through which the sun passes during the night are

enumerated from the cenotaph of Seti I at Abydos, Dynasty 19, in Parker and Neugebauer, *op. cit.*, 82.

15. B. S. Lesko, "True Art in Ancient Egypt," 92.

16. S. E. Thompson, "A Study of the Pyramid Texts."

17. Ibid., 26–27.

18. Mace and Winlock, *Tomb of Senebtisi*, 32.

19. J. Černý, *Ancient Egyptian Religion*, 82.

20. Earth mothers abound, rooted deep in human psychology; see E. Neumann, *The Great Mother*, 48–49.

21. M. Münster, *Untersuchungen zur Göttin Isis*, 198–99.

22. S. T. Hollis, "Women of Ancient Egypt and the Sky Goddess Nut," n. 28, 213. As she points out elsewhere, quoting numerous Egyptologists, the words for "sky" in Egyptian are consistently feminine, and various words for "earth" are masculine. Hollis, "Ancient Egyptian Women," 208.

23. Sir Alan Gardiner (as Hollis, "Ancient Egyptian Women," 210, reminds us) stressed the "unprecedented influence of the Heliopolitan priesthood" at least by the Fifth Dynasty (the period when the religious texts were first engraved in pyramids); see his *Egypt of the Pharaohs*, 84; and Neumann recognized the Heliopolitan recension as "emphatically patriarchal." "The priests of Heliopolis . . . did their best, though not always successfully, to obliterate and overlay the old matriarchal religion." *The Great Mother*, 217.

24. S. N. Kramer, "Poets and Psalmists," 12–16.

25. C. Christ, *Rebirth of the Goddess*, 32–34.

26. B. J. Kemp, *Ancient Egypt*, 88–89.

27. Anthes, "Egyptian Theology," 175–78.

28. Note that both the gods Sobek, a crocodile, and Osiris, the deified dead king, came to be known by the title Lord of Vegetation, and thus again a male deity illogically was made responsible for the earth's fecundity.

29. In the interest of space, I have not discussed the predynastic culture of Lower Egypt. On this, see M. A. Hoffman, *Egypt before the Pharaohs*, as well as the later, but more technical, van den Brink, *Nile Delta in Transition*.

30. L. H. Lesko "Ancient Egyptian Cosmogonies," 91.

31. Kemp, *Ancient Egypt*, 37–43.

32. Manetho *apud* Syncellus, frag. 2.

33. Faulkner, "The King and the Star-Religion," and Wainwright, *Sky Religion in Egypt*.

34. L. H. Lesko, "Ancient Egyptian Cosmogonies," 91.

35. The ancient name of Heliopolis was Iwnw or On, as it is cited in the Bible.

36. S. N. Kramer, "Poets and Psalmists," 13–16. also B. S. Lesko, "Women of Ancient Egypt and Western Asia," 63.

37. The Akkadian Creation Epic, Tablets 3 and 4, in Pritchard, *Ancient Near Eastern Texts*, 64–67.

38. *Eumenides* by Aeschylus, Vallacott translation, 86–87.

39. J. H. Breasted, *Development of Religion and Thought*, 252–57.

40. Coffin from the Washington University Gallery of Art, St. Louis, now in the Cleveland Museum of Art, no. 61.

41. L. Habachi, "The Owner of the Tomb," 19.

42. Piankoff, *Shrines of Tut-Ankh-Amon*, 59.

43. Ibid., fasc. 2, pl. 19.

44. Ibid., 59 n. 27.

45. Shrine 2, fasc. 1, 42.

46. Parker and Neugebauer, *Egyptian Astronomical Texts*, 36–38; 82.

47. Ibid., 68–69.

48. M.-L. Buhl, "Goddesses of the Egyptian Tree Cult," 97.

49. Twelfth Hour, Short Amduat, 281–83. E. Hornung, *Das Amduat*, 24.

50. Parker and Neugebauer, *Egyptian Astronomical Texts*, 82–83.

51. E. Hornung, *Valley of the Kings*, 90.

CHAPTER 3

1. M. Lichtheim, *Ancient Egyptian Literature* 2:215; B. Adams, *Predynastic Egypt*, 51.

2. W. M. F. Petrie, *Diospolis Parva*, pl. 20, 11; A. J. Spencer, *Early Egypt*, fig. 44.

3. E. Hornung, *Conceptions of God*, 103.

4. P. Kaplony, "Der Titel *wnr(w)*," 151n. 69.

5. For the discussion of the beetle, see S. T. Hollis, "Five Egyptian Goddesses," 48–49.

6. K. Sethe, "Der Name der Göttin Neith," 145.

7. A. M. Cooper, "Canaanite Religion," 3:38.

8. H. Kees, *Ancient Egypt*, 28.

9. Hornung, *Conceptions of God*, 108n. 19.

10. E. Drioton and J. Vandier, *L'Égypte*, 83.

11. I. E. S. Edwards, "Early Dynastic Period," 23.

12. Ibid., 25–26.

13. Hollis, "Five Egyptian Goddesses," 49; and W. S. Smith, *Art and Architecture*, fig. 19.

14. Hollis, "Five Egyptian Goddesses," 46.

15. S. T. Hollis records still more, following R. Sayed, in "Queens and Goddesses in Ancient Egypt," 211.

16. Plutarch, as quoted and interpreted by C. J. Bleeker, "The Egyptian Goddess Neith," 41–56.

17. M. Gimbutas, in *The Gods and Goddesses of Old Europe*, 196, writes, "divine bisexuality stresses absolute power," and perhaps the same can be claimed for androgyny.

18. S. Schott, "Ein Kult der Göttin Neith," 128–38, pls. 4 and 7.

19. E. J. Baumgartel, "Scorpion and Rosette," 11.

20. Theban Tomb 57 of Khaemhet, cited by J. Assmann, "Neit spricht als Mutter und Sarg," 125.

21. B. Mundkur, *Cult of the Serpent*, 24, fig. 17. The markings are identified as the bifid tongue of the serpent, who is here labeled the Living God.

22. A. Erman, *Ancient Egyptians*, 10.

23. Lichtheim, *Ancient Egyptian Literature*, 2:215.

24. H. H. Nelson, *The Great Hypostyle Hall*, 1:pt. 1, pl. 70.

25. Assmann, "Neit sprecht als Mutter und Sarg," 126.

26. Book of That Which Is in the Beyond, 4th, 10th, 11th hours.

27. Herodotus 2.131–32.

28. G. Posener, *Le Premier Domination Perse*, 1–26.

29. L. H. Lesko translation, P. Berlin 3008, 5:6–8.

30. L. H. Lesko translation; for text, see S. Sauneron, *Le Temple d'Esna*, 3:137, lines 252.25–26.

31. Sauneron, *Le Temple d'Esna*, 28, lines 206.1–3.

32. C. J. Bleeker, *The Rainbow*, 136–37; G. Daressy, "Neith Protectrice du Sommeil," 177–79.

33. Bleeker, *The Rainbow*, 137.

34. S. Sauneron, "Remarques de Philologie et d'etymologie," 242; and Bleeker, *The Rainbow*, 140.

35. Bleeker, *The Rainbow*, 140.

CHAPTER 4

1. F. A. Hassan, "Primeval Goddess to Divine King," 312; contrary to J. Baines, who states Nekhbet is not known before the Old Kingdom. "Origins of Egyptian Kingship," 100. Her name, however, merely means She of Nekheb, one of the oldest settlements in Egypt. The Two Ladies are attested already in the First Dynasty; see W. M. F. Petrie, *Royal Tombs of the 1st Dynasty*, 1:pl. 11, no. 1; and the vulture appears uniting the Two Lands on a vase of the Second Dynasty; see L. Troy, *Patterns of Queenship*, 116, fig. 80.

2. A. Dodson, "El Kab City of the Vulture-Goddess," 60.

3. Troy, *Patterns of Queenship*, fig. 52.

4. Egyptologists dispute whether Horus the falcon was originally from Hierakonpolis, because it also revered a crocodile god. However, a Horus of Nekhen is attested in historic times.

5. E. W. Gadon, *The Once and Future Goddess*, 25–37.

6. Troy, *Patterns of Queenship*, 118, fig. 82.

7. Ibid., 117.

8. A. Roberts, *Hathor Rising*, 42. For a late representation of such a shrine for Weret Hekau, see M. Eaton-Krauss and E. Graefe, *Small Golden Shrine*, pl. 13; also the exhibition catalog published for the seven American venues of the traveling exhibition: *Treasures of Tutankhamun*, 117–19.

9. A. H. Gardiner, "Coronation of King Haremhab," 24–25.

10. Eaton-Krauss, and Graefe, *Small Golden Shrine*; or I. E. S. Edwards, *Tutankhamun*, 52–57.

11. Eaton-Krauss and Graefe, *Small Golden Shrine*, pl. 13.

12. *Treasures of Tutankhamun* catalog, 132, pl. 13.

13. Ibid., 132.

14. Ibid., 133, pl. 14.

15. J. E. Quibell, *El-Kab*, pl. 21.

16. M. A. Murray, *Egyptian Religious Poetry*, 100.

17. A. H. Gardiner, "The Goddess Nekhbet," 47–51.

18. A. J. Arkell, "The signs ⌐ and ⌐ ," 175–76.

19. S. B. Johnson, *The Cobra Goddess*, 209.

20. M. Gimbutas, *Goddesses and Gods of Old Europe*, 112.

21. S. Johnson, *The Cobra Goddess*, 20, fig. 18.

22. Ibid., 67, fig. 107.

23. Portrayed on an ivory tag of King Den; see M. A. Hoffman, *Egypt before the Pharaohs*, fig. 64.

24. Hymn to the Diadem. A. Erman, *Hymnen an des Diadem*, 48, lines 2–4.

25. Johnson, *The Cobra Goddess*, 71.

26. Troy, *Patterns of Queenship*, 120, fig. 84.

27. Ibid., 116 (citing B. Begelsbacher-Fischer).

28. Ibid.

29. Roberts, *Hathor Rising*, fig. 53.

30. Ibid., figs. 73, 74.

31. *Treasures of Tutankhamun* catalog, 19.

32. Gardiner, "Coronation of King Haremhab," 13–31.

33. H. H. Nelson, *The Great Hypostyle Hall at Karnak*, 1:pt. 1, pl. 74.

34. The udjat is a human eye and eyebrow to which are added the markings of a falcon head. This was the most popular amulet among the ancient Egyptians, having power against illness. Roberts, *Hathor Rising*, fig. 120.

35. A. H. Gardiner, "Horus the Behdetite," 56.

36. Troy, *Patterns of Queenship*, 86.

37. Stele N. 50058; M. Tosi and A. Roccati, *Stele e altere epigrafi*, 94–95, L. H. Lesko translation.

38. L. V. Zabkar, *Hymns to Isis*, 91.

39. D. P. Silverman, *Searching for Ancient Egypt*, 56, pl. 8.

40. Žabkar, *Hymns to Isis*, 93.

CHAPTER 5

1. H. G. Fischer, "The Cult and Nome of the Goddess Bat," 7–18.

2. S. Allam, *Beiträge zum Hathorkult*, 97.

3. B. J. Kemp, *Ancient Egypt*, 62–63.

4. L. H. Lesko, "Ancient Egyptian Cosmogonies," 100.

5. L. Troy, *Patterns of Queenship*, 31.

6. A concept found in much later religious texts; see P. Derchain, *Hathor Quadrifrons*, 46.

7. See the Palermo Stone entries for the reigns of Userkaf, Sahure, and Neferirkare; M. Clagett, *Ancient Egyptian Science*, 1:1, 88, 91, 94.

8. H. Goedicke, "The Story of the Herdsman," 262.

9. H. G. Fischer, *Dendera in the Third Millennium B.C.*, 24–31.

10. D. Eady, "Some Miraculous Wells and Springs of Egypt," 17–22.

11. M. Galvin, *Priestesses of Hathor*, 22, 82.

12. B. Porter and R. L. B. Moss, *Topographical Bibliography*, 3:pt. 2, 746.

13. D. Dunham and Wm K. Simpson, *The Mastaba of Queen Mersyankh III*; Allam, *Beiträge zum Hathorkult*, 14–15; 20.

14. N. Grimal, *History of Ancient Egypt*, 176.

15. For the Admonitions of Ipuwer, see Papyrus Leiden 344, Recto 13, 17, or Lichtheim, *Ancient Egyptian Literature*, 1:160.

16. F. Daumas, *Le Culte d'Isis*, 13. However, in view of its absence among the Old Kingdom monuments studied by Galvin, Southern Sycamore, which appears in New Kingdom sources, may well refer to a Hathoric cult of Upper (southern) Egypt.

17. Galvin, *Priestess of Hathor*, 78; Allam, *Beiträge zum Hathorkult*, 7.

18. As in the Theban Tomb of May; see V. Scheil, *Tombeaux Thébains*, 549.

19. M. Galvin, "Addendum," 29.

20. L. H. Lesko, pers. commun.

21. Galvin, *Priestesses of Hathor*.

22. Ibid., 236.

23. Galvin, *Priestesses of Hathor*, 228–31.

24. Shrine 2, A. Piankoff and N. Rambova, *Mythological Papyri*, pl. 42, n. 102.

25. G. Pinch, *Votive Offerings to Hathor*, 124.

26. Galvin, "Addendum," 26.

27. C. J. Bleeker, *The Rainbow*, 215.

28. H. Brunner, "Das Besänftigungslied im Sinuhe," 10. For the full text in English, see also Lichtheim, *Ancient Egyptian Literature*, 1:232.

29. E. Naville and H. R. Hall, *The XIth Dynasty Temple of Deir el-Bahari*, 1:pl. 20; 2:pl. 13.

30. J. Van Lepp, "The Role of Dance in Funerary Ritual," 385–94.

31. N. de G. Davies, *Tomb of Antefoker*, 22, pls. 23, 23a.

32. Fischer, *Dendera in the Third Millennium B.C.*, 37.

33. Ibid.

34. E. Chassinat, *Le Temple de Dendera*.

35. V. Denon, *Travels in Upper and Lower Egypt*, 1:289.

36. W. Murnane, *Penguin Guide to Ancient Egypt*, 320.

37. An appellation found already in the Old Kingom; see Allam, *Beiträge zum Hathorkult*, 21, 46; A. M. Blackman, *Rock Tombs of Meir*, II.

38. A. Roberts, *Hathor Rising*, 46, pl. 56; 56.

39. N. Jidejian, *Byblos*, 116–18.

40. Ibid., 29, fig. 61.

41. Ibid..

42. Allam, *Beiträge zum Hathorkult*, 132, 142.

43. E. Vassilika, *Egyptian Art*, 72.

44. T. G. H. James, *Pharaoh's People*, 39.

45. Vassilika, *Egyptian Art*.

46. Allam, *Beiträge zum Hathorkult*, 86; and Pinch, *Magic in Ancient Egypt*, 198–245, 302–3.

47. M. Saleh, *Three Old Kingdom Tombs at Thebes*, 19–25.

48. L. H. Lesko translation of Wah'ankh Inyotef, in Hayes, *Scepter of Egypt* 1:fig. 90.

49. C. Lilyquist, *Ancient Egyptian Mirrors*, 98–99.

50. Naville and Hall, *The XIth Dynasty Temple*, 9, pls. 2 and 20; D. Arnold, *Temple of Mentuhotep*.

51. Pinch, *Magic in Ancient Egypt*, 4.

52. V. Donahue, "Goddess of the Theban Mountain," 871–85.

53. H. D. Schneider and M. J. Raven, *De Egyptische Oudheid*, 113–14, pl. 115. For the Ani Papyrus vignette, see the recent reedition by O. Goelet, *The Egyptian Book of the Dead*, pl. 37.

54. Kemp, *Ancient Egypt*, fig. 38c.

55. Arnold, *Temple of Mentuhotep*, 21.

56. G. A. Gaballa and K. A. Kitchen, "The Festival of Sokar."

57. N. de G. Davies, *Tomb of Antefoker*, 10–11, 22–25, pls. 3, 23, 23a,b.

58. Blackman, *Rock Tombs of Meir*, II, 24.

59. E. Brovarski, "Senenu," 59.

60. E. Naville, *The Temple of Deir el-Bahari* 4:pls. 94, 96, 105.

61. Donahue, "Goddess of the Theban Mountain," 873.

62. Ibid., 879, fig. 9.

63. T. Kendall, "Discoveries at Sudan's Sacred Mountain," 96–124.

64. Donahue, "Goddess of the Theban Mountain," 880; Pinch, *Magic in Ancient Egypt*, 29, 36.

65. Naville and Hall, *XIth Dynasty Temple*, 1:7.

66. Donahue, "Goddess of the Theban Mountain," 881; Naville, *Temple of Deir el-Bahari*, 2:pls. 47–49.

67. Naville, *Temple of Deir el-Bahari*, 4:4.

68. Excerpt from L. H. Lesko's translation of the Speos Artemidos inscription in B. S. Lesko, "Rhetoric of Women," 101–2.

69. Hathor in her many forms absorbed those associated with other goddesses. Her awesome powers are the subject of a specialized study, which grew out of a lengthy doctoral dissertation, by A. Roberts, *Hathor Rising*.

70. Inscriptions identify the statue's donor as Thutmose III's son, Amunhotep II, but these may date from a time subsequent to its erection. Naville and Hall, *XIth Dynasty Temple*, 1:66.

71. Donahue, "Goddess of the Theban Mountain," 875.

72. Ibid., 881. The wild, barren mountain scenery of the Thebaid suggests this powerful and untamed aspect of Hathor, who is portrayed in art as emerging from the mountain or in a swamp and thus is a wild, as opposed to a domesticated, cow. Her animal nature is the side depicted at first in the Herdsman's Tale; her appealing human femininity and sexuality appear the next day and delight instead of frighten the herdsman. See Goedicke, "Story of the Herdsman," 244–66.

73. The close association between this instrument and goddesses is emphasized by its temporary disappearance during the reign of the "monotheistic" Akhenaten.

74. Naville, *Deir el-Bahari*, 4:3, pl. 94, 96.

75. Scheil, *Tombeaux Thébains*, 549.

76. Tomb of Iri-nufer, Theban Tomb 290; see Porter and Moss, *Topographical Bibliography*, 1:pt., 372; and pl. 16, this vol.

77. E. Hornung, *Valley of the Kings*, 58.
78. Ibid.
79. J. Lipinska, *Deir el-Bahari*, 4:29.
80. Hornung, *Valley of the Kings*, 58.
81. Pinch, *Magic in Ancient Egypt*, 354.
82. Ibid., 99.
83. Denon, *Travels in Upper and Lower Egypt*, 1:165–66.
84. Turin Love Song no. 28–30.
85. A. H. Gardiner, in N. de G. Davies, *Tomb of Amenemhet*, 96.
86. On a New Kingdom statue of Djaui, see Naville, *XIth Dynasty Temple*, 8.
87. Ibid.
88. Bleeker, *The Rainbow*, 215.
89. Pinch, *Magic in Ancient Egypt*, 12, 222–23.
90. Ibid., 126.
91. L. Manniche, *Sexual Life in Ancient Egypt*, fig. 17.
92. J. A. Omlin, *Der Papyrus 55001*.
93. C. J. Bleeker, *Hathor and Thoth*, 99. Before the modern age, the idea that orgasm was necessary for conception to take place was common and helps to explain the emphasis on sexual excitement in the cult of deities who aided procreation.
94. M. Bierbrier, *Tomb-builders of the Pharaoh*, 32.
95. "Hathor in sieben," in *LA*, 2:1033.
96. A. H. Gardiner, Group A, No. 32. *Chester Beatty Papyrus, No. 1*, 60.
97. B. S. Lesko translation, Ibid., No. 35.
98. Roberts, *Hathor Rising*, 45–48.
99. Ibid., 48.
100. Goedicke, "Story of the Herdsman," 258–62.
101. "The Story of Sinuhe," in Lichtheim, *Ancient Egyptian Literature*, 1:223–33.
102. H. Brünner, *Die Geburt des Gottkönigs*, 122–26, pls. 12–15, 22, 23.
103. R. Johnson, "Images of Amenhotep III," 36–41.
104. L. Habachi, in University of Chicago, Epigraphic Survey, *Kheruef*, 19; E. F. Wente, "Hathor at the Jubilee," 47.
105. Johnson, "Images of Amenhotep III," 41.
106. E. Hornung, *Tomb of Pharaoh Seti I*, pl. 95. Hathor holding out her menat to the king is seen also on the two panels taken from the tomb and now in Paris's Louvre Museum and Florence's Museo Archeologico.
107. Bleeker, *Hathor and Thoth*, 99.
108. Roberts, *Hathor Rising*, 8–9.
109. For "The Contendings of Horus and Seth," see Lichtheim, *Ancient Egyptian Literature*, 2:216.
110. C. Desroches-Noblecourt and C. Kuentz, *Abou Simbel*, 2:123–26.
111. B. Lesko, "Queen Khamerernebty II," 161.
112. Desroches-Noblecourt and Kuentz, *Abou Simbel*.
113. M. V. Fox, *Song of Songs and the Ancient Egyptian Love Songs*, 349.
114. E. R. Russman, *Egyptian Sculpture*, pl. 86.
115. T. G. H. James, *Ancient Egypt*, 179–80.

116. H. Junker, "Poesie aus der Spät Zeit," 106.

117. R. A. Parker, "Lady of the Acacia," 151.

118. E. Chassinat, *Le Temple de Dendera*, 1–11.

119. Lesko translation of Junker, "Poesie aus der Spät Zeit," 104–16.

120. J. C. Darnell, "Hathor Returns to Medamud," 49–50.

121. Bleeker's translation of H. Junker's German translation, in Bleeker *Hathor and Thoth*, 1.

122. H. W. Fairman, "Worship and Festivals," 196–99.

123. Ibid., 200.

124. M. Holmberg-Sandman, *The God Ptah*, 192.

125. C. J. Bleeker, *Egyptian Festivals*, 33; Fairman, "Worship and Festivals," 183.

126. "The Destruction of Mankind"; see Lichtheim, *Ancient Egyptian Literature*, 2:197–99; and L. H. Lesko, "Ancient Egyptian Cosmogonies," 109–11; Bleeker, *Hathor and Thoth*, 49–51.

CHAPTER 6

1. M. Bietak, *Avaris, the Capital of the Hyksos*.

2. Although this goddess was rarely represented, we find her commemorated with a colossal statue by Pharaoh Tutankhamun at Karnak; see back cover of B. S. Lesko, *The Remarkable Women of Ancient Egypt*, 2d rev. ed.

3. H. te Velde, "Mut."

4. Mut is Mistress of Megeb (in the Aphrodiopolite Nome) at the temple of Medinet Habu, south wall of Mut's sanctuary, where Ramses III offers burning incense to her. He also offers bouquets of flowers to a human-headed Mut, Great of Magic and Mistress of the Palace; see Epigraphic Survey, *Temple of Medinet Habu*, 7:pl. 504A and B.

5. D. B. Redford, *History and Chronology*, 68–69.

6. te Velde, "Mut," 247.

7. A. Erman, *Life in Ancient Egypt*, fig. p. 283.

8. A. Roberts, *Hathor Rising*, 75.

9. B. Porter and R. Moss, *Topographical Bibliography*, 2:196.

10. E. Thomas, "The K3y of Queen Inhapy," 85.

11. G. Pinch, *Votive Offerings*, 192.

12. A. Piankoff and N. Rambovaa, *Mythological Papyri*, 3:pl. 15.

13. H. te Velde, "The Cat as Sacred Animal of the Goddess Mut," 133.

14. Berlin Papyrus. Ibid., 133–34.

15. Ibid., 135.

16. S.-A. Naguib, *Le clergé féminin*, 87; H. te Velde, "Towards a Minimal Definition of the Goddess Mut," 8.

17. M. Lichtheim, *Ancient Egyptian Literature* 2:141. This socialization of the young by the mother and acknowledgment of her impact on the character of her children is repeated centuries later in the writings of Ankhsheshonq, 25, 17; see Lichtheim, *Ancient Egyptian Literature*, 3:179; W. H. Peck, "Miss Benson and Mut," 10–19, 63–65.

18. te Velde, "Towards a Minimal Definition of the Goddess Mut," 5, quoting W. C. Hayes, *Scepter of Egypt*, 2:105. Under Thutmose III, Hatshepsut's successor, the

Mistress of Thebes is sometimes identified as a composite Mut-Hathor; see J. H. Breasted, *Ancient Records*, 2:248.

19. L. H. Lesko translation of lines 68–75, pl. 51, in M. Abdul-Qader Muhammed, "Two Theban Tombs."

20. This changing of a name to a newly promoted goddess who reflected Hatshepsut's control of and wearing the crowns is of interest too from the standpoint that *sen* = "brother," a term for lover or husband. Thus in the case of the female pharaoh, the name chosen by her closest adviser may reflect an intimate relationshsip aspired to by its bearer.

21. Probably not all records, however, but the most public of them. Manetho, an ancient historian writing in the Ptolemaic period, recorded a female on the throne for the Eighteenth Dynasty, so obviously he must have had some records at his disposal on which to base this.

22. Lesko, *The Remarkable Women*, 13–22.

23. K. Sethe, *Urkunden*, 4:478–80; H. te Velde, "Mut, the Eye of Re," 397–98.

24. S. Quirke, *Ancient Egyptian Religion*, 120.

25. Pinch, *Magic in Ancient Egypt*, 54; C. Traunecker, "Une Chapelle de Magie Guerisseuse," 68–79.

26. A. Gardiner (quoting J. Barns), *Ramesseum Papyri*, 9.

27. R. K. Ritner, *Mechanics of Ancient Egyptian Magical Practice*, 223.

28. E. Naville, *Deir El-Bahari*, 2:pls. 47–54.

29. L. Bell, "Luxor Temple and the Cult of the Royal K3."

30. te Velde, "Towards a Minimal Definition of the Goddess Mut," 6, also suggests Mut was the divine manifestation of kingship in his article "Mut and Other Ancient Egyptian Goddesses," quoted by R. Fazzini, "Statuette of the goddess Mut," in Capel and Markoe, 128.

31. J. F. Borghouts, "Magical Practices among the Villagers."

32. P. Insinger, 8, 18–19, pertinent lines translated by te Velde in "Towards a Minimal Definition of the Goddess Mut."

33. te Velde, "Towards a Minimal Definition of the Goddess Mut."

34. Fazzini, "Bust from a statue of the goddess Sekhmit," in Capel and Markoe, 134–36.

35. Egyptologists often have equated the goddess's absence with the low Nile and her return with the coming of the inundation, a time that was celebrated but that also could be a disaster. Thus the certainty that the return was a joyous occasion tied to the inundation is not too credible.

36. J. Zandee, Leiden I 350.

37. G. Markoe, "Aegis and Menat onto head of lion-headed goddess," in Capel and Markoe, 136.

38. J. Malek, *The Cat*, 90–91.

39. Stela of Ramose from Deir el-Medina. K. A. Kitchen, *Pharaoh Triumphant*, 200.

40. H. M. Stewart, "A Crossword Hymn to Mut."

41. Ibid., 90.

42. Ibid., 93.

43. Ibid., 95.

44. Naguib, *Le clergé féminin*, 287; K. A. Kitchen, *Third Intermediate Period*, 260.

45. L. H. Lesko, "Some Remarks on the Books of the Dead," 185–86.

46. BD chap. 164; see Goelet, *Egyptian Book of the Dead*, 125–26. An ithyphallic image of a lioness-headed Mut eventually appeared on a temple wall during the Persian period in Egypt; see N. de G. Davies, *Temple of Hibis*, pt. 3, pl. 2d.

47. A. Leahy, "Death by Fire in Ancient Egypt," 199–206. R. Fazzini suggests that at least in the Late Period victims of Mut's brazier included "human sacrifices identified by particular biological characteristics as incarnations of forces inimical to the king, as well as to Ra and Osiris," "Statuette of the goddess Mut," in Capel and Markoe, 128.

48. te Velde, "Mut, the Eye of Re," 401.

49. Lichtheim, *Ancient Egyptian Literature*, 2:214–22.

50. P. Insinger 8, 11, and 8, 18–19, in Lichtheim, *Ancient Egyptian Literature*, 3:191–92. L. Troy, "Good and Bad Women," 77–81.

51. Kitchen, *Third Intermediate Period*, 359.

52. te Velde, "Towards a Minimal Definition of the Goddess Mut," 6.

53. Lichtheim, *Ancient Egyptian Literature*, 32.

54. Malek, 77.

55. Herodotus 2.66–68.

56. Diodorus, recalled in Malek, *The Cat*, 99.

57. M. Benson and J. Gourlay, *The Temple of Mut in Asher*.

58. te Velde, "Mut, the Eye of Re," 401–3.

59. Ibid., 402.

CHAPTER 7

1. Reported in the ancient historian Manetho's *History of Egypt*, bk. 1, frag. 9.

2. Indeed, the Second Dynasty date of this alleged ruling strongly suggests that dynastic struggles such as that recalled in the story of the murder of Osiris actually occurred during the formative decades of the state even though the story can admittedly reflect other sources.

3. S. T. Hollis, "Five Egyptian Goddesses," 82.

4. E. Hornung, *Conceptions of God*, 80.

5. K. Baedeker, *Egypt and the Sudan*, xxv.

6. V. Denon, *Travels in Upper and Lower Egypt*, 1:218.

7. The battle between Horus and Seth has been interpreted as political, recalling the struggle between Upper and Lower Egypt that ended finally in victory for the south and its Horus King over the northerners; see V. A. Tobin, "Divine Conflict in the Pyramid Texts," 102.

8. J. Gwyn Griffiths published Plutarch's *De Iside et Osiride*.

9. R. O. Faulkner, "The Pregnancy of Isis." This reminds one of the later story of Semele and Zeus, except that Isis survived.

10. W. C. Hayes, *Scepter of Egypt*, 2:71.

11. E. Thomas, "Solar Barks Prow to Prow."

12. N. Jenkins, *The Boat Beneath the Pyramid*.

13. W. K. Simpson, *The Terrace of the Great God at Abydos*, 11.

14. K. Pflüger, "The Private Funerary Stelae of the Middle Kingdom," 134.

15. Ibid., 133.

16. M. Münster, *Untersuchungen zur Göttin Isis*, 154.

17. M. Lichtheim, *Ancient Egyptian Literature*, 3:123–25.

18. J. H. Breasted, *Development of Religion and Thought in Ancient Egypt*, 256.

19. R. O. Faulkner, *Ancient Egyptian Coffin Texts.*

20. R. O. Faulkner, *Ancient Egyptian Book of the Dead*; O. Goelet, *Egyptian Book of the Dead.*

21. Goelet, *Egyptian Book of the Dead*, chap. 18, pl. 23.

22. Ibid., chap. 15, pl. 19.

23. L. V. Žabkar, *Hymns to Isis,* 83.

24. *LA*, 195, for Middle Kingdom cult references. The demotic story of Khaemwas (Ptolemaic period) relates the existence of priests of Isis at Koptos; see Lichtheim, *Ancient Egyptian Literature*, 3:126.

25. Stela of Sobk-iry, in Lichtheim, *Ancient Egyptian Literature*, 1:204.

26. Wm. M. F. Petrie, *Koptos*, 7–8, pl. 3.

27. R. A. Caminos, *New Kingdom Temples of Buhen*, 1:18.

28. H. Joachim, *Papyros Ebers*, 2.

29. Lesko translation of A. Moret, *Mélanges V. Loret*, 725–50. For full translation, see M. Lichtheim, *Ancient Egyptian Literature*, 2:81–86.

30. L. H. Lesko translation of "The Lamentations of Isis and Nephthys," Pap. Berlin 3008; full translation in Lichtheim, *Ancient Egyptian Literature*, 3:116–21.

31. L. H. Lesko translation from Papyrus Bremner-Rhind I transcription published by R. O. Faulkner, *The Papyrus Bremner-Rhind.* For Faulkner's translation of the full text, see The Songs of Isis and Nephthys, in R. O. Faulkner, "The Bremner-Rhind Papyrus-I," 121–40.

32. H. Frankfort, *Kingship and the Gods*, 162–80.

33. K. A. Kitchen, *Ramesside Inscriptions* 1:207.

34. G. T. Martin, *The Memphite Tomb of Horemhab*, 93.

35. Lichtheim, *Ancient Egyptian Literature*, 2:214–23; and M. V. Seton-Williams, *Egyptian Legends and Stories*, 30–38.

36. D. Meeks and C. Favard-Meeks, *Daily Life of the Egyptian Gods*, 94–107.

37. Seton-Williams, *Egyptian Legends and Stories*, 44–45.

38. A. Piankoff, *The Shrines of Tut-Ankh-Amon*, Shrine 3.

39. M. Jones and A. Milward, "Survey of the Temple of Isis Mistress-of-the-Pyramid," 147.

40. Ibid., 150.

41. A. Calverly, M. F. Broome, and A. H. Gardiner, *Temple of King Sethos I*, 1:pls. 17–23.

42. Kitchen, *Ramesside Inscriptions*, 1:208, 278.

43. Herodotus, *Histories*, 2.60.

44. G. Pinch, *Magic in Ancient Egypt*, 124.

45. Ibid., 116. Spiritual feminists hold the view that it was the ascendancy of patriarchy that put a stop to the favorable light in which menstrual blood was once held and that taught instead that it was impure. See C. Eller, *Living in the Lap of the Goddess*, 168.

46. J. Bergman, "I Overcome Fate."

47. Lichtheim, *Ancient Egyptian Literature*, 1:220–22, "Three Tales of Wonder."

48. Ibid., 222–33.

49. Bergman, "I Overcame Fate," 37.

50. Žabkar, *Hymns to Isis*, 108

51. Seton-Williams, *Egyptian Legends and Stories*, 41–43.

52. C. J. Bleeker, "Isis as a Saviour-Goddess," 1–16.

53. A. B. Edwards, *A Thousand Miles Up the Nile*, 207–10.

54. Ibid.

55. Hymn 4 in Žabkar, *Hymns to Isis*, 51.

56. R. S. Kraemer, *Her Share of the Blessings*, 77–78.

57. Just such a need and quest for a mother is quoted by Eller, *Living in the Lap of the Goddess*, 143.

58. Kraemer, *Her Share of the Blessings*, 72–73.

59. W. B. Kristensen, *Life out of Death*, 102–5.

60. Žabkar, *Hymns to Isis*,159–60.

61. Ibid., 42, Hymn 3.

62. Ibid., 51, Hymn 4.

63. Ibid., 69, Hymn 5.

64. Ibid.

65. S. A. Takacs, *Isis and Serapis in the Roman World*, 6.

66. R. E. Wit, *Isis in the Graeco–Roman World*, 56–57 (map).

67. S. De Caro, *Il Museo Archeologico Nazionale di Napoli*, pls. 126, 133.

68. Wit, *Isis in the Graeco-Roman World*, pl. 30.

69. See J. G. Griffiths, *The Isis Book*, for Apuleius translation in English; or the earlier translation by H. E. Butler, *The Metamorphoses*.

70. Book XI, Chapter 23.

71. Josephus, *Antiquitates Judaicae*, 18.66–80.

72. J.-C. Grenier, *Museo Gregoriano Egizio*, tav. 16.

73. Ibid., 31, tav. 8.

74. S. K. Heyob, *The Cult of Isis among Women*, 80, 97.

75. Bergman, "I Overcame Fate," 35–51.

76. Apulcius, *Metam.* 11.6.6.

77. Heyob, *The Cult of Isis among Women*, 80; Kraemer, *Her Share of the Blessings*, 77.

78. Xenophon, English translation by G. Anderson, in B. P. Reardon, *Collected Ancient Greek Novels*, 137–45, Isis's identity with love relationships is further shown by her son "Horus the Child," known in the Greco-Roman world as Harpokrates, equated with Eros. Hornung, 144.

79. L. Green, "Isis, the Egyptian Goddess Who Endured," 68.

80. Juvenal 6.511–41.

81. Žabkar, *Hymns to Isis*, 135–43.

82. Ibid., 140–41. Permission of University Press of New England.

83. P. Oxyrhynchus 11.1380, 214–16, or see S. B. Pomeroy, *Goddesses, Whores, Wives and Slaves*, 219.

84. Kraemer, *Her Share of the Blessings*, 79.

85. Žabkar, *Hymns to Isis*, 144.

86. W. Berkert, *Ancient Mystery Cults*, 15.

87. T. A. Brady, *Sarapis and Isis*, 12.

88. J. G. Griffiths, "Isis and the Love of the Gods," 29, 148.

89. Wit, *Isis in the Graeco-Roman World*, 274–77; Zabkar, *Hymns to Isis*, 160

90. Wit, *Isis in the Graeco-Roman World*, 275.

91. Ibid., 183.

92. During the European Renaissance, the Borgias commissioned paintings for their palace which reflected ancient Egyptian cults (Green, "Isis, the Egyptian Goddess Who Endured," 61), so knowledge of Isis's cult did not die out, thanks to both the plethora of ancient Egyptian monuments at Rome and the writings of classical authors.

CHAPTER 8

1. A. Badawy, *History of Egyptian Architecture*, 1:34–36; D. O'Connor and Silverman, "Status of Early Egyptian Temples."

2. B. Shafer, ed., *Religion in Ancient Egypt*, fig. 53.

3. C. Aldred, *Egyptian Art in the Days of the Pharaohs*, 78–80.

4. W. S. Smith, *Art and Architecture of Ancient Egypt*, 168.

5. H. Frankfort, *Ancient Egyptian Religion*, 153–54.

6. A. Badawy, *History of Egyptian Architecture*, 182–83.

7. H. te Velde, "Theology, Priests, and Worship in Ancient Egypt," 1741.

8. F. Nightingale, *Letters from Egypt*, 142–45; J. Rees, *Writings on the Nile*, 53.

9. L. Bell, "The New Kingdom 'Divine' Temple," 133.

10. F. Daumas, *Les Mammisis des temples égyptiens*, pls. via and vib, 152–58.

11. Lesko translation, K. Sethe, *Urkunden*, 4:365, lines 1–4.

12. G. A. Reisner, "The Tomb of Hepzefa"; C. J. Bleeker, *Egyptian Festivals*, 134–36.

13. H. W. Fairman, "Worship and Festivals in an Egyptian Temple," 177.

14. te Velde, "Theology, Priests, and Worship in Ancient Egypt," 1741.

15. L. H. Lesko, *King Tut's Wine Cellar*, 11–14.

16. P. Dils, "Wine for Pouring and Purification," 116–17.

17. te Velde, "Theology, Priests, and Worship in Ancient Egypt," 1743.

18. H. H. Nelson, "Certain Reliefs at Karnak and Medinet Habu," pts. 1 and 2, 201–32, 310–45; Fairman, "Worship and Festivals in an Egyptian Temple," 165–203.

19. Fairman, "Worship and Festivals in an Egyptian Temple," 180.

20. L. Manniche, *Music and Musicians in Ancient Egypt*, 63–64.

21. Nelson, "Certain Reliefs at Karnak and Medinet Habu," 221.

22. Ibid., 329.

23. te Velde, "Theology, Priests, and Worship in Ancient Egypt," 1744.

24. Nelson, "Certain Reliefs at Karnak and Medinet Habu," 225.

25. Stela of Ikhernofret from Abydos, Lichtheim, *Ancient Egyptian Literature*, 1:124.

26. J. F. Borghouts, in Sasson, *Civilizations of the Ancient Near East*, 1775–85.

27. Nelson, "Certain Reliefs at Karnak and Medinet Habu," 310.

28. After Nelson, "Certain Reliefs at Karnak and Medinet Habu," 229.

29. Ibid., pt. 2, 317.

30. Ibid., 319.

31. Fairman, "Worship and Festivals in an Egyptian Temple,"182.

32. Darnell, "Hathor Returns to Medamud," 49–50.

33. Ibid., 60.

34. Ibid., 62–63.

35. Ibid., 73, refers to the Epigraphic Survey, *The Tomb of Kheruet*, pls. 24, 34–40.

36. Ibid., 82.

37. Ibid., 93.

38. Nelson, "Certain Reliefs at Karnak and Medinet Habu," 226.

39. te Velde, "Theology, Priests, and Worship in Ancient Egypt," 1740.

40. Darnell, "Hathor Returns to Medamud," 54.

41. R. K. Ritner, "Denderite Temple Hierarchies."

42. S. Sauneron, "Clergy."

43. Speech of Thothrekh, son of Petosiris; see Lichtheim, *Ancient Egyptian Literature*, 3:53–54.

44. J. Černý, "The Origin of the Name of the Month Tybi."

45. B. Landström, *Ships of the Pharaohs*.

46. H. H. Nelson, *The Great Hypostyle Hall at Karnak*, 1:pt. 1, pls. 38, 53.

47. J. Karkowski, "The Question of the Beautiful Feast of the Valley."

48. J. Baines, "Society, Morality, and Religious Practice," 147–50.

49. Bell, "The New Kingdom 'Divine' Temple," 173–76.

50. Epigraphic Survey, *Temple of Medinet Habu*, 8, 9, 23, 51, 83, 84, 93, 94, 1930–70.

51. E. Chassinat, *Le Temple de Dendera*, 8, pls. 739–801.

52. Fairman, "Worship and Festivals in an Egyptian Temple," 199–290.

53. Ibid.

54. Ibid., 202.

55. D. Montserrat, *Sex and Society in Graeco-Roman Egypt*, 164.

56. Ibid., 165.

57. Diod. 1.85.

58. Ibid., 168.

59. J. A. Omlin, *Der papyrus 55001*.

60. Montserrat, *Sex and Society in Graeco-Roman Egypt*, 170.

61. L. H. Lesko, ed. *Pharaoh's Workers*, 19, 93.

62. Bell, "The New Kingdom 'Divine' Temple," 164–65.

63. Epigraphic Survey, *Temple of Medinet Habu*, 8:xi, pl. 608.

64. G. Pinch, *Votive Offerings to Hathor*, 248–54.

65. Ibid., 334.

66. Ibid., 345; 356.

67. Theban Tomb 2 (at Deir el–Medina), B. Porter, R. Moss, and E. Burney eds., *Topographical Bibliography*, 8.

68. P. Smither, "A Ramesside Love Charm," 131.

69. Borghouts, in Sasson, *Civilizations of the Ancient Near East*, 1778.

70. L. H. Lesko, *op. cit.*, 90; A. I. Sadek, *Popular Religion in Egypt*, 59–74.

71. Instruction of Ani. E. Suys, *La sagesse d'Ani*, 3:3–8.

72. Ibid., 7:15–16.

73. Sadek *Popular Religion in Egypt,* 70; A. H. Bomann, *The Private Chapel in Ancient Egypt,* 71–75.

74. E. Suys, *La sagesse d'Ani,* 4:1–4.

75. A. H. Gardiner, *Library of Chester Beatty,* Group A, no. 35, fifth stanza.

76. L. Troy, *Patterns of Queenship,* 153–54.

77. H. G. Fischer, "Priesterin," cols. 1100–05.

78. M. Galvin, *The Priestesses of Hathor.*

79. M. Galvin, "Hereditary Status of the Titles of the Cult of Hathor."

80. D. Nord, "The Term *hnr* 'Harem' or 'Musical Performers,'" 137.

81. N. de G. Davies, *The Tomb of Antefoker,* 17.

82. A. M. Blackman, *Rock Tombs of Meir II,* pls. 9, 16; 3: pl. 12.

83. R. Gillam, "Priestesses of Hathor," 211–37.

84. Merikare. A. Volten, *Zwei altägyptische politische Schriften,* 63–66.

85. H. W. Fairman, "A Scene of the Offering of Truth," 90.

86. T. G. H. James, *Pharaoh's People,* chap. 3, 373–94.

87. P. Kahun III.3. Letter 101, in E. Wente, *Letters from Ancient Egypt,* 82.

88. B. M. Bryan "In Women Good and Bad Fortune Are on Earth: Status and Roles of Women in Egyptian Cults," 43.

89. S.-A. Naguib, *Le clergé féminin,* pls. 18–19.

90. Wente, *Letters from Ancient Egypt,* 174, letter 290. An indication of the control of wealth is found in the titles of a first prophet of Hathor: "overseer of cattle, overseer of fields, and overseer of the granary." Ritner, "Denderite Temple Hierarchies," 221.

91. Ritner, "Denderite Temple Hierarchies," 213.

92. D. B. Redford, *History and Chronology,* 71; B. S. Lesko, *Remarkable Women of Ancient Egypt,* 14, see also M. Gitton, "Ahmose Nofretere."

93. T. E. Peet, *Tomb Robberies of the Twentieth Egyptian Dynasty,* 39.

94. J. K. MacDonald, *House of Eternity.*

95. C. Desroches-Noblecourt and C. Kuentz, *Abou Simbel,* pls. 124–26.

96. Queen Tiy as Hathor or Isis, in Museo Egizio di Torino, *Civilta' Degli Egizi, le arti della celebrazione,* 143, fig. 223.

97. Troy, *Patterns of Queenship,* 7–12.

98. A. Niwinski, "The Wives of Pinudjem II," 226–30.

99. Ibid., 228.

100. L. H. Lesko, "Some Remarks on the Books of the Dead."

101. A. H. Gardiner, "The Goddess Nekhbet at the Jubilee Festival of Rameses III."

102. Lesko translation of G. Legrain, *Catalogue général des antiquités égyptienne,* 58, c., 11–6; see Lichtheim, *Ancient Egyptian Literature,* 3:19.

103. B. Watterson, *Women in Ancient Egypt,* 62–65.

104. J. Leclant, *Mentouemhet,* 60; Lichtheim, *Ancient Egyptian Literature,* 3:32.

105. R. A. Caminos, "The Nitocris Adoption Stela."

106. R. Bianchi, review of J. Eingartner, *Isis und ihre Dienerinnen,* 201.

107. D. J. Thompson, *Memphis under the Ptolemies,* 144.

108. S. B. Pomeroy, *Women in Hellenistic Egypt,* 39.

109. Thompson, *Memphis under the Ptolemies,* 131.

110. Pomeroy, *Women in Hellenistic Egypt*, 39.

111. Amun to Arsinoe II Philadelphus, deceased. J. Quaegebeur, "Cleopatra VII and the Cults of the Ptolemaic Queens," 43.

112. Thompson, *Memphis under the Ptolemies*, 135.

113. Wit, *Isis in the Graeco-Roman World*, 71.

114. P. Harris 1.4.3–4.4. Author's translation.

115. Epigraphic Survey, *The Temple of Medinet Habu*, 5:pt. 1, pls. 319, 320.

116. Ibid., pl. 322.

117. Ibid., pl. 325.

118. D. A. Warburton, *State and Economy in Ancient Egypt*, 201.

119. Ibid.

120. L. V. Žabkar, *Hymns to Isis*, 91–92.

121. B. J. Kemp, *Ancient Egypt*, 191, 195.

122. Herod. 2.40.

123. A L. Oppenheim, "Babylonian and Assyrian Historical Texts."

CONCLUSION

1. Herod. 2.37.

2. Nefer-abu, artisan in the Valley of the Kings. L. H. Lesko translation of M. Tosi and A. Roccati, *Stele e altere epigrafi di Deir El Medina*, 94–96, 286.

3. B. S. Lesko, "Researching the Role of Women in Ancient Egypt," 14–23; "Rank, Roles and Rights," 15–39; "The Rhetoric of Women," 89–111; *The Remarkable Women of Ancient Egypt*; "Women of Ancient Egypt and Western Asia," 15–45; "Women's Monumental Mark on Ancient Egypt," 4–15.

4. J. Cott, *Isis and Osiris*, 99–195.

ℬIBLIOGRAPHY

Abdul-Qader Muhammed, M. "Two Theban Tombs Kyky and Bak-en-Amon." *Annales* 59 (1966): 159–83.

Adams, B. *Predynastic Egypt.* Aylesbury, U.K.: Shire Egyptology, 1988.

———. "A Predynastic Female Figurine." *KMT: A Modern Journal of Ancient Egypt* 3, no. 2 (1992): 12–13.

Adams, B., with R. F. Friedman. "Imports and Influences in the Predynastic and Proto-dynastic Settlement and Funerary Assemblages at Hierakonpolis." In E. C. M. van den Brink, ed., *The Nile Delta in Transition*, 317–338. Jerusalem: Israel Exploration Society, 1992.

Aldred, C. *Egyptian Art in the Days of the Pharaohs.* New York: Oxford University Press, 1980.

Allam, S. *Beiträge zum Hathorkult bis zum Ende des Mittleren Reich.* Berlin: Verlag Bruno Hessling, 1963.

———. "Women as Owners of Immovables in Pharaonic Egypt." In B. S. Lesko, ed., *Women's Earliest Records*, 123–35. Atlanta: Scholars Press, 1989.

Anthes, R. "Egyptian Theology in the Third Millennium B.C.," *Journal of Near Eastern Studies* 18 (1959): 169–212.

Arkell, A. J. *Shaheinab: An Account of the Excavations of a Neolithic Occupation Site carried out for the Sudan Antiquities Service in 1949–50.* London: Oxford University Press, 1953.

———. "The signs ⌐ and ℞." *JEA* 19 (1933): 175–76.

Arnold, D., ed. *The Temple of Mentuhotep at Deir el-Bahari, from the Notes of Herbert Winlock.* New York: Metropolitan Museum of Art, 1979.

Assman, J. "Neit spricht als Mutter und Sarg." *Mitteilungen des Deutsches Archaeologisches Instituts Abteilung Kairo* 28 (1972): 125.

Badawy, A. *A History of Egyptian Architecture, from the Earliest Times to the End of the Old Kingdom.* Cairo: Privately printed, 1954.

————. *A History of Egyptian Architecture: The Empire (New Kingdom).* Berkeley: University of California Press, 1968.

Baedeker, K. *Egypt and the Sudan: Handbook for Travelers.* 6th ed. Leipzig: Karl Baedeker, 1908.

Baines, J. "Origins of Egyptian Kingship." In D. O'Connor and D. P. Silverman, ed., *Ancient Egyptian Kingship,* 95–156. Leiden: E. J. Brill, 1995.

————. "Society, Morality, and Religious Practice." In B. Shafer, ed., *Religion in Ancient Egypt,* 123–200. Ithaca: Cornell University Press, 1991.

Baumgartel, E. J. *The Cultures of Prehistoric Egypt.* 2 vols. London: Oxford University Press, 1960.

————. "Predynastic Egypt." In *The Cambridge Ancient History,* 3d ed., vol. 1, pt. 1, chap 9. Cambridge: University Press, 1970.

————. Review of Ucko, *Anthropomorphic Figurines. Journal of Egyptian Archaeology* 56 (1970): 201.

————. "Scorpion and Rosette and the Fragment of the Large Hierakonpolis Mace Head." *Zeitschrift für Ägyptische Sprache und Altertumskunde* 93 (1966): 10–11.

Begelsbacher-Fischer, B. *Untersuchungen zur Götterwelt des alten Reiches* (Orbis Biblicus et Orientalis, 37). Freiburg: Universitäts Verlag; Göttingen: Vandenkoeck & Ruprecht, 1981.

Bell, L. "Luxor Temple and the Cult of the Royal K3." *Journal of Near Eastern Studies* 44 (1985): 251–94.

————. "The New Kingdom 'Divine' Temple: The Example of Luxor." In B. Shafer, ed., *Temples in Egypt: Function, Rituals and Meaning,* 127–84. Ithaca: Cornell University Press, 1997.

Benson, M., and J. Gourlay. *The Temple of Mut in Asher.* London: John Murray, 1899.

Bergman, J. "I Overcome Fate, Fate Harkens to Me." In H. Ringgren, ed., *Fatalistic Beliefs in Religion, Folklore, and Literature,* 35–51. (Scripta Instituti Donneriani Aboensis, 2). Stockholm: Almqvist & Wiksell, 1967.

Berkert, W. *Ancient Mystery Cults.* Cambridge, Mass.: Harvard University Press, 1987.

Bianchi, R. Review of J. Eingartner, *Isis und ihre Dienerinnen in der Kunst der römischen Kaiserzeit. Journal of the American Research Center in Egypt* 30 (1993): 200–1.

Bierbrier, M. *The Tomb-Builders of the Pharaoh.* London: British Museum, 1982.

Bietak, M. *Avaris, the Capital of the Hykson: Recent Excavations at Tell el-Dab'a.* London: British Museum, 1996.

Blackman, A. M. *The Rock Tombs of Meir, II.* London: Egypt Exploration Fund, 1915.

Bleeker, C. J. *Egyptian Festivals: Enactments of Religious Renewal.* Leiden: Brill, 1967.

————. "The Egyptian Goddess Neith." In *Studies in Mysticism and Religion presented to Gershom G. Scholem on his Seventieth Birthday,* 41–56. Jerusalem: Magnus Press, 1967.

————. *Hathor and Thoth: Two Key Figures of the Ancient Egyptian Religion.* Leiden: Brill, 1973.

————. "Isis as a Saviour-Goddess." In S. G. F. Brandon, ed., *The Saviour God, Studies . . . E. O. James,* 1–16. Manchester: Manchester University Press, 1963.

————. *The Rainbow: A Collection of Studies in the Science of Religion.* Leiden: Brill, 1975.

Bomann, A. H. *The Private Chapel in Ancient Egypt.* London: Kegan Paul, 1991.

Borghouts, J. F. "Magical Practices among the Villagers." in L. H. Lesko, ed., *Pharaoh's Workers,* 119–30. Ithaca: Cornell, 1994.

Brady, T. A. *Sarapis and Isis: Collected Essays.* Chicago: Ares, 1978.

Breasted, J. H. *Ancient Records of Egypt.* New York: Russell & Russell, 1906. (Reprint 1962.)

———. *Development of Religion and Thought in Ancient Egypt.* New ed. New York: Harper & Brothers, 1959.

Brovarski, E. "Senenu, High Priest of Amun at Deir el-Bahri." *JEA* 67 (1976): 57–73.

Brünner, H. "Das Besänftigungslied im Sinuhe (B269–279)." *Zeitschrift für Ägyptische Sprache und Altertumskunde* 80 (1955): 5–11.

———. *Die Geburt des Gottkönigs.* Ägyptologische Abhandlungen, 10. Wiesbaden: Harrassowitz, 1964.

Brunton, G., and G. Caton-Thompson. *The Badarian Civilisation.* British School of Archaeology in Egypt. London, 1928.

Bryan, B. M. "In Women Good and Bad Fortune Are on Earth: Status and Roles of Women in Egyptian Culture." In A. K. Capel and G. E. Markoe, eds., *Mistress of the House, Mistress of Heaven,* 25–46. New York: Hudson Hills, 1996.

Buhl, M.-L. "The Goddesses of the Egyptian Tree Cult." *Journal of Near Eastern Studies* 6 (1947): 80–97.

Butler, H. E. *The Metamorphoses or Golden Ass of Apuleius of Madaura, II.* Oxford: Clarendon Press, 1910,

Calverly, A., M. F. Broome, and A. H. Gardiner. *The Temple of King Sethos I at Abydos.* London: Egypt Exploration Society, 1933.

Caminos, R. A. *The New Kingdom Temples of Buhen.* Archaeological Survey of Egypt, 33d Memoir. London: Egypt Exploration Society, 1974.

———. "The Nitocris Adoption Stela." *JEA* 50 (1964): 107–18.

Capel, A. K. and G. E. Markoe, eds. *Mistress of the House, Mistress of Heaven.* New York: Hudson Hills, 1996.

Černý, J. *Ancient Egyptian Religion.* London: Hutchinson University Library, 1952.

———. "The Origin of the Name of the Month Tybi." *Annales du Service des Antiquités de l'Égypte* 43 (1943): 174–75.

Chassinat, E. *Le Temple de Dendera.* Cairo: Institut Français d'Archéologie Orientale, 1934–87.

Christ, C. *Rebirth of the Goddess.* Reading, Mass.: Addison-Wesley, 1997.

Clagett, M. *Ancient Egyptian Science: A Source Book.* I:1. Philadelphia: American Philosophical Society, 1989.

Cooper, A. M. "Canaanite Religion, an Overview." In Mircea Eliade, ed., *The Encyclopedia of Religion,* 3:35–45. New York, Macmillan, 1987.

Cott, J. *Isis and Osiris: Exploring the Goddess Myth.* New York: Doubleday, 1994.

Daressy, G. "Neith Protectrice du Sommeil." *Annales du Service des Antiquités Egyptienne* 10 (1910): 177–79.

Darnell, J. C. "Hathor Returns to Medamud." *Studien zur Altägyptischen Kultur* 22 (1995): 49–50

Daumas, F. *Le Culte d'Isis dans le Bassin oriental de la Mediterranée I: Le culte d'Isis et les Ptolemees.* Leiden: Brill, 1973.

————. *Les Mammisis des temples égyptiens.* Paris: Les Belles Lettres, 1958.

Davies, N. de G. *The Temple of Hibis in El Khargeh Oasis.* New York: Metropolitan Museum of Art, 1953.

————. *The Tomb of Amenemhet.* London: Egypt Exploration Fund, 1915.

————. *The Tomb of Antefoker, Vizier of Sesostris I, and of His Wife Senet (No. 60).* London: George Allen & Unwin, 1920.

De Caro, S. *Il Museo Archeologico Nazionale di Napoli.* Naples: Electa Napoli, 1994.

Denon, V. *Travels in Upper and Lower Egypt.* Translated by A. Aikin. London: Longman and Rees, 1803.

Derchain, P. *Hathor Quadrifrons: Recherches sur la syntaxe d'un mythe égyptien.* Istanbul: Nederlands Historisch-Archaeologisch Instituut, 1972.

Desroches-Noblecourt, C., and C. Kuentz. *Abou Simbel, Le Petit Temple.* Cairo: Ministry of Culture, Center of Documentation, Memoires 2, 1968.

Dils, P. "Wine for Pouring and Purification in Ancient Egypt." In J. Quaegebeur, ed., *Ritual and Sacrifice in the Ancient Near East,* 107–23. Orientalia Lovaniensia Analecta 55. Louvain: 1993.

Dodson, A. "El Kab, City of the Vulture-Goddess." *KMT: A Modern Journal of Ancient Egypt* 7, no. 4 (1996–97): 60–68.

Donadoni, A. M., et al. *Civilta' degli Egizi, le arti della celebrazione.* Torino: Museo Egizio, 1989.

Donahue, V. "The Goddess of the Theban Mountain." *Antiquity* 66 (1992): 871–85.

Drioton, E., and J. Vandier. *L'Égypte.* Les Peuples de l'Orient Mediterranean II. Paris: Presses Universitaires de France, 1962.

Dunham, D., and W. K. Simpson. *The Mastaba of Queen Mersyankh III.* Boston: Museum of Fine Arts, 1974.

Duff Gordon, Lucie, Lady. *Letters From Egypt.* Rev. ed. New York: McClure, Phillips & Co., 1904.

Eady, D. "Some Miraculous Wells and Springs of Egypt." *Newsletter of the American Research Center in Egypt* 75 (1968): 17–22.

Eaton-Krauss, M., and E. Graefe. *The Small Golden Shrine from the Tomb of Tutankhamun.* Oxford: Griffith Institute, 1985.

Edwards, A. B. *A Thousand Miles up the Nile.* 2d ed. London: Routledge & Sons, 1890.

Edwards, I. E. S. "The Early Dynastic Period in Egypt." In *Cambridge Ancient History,* 3d ed. Cambridge: University Press, 1971.

————. *Tutankhamun: His Tomb and Its Treasures.* New York: Metropolitan Museum of Art, 1976.

Ehrenberg, M. *Women in Prehistory.* Norman: University of Oklahoma Press, 1989.

Eller, C. *Living in the Lap of the Goddess: The Feminist Spirituality Movement in America.* New York: Crossroad, 1993.

Epigraphic Survey. *The Temple of Medinet Habu.* 8 vols. Oriental Institute Publications, 8, 9, 23, 51, 83, 84, 93, 94. Chicago: University of Chicago Press, 1930–70.

Epigraphic Survey. *The Tomb of Kheruef.* Oriental Institute Publication. Chicago: University of Chicago Press, 1980.

Erman, A. *The Ancient Egyptians: A Source Book of Their Writings.* Translated by A. M. Blackman, introduction by W. K. Simpson. New York: Harper & Row, 1966.

————. *Hymnen an des Diadem.* Berlin: Preussischen Akademie der Wissenschaften zu Berlin, 1911.

————. *Life in Ancient Egypt.* Translated by Tirard. New ed. New York: Dover, 1971.

Fagan, B. "A Sexist View of Prehistory." *Archaeology* (March/April 1992): 14–18, 66.

Fairman, H. W. "A Scene of the Offering of Truth in the Temple of Edfu." *Mitteilungen des Deutschen Archäologischen Instituts, Abteilung Kairo* 16 (1958): 86–92.

————. "Worship and Festivals in an Egyptian Temple." *Bulletin of the John Rylands Library, Manchester,* 37 (1954): 165–203.

Faulkner, R. O. *The Ancient Egyptian Book of the Dead.* Rev. ed. Edited by C. Andrews. Austin: University of Texas Press, 1985.

————. *The Ancient Egyptian Coffin Texts.* 3 vols. Warminster, U.K.: Aris & Phillips, 1973–78.

————. *The Ancient Egyptian Pyramid Texts.* Oxford: Clarendon Press, 1969.

————. "The King and the Star-Religion in the Pyramid Texts." *Journal of Near Eastern Studies* 25 (1966): 153–61.

————. *The Papyrus Bremner-Rhind (British Museum No. 10188).* Bibliotheca Aegyptiaca 3. Bruxelles: La Fondation Égyptologique Reine Élisabeth, 1933.

————. "The Pregnancy of Isis." *JEA* 54 (1968): 40–44.

Fischer, H. G. "The Cult and Nome of the Goddess Bat." *Journal of the American Research Center in Egypt* 1 (1962): 7–23.

————. *Dendera in the Third Millennium B.C.* Locust Valley, N.Y.: J. J. Augustin, 1968.

————. "Priesterin." in W. Helck and E. Otto, eds., *Lexikon der Ägyptologie,* 4:1100–05. Wiesbaden: Harrassowitz, 1982

Flaubert, G. *Flaubert in Egypt: A Sensibility on Tour, Travel Notes and Letters.* Translated and edited by Francis Steegmuller. Chicago: Academy Chicago Publishers, 1972.

Fox, M. V. *The Song of Songs and the Ancient Egyptian Love Songs.* Madison: University of Wisconsin Press, 1985

Frankfort, H. *Ancient Egyptian Religion.* New York: Harper & Brothers, 1948.

————. *Kingship and the Gods: A Study of Ancient Near Eastern Religions as the Integration of Society and Nature.* Chicago: University of Chicago Press, 1948.

Gaballa, G. A., and K. A. Kitchen. "The Festival of Sokar." *Orientalia* 38 (1969): 1–76.

Gadon, E. W. *The Once and Future Goddess: A Symbol for Our Time,* San Francisco: Harper, 1989.

Galvin, M. "Addendum." In B. S. Lesko, ed., *Women's Earliest Records from Ancient Egypt and Western Asia,* 28–30. Brown Judaic Studies, 166. Atlanta: Scholars Press, 1989.

————. "The Hereditary Status of the Titles of the Cult of Hathor." *JEA* 70 (1984): 42–49.

————. *The Priestesses of Hathor in the Old Kingdom and the 1st Intermediate Period.* Ann Arbor: University Microfilms International, 1981.

Gardiner, Sir Alan H. "The Coronation of King Haremhab." *JEA* 39 (1953): 52–57.

————. *Egypt of the Pharaohs.* Oxford: Clarendon Press, 1961.

————. "The Goddess Nekhbet at the Jubilee Festival of Ramses III." *Zeitschrift für Ägyptische Sprache und Altertumskunde* 48 (1910): 47–51.

————. "Horus the Behdetite." *JEA* 30 (1944): 23–60.

————. *The Library of Chester Beatty: The Chester Beatty Papyrus.* No. 1. London: Oxford University Press, 1931.

————. *The Ramesseum Papyri.* Oxford: Oxford University Press, 1955.

Gillam, R. "Priestesses of Hathor: Their Function, Decline and Disappearance." *Journal of the American Research Center in Egypt* 32 (1995): 211–37.

Gimbutas, M. *The Goddesses and Gods of Old Europe: Myths and Cult Images.* Berkeley: University of California Press, 1982.

————. *The Gods and Goddesses of Old Europe, 7000 to 3500 B.C.: Myths, Legends, and Cult Images.* London: Thames & Hudson, 1974.

Gitton, M. "Ahmose Nofretere." In W. Helck and E. Otto, eds., *Lexikon der Ägyptologie,* 1:102–9. Wiesbaden: Harrassowitz, 1975–90.

Goedicke, H. "The Story of the Herdsman." *Chronique d'Égypte* 90 (1970): 244–66.

Goelet, O. *The Egyptian Book of the Dead: The Book of Going Forth by Day.* San Francisco: Chronicle Books, 1994.

Green, L. "Isis, the Egyptian Goddess Who Endured in the Graeco-Roman World." *KMT: A Modern Journal of Ancient Egypt* 5 (1994): 60–68.

Grenier, J.-C. *Museo Gregoriano Egizio.* Guide Cataloghi Musei Vaticani, 2. Roma: L'Erma di Bretschneider, 1993.

Griffiths, J. G. "Isis and the Love of the Gods." *Journal of Theological Studies* 29 (1978): 148.

————. *The Isis Book (Metamorphores XI) Apuleius of Madauros.* Etudes Preliminaries aux Religions Orientales dans l'Empire Romain, 39. Leiden: Brill, 1975.

Griffiths, J. G., ed. *Plutarch's "De Iside et Osiride,"* Cambridge: Cambridge University Press, 1970.

Grimal, N. *A History of Ancient Egypt.* Translated by I. Shaw. Oxford: Blackwell, 1992.

Habachi, L. "The Owner of the Tomb." In Epigraphic Survey, *The Tomb of Kheruef: Theban Tomb 192,* 17–26. Oriental Institute Publication, 102. Chicago: Oriental Institute, 1980.

Hassan, F. "Primeval Goddess to Divine King: The Mythogenesis of Power in the Early Egyptian State." In R. Friedman and B. Adams, eds., *Followers of Horus, Studies Dedicated to Michael Allen Hoffman,* 307–320. Oxford: Oxbow Monographs, 1992.

Hayes, W. C. *Scepter of Egypt.* Vol. 2. Cambridge, Mass.: Harvard University Press, 1959.

Helck, W., and E. Otto, eds. *Lexikon der Ägyptologie.* 7 vols. Wiesbaden: Harrassowitz, 1975–90.

Heyob, S. K. *The Cult of Isis among Women in the Graeco-Roman World.* Etudes Preliminaires aux Religions Orientales dans l'Empire Romain, 51. Leiden: Brill, 1975.

Hill, D. R. "Magic." In Mircea Eliade, ed., *The Encyclopedia of Religion,* 9:89–92. New York: Macmillan, 1987.

Hoffman, M. A. *Egypt before the Pharaohs: The Prehistoric Foundations of Egyptian Civilization.* New York: Alfred A. Knopf, 1984.

Hollis, S. T. "Ancient Egyptian Women and the Sky Goddess Nut." In S. T. Hollis, L. Pershing, and M. J. Young, eds., *Feminist Theory and the Study of Folklore,* 200–18. Urbana: University of Illinois Press, 1993.

————. "Five Egyptian Goddesses in the Third Millennium B.C." *KMT: A Modern Journal of Ancient Egypt* 5, no. 4 (1994): 46–51.

————. "Queens and Goddesses in Ancient Egypt." In K. L. King, ed., *Women and Goddess Traditions in Antiquity and Today,* 210–25. Minneapolis: Fortress Press, 1997.

———. "Women of Ancient Egypt and the Sky Goddess Nut." *Journal of American Folklore* 100 (1987): 496–503.

Holmberg-Sandman, M. *The God Ptah.* Lund: C. M. K. Gleerup, 1946.

Hornung, E. *Das Amduat, die Schrift des verborgenen Raumes III.* Ägyptologische Abhundlungen, 13. Wiesbaden: Otto Harrassowitz, 1967.

———. *Conceptions of God in Ancient Egypt.* Translated by J. Baines. Ithaca: Cornell University Press, 1982.

———. *The Tomb of Pharaoh Seti I.* Zurich: Artemis & Winkler, 1991.

———. *The Valley of the Kings: Horizon of Eternity.* Translated by D. Warburton. New York: Timken, 1990.

Jacobsen, T. "Mesopotamian Religions." In Mircea Eliade, ed., *The Encyclopedia of Religion,* 9:447–69. New York: Macmillan, 1987.

James, E. O. *The Cult of the Mother-Goddess: An Archaeological and Documentary Study.* London: Thames and Hudson, 1959.

James, T. G. H. *Ancient Egypt: The Land and Its Legacy.* Austin: University of Texas Press, 1988.

———. *Pharaoh's People: Scenes from Life in Imperial Egypt.* London: Bodley Head, 1984.

Jenkins, N. *The Boat Beneath the Pyramid: King Cheops' Royal Ship.* New York: Holt, Rinehart and Winston, 1980.

Jidejian, N. *Byblos through the Ages.* Beirut: Dar el-Machreq, 1968.

Joachim, H. *Papyros Ebers, das älteste Buch über Heilkunde.* Berlin: Walter de Gruyter, 1890. Reprint, 1973.

Johnson, R. "Images of Amenhotep III in Thebes: Styles and Intensions." In L. M. Berman, ed., *The Art of Amenhotep III: Art Historical Analysis,* 26–46. Cleveland: Museum of Art, 1990.

Johnson, S. B. *The Cobra Goddess of Ancient Egypt: Predynastic, Early Dynastic, and Old Kingdom Periods.* London: Kegan Paul, 1990.

Jones, M., and A. Milward. "Survey of the Temple of Isis Mistress-of-the-Pyramid at Giza, 1980 Season: Main Temple Area." *Journal of the Society for the Study of Egyptian Antiquity* 12 (1982): 140–51.

Junker, H. "Poesie aus der Spät Zeit." *Zeitschrift für Ägyptische Sprache* 43 (1906): 101–127.

Kaplony, P. "Der Titel *wnr(w)* nach Spruch 820 der Sargtexte." *Mitteilungen des Instituts für Orientforschungen* 11 (1966): 151.

Karkowski, J. "The Question of the Beautiful Feast of the Valley as Represented in the Temple of Hatshepsut at Deir el-Bahri." In W. F. Reineke, ed., *First International Congress of Egyptology,* 356–64. Berlin: Akademie Verlag, 1979.

Kees, H. *Ancient Egypt: A Cultural Topography.* Edited by T. G. H. James. Chicago: University of Chicago Press, 1961.

Kemp, B. J. *Ancient Egypt: Anatomy of a Civilization.* London: Routledge, 1989.

Kendall, T. "Discoveries at Sudan's Sacred Mountain: Jebel Barkal Reveals Secrets of the Kingdom of Kush." *National Geographic,* 178, no. 5 (1990): 96–124.

Kitchen, K. A. *Pharaoh Triumphant: The Life and Times of Ramesses II.* Warminster: Aris & Phillips, 1982.

———. *Ramesside Inscriptions Translated and Annotated, Notes and Comments.* Vol. 1. Oxford: Blackwell, 1993.

————. *The Third Intermediate Period in Egypt.* Warminster: Aris & Phillips, 1973.

Kraemer, R. S. *Her Share of the Blessings: Women's Religions among Pagans, Jews, and Christians in the Greco-Roman World.* New York: Oxford University Press, 1992.

Kramer, S. N. "Poets and Psalmists: Goddesses and Theologians. Literary, Religious and Anthropological Aspects of the Legacy of Sumer." In D. Schmandt-Besserat, ed., *The Legacy of Sumer* 3–21. Bibliotheca Mesopotamica, 4. Malibu: Undena, 1979.

Kristensen, W. B. *Life out of Death: Studies in the Religions of Egypt and of Ancient Greece.* Translated by H. J. Franken and G. R. H. Wright. Louvain: Peeters Press, 1992.

Landström, B. *Ships of the Pharaohs.* London: Allen & Unwin, 1970.

Leacock, E. B. *Myths of Male Dominance.* New York: Monthly Review Press, 1981.

Leahy, A. "Death by Fire in Ancient Egypt." *Journal of the Economic and Social History of the Orient* 27 (1984): 199–206.

Leclant, J. *Montouemhat, quatrième prophète d'Amon, prince de la ville.* Bibliothèque d'étude, 35. Cairo: Institut Français d'Archéologie Orientale, 1961.

Legrain, G. *Catalogue général des antiquités égyptienne du Musée du Caire: Statues et statuettes de Rois et des particuliers.* Cairo: L'Institut Français d'Archeologie Orientale, 1914.

Lesko, B. "Queen Khamerernebty II and Her scultpure." In L. H. Lesko, ed., *Ancient Egyptian and Mediterranean Studies in Memory of William A. Ward*, 149–62. Providence: Brown University, Department of Egyptology, 1998.

————. "Rank, Roles, and Rights." In L. H. Lesko, edl, *Pharaoh's Workers*, 15–39. Ithaca: Cornell University Press, 1994.

————. *The Remarkable Women of Ancient Egypt.* 2d and 3d eds. Providence: B. C. Scribe Publications, 1987, 1996.

————. "Researching the Role of Women in Ancient Egypt." *KMT: A Modern Journal of Ancient Egypt* 5 (1994–95): 14–23.

————. "The Rhetoric of Women in Pharaonic Egypt." In M. M. Wertheimer, ed., *Listening to Their Voices: The Rhetorical Activities of Historical Women.* Columbia: University of South Carolina Press, 1997.

————. "True Art in Ancient Egypt." In L. H. Lesko, ed., *Egyptological Studies in Honor of Richard A. Parker*, 85–97. Hanover: University Press of New England, 1986.

————. "Women of Ancient Egypt and Western Asia." In R. Bridenthal, S. Stuard, and M. E. Wiesner, eds., *Becoming Visible: Women in European History*, 3d rev. ed., 16–45. Boston: Houghton Mifflin, 1998.

————. *Women's Earliest Records.* Atlanta: Scholars Press, 1989.

————. "Women's Monumental Mark on Ancient Egypt." *Biblical Archaeologist* 54, no. 1 (1991): 4–15.

Lesko, L. H. "Ancient Egyptian Cosmogonies and Cosmology." In B. E. Shafer, ed., *Religion in Ancient Egypt: Gods, Myths, and Personal Practice*, 88–92. Ithaca: Cornell University Press, 1991.

————. *King Tut's Wine Cellar.* Berkeley: B. C. Scribe Publications, 1977.

————. *Pharaoh's Workers: The Villagers of Deir el Medina.* Ithaca: Cornell University Press, 1994.

————. "Some Remarks on the Books of the Dead Composed for the High Priests Pinedjem I and II." In D. P. Silverman, ed., *For His Ka: Essays Offered in Memory of*

Klaus Baer, 179–86. Studies in Ancient Oriental Civilization, 55. Chicago: Oriental Institute, 1994.

Lichtheim, M. *Ancient Egyptian Literature.* 3 vols. Berkeley: University of California Press, 1973–80.

Lienhardt, G. *Divinity and Experience: The Religion of the Dinka.* Oxford: Oxford University Press, 1961.

Lilyquist, C. *Ancient Egyptian Mirrors from the Earliest Times through the Middle Kingdom.* Münchner Ägyptologische Studien, 27. Munich: Deutscher Kunstverlag, 1979.

Lipinska, J. *Deir el-Bahari IV: The Temple of Tuthmosis III, Statuary and votive Monuments.* Warsaw: Editions Scientifiques de Pologne, 1984.

Loth, H. *Woman in Ancient Africa.* Translated by S. Marnie. Leipzig: Edition Leipzig, 1987.

Lotti, P. *Egypt (La Mort de Philae).* Translated by W. P. Baines. New York: Duffield & Co., 1910.

MacDonald, J. K. *House of Eternity: The Tomb of Nefertari.* Los Angeles: J. Paul Getty Museum, 1996.

Mace, A. C., and H. E. Winlock. *The Tomb of Senebtisi at Lisht.* New York: Metropolitan Museum of Art, 1916.

McNeill, W. H. *The Rise of the West: A History of the Human Community.* Chicago: University of Chicago Press, 1963.

Malek, J. *The Cat in Ancient Egypt.* London: British Museum, 1993.

Manniche, L. *Music and Musicians in Ancient Egypt.* London: British Museum Press, 1991.

———. *Sexual Life in Ancient Egypt.* London: Routledge & Kegan Paul, 1987.

Martin, G. T. *The Memphite Tomb of Horemhab Commander-in-Chief of Tutankhamun.* 55th Excavation Memoire. London: Egypt Exploration Society, 1989.

Meeks, D., and C. Favard-Meeks. *Daily Life of the Egyptian Gods.* Translated by G. M. Goshgarian. Ithaca: Cornell University Press, 1996.

Mellaart, J. *The Neolithic in the Near East.* New York: Charles Scribner's Sons, 1975.

Meskell, L. "Goddesses, Gimbutas and New Age Archaeology." *Antiquity* 69 (1995): 74–86.

Miles, R. *The Women's History of the World.* Topsfield, Mass.: Salem House, 1989.

Montserrat, D. *Sex and Society in Graeco-Roman Egypt.* London: Kegan Paul International, 1996.

Moret, A. "Mélanges V. Loret." *Bulletin de l'Institut français d'archéologie orientale* 30 (1931): 725–50.

Mundkur, B. *The Cult of the Serpent: An Interdisciplinary Survey of Its Manifestations and Origins.* Albany: State University of New York Press, 1983.

Münster, M. *Untersuchungen zur Göttin Isis vom Alten Reich bis zum end des Neuen Reiches.* Münchner Ägyptologische Studien, 11. Berlin: Bruno Hessling, 1968.

Murnane, W. *The Penguin Guide to Ancient Egypt.* Harmondsworth: Penguin Books, 1983.

Murray, M. A. "Burial Customs and Beliefs on the Hereafter in Predynastic Egypt." *JEA* 42 (1956): 86–96.

———. *Egyptian Religious Poetry.* London: John Murray, 1949.

Museo Eglzio di Torino. *Civilta' Degli Egizi le arti della celabrazione.* Milano: Electa, 1989.

Naguib, S.-A. *Le clergé féminin d'Amon Thébain a la 21ᵗ Dynastie.* Oslo: Ethnografisk Museum, 1988.

Naville, E. *The Temple of Deir el-Bahari.* Vols. 2 and 4. London: Egypt Exploration Fund, 1896–1901.

Naville, E., and H. R. Hall. *The XIth Dynasty Temple of Deir el-Bahari.* Vols. 1 and 2. London: Egypt Exploration Fund, 1907–10.

Nelson, H. H. "Certain Reliefs at Karnak and Medinet Habu and the Ritual of Amenophis I, parts 1 and 2." *Journal of Near Eastern Studies* 8 (1949): 201–32, 310–45.

———. *The Great Hypostyle Hall at Karnak I, Part 1: The Wall Reliefs.* Edited by W. J. Murnane. Oriental Institute Publications, 106. Chicago: Oriental Institute, 1981.

Neumann, E. *The Great Mother: an Analysis of the Archetype.* Translated by R. Manheim. Bollingen Series, 47. Princeton: Princeton University Press, 1974.

Nightingale, F. *Letters from Egypt: A Journey on the Nile 1849–1850.* Edited by A. Sattin. New York: Weidenfeld & Nicolson, 1987.

Niwinski, A. "The Wives of Pinudjem II." *JEA* 74 (1988) 226–30.

Nord, D. "The Term *hnr* 'Harem' or 'Musical Performers.'" In *Studies in Ancient Egypt, the Aegean, and the Sudan,* 137–45. Boston: Museum of Fine Arts, 1981.

O'Connor, D., and D. Silverman. *Ancient Egyptian Kingship.* Leiden: Brill, 1995.

———. "The Status of Early Egyptian Temples: An Alternative Theory." In R. Friedman and B. Adams, eds., *The Followers of Horus: Studies Dedicated to Michael Allen Hoffmann,* 83–98. Oxford: Oxbow Monograph, 1992.

Omlin, J. A. *Der Papyrus 55001 und seine satirisch-erotischen Zeichnungen und Inscriften.* Torino: Edizione d'Arte Fratelli Pozzo, 1973.

Oppenheim, A. L. "Babylonian and Assyrian Historical Texts." In J. B. Pritchard ed., *Ancient Near Eastern Texts Related to the Old Testament,* 2d ed., 295. Princeton: Princeton University Press, 1955.

Parker, R. "Lady of the Acacia." *Journal of the American Research Center in Egypt* 4 (1965): 151.

Parker, R., and O. Neugebauer. *Egyptian Astronomical Texts.* Vol. 1: *The Early Decans.* Brown Egyptological Studies, 3. Providence: Brown University Press, 1960.

Peck, W. H. "Miss Benson and Mut." *KMT: A Modern Journal of Ancient Egypt* 2, no. 1 (1991): 10–19, 63–65.

Peet, T. E. *Tomb Robberies of the Twentieth Egyptian Dynasty.* Oxford: Clarendon Press, 1930.

Petrie, W. M. F. *Diospolis Parva.* London: Egypt Exploration Fund, 1901.

———. *Koptos.* London: B. Quaritch, 1896.

———. *The Royal Tombs of the 1st Dynasty.* Pt. 1. London: Egypt Exploration Fund, 1900.

Petrie, W. M. F., and J. E. Quibell. *Naqada and Ballas.* London: Egypt Exploration Fund, 1896.

Pflüger, K. "The Private Funerary Stelae of the Middle Kingdom and Their importance for the Study of Ancient Egyptian History." *Journal of the American Oriental Society* 67 (1947): 134.

Phillips, J., ed. *Ancient Egypt, the Aegean, and the Near East: Studies in Honor of Martha Rhoads Bell.* San Antonio: Van Siclen Books, 1997.

Piankoff, A. *The Shrines of Tut-Ankh-Amon.* Edited by N. Rambova. New York: Bollingen Foundation, 1955.

Piankoff, A., and N. Rambova. *Mythological Papyri: Egyptian Religious Texts and Representations.* Vol. 3. Bollingen Series, 40. New York: Pantheon Books, 1957.

Pinch, G. *Magic in Ancient Egypt.* Austin: University of Texas Press, 1994.

———. *Votive Offerings to Hathor.* Oxford: Griffith Institute, 1993.

Pomeroy, S. B. *Goddesses, Whores, Wives, and Slaves: Women in Classical Antiquity.* New York: Schocken Books, 1975.

———. *Women in Hellenistic Egypt.* New York: Schocken Books, 1984.

Porter, B., R. L. B. Moss, and E. Burney, eds., *Topographical Bibliography of Ancient Egyptian Hieroglyphic Texts, Reliefs, and Paintings.* 2d ed. Revised by J. Malek. Oxford: Griffith Institute, 1981.

Posener, G. *Le Premier Domination Perse.* Bibliothéque d'étude, 11. Cairo: Institut Français d'Archéologie Orientale, 1936.

Pritchard, J. B., ed. *Ancient Near Eastern Texts Relating to the Old Testament.* 2d ed. Princeton: Princeton University Press, 1955.

Quaegebeur, J. "Cleopatra VII and the Cults of the Ptolemaic Queens." In *Cleopatra's Egypt: Age of the Ptolemies,* 41–54. Exhibition Catalog, 7 October 1988–2 January 1989. Brooklyn: Brooklyn Museum.

Quibell, J. E. *El-Kab.* Egyptian Research Account, 3. London: Egypt Exploration Fund, 1898.

Quirke, S. *Ancient Egyptian Religion.* New York: Dover, 1995.

Raphael, M. *Prehistoric Pottery and Civilization in Egypt.* Translated by N. Guterman. Bollingen Series, 7. New York: Pantheon Books, 1947.

Reardon, B. P., ed. *Collected Ancient Greek Novels.* Berkeley: University of California Press, 1989.

Redford, D. B. *History and Chronology of the Eighteenth Dynasty of Egypt: Seven Studies.* Toronto: University of Toronto Press, 1967.

Rees, J. *Writings on the Nile.* London: Rubicon Press, 1995.

Reisner, G. A. "The Tomb of Hepzefa, Monarch of Siut." *JEA* 5 (1918): 79–98.

Ritner, R. K. "Denderite Temple Hierarchies and the Family of Theban High Priest Nebwenenef: Block Statue OIM 1017729." In D. P. Silverman, ed., *For His Ka: Essays Offered in Memory of Klaus Baer,* 205–26. Studies in Ancient Oriental Civilizations, 55. Chicago: Oriental Institute, 1993.

———. *The Mechanics of Ancient Egyptian Magical Practice.* Studies in Ancient Oriental Civilization, 54. Chicago: Oriental Institute, 1993.

Roberts, A. *Hathor Rising: The Serpent Power of Ancient Egypt.* Totnes, Devon: Northgate, 1995.

Russman, A. *Egyptian Sculpture: Cairo and Luxor.* Austin: University of Texas Press, 1989.

Sadek, A. I. *Popular Religion in Egypt during the New Kingdom.* Hildesheimer Ägyptologische Beiträge, 27. Hildesheim: Gerstenberg Verlag, 1988.

Saleh, M. *Three Old Kingdom Tombs at Thebes.* Archaeologische Veroffentlichungen, 1977.

Sasson, J. M., ed. *Civilizations of the Ancient Near East.* 4 vols. New York: Charles Scribner's Sons, 1995.

Sauneron, S. "Priests." In G. Posener, ed., *Dictionary of Egyptian Civilization*, 223–25. New York: Tudor Publishing, 1959.

———. "Remarques de Philologie et d'etymologie, 14. Le Createur Androgyne." In *Mélanges Mariette*, 229–49. Bibliothèque d'Étude, 32. Cairo: Institut Français d'Archéologie Orientale, 1961.

———. *Le Temple d'Esna*. Vol. 3. Cairo, Institut Français d'Archéologie Orientale, 1968.

Scheil, V. *Tombeaux Thébains*. Mémoire, Mission Archéologique Française du Caire, 5. Paris: Leroux, 1894.

Schneider, H. D., and M. J. Raven. *De Egyptische Oudheid*. Leiden: Rijksmuseum van Oudheden te Leiden, 1981.

Schott, S. "Ein Kult der Göttin Neith." In H. Ricke, *Das Sonnenheiligtum des Konigs Userkaf*, 2:123–48, pls. 1–7. Cairo: Schweizerisches Instituut für ägyptische Bauforschung und Altertumskunde, 1965.

Sethe, K. *Altägyptischen Pyramidentexte*. 4 Bde. Leipzig: J. C. Hinrichs, 1908–22.

———. "Der Name des Göttin Neith." *Zeitschrift für Ägyptische Sprache und Altertumskunde* 43 (1906): 144–47.

———. *Urkunden der 18. Dynastie*. 4 Bde. Leipzig: Hinrichs, 1905–9.

Seton-Williams, M. V. *Egyptian Legends and Stories*. London: Rubicon Press, 1988.

Silverman, D. P., ed. *Searching for Ancient Egypt: Art, Architecture, and Artifacts from the University of Pennsylvania Museum of Archaeology and Anthropology*. Ithaca: Cornell University Press, 1997.

Simpson, W. K. *The Terrace of the Great God at Abydos*. Publication of the Pennsylvania-Yale Expedition, 5. New Haven: Peabody Museum of Yale; Philadelphia: University Museum of the University of Pennsylvania, 1974.

Smith, W. S. *Art and Architecture of Ancient Egypt*. Baltimore: Penguin Books, 1958. Revised with additions by W. K. Simpson New Haven: Yale University Press, 1981.

Smither, P. "A Ramesside Love Charm." *Journal of Egyptian Archaeology* 27 (1941): 131.

Spencer, A. J. *Early Egypt: The Rise of Civilization in the Nile Valley*. Norman: University of Oklahoma Press, 1993.

Stewart, H. M. "A Crossword Hymn to Mut." *JEA* 57 (1971): 87–104.

Suys, E. *La sagesse d'Ani*, Roma: Pontificio Istituto Biblico, 1935.

Takacs, S. A. *Isis and Serapis in the Roman World*. Religion in the Graeco-Roman World, 124. Leiden: Brill, 1995.

te Velde, H. "The Cat as Sacred Animal of the Goddess Mut." In M. Heerma Van Voss et al., eds., *Studies in Egyptian Religion dedicated to Professor Jan Zandee*, 127–37. Leiden: Brill, 1982.

———. "A Few Remarks on the Religious Significance of Animals in Ancient Egypt." *Numen* 27 (1980) 78.

———. "Mut." In W. Helck and E. Otto, eds., *Lexikon der Ägyptologie*, 4:246. Wiesbaden: Harrassowitz, 1975–90.

———. "Mut, the Eye of Re." *SAKB* 3 (1988): 395–403.

———. "Theology, Priests, and Worship in Ancient Egypt." In J. M. Sasson, ed., *Civilizations of the Ancient Near East*, 3:1731–49. New York: Charles Scribner's Sons, 1995.

———. "Towards a Minimal Definition of the Goddess Mut." *Jaarbericht ex Oriente Lux* 26 (1979–80): 3–9.

Thomas, E. "The K3y of Queen Inhapy." *Journal of the American Research Center in Egypt* 16 (1979): 85.

———. "Solar Barks Prow to Prow." *JEA* 42 (1956): 65–79.

Thompson, D. J. *Memphis under the Ptolemies.* Princeton: Princeton University Press, 1988.

Thompson, S. E. "A Study of the Pyramid Texts Occurring on Middle Kingdom Saqqara Coffins." M.A. thesis, Brown University, 1986.

Tobin, V. A. "Divine Conflict in the Pyramid Texts." *Journal of the American Research Center in Egypt* 30 (1993): 102.

Tosi, M., and A. Roccati. *Stele e altere epigrafi di Deir el Medina n.50001–n.50262.* Catalogo del Museo Egizio di Torino, Serie Seconda, Collezioni I. Torino: Fratelli Pozzo, 1972.

Traunecker, C. "Une Chapelle de Magie Guerisseuse sur le parvis du temple de Mout a Karnak." *Journal of the American Research Center in Egypt* 20 (1983): 68–79.

Troy, L. "Good and Bad Women." *Göttinger Miszellen* 80 (1984): 77–81.

———. *Patterns of Queenship in Ancient Egyptian Myth and History.* Uppsala Studies in Ancient Mediterranean and Near Eastern Civilizations, 14. Uppsala: Acta Universitatis, 1986.

Ucko, P. J. *Anthropomorphic Figurines of Predynastic Egypt and Neolithic Crete with Comparative Material for the Prehistoric Near East and Mainland Greece.* London: Andrew Szmidla, 1968.

van den Brink, E. C. M., ed. *The Nile Delta in Transition: 4th–3rd Millennium B.C.* Jerusalem: Israel Exploration Society, 1992.

Van Lepp, J. "The Role of Dance in Funerary Ritual in the Old Kingdom." In S. Schoske, ed., *Akten des vierten Internationalen Ägyptologen Kongresses*, 385–90. Hamburg: H. Buske Verlag, 1991.

Vassilika, E. *Egyptian Art, Fitzwilliam Museum Handbook.* Cambridge: Cambridge University Press, 1995.

Vellacott, P., trans. *The Oresteian Trilogy of Aeschylus.* Harmondsworth: Penguin Books, 1956. Reprint 1985.

Volten, A. *Zwei altägyptische politissche Schriften.* Analectal Aegyptiaca, 4. Copenhagen: Munksgaard, 1945.

Wainwright, G. A. *The Sky-Religion in Egypt.* Cambridge: Cambridge University Press, 1938.

Warburton, D. A. *State and Economy in Ancient Egypt: Fiscal Vocabulary of the New Kingdom.* Orbis Biblicus et Orientalis, 151. Fribourg: University Press, 1997.

Watterson, B. *Women in Ancient Egypt.* New York: St. Martin's Press, 1991.

Weeramunda, A. J. "The Milk Overflowing Ceremony in Sri Lanka." In J. J. Preston, ed., *Mother Worship Theme and Variations*, 252–61. Chapel Hill: University of North Carolina Press, 1982.

Wells, R. A. "The Mythology of Nut and the Birth of Ra." *Studien zur Altägyptischen Kultur* 19 (1992): 305–21.

Wente, E. F. "Hathor at the Jubilee." In *Studies in Honor of John A. Wilson*, 83–91. Studies in Ancient Oriental Civilizations, 38. Chicago: University of Chicago Press, 1969.

———. *Letters from Ancient Egypt.* Society of Biblical Literature, Writings from the Ancient World, 1. Atlanta: Scholars Press, 1990.

BIBLIOGRAPHY

Wilson, J. A. "The Theban Tomb (No. 409) of Si-Mut, Called Kiki." *Journal of Near Eastern Studies* 29 (1970): 187–92.

Wit, R. E. *Isis in the Graeco-Roman World.* Ithaca: Cornell University Press, 1971.

Žabkar, L. V. *Hymns to Isis in Her Temple at Philae.* Hanover: University Press of New England, 1988.

Zandee, J. *De Hymnen aan Amon von Papyrus Leiden I 350.* Oudheid Rundiage Mededelingen uit het Rijksmuseum van Oudheden te Leiden 28. Leiden: Rijksmuseum van Oudheden, 1947.

INDEX

Abu Gurob, 89, 205
Abu Simbel, 75, 124, 208, 246
Abu Sir, 205, 206
Abydos: cenotaph of Seti I, 42; gods of cemetery of, 159; Isis at, 213; Middle Kingdom stelae from, 16; Osiris's shrine at, 172, 178; temple of Seti I, 120, 213
Adams, Barbara, 11
Aeschylus, 37–38
Africa, cultural roots for Egypt, 8, 12–16, 69, 156
Africanus, 51
Afterlife:7, 23–24, 27, 129–30. *See also* Eternal life
Agilqiyya Island, 183, 264
Agriculture: Egyptian, 14; first, 7; revolution, 10
Aha (king), 45
Ahmose (queen), 106
Ahmose-Nefertari (queen): deified, 236; regent for son, 265; temple role, 245–46
Akhenaton, 24, 109, 246
Akhmim, 140, 168–69, 181
Alexander the Great, 43–44; conquest of Egypt, 185–86
Alexandria, 188, 252, 253
Amarna interlude, 24; impact on religion, 119–20
Amasis (king), 59
Amulets, 8, 179
Amun (god), 104, 117, 131

Amunemhet, 114
Amunemhet (king): I, 104; II, 206; III, 74, 206
Amunet (goddess), 131, 265–66
Amunhotep (king): I, 136, 236, deified after death, 237, 265; II, 68, 74; III, 40, 68, 111, divine birth of, 119
Amunhotep, son of Hapu, 234
Amunirdis (princess), 250
Amunmose, 170
Amun-Re: divine father of Hatshepsut, 55–56; Feast of Opet, 141; fused with sun god,132; god of empire, 102, 114; husband of Mut, 120, 136; at Karnak, 245, 255; king of gods, 75–76, 220; at Thebes, 128; waning of cult, 259
Anath (goddess), 47, 266
Anatolian cult, 66
Ani, maxims of, 101, 136, 237
Animals: models of, 7; respect for, 8, 14; sensitivity to, 260; worship of, 124
Ankhnesneferibre (princess), 250
Antef-Nubkheperre, 134
Antefoker, 92
Anthes, Rudolf, 31
Anubis (god), 110, 191, 194, 266
Apis (god), 230
Aphrodisiac, 169
Apop, 134–35
Apuleius, 192, 199
Arensnuphis (god), 185

James, E. O., 13, 18
Jerusalem, 233
Jesus Christ, 199
Judaism, 230
Judgment, 55, 167, 221
Julius Caesar, 192
Justinian (emperor), 254

Kadesh, battle of, 273
Kamutef (god), 142
Karnak temple, 74, 98, 137, 142–43; Hener at, 246; Hypostyle Hall of, 144; priests of, 146–47, 150, 247–50; Mut at, 153, 270; queen at, 265
Kauket (goddess), 268
Kees, Hermann, 47
Kemp, Barry, 14, 31, 82, 255
Khafre (king), 85, 87, 239; Temple of, at Giza, 205
Khasekhemui (king), 97
Kheftherrnebes (goddess), 265
Khentiamentiu (god), 159
Kheruef, 40, 118
Khnum (god), 60, 106, 227, 266–67, 270–71
Khonsu (god), 130–31, 151, 240, 349
Khufu (king), 49, 85; boat of, 97; prophetess in cult of, 239; queen's pyramid, 178
Ki (goddess), 37
Kiki, 137
Kingship, divine: birth scenes, 106; motivation for, 21, 158, 260; son of Horus, 32; son of sun god, 33, 37; and titulary goddesses, 64
Koptos, 168–69, 181
Kronos, 196
Kusae, 89
Kushite Dynasty, 78, 144

Lamentations of Isis and Nephthys, 172
Lamps, 212–13
Late Period, 150, 272
Lebanon, 185
Leiden, Museum of Near East, 102, 122
Lesko, Leonard H., 27, 36, 89
Library, 210
Libya, 126
Libyans, 47, 58; dances, 219; Egyptian Dynasty of, 248–49; war against, 253
Licentiousness, 230
Lienhardt, Godfrey, 14–15
Linen, 216, 240
Lion, 273
Lioness: Mut, 131, 137; Pakhet, 147, 151; Sekhmet, 55, 139–41, 145. See also Eye of Re
Livingstone, David, 13
Loti, Pierre, 183

Love: charm, 179; sexually acceptable, 200; songs, 27
Lucius, 192, 199
Luxor, 65, 76; temple of, 118, 135, 141–42

Ma'at (goddess), 119, 196, 215, 268
Ma'atkare, 247
Macedonia, 186
Mafdet (goddess), 151–52, 269
Magic, 145, 273; instruments of, 259–60; Isis Great of, 170, 177, 180–82, 221, 244; Wadjet's, 73
Magicians: of Mut and Sekhmet, 139; women as, 9–10
Malek, Jaromir, 152
Mammisi, 96, 210, 227
Manetho, 130
Marduk, 37
Meat, 215–16; offerings, 238, 256
Medamud, 126, 219
Medicine, 139; and Isis, 181–82; and Serapis, 191
Medinet Habu temple, 209, 220, 227, 233, 250
Medinet Maadi, 206, 273
Mehet-Weret (goddess), 17, 21, 23, 26, 30, 55, 62, 81, 102, 235, 269
Meir (Kusae), 92, 96, 103–104, 107, 166
Mekhit (goddess), 269
Memphis, 22, 35–37, 48, 53–54, 111, 120, 128, 131, 148, 205
Menat, 100, 103–104, 109, 114, 117–18, 143, 145, 214, 260
Mendes, 47, 54
Menkaure (king), 85
Menstrual blood, 179
Mentuemhet, 151
Mentuhotep II (king), 92–93, 96, 101–102, 104–105, 223, 241
Merenre (king), 30
Meret priestess, 240
Meretseger (goddess), 76–77, 101, 237, 258, 269, 272
Merhyt (goddess), 269
Merit (goddess), 269
Meritamun (princess), 246
Mer(it)-Neith (queen), 49
Merneptah (king), 57
Mersyankh (queen), 85, 239
Meskhenit (goddess), 269, 272
Mesopotamia, 37, 55
Metternich Stela, 234
Middle Kingdom temples, 204–206
Milk, 17; of Hathor, 92, 107; of Isis, 161, 191
Milky Way, 6, 25
Min (god), 18, 46, 169, 245, 266, 272